# The U.N. Commission
# on Human Rights

# About the Book and Author

In 1946, the United Nations Commission on Human Rights became the first international body empowered to promote global human rights. During its first twenty years, the Commission established most of the contemporary standards of human rights. Increased social awareness in the 1960s enabled the Commission to respond to specific complaints from individuals and nongovernmental organizations and to pressure offending governments by using various measures that ranged from exhortation and mediation to sanctions designed to isolate violators. These enforcement activities have increased the Commission's visibility and have dramatically transformed its operation.

Dr. Tolley's thematic history of the Commission offers important insights into states' political conduct in international human rights organizations, the evolving legal and institutional means of preventing human rights violations, and the difficulties encountered when an intergovernmental body is pressed to provide impartial protection to citizens against abuse by their own government.

Howard Tolley, Jr., is associate professor of political science at the University of Cincinnati and a fellow of the Urban Morgan Institute for Human Rights.

Sponsored by the
Urban Morgan Institute for Human Rights

College of Law, University of Cincinnati

# The U.N. Commission on Human Rights

Howard Tolley, Jr.

Westview Press / Boulder and London

*Westview Special Studies in International Relations*

Copyright © 1987 by Howard Tolley, Jr.

Published in 1987 in the United States of America by Westview
Press, Inc.; Frederick A. Praeger, Publisher; 5500 Central Avenue,
Boulder, Colorado 80301

Library of Congress Cataloging-in-Publication Data
Tolley, Howard.
    The U.N. Commission on Human Rights.
    Bibliography: p.
    Includes index.
    1. United Nations. Commission on Human Rights.
I. Title. II. Title: UN Commission on Human Rights.
JC571.T66 1987    341.4'81    86-32580
ISBN 0-8133-7288-7

Composition for this book was created by conversion of the author's word-processor disks.
This book was produced without formal editing by the publisher.

Printed and bound in the United States of America

The paper used in this publication meets the requirements
of the American National Standard for Permanence of Paper
for Printed Library Materials Z39.48-1984.

6   5   4   3   2   1

To our family

# Contents

# Tables and Illustrations

*Chart*

*Photograph*

# Preface

After centuries of inadequate, piecemeal efforts to protect citizens from abuse by their own governments, in 1946 the international community founded a global human rights institution. The United Nations Commission on Human Rights became the first international body empowered to promote all the human rights of all the world's peoples. The founders assumed that improved respect for human rights would help individuals and would also serve the United Nations' primary peacekeeping goal by eliminating repressive practices which provoked war.

During its first forty years, the Commission has contributed to the inadequate but nevertheless incremental growth of supranational authority capable of scrutinizing practices that had previously been exclusively within governments' sovereign jurisdiction. After two decades spent in fashioning and promoting human rights law, the Commission shifted to enforcement activities, responding to specific complaints against over seventy governments. The process has increased the Commission's visibility and dramatically transformed its operation while exacerbating fundamental differences over whether political or economic, individual or collective rights deserve priority. This monograph describes the Commission's historical development from 1947 to 1986 in order to answer several important questions. Can a policymaking organ responsible for drafting international norms successfully perform enforcement activities? Can a political organ composed of government representatives provide impartial and effective protection to citizens against abuse by their own governments? The Commission's history offers significant lessons about states' political conduct in international human rights organizations and about the evolving legal and institutional means to prevent human rights violations.

The introductory chapter identifies the Commission's forerunners and recounts its founding. The following six chapters follow the Commission's evolution through four stages of development distinguished by increased membership and new priorities. Chapter 2 examines the Commission's Western dominated formative years, 1947–1954, devoted to drafting the International Bill of Rights. Chapter 3 covers the second stage, a twelve-year period of relative inactivity after 1954 spent primarily on research studies, seminars, and promotional undertakings. Chapter 4 reports the dramatic shift toward implementation efforts directed at South Africa and Israel resulting from the addition of Afro-Asian members to the Commission in 1967. Chapter 5 describes the Commission's standard-setting and promotional activities in that 1967–1979 period.

Chapter 6 identifies a fourth stage of development marked by a membership increase in 1980 and characterized by greater balance in enforcement activity, with heightened scrutiny of violations in all regions of the world. Chapter 7 reviews the Commission's standard-setting, promotion, and institutional reform activities between 1980 and 1986. Chapter 8 examines the parallel development of the Commission's independent agent, the Sub-Commission on Prevention of Discrimination and Protection of Minorities. The concluding chapter evaluates the Commission's impact, impartiality, institutional effectiveness, and future prospects.

Three appendices and a select bibliography provide supplementary references. Appendix A presents the text of the major ECOSOC resolutions granting authority to the Commission. Appendix B lists by region all governments elected to the Commission between 1947 and 1987 with dates of service. Readers confused by the U.N. symbols appearing in the notes will find an explanation of the system in Appendix C along with lists giving the identifying symbols for annual reports of both the Commission and Sub-Commission.

English language journals and periodicals listed in the bibliography have frequently examined one session or a significant Commission initiative. Jean Bernard Marie published a comprehensive monograph *La Commission des droits de l'Homme de l'O.N.U.* in 1974, after which the Commission significantly expanded its implementation activities. This study builds upon prior secondary sources with personal interviews and documentary research to describe, explain, and evaluate the Commission's work through 1986.

Sponsorship and financial support of the Urban Morgan Institute for Human Rights of the University of Cincinnati College of Law permitted eight weeks of field research in Geneva during summer 1982 and attendance at the Commission's 39th to 41st Sessions in the following three years. Two articles based on that research have appeared in the Institute's *Human Rights Quarterly* published by The Johns Hopkins University Press, which has authorized republication of selected material. A 1985 summer research fellowship from the University of Cincinnati supported the project in its final stages. The author also gratefully acknowledges the cooperation of Secretariat staff at the United Nations Centre for Human Rights and the assistance of Commission representatives, government advisors, and officers of nongovernmental organizations who gave personal interviews.

This study has also benefited from critical reviews by a number of scholars, students, and participants including Professors David Forsythe, Paul G. Lauren, Richard Lillich, David Weissbrodt, and Roger Clark; Morgan Fellows Tom O'Donnell, Fred Woodbridge, and Richard Rosswurm; as well as John

Humphrey, Sidney Liskofsky and others who commented on different sections of the manuscript. Diddi Mastrullo provided invaluable editorial assistance in preparing the final text and references for publication. Clerical support from Marie Toland and Nancy Ent appreciably lightened my burden. Professor Bert B. Lockwood, Jr., Director of the Urban Morgan Institute for Human Rights, has provided the indispensable guidance and sponsorship which made the project possible.

*Howard Tolley, Jr.*

# The U.N. Commission
# on Human Rights

# 1

## The Commission's Genesis

The 1940s proponents of a United Nations Commission on Human Rights sought to improve on a framework of pre-war international law and organization that proved unable to prevent the Nazi holocaust. This introductory chapter describes and explains the Commission's precursors, founders, origins, and initial mandate.

### Forerunners

Centuries of Western reforms advancing individual rights at the national level preceded the first international human rights initiatives.[1] The English Magna Carta and Bill of Rights, the United States Declaration of Independence and Constitution, and the French Declaration of the Rights of Man and the Citizen all contributed to the Western tradition of individual civil and political rights. Shamed by their own violations of these rights in Africa, Europeans convened meetings and drafted conventions to suppress the slave trade.[2] Mistreatment of Christians in Turkey, pogroms against Jews in Russia, and violations of religious liberties in Spain generated increasing pressure for humanitarian intervention and improved forms of international protection.[3] European wars produced the most important efforts to safeguard individual rights. Following the Napoleonic wars, the Treaty of Vienna guaranteed religious liberties and civil rights for citizens of the projected union between Belgium and Holland. In 1878 The Treaty of Berlin recognized the rights of certain minorities.[4] Various Geneva Conventions adopted after 1863 authorized the Red Cross to provide humanitarian relief to combatants and civilians during war.

The 1919 Versailles Treaty concluding World War I created the first permanent mechanisms for international supervision of human rights violations. The 1919 Treaty established a mandates system for governing territories taken from the German and Ottoman Empires. Administering powers accepted, as a "sacred trust," responsibility for the well-being and development of subject peoples. Individuals both within and without the trust territories could petition the League Council to redress grievances through a Permanent Mandates Commission. For the first time some nation states became regularly accountable for an international body for mistreatment of individuals subject to their rule.[5] The Treaty also established the International Labour Organization (ILO), a tripartite body of government, employer, and worker representatives. The ILO was empowered to draft conventions protecting specific worker rights, such as minimum age and maximum hours, for implementation by the permanent staff of The International Labour Office.[6] Under Treaty provisions comprising the League of Nations Covenant states promised "to endeavor to secure and maintain fair and humane conditions of labor for men, women and children."[7]

A series of postwar "minorities treaties" provided comprehensive human rights norms and supervisory machinery in states separated from the German and Ottoman Empire—Czechoslovakia, Greece, Poland, Romania and Yugoslavia. The instruments guaranteed "protection of life and liberty, freedom of religious worship, citizenship rights, equality of civil and political rights, free use of the mother tongue" and educational opportunities. To enforce their rights, minorities could petition the League Council directly.[8] The victorious allies imposed similar obligations on Austria, Bulgaria, Hungary, and Turkey. In addition, Albania, Estonia, Iraq, Latvia, Lithuania, and Finland made declarations before the Council upon joining the League. Germany and Poland agreed to a convention delineating citizens' rights in Upper Silesia.

The Covenant of the League of Nations did not, however, include any general reference to human rights. Nor in practice did the Assembly or Council ever investigate massive political repression by Stalin, Hitler, or Mussolini. International efforts to protect human rights before World War II thus amounted to sporadic, fragmentary measures affecting only a few target states or narrow groups of rights. Despite hopes raised by the ILO, the mandates system, and the minorities treaties, inter-war initiatives never overcame the prevailing belief "that international law covered relations between states and not the relation of the citizen to the state."[9] Hitler demonstrated the total inadequacy of the League's patchwork system when he occupied Czechoslovakia, ostensibly to protect that country's German minority.

## Wartime Conceptions

The holocaust which accompanied Nazi aggression persuaded the allies of World War II to move beyond the rudimentary forms of international cooperation that had thus far insured neither peace nor the observance of human rights. Planning for a new, stronger international organization had top priority in the United States. A State Department committee began planning postwar foreign policy even before the United States entered the war. President Franklin

D. Roosevelt sought to overcome the isolationist sentiment that had kept the United States out of the League. A month after the Japanese attacked Pearl Harbor, Roosevelt linked the war effort to human rights goals in his "Four Freedoms" message: freedom of speech and expression, freedom of worship, freedom from want, and freedom from fear. The Atlantic Charter of August 1941 declared Anglo-American support for freedom from want and freedom from fear as well as respect for "the right of all peoples to choose the form of government under which they will live." Twenty-six states made a similar affirmation in a "Declaration by the United Nations" on January 1, 1942; other states joined in principle as the war progressed.[10]

Encouraged by allied support for a new postwar international organization, technical advisory committees of the United States State Department had drafted a proposed constitution by June 1943. From the outset, planners had difficulty deciding where to assign responsibility for human rights. On the one hand, if human rights violations caused political disputes leading to war, then a collective security organ must have the power to prevent violations. On the other hand, if human rights problems resembled social disorders such as drug addiction, the international community should promote humanitarian cooperation rather than international coercion. Finally, if human rights entailed substantive legal guarantees for the individual against the state, then victims would need an international tribunal to adjudicate and enforce their claims. A State Department legal subcommittee tentatively advanced an adjudicatory approach by proposing an International Bill of Rights for the constitution. That low-level planning group decided not to recommend any enforcement machinery, concluding that an international court or commission would be "against all previous experience."[11]

Secretary of State Cordell Hull then created a high level Political Agenda Group which reworked the committee proposals. The Agenda Group's outline submitted to President Roosevelt in December 1943, contained no reference whatever to human rights. In 1944 the Agenda Group drafted proposals for an Economic and Social Council (ECOSOC) responsible for human rights concerns. The group concluded that a general provision for subsidiary commissions would be sufficient without express reference to a human rights commission. "There was no clear feeling . . . whether this broad subject was primarily political, social, or cultural in nature."[12] Once the Soviet leaders gave assurances that the U.S.S.R. would participate in the new postwar organization, the State Department completed tentative proposals for a United Nations Charter by July 1944.

Subsequently the United States, United Kingdom, and U.S.S.R., and later China (Big Four) met at Dumbarton Oaks to plan a postwar international security organization. None of the organization's general purposes, nor any specific functions proposed for the General Assembly or Security Council referred to human rights. China unsuccessfully sought to include provisions for nondiscrimination and equal rights. The United States and United Kingdom hesitated to approve broad human rights provisions because of their racial segregation and exclusionary immigration policies.[13] The single reference to human rights in the Dumbarton Oaks proposals appears in the Chapters on Economic and Social Cooperation.[14] In accord with the United States tentative proposals, ECOSOC would be able to create subsidiary commissions, but no human rights commission was expressly specified. The Big Four agreed on a security council that could "protect" the peace by imposing sanctions on states committing aggression. By contrast, they maintained that the organization should "promote" human rights and did not authorize any organ to sanction violations. In 1945 the Big Four sponsoring states invited the other United Nations to discuss the Dumbarton Oaks proposals at a conference on international organization to be hosted by the United States at San Francisco.

Nongovernmental organizations (NGOs) and Latin American states complained vehemently about the inadequate provision for human rights in the Dumbarton Oaks proposals. To overcome the isolationism that had doomed American participation in the League the Democratic administration had cultivated both public and Republican supporters for the United Nations. Throughout the war, the State Department had received advice from citizen groups such as the Commission to Study the Organization of the Peace, the Council on Foreign Relations, the American Association of the United Nations, the Foreign Policy Association and the Federal Council of the Churches of Christ.[15] The State Department appointed a committee of NGO consultants for its delegation to San Francisco. Twenty-two advisory NGOs submitted an amendment to the Dumbarton Oaks proposals providing for creation of a human rights commission under ECOSOC.[16] A prominent Republican member of the United States delegation, Senator Arthur Vandenberg, also supported stronger human rights language.[17]

The United States also had to accommodate the human rights concerns of Latin American neighbors who had not been involved in the great power conferences. After the U.S.S.R. had agreed to attend the San Francisco conference, Secretary of State Hull flew directly from Yalta to an inter-American meeting in Mexico City.[18] Latin American states adopted a sweeping resolution on essential rights as the Final Act of the Inter-American Conference on War and Peace at Chapultepec in March 1945.[19] By the time the San Francisco conference began, the United States responded to its advisory NGOs and Latin American neighbors by committing its delegation to support the creation of a commission for the promotion of human rights under the proposed ECOSOC.[20]

## Delivery in San Francisco

The Conference on International Organization convened in San Francisco on April 25, 1945. The United States led the Big Four sponsors in recommending modest amendments making the promotion of human rights both a main purpose of the organization and a specific responsibility of the General Assembly and ECOSOC. "The General Assembly shall initiate studies and make recommendations for the purpose of: . . . b) promoting . . . and assisting in the realization of human rights and fundamental freedoms for all without distinction as to race, sex, language or religion."[21] A similar amendment authorized ECOSOC to make recommendations to promote human rights. In addition, the sponsoring powers recommended a special commission under ECOSOC "for the promotion of human rights."[22]

A minority favoring United Nations "protection" of human rights would have granted enforcement powers to a main political organ such as the Security Council, General Assembly, or the ECOSOC. France proposed that the "General Assembly and the Economic and Social Council cooperate with the Security Council in the execution of these [human rights] functions."[23] At one point the French delegate also proposed a separate council to deal with human rights.[24] Three Jewish NGOs proposed that ECOSOC have the power to make binding human rights decisions and "be empowered to act in cases of infraction in the same way as the Security Council."[25]

Dissatisfied Latin American states unsuccessfully attempted to strengthen the major power's amendments. Panama wanted the United Nations to "safeguard and protect" rather than to "promote" human rights.[26] Panama was also unable to obtain approval for an international bill of rights as part of the basic Charter. Mexico and Uruguay introduced separate amendments calling for permanent human rights organizations for the protection of international rights and the promotion of equality. Canada, Australia, and Chile also proposed terms that would have imposed greater obligations on members.[27]

The final compromise language provides for something more than mere promotion of human rights, but does not promise United Nations protection. By the terms of article 55, the United Nations would "promote . . . universal respect for, and observance of human rights and fundamental freedoms for all without distinction as to race, language, religion, or sex;" then in the article 56, "[a]ll members pledge themselves to take joint and separate action in co-operation with the organization for the achievement of the purposes set forth in Article 55."[28]

Would the United Nations require a separate commission to promote such joint action? The sponsoring powers had originally proposed broad authorization for the Economic and Social Council to create any subsidiary commissions needed to foster cooperative activities. A Four Power amendment to the Dumbarton Oaks Proposals would have created both a human rights commission and a cultural commission. Brazil also wanted a health commission named, and Panama sought "permanent offices" for migration and maritime transportation.[29] Canada and New Zealand favored only a general authorization to ECOSOC without reference to any specific commission. The delegates agreed to drop the proposed cultural commission in deference to a London Conference of Allied Ministers of Education that had begun planning for The United Nations Educational, Scientific and Cultural Organization (UNESCO).

The United States, however, insisted on the naming of a human rights commission. Consultants from forty-two nongovernmental organizations pressed Secretary of State Stettinius at a meeting in May 1945 described by Walter Kotschnig, a delegation member. In an impassioned plea, Judge Proskauer stressed the need for United Nations human rights machinery beyond the Charter's general statements of principles; he charged Stettinius and the American delegation with particular responsibility for obtaining the necessary article. Other NGO speakers appealed with similar conviction. Several years later Kotschnig addressed an NGO group and described the Secretary's response to the meeting in San Francisco:

I accompanied Mr. Stettinius at the end of that meeting to a meeting of the American delegation. We went straight there. And all the way up in the elevator, then way down the long corridor on the fifth floor, down to the corner room where the American delegation was meeting, he didn't say a word. He was obviously moved. But he did speak strongly and convincingly at the delegation meeting. It was that afternoon that the Commission on Human Rights was born.[30]

Stettinius, Chairman of the United States delegation, characterized the proposed commission as "the heart of the matter."[31] Other delegations from smaller states, even more than the United States, insisted on human rights machinery. Considerable publicity had aroused expectations that a human rights commission would be expressly named.[32] After several more weeks of deliberation, the final compromise text of Article 68 mandated the establishment of commissions generally, but only one in particular. ECOSOC shall "set up commissions in economic and social fields and for the promotion of human rights and such other commissions as may be required for the performance of its functions."[33]

That mandate for a human rights commission won unanimous approval in the conference drafting committee, and only one state voted against the Article 55 pledge by members to take joint and separate action in cooperation with the organization.[34] The delegates did not, however, approve human rights commission enforcement of individual rights against member states. To the contrary, the official record shows the founders' respect for national sovereignty:

The members of Committee 3 of Commission II are in full agreement that nothing contained in Chapter IX can be construed as giving authority to the Organization to intervene in the domestic affairs of Member States.[35]

In addition, the Big Four sponsored a critical limitation on United Nations authority that became Charter article 2(7) with full support of even the most ardent Latin American human rights advocates.[36]

> Nothing contained in the present Charter shall authorize the United Nations to intervene in matters which are essentially within the domestic jurisdiction of any state or shall require the Members to submit such matters to settlement under the present Charter; but this principle shall not prejudice the application of enforcement measures under Chapter VII.

Intervention would only be justified under Chapter VII when the Security Council found a "threat to the peace, breach of the peace, or act of aggression."[37] Chapters V to VII of the Charter concerning the Security Council, peaceful settlement, and threats to the peace make no reference to human rights, although conceivably the Security Council might find that a gross human rights violation posed a threat of war.

Human rights advocates did however succeed in adding to other articles provisions that subsequently supported United Nations actions which appeared to invade traditional spheres of domestic jurisdiction. The preamble and article 1 affirm the United Nations purpose to promote human rights and to respect principles of nondiscrimination. Article 13 empowers the General Assembly to initiate studies and to make recommendations for the purpose of "promoting . . . and assisting in the realization of human rights and fundamental freedoms for all. . . ." Similarly, article 62(2) authorizes ECOSOC to make recommenda - tions for promoting "respect for, and observance of, human rights." Article 68 expressly names a commission for the promotion of human rights and article 76 affirms human rights ideals in the trusteeship system. Finally, broad language that might justify intervention by the Commission, ECOSOC or the General Assembly appears in Articles 55 and 56 and refers to the promotion of "observance" of human rights and the "pledge" by states to cooperate in joint action.

## Expectations and Choices

The compromise Charter formula created a legal framework but left unresolved the question of how much power and authority the Commission would exercise. What functions should the General Assembly and ECOSOC delegate to the Commission? Would the Commission be composed of state representatives or individual experts? What staff would be required? Should the Commission respond to alleged violations? Should it follow the ILO model of drafting narrow conventions or formulate a comprehensive bill of rights? The Charter offered no clear answers. From June 1945 until the full Commission on Human Rights first convened in January 1947, legal experts and United

Nations representatives debated and decided important threshold questions about the Commission's membership and mandate.

In his closing address to the San Francisco Conference, President Harry Truman had suggested that the Commission give first priority to drafting an international bill of rights. Many states and private organizations expected the Commission to proceed immediately with that task. Twelve different drafts had been proposed by early 1946.[38] The noted Cambridge international law scholar Hersch Lauterpacht advocated not only a binding bill of rights but sweeping powers of inquiry for the Commission to enforce the provisions.[39] O. Frederick Nolde agreed with Lauterpacht that the Commission should identify, for consideration by the Security Council, human rights violations that posed a threat to the peace.[40]

Three legal scholars in the United States urged the Commission to proceed more cautiously. Percy Corbett opposed Lauterpacht's vision of a universal code. Instead, he advocated a step-by-step approach beginning with covenants affirming particular rights such as racial equality, religious liberty, freedom from arbitrary arrest, and freedom of information.[41] Corbett's proposal that commission staff be empowered to review individual communications and to investigate alleged violations by governments aroused strong objections from two other American commentators. Philip C. Jessup wrote that years of careful study would be required to build an international consensus. Referring to the as yet unnamed body as "The Commission for the Promotion of Human Rights," Jessup argued against a strategy of frontal attack on evil that might estrange potential allies.[42] Nathaniel Peffer characterized the proposed universal declaration of rights as a "cruelly deceptive" gesture that would raise false hopes for unachievable ideals.[43] Yale law professor and former assistant solicitor in the State Department Edwin Borchard concluded pessimistically:

> Yet the times seem hardly propitious for the much greater advance involved in affording the individual protection for the enforcement or international guaranty of his rights against his own state . . . the chances that the United Nations will implement their promises and hopes by provisions of positive law, and especially that they will enforce these provisions effectively are rather less than rosy.[44]

By contrast, Senator Arthur Vandenberg spoke optimistically about "the protection for human rights and fundamental freedoms inherent in the San Francisco Charter."[45] Secretary of State Stettinius expected the Commission to focus world attention on violations by submitting recommendations to ECOSOC and to the General Assembly. Reporting as Chairman of the United States delegation, Stettinius declared that acceptance of the Commission might "well prove one of the most important and significant achievements of the San Francisco conference."[46] The Secretary noted however that years of hard work, careful study, and long-range planning were needed. He quoted Jefferson's statement: "the people of every country are the only safeguardian of their own rights."[47] Most important, Stettinius acknowledged the limits on human rights enforcement. "The provisions are not made enforceable by any international ma - chinery. . . . [R]esponsibility rests with the member governments to carry them out. . . . Whether the opportunity is used effectively or not will depend . . . upon the governments of the member Nations and upon the peoples who elect them to office.[48]

A fourteen-member Executive Committee of the United Nations Preparatory Commission meeting in London from August to October 1945 recommended that ECOSOC create six commissions. The Commission on Human Rights headed the list. The Executive Committee proposed that the Commission on Human Rights make studies and recommendations at the request of "the General Assembly or of the Economic and Social Council whether on its own initiative or at the request of the Security Council or Trusteeship Council," in order to "help to check and eliminate discrimination and other abuses."[49] The Executive committee used unexpectedly strong language in listing among the objectives for the Commission the "protection of minorities" and "prevention of discrimination."[50] The full Preparatory Commission approved the Executive Committee proposals in December without resolving whether the Commission would be composed of government representatives or experts serving in their individual capacity.[51]

At its initial session in 1946 the General Assembly established numbered Main Committees. The Assembly's Third Committee (Social, Humanitarian and Cultural Questions) approved the Preparatory Commission's recommendations for the Commission on Human Rights. Panama sought Assembly approval in both the First (Political) and Third Committees for the draft bill of rights it had submitted in San Francisco. Mrs. Franklin Roosevelt successfully persuaded the Assembly to refer the Panamanian proposal to the Commission on Human Rights.[52] The first General Assembly nevertheless acted on a variety of other human rights items without awaiting recommendations from the yet to be convened commission. Politically sensitive issues such as the treatment of Indians in South Africa went to the First rather than to the Third Committee. The Assembly also adopted a resolution on religious and racial persecution and requested ECOSOC to draft a genocide convention.[53]

At its first meeting in January 1946, ECOSOC appointed nine individuals to a "nuclear" Commission on Human Rights to recommend the functions and composition of the full Commission. The group met at Hunter College with Eleanor Roosevelt as chair. In addition to calling for an international bill of rights, the group identified the "need for an international agency of implementation entrusted with the task of watching over the general observance of human rights."[54] Specifically, the nuclear Commission proposed:

> Pending the eventual establishment of an agency of implementation the Commission on Human Rights might be recognised as qualified to aid the appropriate organs of the United Nations in the tasks defined for the General Assembly and the Economic and Social Council in Articles 13, 15 and 62 of the Charter concerning the promotion and observance of human rights and fundamental freedoms for all, and to aid the Security Council in the task entrusted to it by Article 39 of the Charter, by pointing to cases where violation of human rights committed in one country may, by its gravity, its frequency, or its systematic nature, constitute a threat to peace.[55]

The members apparently believed that human rights violations which might lead to war justified United Nations intervention.  Charter article 2(7) authorized intervention in a state's domestic affairs in situations which threatened the peace, so the Commission attempted to extend that authority to enforce human rights norms.  ECOSOC, however, did not fully accept that expansive vision of the Commission's role.  At its June 1947 session, ECOSOC merely directed the full Commission to "submit at an early date suggestions regarding the ways and means for the effective implementation of human rights and freedoms."[56]

In fashioning a mandate for the Commission, ECOSOC accepted the list of functions developed by the Preparatory Commission a year earlier, giving top priority to the drafting of an international bill of rights.  ECOSOC also authorized the Commission to submit recommendations on "any other matter concerning human rights not covered," to propose changes in its terms of reference and to make recommendations for any subcommission it wished to establish.  The Council only mandated studies that it requested.  Unlike the Preparatory Commission, ECOSOC did not mention possible requests for studies from the General Assembly or the Security Council.[57]

Nor did ECOSOC accept the nuclear Commission's recommmendation that members continue to serve in their individual capacity.  The group's report noted that since government delegates served on both the General Assembly and ECOSOC, the Commission should reflect the perspective of independent experts.  Lauterpacht had argued that the Commission could exercise greater moral persuasion if its members were "independent persons of the highest distinction."[58]  Government representatives might be too protective of national sovereignty and too politically inclined to express credibly the world's conscience.  The United States originally favored individual experts.  The U.S.S.R. by contrast reasoned that "instructed representatives would be more qualified to develop practical solutions."[59]  Several European states wanted government representatives to do the politically sensitive drafting of an international bill of rights.  As a result, ECOSOC provided for the election of eighteen *state* members to the full Commission.  "With a view to securing balanced representation"[60] of private experts and public officials, government representatives were to be selected after consultation with the Secretary-General and confirmation by ECOSOC.[61] To provide continuity, ECOSOC established staggered three-year terms, six member states to be elected each year. The eighteen states ECOSOC elected for the Commission's first session included all five permanent members of the Security Council.[62] The United States, its European, Latin American and Asian allies obtained an insurmountable majority over the three Soviet Republics and Yugoslavia. Australia, Belgium, France, United Kingdom, and the United States comprised a five member Western contingent. There were also five Asian members—China, India, Iran, Lebanon, and the Philippines. Chile, Panama, and Uruguay represented Latin America, and Egypt was the only member from Africa. Appendix B lists all member governments and years of service from 1947–1986.

The governments appointed highly qualified, instructed representatives of considerable stature, including several individuals who represented their countries on the Commission and its parent organs. Eleanor Roosevelt and P.C. Chang served both at the Commission and on the Assembly's Third Committee. Colonel Hodgson represented Australia on both the Commission and the Security Council.[63] Members Carlos Romulos of the Philippines and Lebanon's Charles Malik served terms as Presidents of the General Assembly. The Commission's doyen, René Cassin, had served the League of Nations. A former Vice-President of the French Conseil D'Etat, he later served as President of the European Court of Human Rights.[64] Influential diplomat P.C. Chang of China held a Columbia University Ph.D., but challenged the Western orientation of the Harvard-educated Malik.[65]

The United Nations first Secretary-General, Trygve Lie, was elected by the General Assembly to head the Secretariat responsible for staffing policymaking organs such as the new Commission. The Commission required essential conference services, staff assistance, and program administration from different departments of the Secretariat. The Charter directs the Secretary-General to assign appropriate staffs permanently to the ECOSOC and the Trusteeship Council and, "as required, to other organs of the United Nation."[66] The Secretary-General could have assigned a small permanent Secretariat to the Commission, but instead he created a Human Rights Division to serve committees of ECOSOC and the General Assembly as well as subsidiary Commissions. Unlike committees of a national legislature, the Commission would not select and control its own staff. Representatives of the major powers could rely on political and technical advisers provided by their governments; other members, such as Lebanon's Malik, depended heavily on the United Nations Secretariat.[67]

Just as the member governments had concluded that the Commission should report to the Assembly's Third (Social and Humanitarian) rather than its First (Political) Committee, Secretary-General Lie placed the Human Rights Division under the Assistant Secretary-General for Social Affairs, rather than under his political assistant. Before the Commission convened its first session, Assistant

CHART 1.1
Commission's Relationship to Principal U.N. Organs, 1947

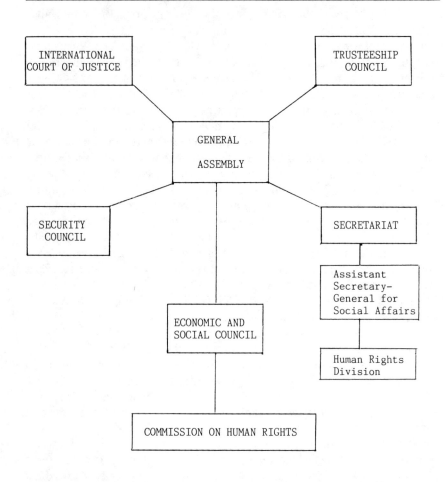

Secretary-General Henri Laugier appointed Canadian John Humphrey as Director of the Human Rights Division. In recruiting the division's professional staff, Humphrey had to reconcile the Charter's mandate for "efficiency, competence, and integrity" with its concern for geographical representation.[68] Despite a Charter provision requiring members to "respect the exclusively international character of the responsibilities of the Secretary-General,"[69] the U.S.S.R. posted officials from its foreign service to the Division for a limited tour and lobbied for appointment of a Soviet national as deputy director.[70]

Chart 1.1 illustrates the Commission's subordinate relations to the principal United Nations organs in January 1947 when eighteen approved state representatives convened the Commission's first session at Lake Success in New York. Since that initial three-week session, the Commission has evolved into a far larger organ with significantly different responsibilities. Major changes in 1954, 1967, and 1980 delineate cumulative stages of growth. The following six chapters describe those distinct periods, explaining how shifting political alignments generated new programs and priorities.

# 2

# A Quest for Consensus on
# Universal Norms, 1947–1954

In ten sessions between 1947 and 1954 the founding members established the new Commission's procedures and priorities, successfully completed a Universal Declaration of Human Rights, and recommended two covenants to the General Assembly. Table 2.1 identifies the governments sending representatives to the Commission during its formative years. In that eight year period, Western governments comprised 34% of the membership and enjoyed considerable support from Asian and Latin American representatives who constituted another 40% of the total.

### Participants, Procedures, and Priorities

The Commission convened its first two week session in New York on January 27, 1947. Rules of Procedure established by ECOSOC governed the selection of officers, preparation of an agenda, conduct of business, voting, and participation by non-members. The United States' Eleanor Roosevelt was selected chair (a position she held for six sessions until 1951). Charles Malik of Lebanon was named rapporteur (and chaired the Commission's seventh and eighth sessions). China's P. C. Chang served as vice-chairman. Canada's John Humphrey, Director of the Secretariat's Division of Human Rights, represented the Secretary-General. Representatives from two specialized agencies, ILO and UNESCO, also attended the first session.

The United Nations Charter provided fewer opportunities for participation by nongovernmental organizations than those groups had enjoyed in the League of Nations and the ILO. Specialized agencies could "participate, without vote,"[1] but the Charter limited NGO involvement to the Economic and Social Council and allowed only consultation. The largest NGOs, classified in "Category A," could propose agenda items and prepare brief statements for distribution by the

*14*

TABLE 2.1
Commission Membership, 1947-1954 (18 seats)

| Year 19-<br>Session | 47<br>1 | 47<br>2 | 48<br>3 | 49<br>4 | 49<br>5 | 50<br>6 | 51<br>7 | 52<br>8 | 53<br>9 | 54<br>10 | Total |
|---|---|---|---|---|---|---|---|---|---|---|---|
| **Africa** | | | | | | | | | | | |
| Egypt | XX | XX | XX | XX | XX | XX | XX | XX | CH | CH | 10 |
| **Asia** | | | | | | | | | | | |
| China | XX | XX | XX | XX | XX | XX | XX | XX | XX | XX | 10 |
| India | XX | XX | XX | XX | XX | XX | XX | XX | XX | XX | 10 |
| Iran | XX | XX | AA | XX | XX | | | | | | 4 |
| Lebanon | XX | XX | XX | XX | XX | XX | CH | CH | XX | XX | 10 |
| Pakistan | | | | | | | XX | XX | XX | XX | 4 |
| Philippines | XX | XX | XX | XX | XX | XX | | | XX | XX | 8 |
| **Eastern Europe** | | | | | | | | | | | |
| Byelorussia | XX | XX | XX | | | | | | | | 3 |
| Poland | | | | | | | | XX | XX | XX | 3 |
| Ukraine | XX | XX | XX | XX | XX | XX | XX | XX | XX | XX | 10 |
| USSR | XX | XX | XX | XX | XX | XX | XX | XX | XX | XX | 10 |
| Yugoslavia | XX | XX | XX | XX | XX | XX | XX | XX | XX | | 9 |
| **Latin America** | | | | | | | | | | | |
| Chile | XX | XX | XX | XX | XX | XX | XX | XX | XX | XX | 10 |
| Guatemala | | | | | | XX | XX | AA | XX | | 3 |
| Panama | XX | XX | XX | | | | | | | | 3 |
| Uruguay | XX | XX | XX | XX | XX | XX | XX | XX | XX | XX | 10 |
| **W. Eur. + Other** | | | | | | | | | | | |
| Australia | XX | XX | XX | XX | XX | XX | XX | XX | XX | XX | 10 |
| Belgium | XX | XX | XX | XX | XX | XX | | XX | XX | XX | 9 |
| Denmark | | | XX | XX | XX | XX | | | | | 4 |
| France | XX | XX | XX | XX | XX | XX | XX | XX | XX | XX | 10 |
| Greece | | | | | | XX | XX | XX | | XX | 4 |
| Norway | | | | | | | | | | XX | 1 |
| Turkey | | | | | | | XX | XX | XX | | 3 |
| United Kingdom | XX | XX | XX | XX | XX | XX | XX | XX | XX | XX | 10 |
| United States | CH | CH | CH | CH | CH | CH | XX | XX | XX | XX | 10 |

CH designates Chairman          AA denotes absence

Secretariat. Most human rights NGOs were placed in "Category B" or listed on the "Register" with smaller, more specialized groups allowed only to circulate short statements and to make brief oral presentations. (ECOSOC later redesignated the three consultative classes as Categories I and II and the Roster.) Fourteen groups, primarily labor and religious organizations, attended the Commission's second session of 1947 held in Geneva.

ECOSOC had authorized the Commission to create three sub-commissions, and the members decided to elect independent experts to three-year terms. The United States initially proposed a Sub-Commission on Freedom of Information and the Press, which met only from 1947–1952. The Soviet Union insisted on two additional sub-commissions, one for the prevention of discrimination and another for the protection of minorities. The single Sub-Commission on the Prevention of Discrimination and Protection of Minorities which resulted became the Commission's only permanent expert group.[2] Chapter 8 examines the Commission's often difficult relationship with that Sub-Commission. In setting its own agenda, the Commission heard state representatives, nongovernmental organizations and individual petitioners complain about violations against specific victims. By denying themselves the authority to respond, the members effectively limited the Commission agenda to the drafting of an International Bill of Rights.

## Disclaiming the Power to Act on Violations

Prior to the United Nations Charter, few international agreements provided for complaints against governments. The League of Nations had granted individuals a right of petition in the Mandate System and in the Minorities Treaties.[3] The 1919 International Labor Organization Constitution allows states, employers and employee organizations, but not individuals, to file complaints. Interstate complaints are both infrequent and politically motivated. Private complaints from employee organizations have been the most common and effective vehicle for exposing violations of workers' rights.

The United Nations Charter created a system of interstate complaints in the Security Council for threats to the peace and acts of aggression,[4] as well as a right of individual petition in the Trusteeship Council.[5] Hersch Lauterpacht insisted that the Charter also created an implied right to petition the United Nations when governments violated individual liberties. Strict constructionists countered that the Charter's Article 2(7) expressly bars United Nations intervention in matters "essentially within the domestic jurisdiction of any state." Citizens' complaints against their government are domestic questions unless the situation creates a "threat to the peace, breach of the peace, or act of aggression."[6] The first General Assembly debated state allegations of violations against individuals by Hungary, Bulgaria, the Soviet Union, Spain, and Greece. The Assembly established *ad hoc* investigatory committees on forced labor and slavery and for South Africa.

Faced with competing views of its authority and mission, the Commission made a critical declaration of impotence at its first session. ECOSOC's original charge authorized the Commission to make recommendations in "any other matter concerning human rights" and to call in *ad hoc* working groups of nongovernmental experts in specialized fields.[7] At the first session, India's representative Hansa Mehta challenged South Africa's *apartheid* policy, and the Secretariat reported on thousands of individual communications alleging violations by other states. Despite the ambitious recommendations of members on the "nuclear" Commission, the state appointed representatives were far more cautious about assuming the power either to hear interstate complaints or to review individual petitions.

General Romulos of the Philippines urged the Commission to conduct itself like a court of appeal, guaranteeing immunity to plaintiffs from any nation. Mrs. Roosevelt reasoned that the Commission had power to make recommendations to ECOSOC but not to conduct an inquiry. Australia, the United Kingdom, and the U.S.S.R. opposed Commission review of individual petitions. A three member subcommittee recommended that in future the Secretariat prepare a confidential list of communications and then grant members access to the originals.[8] The Commission conclusively resolved that "it had no power to take any action in regard to any complaints concerning human rights."[9] Professor René Cassin of France wanted to call ECOSOC's attention to the void created by limiting the Commission's power, but Mrs. Roosevelt successfully insisted that an oral explanation would be sufficient.[10] The Commission thus repudiated its powers to investigate and to make recommendations, beginning a twenty year period of self-denial.

ECOSOC not only resolved that the Commission had no power to act on complaints, but also decided that the members should not review the original text of specific complaints by individuals.[11] The Commission could only review the originals of communications about general principles of human rights. For specific complaints, the Secretariat prepared a confidential list of the communications received with a brief summary of their substance. The Commission had proposed to identify authors who had no objection to public disclosure; ECOSOC would only allow such complainants to be named on the confidential list, not in public documents.[12] Governments would receive a copy which concealed the name of the author and could respond to complaints made against them. The authors in turn were to be told only that their communications had been received and that the Commission had no power to act in response to complaints.

In 1950, 7,850 of the 9,524 confidential communications involved violations of religious liberty. Over half of the 37,660 communications received between 1952 and 1954 were "mass communications of an almost identical character alleging persecution in two countries."[13] The Commission's 1953 report reproduced the Secretariat's analysis of the complaints in 25,279 communications received between April 1951 and May 1952:

- 24,294 persecution on political grounds
- 305 genocide
- 119 freedom of assembly and association

- 64 discrimination and the rights of minorities
- 83 trade union rights
- 478 other
- 36 general principles unrelated to violations[14]

Only thirteen governments replied to summaries in 1953–54[15] and some simply returned the "libelous" allegations to the Secretariat.

The Secretariat prepared two lists of confidential and non-confidential communications received. A Commission working group first of five, later of eight members reviewed the petitions. "At every session the Commission went through the farce of clearing the conference room for a secret meeting which lasted only a few minutes, time enough for the Commission to adopt a resolution taking note of the list."[16] In 1949 a Secretariat report objected to notifying petitioners that the Commission had no power to act. The required disclaimer

> is bound to lower the prestige and authority not only of the Commission on Human Rights but of the United Nations in the opinion of the general public. . . . This irritates the general public and brings disappointment and disillusionment to thousands of persons all over the world. . . .[17]

Frustrated at his inability to provide an effective response to the numerous requests for assistance, Humphrey characterized the restrictive procedure as "probably the most elaborate wastepaper basket ever invented."[18]

Efforts to make the Commission a forum for reviewing human rights complaints all failed. In 1949 only 10 members favored studying the receiv - ability of petitions. When the Sub-Commission on Prevention of Discrimina - tion and Protection of Minorities inquired whether they could make "urgent proposals" the Commission eliminated from the experts' mandate their original authorization to make recommendations on "urgent problems."[19] At its last session in 1952, the Sub-Commission on Freedom of Information and the Press condemned Argentina for suppressing the newspaper *La Prensa*. Neither the Commission nor its other Sub-Commission criticized a member state for a specific human rights violation. Asian and Latin American states such as Egypt, India, and Uruguay repeatedly sought to have the Commission's parent organs reconsider and allow review of individual petitions. Only eleven states voted for reform at the General Assembly in 1953.[20]

Why did the Commission so firmly close the door to victims claiming denial of human rights? The prevailing majority in 1947 may have reasoned that under Article 2(7) a government's treatment of its citizens was essentially a domestic matter which did not threaten the peace. Undoubtedly many members also recognized that international scrutiny of petitions challenging national human rights practices would threaten their government's authority. The Western oriented majority advocated international enforcement in principle, but insisted that states could not be legally bound without prior consent to both the norms and the implementation procedures. The Soviet bloc minority supported only cooperative arrangements and opposed enforcement tools for any international body.

Even if its members had possessed the political will and legal authority to review thousands of individual communications and contentious interstate complaints, the Commission had good reason to make standard-setting its first priority. Since the United Nations had not formulated any legally binding bill of rights, its main organs had no appropriate standards by which to judge alleged violations. The Commission could more effectively sanction misconduct after states had made legal commitments. A premature effort to enforce undefined norms against unwilling states might have frustrated agreement on the essential basis for United Nations action. Cold War rivalry led the U.S.S.R. to boycott the 1950 session to protest the seating of nationalist China's representative. Debating complaints about Stalin's forced labor camps or American racial segregation might have precluded action on an International Bill of Rights. Drafting thus became the Commission's primary task, an obvious priority and a logical prerequisite to enforcement. Human rights standard-setting, however, was not to be exclusively the Commission's responsibility. A special committee of ECOSOC drafted a Genocide Convention while the Commission prepared a more comprehensive bill of rights.

## The Universal Declaration of Human Rights[21]

*Origins and Adoption*

The Declaration's major provisions had been advocated by so many for so long that no original sponsor or principal author emerges as its "Thomas Jefferson." State Department planners in Washington had initially favored incorporating a bill of rights into the charter of the postwar international organization.[22] At the San Francisco conference, Cuba, Mexico, and Panama introduced a Declaration on the Essential Rights of Man.[23] In his closing remarks at San Francisco, President Harry Truman had identified a bill of rights as the first priority for the United Nations organization. Panama sought immediate passage of a declaration in the first General Assembly, but Eleanor Roosevelt managed to have it referred to the new Human Rights Commission. "Twenty-one American nations meeting in Bogota adopted a Declaration on the Rights and Duties of Man seven months before the United Nations ratified its Declaration."[24] The Division of Human Rights received scores of proposals, from individuals such as Professor Hersch Lauterpacht and H. G. Wells, and from organizations such as the American Law Institute, the American Jewish

Congress, and the *Institut de droit international*. All drafts came from the democratic West, and all but two were in English.[25]

With remarkable speed the Commission proposed the text of a Universal Declaration of Human Rights by the end of its third session in 1948. In January 1947, the Commission appointed a three member drafting committee of its officers, Eleanor Roosevelt (U.S.) as chair. Charles Malik (Lebanon), and P. C. Chang (China). The committee asked John Humphrey to prepare a Secretariat outline for review. At the next ECOSOC meeting the Soviet Union challenged the exclusion of Europeans from the drafting committee. Mrs. Roosevelt agreed to the appointment of five additional members from the Soviet Union, the United Kingdom, France, Australia, and Chile.

In early June 1947 the enlarged drafting committee met to review a detailed Secretariat outline for a declaration including 48 articles prepared by Humphrey.[26] The United Kingdom had also submitted a draft convention protecting civil and political rights, but the committee concentrated on a declaration as the first step. A sub-committee of four invited René Cassin of France to revise the Secretariat proposals.[27] The full drafting committee spent two weeks debating Cassin's text before adjourning. Prior to the Commission's second session in December, the Sub-Commission on Discrimination and Minorities recommended language for two articles.

During two weeks of lengthy meetings that often extended into the early morning, the Commission completed draft texts of both a declaration and a convention before Christmas of 1947. The Commission referred both documents to ECOSOC, member governments, and other United Nations bodies for review. ECOSOC created a special Human Rights Committee, but it had no time to consider the Commission's text. The Commission's own drafting committee reconvened in May 1948 to consider replies from governments. The full Commission had no time for further consideration of the covenant, but managed to adopt the Declaration by June 18 with a recorded vote of twelve in favor, none opposed and four Eastern European members abstaining.

ECOSOC made no substantive changes, as the Declaration proceeded to its major hurdle in the General Assembly's Third Committee on September 30. Fifty-nine delegations participated in the committee's eighty-one meetings that considered sixty-eight proposed amendments. With the Commission's Charles Malik presiding, the declaration had a friendly supporter as chair. A one a.m. vote of approval in committee December 8 made possible final passage by the General Assembly two days later. Within two years and after only three sessions the Commission had achieved its first legislative success, both in procedure and in substance.

The unusual procedural efficiency was possible because the Commission had only eighteen members subject to the control of a single-minded majority. Swift passage of the Declaration without a dissenting vote neither resulted from nor established a consensus on fundamental substantive questions. In fact the members have subsequently disagreed about adopting language verbatim from the Universal Declaration in later instruments for provisions affirming property rights and religious liberty. Even in 1947 ideological differences and partisan cold war disputes resulted in sharp debate on a number of critical provisions.

*Values in Conflict*

At the outset the members debated whether to draft a simple declaration or a binding convention which would include enforcement measures. The British initially proposed a convention as the first step and introduced a draft text. The Indian representative Hansa Mehta advocated international protection for individual victims; the Australian Colonel Hodgson proposed creation of an International Court of Human Rights. In opposition, the Soviet member Vladimir Koretsky (who later served on the International Court of Justice) insisted on implementation exclusively by sovereign national institutions. Mrs. Roosevelt initially favored a two-stage process patterned after the United States' Declaration of Independence and later Bill of Rights. Segregationalist Senators strongly opposed any treaty after the NAACP's W.E.B. DuBois filed a 155-page petition seeking United Nations assistance for black victims of United States human rights violations.[28]   China's P.C. Chang proposed the ultimate solution, a tri-partite approach beginning with a declaration, followed by a convention, and finally implementation measures.[29]

Deliberations by the Commission and its drafting committee revealed profound ideological differences over what constituted universal rights. Even the Charter's authors seemed divided, referring both to "human rights" and to "fundamental freedoms." Conflicting value judgments generated lengthy debate. Are human rights truly indivisible and interdependent, or must political liberties be sacrificed for economic development? Does the individual have inviolable personal freedom, or do the collective needs of society take priority?

Western members favored an international law that would impose minimum enforceable standards limiting state power. Asian and Latin members on the other hand advocated maximum goals that all states should strive to attain. The West stressed the preeminence of individual political and civil liberties—freedom of expression, association, religion, and due process of law. The Eastern bloc gave priority to economic and social rights—to a job, an education, health care and social security. The trust powers administering non–self-governing territories objected to attempts by non-administering states to add the right of collective self-determination to guarantees of individual rights. Eastern bloc and nonwhite nations advocated group rights for minorities beyond general principles of nondiscrimination. Proponents of individual property rights clashed with those advocating community needs. The American and Canadian Bar Associations urged delay and raised the specter of state socialism.[30]

Since the Declaration would not have the same legal effect as a convention, the drafters could include provisions for economic, social and cultural rights of a nonjusticiable character. The British proposed only classical Western civil and political rights in their draft convention. President Franklin Roosevelt however had publicly advocated "freedom from want."[31] Humphrey included economic and social rights in the Secretariat outline, describing his approach as a combination of "humanitarian liberalism with social democracy."[32] The Soviets challenged the preponderance of Western civil liberties, but recognized that their own support for economic rights could threaten vital precepts of national sovereignty. Of the twenty-five articles in the final Declaration, only six refer to economic, social and cultural rights. Personal liberties come first in the Declaration and account for the largest number of provisions, twelve. Another five articles establish procedural guarantees for criminal defendants, and two affirm political rights.

Political differences over several key individual liberties produced weak compromise formulations or gaps in the Declaration that continue to stimulate proposals for stronger norms. Malik unsuccessfully attempted to add language guaranteeing the right to life "from the time of conception."[33] Arab states failed to remove the right to change religion proscribed by the Koran. When Catholic representatives sought to incorporate reference to the deity, the Commission resolved that persons are born with rights, rather than endowed with them by either nature or a creator.[34] A Sub-Commission proposal to affirm the rights of minorities failed completely. A weak provision on asylum simply allowed individuals to seek the right, without requiring states to admit victims of persecution.[35] Though protected from arbitrary seizure, private property owners were not assured "just compensation" when properly deprived of their possessions.[36] The Declaration pronounced a qualified right to social security "in accordance with the organization and resources of each State."[37]

The Declaration's strongest provisions unequivocally proclaim traditional Western civil liberties and political rights found in the United States Constitution, the English Bill of Rights and the French Declaration on the Rights of Man.

*Everyone* has the right to:

- "life, liberty and security of person" (Article 3)
- "recognition everywhere as a person before the law" (Article 6)[38]
- "freedom of movement . . . to leave any country, including his own" (Article 13)
- "a nationality" (Article 15)
- "freedom of thought, conscience and religion" (Article 18)
- "freedom of peaceful assembly and association" (Article 20)
- "take part in the government of his country" (Article 21)

*No one* shall be:

- "held in slavery" (Article 4)
- "subjected to torture" (Article 5)
- "subjected to arbitrary arrest, detention or exile" (Article 9)

Although the provision affirming everyone's right to freedom of expression[39] appears unequivocal, the Declaration's anti-discrimination language prohibits racist propaganda: "All are entitled to equal protection against any discrimination in violation of this Declaration and against any incitement to such discrimination."[40] A provision asserting that everyone has duties to the community[41] also departed from United States Constitutional precepts. Some representatives of Western liberal regimes accepted as consistent with emerging welfare state ideals promises of free public education,[42] food, clothing, housing, medical care and necessary social services,[43] the right to work,[44] and to paid holidays.[45]

Humphrey and several state rperesentatives proposed an individual right to petition the United Nations that was deleted from the Declaration's final text.

> Everyone has the right, either individually or in association with others, to petition or to communicate with the public authorities of the State of which he is a national or in which he resides, or with the United Nations.

The United Kingdom proposed removing the right of petition from the Declaration, so the remedy could be considered with other implementation procedures in a covenant. When referring the Universal Declaration to ECOSOC, the Commission separately appended a provision on the right to petition which had not yet been studied.[46] In the General Assembly's Third Committee the United Kingdom proposed a resolution seeking further study of the right by the Commission. The Assembly eventually approved a Cuban amendment affirming a right of petition at the national level: "the right of petition is an essential human right, as is recognized in the Constitutions of a great number of countries."[47]

*Legal Effect*

Commentators have argued at length about whether the Declaration's sweeping provisions constitute customary international law.[48] The broad proposition introduced by René Cassin as the first article affirms a moral ideal rather than a legal mandate: "All human beings are born free and equal in dignity and rights. They are endowed with reason and conscience and should act towards one another in a spirit of brotherhood." Eleanor Roosevelt expressly campaigned for United States support by arguing that the Declaration would not be legally binding. Ordinarily a General Assembly resolution does not bind the members, particularly those who voted against. Governments at the time anticipated that further drafting of a convention would occur before states would become legally bound by norms established through traditional ratification procedures.

A few in the Assembly such as South Africa and the Soviet Union nevertheless expressed fears that the Declaration would impose new legal obligations; eight abstained from the final vote. The Declaration's preamble makes several references to human rights articles of the United Nations Charter, provisions that established undefined legal duties. If the Declaration constitutes an authoritative interpretation of those Charter articles, then it has the binding legal effect of an international treaty.[49]   By its own terms, the Declaration represents a "common standard of achievement."

## The Covenants

Between May 1949 and April 1954 the Commission completed its contribution to the International Bill of Rights in six sessions that ranged in length from five to eight weeks.[50] External actors shaped both the procedural deliberations and substantive results far more than in the drafting of the Declaration. The General Assembly at first directed the Commission to draft a single covenant including both political and economic rights; then in response to Western pressure the Assembly called for two separate covenants. Developing states in the Assembly pressed the Commission to include an article on self-determination in both covenants. In contrast to the Third Committee's swift action on the Declaration, the Assembly took twelve years before approving the covenants. Representatives from three specialized agencies, the ILO, UNESCO, and the World Health Organization (WHO) participated in drafting articles for the International Covenant on Economic, Social and Cultural Rights.[51] The Sub-Commission contributed an article on minorities for the International Covenant on Civil and Political Rights. Secretariat officials and NGO representatives lobbied vigorously for strong implementation measures through friendly delegations and in public speeches.[52]

As the draft covenants passed back and forth between the Commission, ECOSOC, and the General Assembly from 1948 to 1954, the drafters struggled to resolve three major issues. First, the members could not agree on the relationship, enforceability, and priority of civil and political rights on the one hand and economic and social rights on the other. Second, the representatives disagreed on whether national means of implementation would suffice or whether international agencies would be required. Third, varying political interests sought to add rights not covered in the Declaration, or to weaken principles already formulated. Most of the compromises and decisions taken by the Commission survived in the Assembly's lengthy deliberations. The ideological diversity in the world organization was so great, however, that the two United Nations covenants did not come into force until 1976, twenty-five years after the more homogeneous European governments had adopted a considerably stronger regional convention.

*Political vs. Economic Rights*

The Commission had forwarded a draft covenant to ECOSOC along with the Declaration in 1947. That preliminary text embraced the British and American view that only civil and political rights could be included in a legally binding treaty. When the Soviets proposed discussion of economic rights at the Commission's 1949 session, Mrs. Roosevelt as chair "announced that the new articles would have to be considered *en bloc* and that there would be no voting."[53] The Soviets won a vote on their right to separate voting on the economic articles, so that a requirement of consensus would not frustrate approval of their proposals. The Soviet boycott of the 1950 session to protest nationalist China's participation created a new opportunity for the West. The Commission proposed first a draft covenant limited to civil and political rights and second a covenant for economic rights to be drafted later. The General Assembly, more responsive to developing states and the Eastern bloc, directed the Commission to prepare a single comprehensive covenant, resolving: "[T]he enjoyment of civil and political freedoms and of economic, social and cultural rights are interconnected and interdependent. . . . [W]hen deprived of econom - ic, social and cultural rights man does not represent the human person whom the Universal Declaration regards as the ideal of the free man."[54]

In 1951 the Commission drafted fourteen articles on economic and social rights with considerable input from the ILO on the right to work, from UNESCO on the right to education, and from WHO on the right to health. The United States sponsored language authorizing the right to strike that was approved with the qualification that the right be "exercised in conformity with the laws of the particular country."[55] The British remained hostile to the very concept of economic rights.

The Western states collaborated in a successful effort to persuade the General Assembly to reconsider its decision on a single covenant. Western representatives argued that an instrument designed to curtail government abuse of personal liberties required measures of legal enforcement incompatible with efforts to promote state welfare programs of benefit to individuals. Government was alternately conceived as a potential oppressor or benefactor. Realistically it appeared that if Western governments would obstruct a comprehensive covenant, two agreements would be preferable to none. After the United States suggested that separate covenants could be approved and opened for signature at the same time, the Assembly finally resolved the issue in favor of separate covenants for political and economic rights. The Commission was directed, however, to include as many similar provisions as possible in the two documents to illustrate their unity of purpose.[56]

*Implementation*

Disagreement over how to implement the binding provisions of the civil and political covenant never was resolved in the Commission. The Soviets insisted that national institutions alone had the sole authority to enforce the provisions of international law. Each state must undertake a solemn obligation to bring its laws and practices into accord with international law, but there could be no supranational institutions that impaired a sovereign's prerogative over citizens within its own territory. At the opposite extreme, the Australians advocated an International Court of Human Rights with authority to protect individuals against their own governments. Ultimately, the political covenant included both state pledges to provide rights and remedies for individuals as well as a new international agency. A Human Rights Committee would be created to review reports from governments about how they had modified their laws and practice to comply with their covenant obligations. In addition states could make an optional declaration under Article 41 authorizing the Committee to receive state complaints against them from other parties making the same declaration. If the Committee's good offices failed to resolve the dispute, it could appoint a five member Conciliation Commission.

Neither individuals nor nongovernmental organizations could petition the committee directly. The Commission had split eight to eight on a proposal for an individual right of petition in 1949, and thereafter gave no serious consideration to the proposal.[57] By providing that the Committee submit its own annual report to the General Assembly through ECOSOC, the covenant left the Commission itself out of the implementation system. The Soviet Union repeatedly attempted to eliminate the international implementation provisions; the United States totally repudiated the covenants.[58] In 1953 the new Eisenhower administration responded immediately to domestic protest about United Nations intervention by publicly withdrawing United States support for both covenants. Ohio Senator John Bricker objected to any international supervision of human rights by nonelected United Nations officials controlled by a socialist-communist majority.[59]

The General Assembly redrafted the Commission's implementation articles to delete all reference to the International Court of Justice. The Commission had proposed that the International Court appoint the members of the Human Rights Committee and also be empowered to give advisory opinions in specific cases. The Assembly decided that states parties would elect the committee members. The Assembly also added an optional protocol by which states could authorize the committee to receive and consider individual petitions from their own nationals.[60]

The economic covenant had far fewer articles on implementation. To implement the provisions of the economic and social covenant, the Commission proposed that states report to ECOSOC. Charles Malik, as chair in 1951, introduced proposals drafted by Humphrey who sought to establish

United Nations review comparable to the oversight exercised by the International Labour Office. ILO representatives sought to expand and protect their own jurisdiction by proposing that states party to the economic covenant report to specialized agencies.[61] The ultimate compromise requires states to report to the United Nations, but allows them to refer to special agency reports without duplicating the information.[62] ECOSOC initially appointed a sessional working group of members to review country reports, but in 1983 assigned the responsibility to a "Group of Experts" from fifteen states.[63]

The political rights are also expressed in more absolute terms—"*Everyone* has the right to . . . ," and "*No one* shall be subjected to . . ." Under the economic covenant's eleven substantive articles a state party undertakes to provide welfare benefits "to the maximum of its available resources." "The States parties" are the operative beneficiaries of each article, and citizens are the recipient beneficiaries of economic rights the governments pledge to confer. The economic covenant relieves developing countries of the obligation to guarantee economic rights to nonnationals."[64]

### Rights Beyond the Declaration

In its final version the International Covenant on Civil and Political Rights has 51 articles. In addition to 22 articles which parallel substantive provisions of the Declaration, the Commission and Assembly included in the covenants several new substantive rights. Arab states sponsored an Assembly Resolution calling for a provision on self-determination that became the first article in each of the covenants. The Western powers fruitlessly objected that vague collective rights did not belong with guarantees of individual freedom, but could not block the anti-colonial majority.[65] In defining the newly proclaimed collective right to political independence, the Chilean representative proposed:

> The right of the peoples to self-determination shall also include permanent sovereignty over their natural wealth and resources. In no case may a people be deprived of its own means of subsistence on the grounds of any rights that may be claimed by other states.[66]

Western representatives were unable to obtain language in the Commission draft assuring just compensation for nationalized property. The final text approved by the Assembly makes sovereignty over resources subject to "obligations arising out of international economic cooperation, . . . and international law."[67]

The covenants also included civil and political rights for groups not recognized in the Declaration. The political covenant prohibits imprisonment "merely on the ground of inability to fulfill a contractual obligation."[68] The Commission accepted a weak Sub-Commission draft on the rights of minorities; the Assembly added a provision on the rights of children.

In several cases the covenants either omitted or qualified rights proclaimed by the Declaration. The debate over property rights departed from strict cold war ideology, since the Soviets recognized the right of individuals to personal belongings. When the members could not agree on a procedure for compensation, however, the United States preferred to leave out the provision altogether, rather than to weaken the Universal Declaration's provision. Nor does the covenant contain the promise of a right to seek asylum included in the Declaration.

Several other covenant articles elaborating rights affirmed by the Declaration opened significant exceptions. The United States lost one negotiating battle over guarantees for free speech. Nonwhite representatives of developing states as well as Europeans victimized by Hitler's propaganda favored language prohibiting advocacy of racial hatred and war. Representatives from China, the Soviet Union, and France joined in rare agreement on restricting free speech, despite American objections. In 1947, 1949, and again in 1950 the United States prevailed over restrictive proposals and a recommendation of the Sub-Commission. By 1953 supporters had an 11 to 3 majority with three abstentions for the following text: "Any advocacy of national, racial or religious hostility that constitutes an incitement to hatred and violence shall be prohibited by the law of the States."[69] Moreover, the right to freedom of expression may be subject to

> certain restrictions, but these shall only be such as are provided by law and are necessary: (a) for respect of the rights or reputations of others; (b) For the protection of national security or of public order *ordre public* or of public health or morals.[70]

The article on religious freedom omitted the Declaration's assurance of the right to change religion and qualified the right to free exercise "[f]reedom . . . to manifest [one's] religion or beliefs may be subject only to such limitations as are prescribed by law and are necessary to protect public safety, order, health, or morals of the fundamental rights and freedoms of others."[71] A similar qualification applies to freedom of association. "No restrictions may be placed on the exercise of [the right of peaceful assembly] other than those imposed in conformity with the law and which are necessary in a democratic society in the interests of national security or public safety."[72] Finally, Article 4 affords a general escape clause that Chile, Colombia, the United Kingdom, Uruguay, and Poland have subsequently invoked to defend martial law:

> In time of public emergency which threatens the life of the nation and the existence of which is officially proclaimed, the States Parties to the present Covenant may take measures derogating from their obligations under the present Covenant to the extent strictly required by the exigencies of the situation.[73]

There can be no derogation even during public emergencies from fundamental rights contained in seven articles listed in Article 4.[74]

*Final Provisions*

Both covenants conclude with six final articles on procedures for ratification and amendment. A United States' proposal for a federal state clause stimulated the most debate. In 1951 Ohio's Senator Bricker sponsored a popular constitutional amendment to protect states' rights against treaties authorizing "any international organization to supervise, control, or adjudicate rights of citizens of the United States."[75] A draft article favored by Australia, Canada, and the United States would have allowed federal states to meet their covenant obligations merely by recommending implementation to their constituent states.[76] States rights' opponents of international human rights procedures grew so strong in the United States, that the newly elected Eisenhower administration formally declared in 1953 that it would not become a party to the covenants. Secretary of State Dulles replaced Mrs. Roosevelt with Mrs. Oswald Lord, and the United States contributed nothing further to the drafting effort.[77] The Soviets then sponsored an article extending the covenants' reach to "all parts of federal states without any limitations or exceptions."[78] By 1954 the United States would not even support Australia and Canada in opposition, and the Commission adopted the Soviet proposal.

## Power and Principle in Conflict

The struggle for power and national self-interest frequently exacerbated the philosophical disputes over human rights principles. As representatives of governments, the Commission members operated to varying degrees on instructions from their foreign ministries. Humphrey reports that England's Marguerite Bowie resigned as a result of "reactionary," detailed instructions on every question from the foreign office. By contrast, Humphrey found Malik so independent that the Lebanese representative agreed to introduce covenant implementation proposals drafted by the Secretariat. A new Republican administration replaced Eleanor Roosevelt two years before the end of her term;[79] the Indian government replaced its "independent" expert on the Sub-Commission.

As a result of such control, the Commission often became a forum for political conflict. The United States had the greatest success in defeating its Soviet bloc cold war adversaries. State Department advisers instructed Eleanor Roosevelt not only on substantive questions but also on procedural rulings that reflected cold war partisanship.[80] The Soviet and United States representatives frequently exchanged vitriolic denunciations. When the Western majority refused to accept the credentials of the new Communist Chinese regime, the

Soviet bloc walked out of the 1950 session. In later years the Eastern bloc could only win six votes for unseating nationalist China's representative. No Soviet bloc representative was ever elected to Commission office as chairman, vice chairman, or rapporteur in the first ten sessions.

The United States objected when the International Organization of Journalists and The Women's International Democratic Federation (WIDF) criticized United Nations intervention in Korea. The United States characterized International Association of Democratic Lawyers (IADL) complaints to the Commission as "pure propaganda."[81] In 1952 ECOSOC accepted a United States proposal to withdraw consultative status from the three nongovernmental groups because they failed to meet the requirement that "the organization shall undertake to support the work of the United Nations."[82]

Neither great power honored a Charter provision requiring members to "respect the exclusively international character of the responsibilities of the Secretary-General."[83] The Soviets lobbied Humphrey for an appointment and closely controlled their nationals working in the Secretariat. During the McCarthy era, United States officials subpoenaed one American employee of the Human Rights Division for both grand jury and Senate committee investigations. United States pressure also forced the dismissal of a suspected homosexual from the Division because of susceptibility to blackmail.[84] Personal jealousies and bureaucratic rivalry also appeared among proud individuals jockeying to become Commission chair, to claim credit for new human rights norms, or to assert their institution's authority over new procedures.

Some members and NGOs had a principled interest in extending the protections for minorities fashioned by the League of Nations. When the Sub-Commission defined "minorities" and recommended interim measures for their protection, however, the government representatives proved more committed to indivisible national sovereignty and assimilation.[85] The Soviets used NGO complaints to the Sub-Commission to embarrass the United States, and the Commission's Western bloc resolved to terminate the group of experts. An alliance of socialist and nonwhite states rescued the Sub-Commission in the General Assembly. Third World representatives were far more interested in decolonization than minority rights, however, and they made self-determination a priority on the Commission's agenda.

As work on the covenants proceeded, the Commission began adding other new agenda items on asylum, the rights of children, spousal choice, old age, local human rights committees, and an international court of human rights. By 1953 the agenda included sixteen items, but the members only considered six. In practice the next priorities after standard-setting were Commission intiatives, publications, and celebrations to improve public understanding of human rights. Beginning in 1946 the Secretariat published English and French editions of a *Yearbook of Human Rights*, a reference volume with all the declarations and national bills on human rights in force.[86] The Commission solicited statements on categories of rights, and fifty-six governments submitted information on the Universal Declaration's provision on arbitrary arrest and detention. As the volumes increased in size, publication fell several years behind schedule.

After drafting the Universal Declaration, the Commission approved a Belgian recommendation that governments provide compulsory instruction in the rights, especially in military schools. The U.N. Office of Public Information produced pamphlets using the text as a promotional tool. Assembly approval of the Declaration on December 10 established Human Rights day as a key anniversary for celebrating fundamental rights. The Commission encouraged Secretariat planning for commemorative observances and celebrations.

Repeated references to the Declaration after 1948 in treaties, conventions, resolutions and later declarations both in and out of the United Nations illustrate the potential impact of the Commission's work. "[E]xamples include the Trusteeship Agreement with Italy concerning Somaliland . . . of 1950, the Peace Treaty with Japan of 1951, [a]nd the Special Statute concerning Trieste of 1954."[87] The United States Department of Justice reported that in the period 1948–1973 the constitutions or other important laws of over seventy-five states either expressly referred to or clearly borrowed from the Universal Declaration of Human Rights. "In the same period, the Declaration was referred to in at least sixteen cases in domestic courts of various nations."[88]

The Declaration's early impact was not a result of any special promotion campaign by the Commission, which remained preoccupied with drafting the covenants until 1954. Once that task was completed, however, the United States prevailed on the members to eschew further standard-setting and instead to give top priority to measures promoting respect for human rights. That fundamental reorientation of its agenda initiated a distinct second stage in the Commission's development.

# 3

## Promoting Human Rights Ideals, 1955–1966

After completing work on the covenants the Commission had several options.[1] It might have proceeded like the ILO to draft narrow standards for specific groups of rights such as religious liberty, nondiscrimination, and asylum. The Commission could have also developed implementation machinery for review of individual communications and interstate complaints. The Universal Declaration and the two draft covenants now offered standards that would support such protection activities.

Instead of measures to protect victims, however, the United States persuaded the Commission to promote human rights ideals. The American sponsored "Action Plan" of education and persuasion included (1) advisory services, (2) global studies, and (3) annual country reports. For twelve sessions from 1955 to 1966 those promotional activities became the Commission's top priority. Standard-setting also continued, but the members completed work on only one convention and several declarations.

Critics regarded the "Action Plan" as a euphemism for inaction and questioned the motives of the Western members.[2] The United Kingdom, represented by Samuel Hoare, opposed significant new initiatives. French delegate René Cassin served two years as chair, and then Asian and Latin American delegates chaired the Commission for a decade after 1956. Table 3.1 lists Commission members from 1955–1966. As newly independent African states joined the United Nations, membership was increased from 18 to 21 members in 1962. Pressures mounted to move beyond promotion into effective protection activities. This chapter describes the transitional decade of uncontroversial, Western initiatives which preceded the Commission's expansion to 32 members and capture by Third World activists in 1967.

TABLE 3.1
Commission Membership, 1955-1966

| | 18 Members | | | | | | | 21 Members | | | | | |
|---|---|---|---|---|---|---|---|---|---|---|---|---|---|
| Year 19- | 55 | 56 | 57 | 58 | 59 | 60 | 61 | 62 | 63 | 64 | 65 | 66 | Total |
| Session | 11 | 12 | 13 | 14 | 15 | 16 | 17 | 18 | 19 | 20 | 21 | 22 | |
| **Africa** | | | | | | | | | | | | | |
| Benin | | | | | | | | | | XX | XX | XX | 3 |
| Egypt | XX | | | | | | | | | | | | 1 |
| Liberia | | | | | | | | | XX | XX | XX | | 3 |
| Senegal | | | | | | | | | | | | XX | 1 |
| **Asia** | | | | | | | | | | | | | |
| Afghanistan | | | | | | | XX | XX | CH | | | | 3 |
| Ceylon | | | XX | CH | CH | | | | | | | | 3 |
| China | XX | XX | XX | XX | XX | XX | XX | XX | XX | | | | 9 |
| India | XX | XX | XX | XX | XX | XX | CH | XX | XX | XX | XX | XX | 12 |
| Iran | | | XX | XX | XX | | | | | | | | 3 |
| Iraq | | XX | XX | XX | XX | XX | XX | | | | XX | XX | 8 |
| Israel | | | XX | XX | XX | | | | | | XX | XX | 5 |
| Lebanon | XX | XX | XX | XX | XX | XX | | CH | XX | XX | | | 9 |
| Pakistan | XX | XX | | | | XX | XX | XX | | | | | 3 |
| Philippines | XX | XX | CH | XX | XX | XX | XX | XX | XX | XX | CH | XX | 12 |
| **Eastern Europe** | | | | | | | | | | | | | |
| Poland | XX | XX | XX | XX | XX | XX | XX | XX | XX | XX | XX | XX | 12 |
| Ukraine | XX | XX | XX | XX | XX | XX | XX | XX | XX | XX | XX | XX | 12 |
| USSR | XX | XX | XX | XX | XX | XX | XX | XX | XX | XX | XX | XX | 12 |
| **Latin America** | | | | | | | | | | | | | |
| Argentina | | | XX | XX | XX | CH | XX | XX | | | | XX | 7 |
| Chile | XX | XX | | | | | | | XX | XX | XX | XX | 6 |
| Costa Rica | | | | | | | | | | XX | XX | CH | 3 |
| Ecuador | | | | | | | | | XX | CH | XX | | 3 |
| El Salvador | | | | | | | | XX | AA | XX | | | 2 |
| Jamaica | | | | | | | | | | | XX | XX | 2 |
| Mexico | XX | XX | XX | XX | XX | XX | | | | | | | 6 |
| Panama | | | | | | | XX | XX | XX | | | | 3 |
| Venezuela | | | | | | XX | XX | XX | | | | | 3 |
| **W. Eur. + Other** | | | | | | | | | | | | | |
| Australia | XX | XX | | | | | | | | | | | 2 |
| Austria | | | | | | XX | XX | XX | | XX | XX | XX | 7 |
| Belgium | | | | XX | XX | XX | | | | | | | 3 |
| Canada | | | | | | | | | XX | XX | XX | | 3 |
| Denmark | | | | | | XX | XX | XX | XX | XX | XX | | 6 |
| France | CH | CH | XX | XX | XX | XX | XX | XX | XX | XX | XX | XX | 12 |
| Greece | XX | XX | | | | | | | | | | | 2 |
| Italy | | | XX | XX | XX | | | XX | XX | XX | XX | XX | 8 |
| Netherlands | | | | | | | XX | XX | XX | XX | XX | XX | 6 |
| New Zealand | | | | | | | | | | | | XX | 1 |
| Norway | XX | XX | XX | | | | | | | | | | 3 |
| Sweden | | | | | | | | | | | | XX | 1 |
| Turkey | XX | XX | | | | | | XX | XX | XX | | | 5 |
| U.K. | XX | XX | XX | XX | XX | XX | XX | XX | XX | XX | XX | XX | 12 |
| U.S. | XX | XX | XX | XX | XX | XX | XX | XX | XX | XX | XX | XX | 12 |

CH  designates Chairman      AA  denotes absence

## Approving the "Action Plan"

When Mary Lord replaced Eleanor Roosevelt as the Eisenhower administration's representative to the Commission in 1953, she introduced three resolutions proposing (1) advisory services, (2) annual country reports, and (3) global studies. ECOSOC referred the proposals to governments for comment,[3] and the United States lobbied effectively for support in the General Assembly. The Commission had no time to consider the proposals when the members completed drafting the covenants in 1954. With France's René Cassin as chair the Commission approved, over Soviet objections, first the advisory services proposal in 1955[4] and then the country reports and global studies in 1956.

### Advisory Services

Initially the United States proposed three advisory services: seminars, expert assistance, and fellowships and scholarships.[5] Group seminars would help educate a global constituency about the rights affirmed in the Universal Declaration. Individual fellowships would permit intensive study of particular subjects of concern. Governments with human rights problems could call on United Nations technical experts for advice and guidance in projects such as drafting an election law or a criminal code. The sponsors planned to incorporate the new advisory services into the existing United Nations technical assistance program. Pakistan had previously requested assistance in organizing women's groups, and ECOSOC had approved technical assistance programs on freedom of information and women's rights.

In opposing the United States proposals in 1955, the Soviet representative objected to any initiative that would be an alternative to the covenants. Eastern bloc representatives also stressed the importance of promoting economic and social rights; but the United States warned that the Commission should not duplicate the economic programs of specialized agencies such as the ILO, UNESCO, and WHO. In addition, the United States proposed support for creating new nongovernmental and governmental organizations to protect human rights. The United Kingdom successfully amended the draft to remove a provision authorizing assistance from nongovernmental organizations. The United States draft envisioned United Nations aid to governments facing problems with criminal procedure and law, political participation, women's rights, freedom of information, slavery, and discrimination and minorities. The Soviet Union sought to add to the list self-determination, social insurance, medical aid and education. The final compromise text deleted reference to any specific rights, recommending assistance for

> any subject in the field of human rights . . . provided however that the subject shall be one for which adequate assistance is not available through a specialized agency and which does not fall within the scope of existing technical assistance programmes.[6]

The United States initially proposed advisory services of experts as a new form of technical assistance for improving political and legal institutions. Just as less developed countries invited agricultural experts to advise on modern farming methods, the sponsors hoped that predemocratic societies would solicit legal advice on fashioning a constitution, criminal code, or election procedures. Skeptics questioned the connection between economic development and human rights aid. Hugh Keenleyside, Director of the United Nations Technical Assistance Administration, reportedly opposed confusing his economic assistance program with an unrelated human rights campaign.[7]

Secretary-General Dag Hammarskjold opposed the new program. As part of a comprehensive reorganization and retrenchment in 1955, Hammerskjold had proposed eliminating ten professionals from the Human Rights Division, one-third of the staff. The Secretary-General directed John Humphrey to limit the human rights program to "minimum flying speed," and he twice refused to meet Commission Chair René Cassin to discuss objections to the retrenchment.[8] Hammarskjold also attempted to eliminate the *Yearbook on Human Rights* but the Commission instructed the Secretariat to add material to the reference volume. The Commission similarly disregarded the Secretary-General's objections to the other promotional initiatives.

By a vote of 14-2-1 in 1955 the Commission approved an advisory services program of expert assistance, fellowships for study, and international seminars.[9] In approving the advisory services program, the General Assembly directed that the seminar component incorporate the existing technical assistance programs on freedom of information and women's rights. The Assembly authorized only $50,000 for the first year of all three advisory services and included those funds in the technical assistance budget.[10]

## Global Studies

As a second component of the action program proposed in 1953, the United States advocated global studies on specific rights or groups of rights. Charter Article 62 authorizes ECOSOC and subsidiary bodies such as the Commission to "make or initiate studies" and to "make recommendations for the purpose of promoting respect for, and observance of, human rights." Sub-Commission rapporteurs had already begun studies on discrimination. The United States wanted the Commission to study the question of arbitrary arrest, detention and exile, ostensibly as a basis for recommendations to ECOSOC and the Assembly, and to educate world opinion.[11] By soliciting government response to specific queries about current laws and practice, the survey research might also expose problems and promote reform.

The Commission directed that studies report on general developments, progress achieved, and measures taken to safeguard particular liberties.[12] As a result of American pressure, the resolution barred Secretariat officials from contacting states such as communist China which did not belong to the United Nations. In most cases, governments would be given an opportunity to review a summary of information about their country before the study's final recommendations were prepared. By a vote of 12-3-3 the Commission decided the studies would not direct recommendations to particular countries. The United States developed serious reservations about the financial costs of the studies. The United Kingdom voted against the final resolution. Only eleven members voted in favor.[13]

## Annual Country Reports

Formal reporting on human rights by each member of the United Nations became the third component of the United States "Action Plan." International organizations such as the League of Nations and the ILO had previously used reports as an implementation procedure to assure compliance with legal obligations. The United Nations Charter similarly authorizes ECOSOC to give effect to its recommendations by seeking reports from both the specialized agencies and member governments. In 1950, France first proposed a system of annual reports from governments on how they had "promoted respect for, and the progress of, human rights in the preceding year."[14]

The United States strongly preferred such reporting obligations to direct international oversight of domestic practices. The draft resolution envisioned a useful exchange of information "to stimulate Governments of Member States to press forward toward attaining the goals set forth in the Universal Declaration of Human Rights." In the process of conveying information to the Commission, government officials would develop an appreciation for the human rights goals being pursued.

The Soviets objected that the program would serve as an unsatisfactory alternative to the reporting requirements of the proposed covenants, and the United Kingdom also disapproved. The Commission nevertheless adopted the plan 13-4-1, stating the resolution was

> without prejudice to the adoption and ratification of the covenants . . . this resolution shall be subject to review upon the coming into force of the covenants together with measures of implementation.[15]

In deference to the anti-colonial movement, the colonial powers were to report on the right of peoples to self-determination and the status of liberty in non-selfgoverning territories. The resolution called on all governments to report general developments, progress achieved, and measures taken to safeguard human liberty; it also recommended the setting up of national advisory bodies to assist in preparing the reports.

## Implementing Promotional Activities

Just as Western interests determined the creation of a program to promote human rights, Western concepts of individual liberty dominated the first seminars and studies conducted under the program. The Western members and their ideological allies in Asia and Latin America who controlled the Commission through the 1950's promoted a classical liberal conception of human rights. Unlike their Eastern bloc adversaries who regarded the state as a source of economic benefit, Western representatives sought to check arbitrary state power which denied personal freedom and impaired the operation of a free market.

The depression era need for welfare state programs persuaded some Western representatives to support individual economic rights for housing, jobs and education in the Universal Declaration. Such economic assistance from the state, however, could not become an enforceable right in the same way that personal freedom from oppressive government must be guaranteed. States would be encouraged to provide as many welfare benefits as they could afford, but had to be more effectively compelled to respect fundamental civil and political rights. According to the traditional liberal view, a truly free people would provide for their own economic well-being.

Democratic governments of Latin America and Asia joined with the West to give the Commission's early promotional efforts an exclusive focus on individual civil and political rights. The 1950s seminars and studies gave first priority to freedom of information, individual liberty and most importantly, due process in criminal procedure. Non-aligned and socialist representatives advocated more support for group rights of disadvantaged classes, youth, minorities, and especially women. As newly independent African governments joined the United Nations after 1960, Third World states gave greater emphasis to self-determination, equal rights and nondiscrimination.

### Advisory Services Seminars

In setting up the advisory services program, the first Director of the Secretariat's Human Rights Division, John Humphrey, confronted opposition from the Secretary-General as well as a natural reluctance of governments with human rights problems to acknowledge a need for aid. Not surprisingly, Humphrey, a former Canadian law professor, gave top priority to arranging seminars on criminal procedure. He actively sought to persuade governments to host seminars on subjects where they had a good record that might serve as a model to others.

Rather than wait for states to extend invitations, Humphrey traveled extensively to solicit government sponsors. In seeking hosts for the seminars, Humphrey concluded it was "unrealistic to think that governments would ask the United Nations for technical assistance in a matter as politically delicate as

TABLE 3.2
Advisory Services Seminar Topics and Hosts by Region, 1955-1966

| Topic | Total | Africa | Asia | East Europe | Latin America | West Europe |
|---|---|---|---|---|---|---|
| Civil Rights+ Liberties | 13 | 0 | 4 | 1 | 3 | 5 |
| Economic Devel. | 2 | 2 | 0 | 0 | 0 | 0 |
| Women's Rights | 10 | 2 | 4 | 2 | 2 | 0 |
| Minorities/Youth | 3 | 0 | 0 | 2 | 1 | 0 |
| Total | 28 | 4 | 8 | 3 | 7 | 6 |

human rights."[16] Thus Humphrey encouraged officials to hold seminars which revealed their country's strengths. Sweden convened a seminar on the role of parliamentary institutions, with particular emphasis on the ombudsman. Seminars in the United Kingdom on freedom of association, Poland on children's rights, and Yugoslavia on national minorities, further illustrate efforts to provide international leadership rather than to address national weaknesses. Table 3.2 displays the distribution of topics by regional hosts and reveals the strong preference of Western governments for themes related to criminal due process.

When Humphrey urged governments to arrange meetings that might stimulate domestic reform, he had less success. Although many Third World governments held meetings on women's rights, he never could find an Arab government willing to do so; Brazilian officials, sensitive to tension within their multiracial society, were unwilling to conduct a seminar on race relations until the issue could be safely addressed under the rubric of apartheid in 1966. Regimes which violate human rights obviously refuse to create an international forum for discussion of their abuses. The United Nations, however, has conducted conferences in states accused of human rights violations without discussion of abuses by the host government.[17] Local events during some seminars did, nevertheless, cause political embarrassment for the sponsoring government. In 1959 an attempted coup in Argentina provided a timely case study for the Buenos Aires Seminar on "judicial and other remedies against the illegal exercise or abuse of administrative authority." Rebel forces temporarily seized control of Addis Ababa, Ethiopia, during a 1960 seminar on the participation of women in public life. Dissidents in Mexico City staged a protest in 1961 at a seminar on *amparo* and *habeas corpus*.[18]

Humphrey reports that political and ideological pressures influenced both the selection of hosts and participants. The United States initially pressured him to exclude communist participants and opposed Eastern bloc sponsorship of any seminar.[19] Not until 1961, after ten seminars in non-communist states, did an Eastern bloc member, Romania, play host for a meeting on the status of women in family law. When Mongolia sponsored a regional seminar on the participa - tion of women in public life, its government attempted to exclude participants from Taiwan, South Vietnam, and South Korea; participants from those states though invited, refused to attend without guarantees for their safety. Egypt refused to hold a regional meeting that would require participation by Israel.

After agreeing on an appropriate topic, Humphrey would negotiate a cost sharing agreement as directed by Commission guidelines. For a regional meeting the United Nations paid for the travel and subsistence of participants, and preparation of background papers by expert consultants, and Secretariat personnel to staff the conference.[20] The host government furnished conference facilities and personnel, interpreters, translators and support staff.[21] In preparing for a two-week seminar, the Secretariat commissioned several twenty to thirty page background papers on the seminar's theme from experts representing different ideological perspectives. Participants prepared 10 to 20 page working papers for duplication and distribution. After the first few seminars, funds were unavailable for working party sessions before the regular meeting.

Following greetings by a host country official and a Secretariat representa - tive, the members elected a chairman from the host country. The informal seminar discussions were not recorded, and with one exception the groups did not vote or adopt formal resolutions. Activists did, however, seek approval for recommendations that might be useful in representations to policy organs. A final report prepared by Secretariat staff summarized the discussion, highlighted areas of consensus, and included proposed recommendations. The United Nations office of public information published the reports as sales documents.[22]

The topics selected for the first seminars reflected the legal interests of Humphrey, a Canadian, and host governments in Asia and Latin America seeking to promote reforms in criminal procedure. The Commission initially recommended seminars on prevention of discrimination and protection of minorities[23] and in 1960 lamented that no governments had offered to sponsor a seminar on discrimination. France's representative, René Cassin, reportedly selected the seminar topic on remedies for the illegal exercise of administrative authority.[24] The Commission on the Status of Women often gave more direction than the Commission in recommending seminar topics. In the program's first decade, narrowly defined topics on criminal justice, individual, and women's rights were repeated in seminars organized on a regional basis. The Eastern bloc minority on the Commission unsuccessfully urged the Secretariat to arrange for more seminars on economic and social rights and to move beyond regional meetings to larger international seminars.

*Women's Rights.* In 1957 Thailand sponsored the very first seminar in the Advisory Services Program: "The civic responsibilities and increased participation of Asian Women in public life." Colombia, Ethiopia, and Mongolia subsequently hosted seminars on increased participation by women in their regions. Despite United States objections about inadmissible NGO and East German propaganda, anti-American speeches at the seminar in Mongolia condemned policies in Vietnam unrelated to women's issues. Participants at the 1966 Philippines seminar on the advancement of women addressed the need for a long-range program. Regional seminars on "The status of women in family law" convened in Romania, Japan, Colombia, and Togo. Romania also arranged meetings on "The effects of scientific and technological developments on the status of women."

*Criminal Procedure.* Four regional seminars hosted by the Philippines, Chile, Austria, and New Zealand considered "The protection of human rights in criminal law and procedures." All the participants in the Philippines were English speaking lawyers, none representing their governments. The Vienna seminar in 1960 was the first attended by a participant from the U.S.S.R., a vice president of its Supreme Court.

Sri Lanka, Argentina, and Sweden sponsored meetings on "Judicial and other remedies against the illegal exercise or abuse of administrative authority." New Zealand reportedly created an ombudsman following the seminar in Kandy, Sri Lanka.[25] Mexico hosted a seminar on *amparo, habeas corpus* and similar remedies, Australia a session on the role of police in protecting human rights, and Japan a meeting on the substantive criminal law and penal sanctions. Humphrey regarded the Australian seminar at Canberra as one of the best, because of participation by Australian judges and police commissioners, good press coverage, and an excellent report.[26] Participation by police and magistrates at Canberra suggested a model for a different type of seminar—a training course to persuade junior and intermediate officials responsible for daily operations of the criminal justice system to respect due process guarantees. A Canadian member of the Commission in 1963 proposed adding training courses to the advisory service program.[27] Following the ten criminal justice seminars held between 1958 and 1963, no other government sponsored a seminar on due process until 1980.

*Individual Rights.* Two regional and two international seminars promoted individual civil liberties central to democratic theory. India's Prime Minister Nehru addressed the 1962 seminar on Freedom of Information in New Delhi. Two years later, a seminar on the same topic meeting in Rome adopted a resolution on a code of ethics and international machinery for promoting freedom of information. A Commission committee on Freedom of Information created in the 1950s revealed early differences between Western members promoting freedom of the press and Third World representatives seeking greater technical aid for the acquisition of communications media.

*Economic Rights.* During the program's first decade, the United Nations funded an average of three regional seminars annually, but only two concerned economic issues. Regional seminars in Afghanistan and Senegal considered the difficulty of reconciling economic development with individual rights. Not until 1966 did the Commission approve a seminar proposed by Poland on the Universal Declaration's economic and social provisions.

### Advisory Services Fellowships and Expert Advisers

In contrast to the popularity and success of the seminars, the other two elements of the advisory services program had minimal impact. The United Nations funded only two fellowships for individuals before 1962 and only two governments requested expert advice. The initial fellowships on judicial administration enabled grant recipients to observe criminal investigation, interrogation, and trial procedures. A few judges and prosecutors studied alternatives to judicial remedies including the use of administrative tribunals and the ombudsman.[28]

Since governments were more willing to acknowledge economic needs than human rights deficiencies, there was little demand for legal advisers. Without identifying the beneficiaries, the Secretariat discreetly reported that:

> a few governments only have availed themselves so far of the experts' services. . . . Two Governments, for example, received advice concerning elections, electoral laws, procedures and techniques, . . . It may be that this part of the programme should be made better known.[29]

The unnamed countries were Haiti and Costa Rica. In response to Haiti's 1957 request for an election expert, Guy Perior de Feral of France's Conseil d'État visited for eight days, just before the host government was overthrown.[30] Beginning in 1958, Costa Rica's more stable democracy benefited from several visits by experts who recommended improvements in the electoral laws. Election observers from Canada, Sweden, and Uruguay made suggestions which led the government to seek further advice from individual experts.[31] After several years of perfunctory acceptance and approval of the Secretary-General's annual report, the Commission routinely postponed consideration of the advisory services program altogether.

### Studies on Detainees

To prepare its first two global studies the Commission appointed a committee of four members that examined the rights of criminal defendants. The United States proposed the first study on the right of everyone to be free from arbitrary arrest, detention, and exile. Changing membership and divided responsibility on the committee resulted in major delays. Representatives of Chile, Norway, Pakistan, and the Philippines comprised the original committee.

As those governments left the Commission, Argentina, Ceylon, and Belgium, but no Eastern bloc member, assumed responsibility for the study.

The study committee used survey responses and material from five sources: (1) governments belonging to the United Nations; (2) the Secretary-General; (3) specialized agencies; (4) nongovernmental organizations; and (5) scholarly writings.[32]  The Secretariat prepared and forwarded country monographs to governments for comment before the completed study was submitted to the Commission in 1961.[33]  The Commission asked the committee to revise the study by including draft principles on freedom from arbitrary arrest, detention, and exile[34] and to prepare another study.  For its second project the committee studied the right of arrested persons to communicate with those necessary to ensure their defense or to protect their essential interests.[35]  The Commission referred both studies and the draft principles to governments for further comment but took no further action until the mid-1970s.[36]

In addition to studies conducted by its own members, the Commission had indirect responsibility for research conducted by independent experts on the Sub-Commission described in Chapter 8.  The experts learned by the early 1950s that the government representatives on the Commission were more interested in assimilating than in protecting minorities.  As a result, they investigated a series of relatively more acceptable topics related to discrimination in education, religion, political rights, and emigration.  Individual rapporteurs conducted global surveys as the basis for comprehensive reports which received only belated and perfunctory review by the Commission.

*Periodic Reports*

By requiring United Nations members to report regularly on human rights conditions, the Commission created a potential tool for monitoring compliance with international norms.  The ILO used a similar procedure to make specific inquiries about shortcomings identified in reports on labor conditions.  Searching inquiry into specific failings would have enabled the Commission to target precise recommendations and to shame governments into accepting their obligations to respect international norms.  With sufficient political will, the Commission could have used the reports to expose local abuses and to propose specific reforms.  Not surprisingly, the reporting governments promoted their own virtues as much as the human rights values of the Universal Declaration.

The Commission and ECOSOC repeatedly changed the reporting schedule, format, and review procedures.  The Commission initially recommended annual reports, but ECOSOC established a triennial reporting schedule, setting the first period for 1954–1956.  As required by the initial authorizing resolution, the Secretariat assisted Commission review in 1959 by preparing a summary of the first group of 41 countries[37] and specialized agency reports.  For the second cycle, 1957–1959, the Comission created an *ad hoc* Committee of six members to screen reports from 59 governments in 1961.  The government representatives never seriously scrutinized the information provided, but merely urged more states to submit reports with details of actual conditions. After the third triennial reporting period in 1962, ECOSOC shifted to annual reports covering a three-year period on one of three separate groups of rights—political and civil rights in the first year, economic, social and cultural rights in the second, and freedom of information in the third.

NGOs eager and willing to provide concrete information were first authorized to make "objective" observations about reports in the third period, 1960–1962. In 1964 the Commission appointed an *ad hoc* committee of eight which held 16 meetings to review 48 reports and accompanying NGO commentary. The United States attempted to get NGO comments distributed as conference room documents, but the chair simply gave the unofficial observations to members expressing an interest. Against the wishes of members who characterized them as superficial and tendentious, the committee did propose giving governments an opportunity to reply to the NGO comments.

The "independent" experts on the Sub-Commission failed to take advantage of their one opportunity to give meaningful scrutiny to the reports for the 1965 to 1967 period. The United States proposed the appointment of Israel's Judge Zeev Zeltner as rapporteur to review the reports. In four annexes to his report, the rapporteur summarized the observations of nongovernmental organizations, some critical of Arab governments. The Soviets prevailed 8-6-4 in a Sub-Commission vote to withdraw the annexes; ECOSOC subsequently withdrew the Sub-Commission's authority to review further reports. By 1966 the General Assembly had completed work on the covenants which, once ratified, would provide a more comprehensive reporting system independent of the Commission.

In practice, the reports contained little information about actual conditions and far too much detail about constitutional or statutory guarantees which might only exist on paper. The Commission took little notice and overlooked widespread disregard for its resolutions calling on governments to report. Rather than criticize or make suggestions to specific governments, the members used the reports as a vehicle for sharing experiences and as a basis for general recommendations.[38] Frustrated activists viewed the reports as the least effective part of the Action Program.[39]

*Other Promotional Activities*

Despite opposition from Secretary-General Hammarskjold, the Commission directed the Secretariat to continue publication of an annual *Yearbook of Human Rights*. The first volume for 1946 included all the declarations and bills on human rights in force in various countries.[40] For succeeding volumes of the *Yearbook* national correspondents provided appropriate commentary on texts of statutes, Constitutions and judicial decisions. The Secretariat published English and French editions. The Commission solicited statements on categories of rights, but soon found there was too much material for publication. Fifty-six governments submitted information on the Universal Declaration's provision on arbitrary arrest and detention. In 1958 the Commission set a limit of 320 pages in the English edition. By then publication of the *Yearbook* had fallen several years behind schedule.

To commemorate the Universal Declaration's 10th anniversary in 1958[41] Afghanistan, India, and Pakistan sponsored a resolution disregarded by ECOSOC to proclaim a Freedom from Prejudice and Discrimination Day. After the General Assembly designated the Declaration's 20th anniversary as a year for human rights,[42] The Commission formed a 34-member committee to plan for a major international conference in 1968.[43] Jamaica chaired the committee which held four meetings over a ten-month period, appointed a working party, and recommended an interim public education program.

## Drafting Principles, Declarations, and Conventions

### Declarations on Children's Rights and Asylum

By 1957 the Commission had approved and the Secretariat had begun to implement the promotional activities proposed by the United States. At that time, other members more interested than the United States in further standard-setting persuaded the Commission to recommend to the Assembly declarations on the rights of the child and on asylum.

International sympathy for the plight of the young has prompted both the League of Nations and the United Nations to proclaim the rights of children. At its inception the United Nations resolved to reaffirm the 1924 Geneva Declaration of the Rights of the Child. Polish children had suffered particularly from the break-up of families, Nazi persecution, and medical experimentation in World War II. Poland's representatives have assiduously pressed the Commis-sion to address problems such as adoption, children of separated parents of different nationalities, children kidnapped and taken across frontiers, children temporarily or permanently deprived of parental care owing to imprisonment, exile, deportation or other judicial or administrative sanctions.[44] The United Nations Social Commission had referred a draft Declaration to the Commission on Human Rights in 1949. Not until 1957 did the Commission find an opportunity to revise the text. After further changes in the Third Committee, the Assembly unanimously approved the Declaration on the Rights of the Child in 1959.[45] Poland continued to advocate a binding convention guaranteeing children's rights, and in the 1970s the Commission began a drafting effort.

France took the lead in proposing a declaration on the right to asylum at the 1957 session. Whether crossing international boundaries en masse or seeking refuge individually, political exiles have sought protection that governments have been reluctant to acknowledge as a right in international law. The

Universal Declaration of Human Rights proclaimed the right of everyone "to seek and to enjoy in other countries asylum from persecution."[46] The draft covenants, however, made no provision for a right to asylum. Recognizing that governments were unlikely to agree to a convention, France proposed instead a simple declaration. Following adoption by the Commission in 1960, the Third and Sixth Committees took seven years to review and revise the text before the Assembly passed the Declaration on Territorial Asylum in 1967.

The Declaration's "chief purpose seems to be to protect states."[47] The Assembly carefully guarded state sovereignty against unwelcome victims of persecution by providing: "It shall rest with the State granting asylum to evaluate the grounds for the grant of asylum." The Declaration encourages protection for persons struggling against colonialism, but denies aid to those guilty of crimes against humanity. Joint international undertakings are recommended to relieve states burdened by an overwhelming number of exiles. The most significant protection affirmed in the Assembly Declaration had already been included in the 1951 Refugee Convention. That is, except for overriding reasons of national security, no exile should be rejected at the frontier, expelled, or compelled to return to a territory where persecution was likely. If unable to accommodate a mass influx, a government should attempt to send refugees to another state rather than return them to certain oppression.

The Commission took up only one other standard-setting task in the 1950s when it directed the Committee studying the rights of detainees to draft principles for their protection. The United Nations had previously adopted the highly regarded Standard Rules for the Treatment of Prisoners which did not apply to detainees awaiting trial. The draft principles referred to governments by the Commission in 1962 did not lead to a meaningful follow-up until the 1970s.[48]

*The Convention Against Racial Discrimination*

After 1960 Third World states significantly redirected the Commission's standard-setting agenda. Seventeen newly independent African governments joined the United Nations in 1960. The Commission membership was increased from 18 to 21 members in 1962, but the African states still had no representation. The Non-Aligned Movement (NAM) held its first Summit conference at Belgrade, Yugoslavia in 1961, and the members agreed to consult at the United Nations. Not surprisingly, nonwhite subjects of European rule viewed racial discrimination as an overriding human rights problem requiring new international standards.

The campaign to legislate stronger international norms guaranteeing racial equality began long before the United Nations created a Commission on Human Rights. Nonwhites subject to the European slave trade and colonial rule had progressively challenged doctrines of white supremacy that have persisted into the twentieth century. Prior to World War I publicists sought to elaborate on the slogans of "The White Man's Burden," "Nordic Superiority," and "The Yellow Peril," among others. While some proclaimed that Asiatic control of territory surely would result in "racial retrogression," others spoke contemptuously of "those whose skins are black, yellow, or red." . . . These statements were accompanied by "scientific" studies of skull types, bone structures, speech patterns, and skin color designed to "prove" the superiority of one race over all others in the world.[49]

Asian governments had vainly protested the exclusionary immigration policies of the United States, United Kingdom, and Australia.

Japan antagonized its World War I allies by proposing an amendment on racial equality to an article on religious toleration proposed for the League of Nations Covenant by President Wilson.

The equality of nations being a basic principle of the League of Nations, the High Contracting Parties agree to accord, as soon as possible, to all alien nationals' of States members of the League equal and just treatment in every respect, making no distinction, either in law or in fact, on account of their race or nationality.[50]

When the British and Americans unequivocally refused to consider that text, the Japanese representatives deleted all reference to race from a revised proposal that League members support "the principle of equality of nations and just treatment of their nationals."[51]    Although the amendment carried eleven votes out of seventeen, Wilson as chair applied the unanimity rule in concluding the proposal had not been adopted.[52]

The Western sponsors of the United Nations Conference at San Francisco initially opposed nondiscrimination provisions for the Charter in the same manner. Britain and the United States rejected China's attempts to include a provision on racial equality in the Dumbarton Oaks proposals.[53] As described in Chapter 1, pressure from Latin American representatives and nongovernmental organizations led the sponsoring powers to propose modest human rights provisions for the Charter at San Francisco. As a result, one purpose of the United Nations proclaimed in Article 1 is to "achieve international cooperation in . . . promoting and encouraging respect for human rights and for fundamental freedoms for all without distinction as to race, sex, language, or religion."

Whatever moral imperative that statement imposed, however, was weakened by the express protection of national sovereignty in the Article 2(7) prohibition on United Nations interference with domestic jurisdiction. When asked during Senate ratification hearings whether the United Nations would have jurisdiction to examine racial discrimination in the United States, Senator Vandenberg declared that Article 2(7) "would prevent any compulsion of enforcement whatever."[54]    Mrs. Roosevelt similarly took refuge in the unenforceable character of the Universal Declaration of Human Rights when critics worried about international challenges to American domestic practice.

The Declaration's single reference to racial equality in Article 2 provides: "Everyone is entitled to all the rights and freedoms set forth in this Declaration, without distinction of any kind, such as race, colour, sex, language, religion ..." The Commission included identical language in both covenants, but those drafts were stalled in the General Assembly when events indicated a need for more effective international protection. In 1960 the International League for the Rights of Man presented the Sub-Commission with evidence of Neo-Nazi activity in several European countries, including West Germany.[55] The Sub-Commission and Commission both condemned the practices and called on the Secretariat to obtain additional information.[56] The Commission asked the Sub-Commission to evaluate material received from governments and to make recommendations. Western members opposed to anti-semitic religious prejudice found African representatives coming to the United Nations for the first time more determined to prohibit racial discrimination. The Eastern bloc traditionally expressed greater sympathy for racial than for religious minorities and supported the anti-colonial goals of the Afro-Asian states. In 1962 the General Assembly directed preparation of declarations and conventions on both racial discrimination and religious intolerance. The United Nations completed work on the race discrimination convention within three years, but took until 1981 to agree on the Declaration Against Religious Intolerance.

Drafting began in the Sub-Commission which recommended a declaration on race discrimination to the Commission in 1963. The Commission spent seventeen of thirty-five meetings on the Declaration and appointed a working group to reconcile conflicting drafts.[57] The Commission unanimously approved a revised draft which the General Assembly adopted on November 20, 1963.[58] The following year the Sub-Commission drafted a convention on race discrimination as well as a proposed declaration on religious intolerance. The Commission gave no consideration to the latter, but promptly forwarded an amended version of the race convention to the General Assembly. After avoiding any formal votes in 1964 (because of a dispute over the Soviet Union's financial contribution), the Assembly unanimously approved a revised International Convention on the Elimination of All Forms of Racial Discrimination in 1965, one year before enacting the two covenants.[59]

In substance the Race Convention "represents a synthesis of the 'individual' and 'group' conceptions of human rights."[60] The text's preliminary clauses refer both to the Universal Declaration and to the Declaration on the Granting of Independence to Colonial Countries and Peoples.[61] The seven substantive articles not only prohibit discrimination against individuals, but also support "when circumstances so warrant, ... special and concrete measures to ensure the adequate development and protection of certain racial groups."[62] The Convention does not, however, "apply to distinction, exclusions, restrictions or preferences made by a State Party . . . between citizens and noncitizens."[63] Western states could legally continue to limit nonwhite immigration since

> [n]othing in this Convention may be interpreted as affecting in any way the legal provisions of States Parties concerning nationality, citizenship or naturalization, provided that such provisions do not discriminate against any particular nationality.[64]

The Convention's general definition of "racial discrimination" applies to more than prejudice based on mere skin color: "any distinction, exclusion, restriction or preference based on race, colour, descent, or national or ethnic origin . . . "[65]    The United States nevertheless proposed both in the Commission and the Assembly language proscribing anti-semitism.    The Soviet Union countered with an amendment adding Nazism, including all its manifestations (neo-Nazism), and a provision that equated anti-semitism with Zionism and colonialism.    Afro-Asian members opposed to Israeli policies in the Middle East buried the United States proposal 82 to 12 with 10 abstentions in the Third Committee.[66]

In the Commission, Western members had negotiated an article on racist propaganda that made incitement to racial discrimination a criminal offense only when it resulted in an act of violence.    The Assembly revised the text so that states parties "[s]hall declare an offence punishable by law all dissemination of ideas based on racial superiority or hatred, incitement to racial discrimination, as well as all acts of violence or incitement to such acts against any race or group of persons."[67]    In addition, states parties pledged to prohibit organizations which incite racial discrimination and to punish participation in such organizations. Qualifying language insisted on by the West gave "due regard to the principles embodied in the Universal Declaration of Human Rights"[68] and to rights listed in Article 5 of the Convention, including freedom of speech and association.    In view of the apparent conflict between the provisions, Western states ratifying the convention have expressed reservations indicating their intent to give priority to free speech and association.

Like the economic covenant, the race convention obliges state parties to undertake national legislative, administrative, and judicial reforms.    States undertake to pursue a policy of eliminating racial discrimination in all its forms,[69] to prevent, prohibit and eradicate racial segregation and apartheid,[70] to guarantee everyone equality before the law,[71] and "to adopt immediate and effective measures (particularly in the fields of teaching, education, culture, and information) with a view to combating prejudices which lead to racial discrimination."[72]    The convention encourages affirmative action in social, economic, cultural, and other fields so long as separate rights are not maintained "after the objectives for which they were taken have been achieved."[73]    The

Commission proposed no measures of international implementation to enforce state compliance with their obligations.

Ghana's delegation proposed implementation provisions in the Assembly.

> When they continued to push their suggestions notwithstanding the objections of some of the other African countries, the speculation in the corridors was that they did so because they were annoyed by the Russians who had, it seems, reproached them for playing into the hands of the United States—an accusation that so infuriated them that they pushed proposals which had been originally launched more or less as a kite.[74]

In several respects the implementation provisions finally accepted for the race convention go beyond the procedures under the political covenant. Both instruments establish a committee of eighteen experts empowered to create a conciliation commission to hear interstate disputes. The Committee on the Elimination of Racial Discrimination, however, need not await a party's optional declaration before receiving interstate complaints of noncompliance.[75] The race convention requires states to report at two-year intervals,[76] while the political covenant leaves the reporting schedule to the discretion of the Human Rights Committee. Under an optional declaration provided for in the race convention rather than in a separate protocol, states may authorize the Committee on Race Discrimination to receive complaints from their nationals.[77] The Committee submits its own annual reports and recommendations to the General Assembly via the Secretary General rather than through the Commission.[78]

As with the Universal Declaration, the swift preparation and general acceptance can be attributed to domination by a single-minded majority. Even if Western officials had been unwilling to repudiate offensive doctrines of white supremacy, formerly subject peoples now had sufficient votes to establish binding principles of nondiscrimination. The drafting process involved a rare collaboration of Sub-Commission experts with the Commission's government representatives that helped contribute to an unusual consensus.[79] As the Commission turned to draft more precise instruments on religious intolerance and apartheid, fundamental ideological differences reappeared.

*Religious Intolerance.* Considering how religious controversies have spawned crusades, jihads, genocide, civil war, revolution, and individual persecution, it is not surprising that the Commission attempted to formulate standards protecting fundamental religious liberties. It is perhaps more surprising that Western Protestants and Catholics, communist atheists, Indian Hindus, Arab Muslims and Jews were able to agree on The Universal Declaration's provision for freedom of thought, conscience, and religion. Arabs successfully opposed including a right to change religion from the similar article in the International Covenant on Civil and Political Rights.[80]

Even before the Assembly approved the Covenants in 1966, the Sub-Commission had completed a study on religious discrimination and had drafted a declaration. The United States expert P. Halpern began the Sub-Commission study in 1955, but Arcot Krishnaswami of India became the rapporteur.[81] The Sub-Commission referred draft principles from the Krishnaswami report to governments for review in 1960. In response to anti-semitic acts in Europe, the Sub-Commission made recommendations that led to a General Assembly directive to prepare instruments on both race discrimination and religious intolerance. The Commission postponed work on the Sub-Commission's draft on religion, and proceeded instead to the declaration and convention on race discrimination described above. After completing the race convention, the Commission spent one session drafting five articles for a declaration on religion without completing a resolution. Not until 1974 did the Commission create a working group to return to the task.[82]

*War Crimes*

In contrast to the impressive consensus on racial discrimination, cold war rivalry over West Germany divided the Commission's drafting of a Convention on the Non-Applicability of Statutory Limitations to War Crimes and Crimes Against Humanity. Poland proposed the treaty as part of a campaign to force West Germany to extend its statute of limitations for Nazi war criminals beyond 1965. As many as 18,000 Nazis suspected of war crimes remained free.[83] The West German government made temporary extensions, first until 1969 and subsequently until 1979, but objected to Soviet demands that individuals already beyond the statutory period be subjected to further liability. NATO allies the United States and the United Kingdom opposed the effort to draft an international convention.

Following complaints of Neo-Nazi practices, in 1965 the Sub-Commission and Commission urged all states to trace, apprehend and punish criminals responsible for war crimes and "invited eligible States which had not done so to accede as soon as possible to the Convention on the Prevention and Punishment of the Crime of Genocide."[84] At the Commission's request, ECOSOC asked states to provide any available information about war criminals.

In 1965 the Commission asked the Secretary-General to draft a convention that would oblige states to eliminate any statute of limitation to the prosecution of war criminals. The Commission revised the Secretariat draft, but failed to reach agreement in 1967, when West Germany had conditionally agreed to sign. A joint working group of the Assembly's Third and Sixth committees prepared the final text.[85] The General Assembly passed the convention in November 1968[86] and it entered into force two years later.[87] The convention provides for states party to eliminate all statutory limitations both for war crimes and for peace time crimes against humanity, including genocide and inhuman acts resulting from apartheid: "[T]here is no period of limitation for war crimes and crimes against humanity comparable to the rules of municipal law providing a period of limitation for ordinary crimes."[88]

Over Eastern bloc objections, the convention only remained open for signature for one year, until December 1969, and was only open to accession by states which signed before that deadline. Of the twenty-three states parties, thirteen are from Eastern Europe, including the German Democratic Republic. The Council of Europe subsequently drafted a regional convention on the non-applicability of statutory limitations[89] and in 1979 the West German parliament abolished its statute of limitations.[90]

## Pressures for Change

The Commission's emphasis on promotional initiatives and further standard-setting after 1954 caused widespread dissatisfaction and prompted conflicting proposals for institutional reform. After sponsoring the "Action Plan," the United States sought to economize by holding Commission meetings only in alternate years rather than annually.[91] ECOSOC budgeted no money for a 1964 session, but the General Assembly approved the necessary funds. Asian and Latin American members enlisted Commission support for the anti-colonial struggle with resolutions recommending the creation of a new United Nations Commission on Self Determination which the General Assembly never approved.

Activists seeking improved international machinery to protect victims of human rights violations complained that the Commission was in the doldrums.[92] The Commission did draft two measures which established two long-awaited enforcement bodies but conducted no investigations of its own during the delay. The proposed International Covenant on Civil and Political Rights included an optional interstate complaint procedure to be conducted by a new Human Rights Committee; the General Assembly added an Optional Protocol allowing an individual right of petition. In 1965 the Commission approved a separate optional petition procedure and a review committee as part of the International Convention on the Elimination of All Forms of Racial Discrimination.[93] A decade before those United Nations instruments were adopted, the European Commission on Human Rights and The European Court of Human Rights had begun to investigate and adjudicate individual complaints. In 1963 the General Assembly sent a fact finding mission to South Vietnam to investigate allegations that Saigon's Catholic government had violated Buddhist rights.

The Commission remained unresponsive to individual communications and to interstate complaints, despite the best efforts of Secretariat officials, nongovernmental observers, and Third World members to change the policy of self-denial. Nongovernmental organizations sponsored a 1958 conference which urged the Commission to help eradicate prejudice and discrimination. The

International League for the Rights of Man documented anti-semitic acts in Germany, but the Commission adopted only a general condemnation of racial prejudice. After its founding in 1961, Amnesty International began lobbying on behalf of prisoners of conscience. In 1966 the ILO called the Commission's attention to violation of workers' rights in Burundi. France objected when Ceylon's member of the Committee on Detainees complained about violations in Algeria. Egypt, India, and the Philippines attempted in both the Assembly and Commission to eliminate the restrictions on access to individual communications, and the Commission appointed a seven-member group to study the restrictive procedures.

ECOSOC responded in 1959 by approving only technical changes[94] which consolidated several procedural amendments and reiterated the Commission's impotence.[95] The resolution directed the Secretary-General to provide the Commission with government replies to complaints as well as with a confidential statistical analysis of how the communications related to articles of the Universal Declaration. ECOSOC required the Secretary-General to notify *all* petitioners that the Commission had no power to take any action. (See Appendix A for the complete text of ECOSOC Resolution 728 (XXVIII) F of 1959.)

Since the Commission could not and would not take meaningful action on reported violations, reformers proposed alternative institutional remedies. Commission Chair R.S.S. Gunewardene of Ceylon added an agenda item to help establish national advisory committees, while other activists revived a proposal for an international criminal court. An alternative proposal to appoint a United Nations Commissioner for Human Rights won the most support. In the early 1950s Uruguay had introduced an NGO proposal attributed to Moses Moskowitz for a United Nations "Attorney General" who could screen individual complaints.[96] Shortly before his assassination in 1963, President Kennedy suggested the possibility of authorizing the Commission chair to perform a kind of ombudsman function between sessions. John Humphrey preferred instead an independent Commissioner for Human Rights appointed by the General Assembly to assist the Commission in reviewing country reports as well as to investigate situations and to mediate disputes.[97]

Sean MacBride of the International Commission of Jurists helped draft a resolution in 1964, and Costa Rica's Ambassador Fernando Volio Jiménez proposed the High Commissioner in the Assembly which referred the matter to the Commission. Eastern bloc representatives bitterly denounced the perceived threat to national sovereignty. The Commission appointed a nine member working group which studied and approved the proposal; ECOSOC subsequently forwarded the recommendation to the General Assembly without result.[98]

United Nations organs concerned with decolonization and racial discrimina - tion never adopted the type of self-imposed restraint approved by the Commission. The Trusteeship Council received petitions in accord with Article

87(b) of the Charter. The General Assembly's Special Committee on the Policies of Apartheid also reviewed communications from South Africa.[99] Despite its professed commitment to national sovereignty, the Soviet Union sponsored measures for decolonization which brought the policies of European administering powers under United Nations scrutiny.[100] In 1961 the Assembly gave the power to receive individual communications to a Special Committee on the Situation with regard to the Implementation of the Declaration on the Granting of Independence to Colonial Countries and Peoples.[101] After investigatory hearings in several African states, that Committee presented evidence to the Commission in 1965 showing widespread violation of human rights in the territories of Southern Africa.

The Third World quest for self-determination produced a procedural breakthrough which empowered the Commission to investigate complaints. After the Special Committee's initiative, ECOSOC invited the Commission to consider "the question of violation of human rights and fundamental freedoms, including policies of racial discrimination and segregation and of apartheid, in all countries, with particular reference to colonial and other dependent countries and territories"[102] and to make recommendations on how to stop violations. The resolution's sponsors—Algeria, Cameroon, the U.S.S.R., and Tanzania— wanted the Commission to focus exclusively on problems in colonial and dependent territories. The Western members succeeded in ensuring reference to "all countries."[103]

At the Commission's 1966 session, the United States and Soviet representatives debated whether the procedures should apply to violations in independent as well as dependent territories.[104] In a Soviet resolution amended to cover all countries the Commission condemned human rights violations and sought authority to review its tasks and functions. The Commission also asked the Sub-Commission for recommendations.[105] Recognizing the significance of its action, ECOSOC then asked the General Assembly to authorize Commission recommendations on "ways and means of improving the capacity of the United Nations to put a stop to violations of human rights wherever they may occur." The Assembly approved.[106]

The United States and Soviet experts in the Sub-Commission introduced competing resolutions on proposed reforms. United States expert Clyde Ferguson proposed quasi-judicial procedures that would make the Sub-Commission an investigative body empowered to use communications as evidence.[107] Ferguson proposed that the Sub-Commission consider whether the communications, in conjunction with other material, revealed "any consistent pattern of violations . . . including policies of racial discrimination, segregation and apartheid, in any country, with particular reference to colonial and other dependent territories."[108] The Sub-Commission did not accept Ferguson's text, but instead approved Soviet expert Nasinovsky's recommendations for information gathering which made no reference to communications. Ferguson's draft was forwarded to the Commission "without approval or disapproval, as illustrative of a possible method"[109]

The Commission receiving that proposal in 1967 would dramatically differ from the group which had given top priority to promotion in the 1955–1966 period.  The Non-Aligned Movement had steadily grown in size and cohesion with important consequences for all policy making organs in the United Nations system.  ECOSOC enlarged the Commission's membership from 21 to 32 and allocated 20 seats to Third World states according to a strict regional formula: Africa–8; Asia–6; Eastern Europe–4; Latin America–6; and Western Europe and other–8.  In future the Commission would elect three vice-chairmen and a rapporteur in addition to the chairman, so that each region would have one representative on a bureau of five officers.  After twenty years without an Eastern bloc chair or effective African representation, the Commission would no longer be controlled by its dominant Western members.  The 1967 session initiated a third stage in the Commission's growth devoted to a protection agenda reflecting the concerns of a new non-Western majority.

# 4

# Non-Aligned Protection
# Initiatives, 1967–1979

The new African and Asian representatives joining the Commission in 1967 came determined to combat racial discrimination and to advance the right of self-determination.[1]  Table 4.1 lists member governments from all five regions for the 1967–1979 period.  Not content with drafting international laws criminalizing *apartheid* and conducting studies on self-determination, the Non-Aligned Movement (NAM) promptly sought enforcement powers to halt egregious violations.  As a result, the Commission repudiated the policy of self denial in effect since 1947.[2]  The Commission asked ECOSOC for an express mandate to "recommend and adopt general and specific measures to deal with violations of human rights."[3]  For the first time since authorized by ECOSOC in 1947, the Commission appointed experts to an advisory panel.

## Approving New Procedures

*Public Complaints: ECOSOC Resolution 1235*

Commission Resolution 8 (XXIII) of 1967 initiated the most significant changes.  The Commission added an agenda item on the "Question of Violations . . ." and authorized the Sub-Commission to do the same.  In accord with Sub-Commission expert Clyde Ferguson's proposals, the Commission radically expanded the Sub-Commission's competence beyond the prevention of discrimination and protection of minorities.  The Sub-Commission was directed "to bring to the attention of the Commission any situation which it has reasonable cause to believe reveals a consistent pattern of violations . . ." and to prepare a "report containing information on violations of human rights and fundamental freedoms from all available sources."  The Commission also sought authority from ECOSOC to examine the individual communications that had been placed beyond its review since 1947.  Following language from the

TABLE 4.1
Commission Membership, 1967-1979 (32 members)

| Year 19- | 67 | 68 | 69 | 70 | 71 | 72 | 73 | 74 | 75 | 76 | 77 | 78 | 79 |
|---|---|---|---|---|---|---|---|---|---|---|---|---|---|
| Session | 23 | 24 | 25 | 26 | 27 | 28 | 29 | 30 | 31 | 32 | 33 | 34 | 35 |
| **Africa (8)** | | | | | | | | | | | | | |
| Benin | XX | XX | | | | | | | | | | | XX |
| Burundi | | | | | | | | | | | | | XX |
| Egypt | XX | XX | XX | XX | XX | XX | XX | XX | XX | XX | XX | XX | XX |
| Ghana | | | | XX | XX | XX | XX | XX | XX | | | | |
| Ivory Coast | | | | | | | | | | | | XX | XX |
| Lesotho | | | | | | | | | | XX | XX | XX | |
| Libya | | | | | | | | | | XX | XX | XX | |
| Madagascar | | XX | XX | XX | | | | | | | | | |
| Mauritania | | | XX | XX | XX | | | | | | | | |
| Mauritius | | | | | | XX | XX | CH | | | | | |
| Morocco | XX | XX | XX | XX | XX | XX | | | | | | | XX |
| Nigeria | XX | XX | XX | | | XX | XX | XX | | | XX | XX | XX |
| Rwanda | | | | | | | | | | XX | XX | XX | |
| Senegal | XX | XX | XX | XX | XX | XX | XX | XX | XX | XX | XX | CH | XX |
| Sierra Leone | | | | | | | | XX | XX | XX | | | |
| Somalia | AA | | | | | | | | | | | | |
| Tanzania | XX | XX | XX | XX | XX | XX | XX | XX | XX | XX | | | |
| Tunisia | | | | | | | XX | XX | XX | | | | |
| Uganda | | | | | | | | | | | XX | XX | XX |
| Upper Volta | | | | | | | | | XX | XX | XX | | |
| Zaire | XX | XX | XX | XX | XX | XX | XX | XX | XX | | | | |
| **Asia (6)** | | | | | | | | | | | | | |
| Cyprus | | | | | | | | XX | XX | XX | XX | XX | XX |
| India | XX | XX | XX | XX | XX | XX | XX | XX | XX | XX | XX | XX | XX |
| Iran | XX | XX | XX | CH | XX | XX | XX | XX | XX | XX | XX | XX | XX |
| Iraq | XX | | | XX | XX | XX | XX | XX | XX | | | | XX |
| Israel | XX | XX | XX | XX | | | | | | | | | |
| Jordan | | | | | | | | | | XX | XX | XX | |
| Lebanon | | XX | XX | XX | XX | XX | XX | XX | XX | XX | | | |
| Pakistan | XX | XX | XX | | XX | XX | XX | XX | XX | XX | XX | XX | XX |
| Philippines | XX | XX | XX | XX | XX | XX | XX | | | | | | |
| Syria | | | | | | | | | | | XX | XX | XX |

(cont.)

TABLE 4.1 cont.

| Year 19- | 67 | 68 | 69 | 70 | 71 | 72 | 73 | 74 | 75 | 76 | 77 | 78 | 79 |
| --- | --- | --- | --- | --- | --- | --- | --- | --- | --- | --- | --- | --- | --- |
| Session | 23 | 24 | 25 | 26 | 27 | 28 | 29 | 30 | 31 | 32 | 33 | 34 | 35 |
| **Eastern Europe (4)** | | | | | | | | | | | | | |
| Bulgaria | | | | | | | XX | XX | XX | XX | XX | XX | XX |
| Byelorussia | | | | | | XX | XX | XX | XX | XX | XX | | |
| Poland | XX | XX | XX | XX | XX | CH | | | | XX | XX | | |
| Romania | | | | | | XX | XX | XX | | | | | |
| Ukraine | CH | XX | XX | XX | XX | | | | | | | | |
| USSR | XX | XX | XX | XX | XX | XX | XX | XX | XX | XX | XX | XX | XX |
| Yugoslavia | XX | XX | XX | XX | XX | | | | XX | XX | CH | XX | XX |
| **Latin America (6)** | | | | | | | | | | | | | |
| Argentina | XX | XX | | | | | | | | | | | |
| Brazil | | | | | | | | | | | | | XX |
| Chile | XX | XX | XX | XX | XX | XX | XX | XX | | | | | |
| Colombia | | | | | | | | | | | | XX | XX |
| Costa Rica | XX | | | | | | | | XX | XX | XX | | |
| Cuba | | | | | | | | | | XX | XX | XX | XX |
| Dominican Rep. | | | | | | | XX | XX | XX | | | | |
| Ecuador | | | | | | XX | XX | XX | XX | CH | XX | | |
| Guatemala | XX | XX | XX | XX | XX | XX | | | | | | | |
| Jamaica | XX | XX | XX | XX | | | | | | | | | |
| Mexico | | | | | | XX | XX | XX | | | | | |
| Nicaragua | | | | | | | | XX | XX | XX | | | |
| Panama | | | | | | | | | XX | XX | XX | XX | XX |
| Peru | XX | XX | XX | XX | XX | XX | | | XX | XX | XX | XX | XX |
| Uruguay | | | XX | XX | XX | | | | XX | XX | XX | XX | |
| Venezuela | | XX | XX | XX | CH | XX | XX | | | | | | |
| **W. Eur. + Other (8)** | | | | | | | | | | | | | |
| Australia | | | | | | | | | | | | XX | XX |
| Austria | XX | XX | XX | XX | XX | XX | XX | CH | XX | | XX | XX | XX |
| Canada | | | | | | | | | | XX | XX | XX | CH |
| Finland | | | XX | XX | XX | | | | | | | | |
| France | XX | XX | XX | XX | XX | XX | XX | XX | XX | XX | | XX | XX |
| Fed. Rep. Germ | | | | | | | | | | XX | XX | XX | XX |
| Greece | XX | XX | XX | | | | | | | | | | |
| Italy | XX | XX | XX | | | XX | XX | XX | XX | XX | XX | | |
| Netherlands | | | | XX | XX | XX | XX | XX | XX | | | | |
| New Zealand | XX | XX | CH | XX | XX | | | | | | | | |
| Norway | | | | | | XX | XX | XX | | | | | |
| Portugal | | | | | | | | | | | | | XX |
| Sweden | | | | | | | | | | | XX | XX | XX |
| Turkey | XX | XX | | XX | XX | XX | XX | XX | XX | XX | XX | XX | |
| U.K. | XX | XX | XX | XX | XX | XX | XX | XX | XX | XX | XX | XX | |
| U.S. | XX | XX | XX | XX | XX | XX | XX | XX | XX | XX | XX | XX | XX |

CH  designates Chairman    AA indicates absence

Ferguson draft, the Sub-Commission experts would have similar access and could use any other available information to study situations which revealed "gross violations" or a "consistent pattern of violations." By the narrowest of margins, the Commission requested for itself authority to make a thorough study and "investigation" of situations.

ECOSOC granted both the Commission and Sub-Commission access to the individual communications, but rejected the request for investigatory power. Representatives of the United Kingdom, the Philippines, and Tanzania objected to investigations without a target state's consent.[4] Instead, ECOSOC Res. 1235 (XLII) empowers the Commission to make a "thorough study" of situations and to submit reports. (See Appendix A for the resolution's complete text.) The Afro-Asian and Soviet bloc representatives added a provision designed to focus primary attention on self-determination and racial equality. The "gross violations" evidenced by the communications and the studies of "consistent patterns of violations" are

> as exemplified by the policy of apartheid as practised in the Republic of South Africa and in the Territory of South West Africa under the direct responsibility of the United Nations and now illegally occupied by the government of the Republic of South Africa, and racial discrimination as practised notably in Southern Rhodesia.[5]

ECOSOC further resolved to reconsider the Commission's need for the added powers conferred following implementation of the Covenant's enforcement procedures.

Since the Covenant would only apply to states parties, the review of all situations authorized by Resolution 1235 could be challenged as a violation of Charter Article 2(7). Proponents favoring United Nations scrutiny of all countries offered two responses. First, when human rights offenses become a consistent pattern of gross violations they are no longer a matter of domestic jurisdiction. Second, the type of "thorough study" authorized would not amount to "intervention" in a nation's internal affairs. Target states placed in the new Commission dock might challenge that rationale of state accountability, but after twenty years the Commission had obtained the authority to investigate human rights violations. Unexpectedly, this procedure evolved into a dual complaint system—a public procedure dominated by interstate complaints under Resolution 1235, and a confidential process authorized by ECOSOC Resolution 1503 for reviewing individual and NGO complaints.[6]

*Confidential Communications: Resolution 1503*

The Resolution 1503 confidential procedure was fashioned during four years of struggle over whether to expand or curtail the Commission's new power to study violations. After retiring from his position as Director of the Division of

Human Rights, John Humphrey worked for stronger implementation measures as a Sub-Commission expert from Canada. In 1967 Humphrey introduced a resolution calling for a Commission study of the situations in Greece and Haiti. John Carey, an alternate from the United States, annexed a report to the proposal presenting as evidence code numbers referring to confidential communications.[7] The Sub-Commission also referred four situations in Southern Africa and the Middle East to the Commission but without a supporting report.

Political interests shaped the Commission response. The Soviet representative, while opposed to using communications for international scrutiny, welcomed the opportunity to castigate the Greek and Israeli regimes.[8] The Tanzanian representative introduced, but later withdrew, a resolution rebuking the Sub-Commission for calling attention to noncolonial situations.[9] The United States argued that the charges against Greece and Haiti lacked sufficient evidence.[10] In 1968 the Commission disregarded the evidence about Greece and Haiti and approved only the Sub-Commission recommendations on Southern Africa and the Middle East. The Commission approved another Tanzanian proposal designed to produce anticolonial results by increasing the Sub-Commission's membership in 1969 from 18 to 26, with 12 experts from Afro-Asian states. These additional experts joined the Sub-Commission in 1969. After the Commission elected only five African experts in 1978, the African states were assured of seven positions in future elections.[11]

The Sub-Commission never again referred to confidential communications in a public report to the Commission identifying a government charged with gross violations. United States alternate John Carey twice introduced resolutions identifying six general situations such as torture, killing, and violation of freedom of expression. The draft proposals did not identify particular states, but called the Commission's attention to confidential communications cited by serial number. The Soviet expert raised procedural objections. The Sub-Commission never formally adopted Carey's resolutions but did forward them to the Commission.[12]

In order to recommend an acceptable procedure for referring communications to the Commission, the Sub-Commission designated a three-member working group chaired by Humphrey. At its 1968 session, the Sub-Commission approved the working group's recommendations for a three stage communications screening procedure by: (1) a Sub-Commission working group, (2) the full Sub-Commission, and (3) the Commission.[13] The Commission approved the proposal in a series of votes that passed by the narrowest of margins: 15-10-7; 12-14; 13-13-3; 14-13-5; and 15-10-7.[14] Supporters included all of the Western European and Latin American members, Austria, and the Philippines. Senegal, Turkey, and Lebanon gave qualified support to some provisions. The other Asian and African members joined the Eastern European bloc in solid opposition.[15]

The Soviet Union favored Commission action only against colonialism and racism, when governments committed gross violations against large groups. The U.S.S.R. representative vigorously opposed any international scrutiny of how sovereign states treated individual citizens.[16] Tanzania also opposed the complaint procedure and successfully moved to have all deliberations on the communications treated in confidence.

> all actions envisaged in the implementation of the present resolution by the Sub-Commission . . . or the Commission on Human Rights shall remain confidential until such time as the Commission may decide to make recommendations to the Economic and Social Council.[17]

An amendment proposed by the United Kingdom authorized the Sub-Commission to consider other available information when preparing reports based on the communications. The Commission also sought authority for investigations based on the communications, but only when the target state expressly agreed to cooperate. The entire review procedure would be reconsidered if any new organ was created to deal with such communications.[18]

Despite the various protections provided for target states, ECOSOC found the proposed procedure so contentious that governments were given a year to comment. Thirty-one did so, after which the Commission reaffirmed its recommendations to ECOSOC. In 1970 by a vote of 12 to 12 with 3 abstentions, the Council's Social Committee defeated a further postponement proposed by Bulgaria and Sudan.[19] By a vote of 14-7-6, ECOSOC then approved the Resolution 1503 (XLVIII) procedure for Sub-Commission screening and Commission review of "communications relating to violations of human rights and fundamental freedoms."[20] (See Appendix A for the resolution's complete text.) In an unsuccessful effort to reverse that ECOSOC decision, the U.S.S.R. submitted a draft resolution in the General Assembly's Third Committee.[21]

## Implementing the Public Procedures

Commission Resolution 8 (XXIII) and ECOSOC Resolution 1235 of 1967 ended the no-power doctrine and created the possibility for significant enforcement initiatives. The compromise resolutions authorizing the Commission to identify human rights violations provided no clear answers to contentious substantive, procedural, and political questions. Who would have standing to bring complaints to the Commission—individual victims and NGOs or only states and intergovernmental bodies? Which complaints would be considered "gross violations" justifying United Nations action? Would the Commission accept partisan and unsubstantiated allegations or undertake impartial investigations before finding culpability? The Commission's new

NAM majority answered each question in accord with its own ideological priorities for liberation in Southern Africa and the Middle East.[22]

*Standing to Bring Complaints*

When the new agenda item on violations assumed top priority, the Commission began receiving public complaints against governments made by parent organs and United Nations Committees, by Commission members and nonmember states, by specialized agencies, and by the Sub-Commission. The General Assembly's Special Committee on the Policies of Apartheid provided evidence about mistreatment of prisoners, and ECOSOC asked the Commission to investigate rights of South African workers. The "front line" states, particularly Tanzania, challenged South Africa's domestic apartheid policy and illegal occupation of Namibia. Following Israel's territorial acquisitions in 1967, Arab states complained about human rights violations in the occupied territories.

NGO representatives also presented evidence of violations to the Commission but could only speak at the end of the debate and were repeatedly warned not to make allegations against governments identifying new situations. Commission members assiduously objected when NGO speakers named regimes other than South Africa or Israel. NGOs could only refer generally to "certain governments" rather than to particular offenders. When several NGOs identified specific situations in debate, NAM and Soviet bloc members sought to revoke their consultative status.[23]

The Tanzanian representative Waldron-Ramsey initiated a major review by ECOSOC in response to press accounts of CIA support for Western organizations and as a reaction to the considerable geographic imbalance of NGO representation.

[O]f the 166 organizations reviewed by the committee, more than 90 per cent had their headquarters in Western countries, while "only two organizations have their headquarters in socialist countries, seven in Latin American countries, six in Asian countries and only one in an African country."[24]

Ironically, the Third World states had to temper their objections to government funding of NGOs in order to redress the geographic imbalance. Arabs challenged Zionist organizations that opposed U.N. initiatives on Palestinian lands. Third World states complained that even genuinely private organizations represented an exclusively Western viewpoint. Africans suspected that Western groups had connections in Southern Africa that undermined the U.N. program against *apartheid*. The Eastern bloc challenged the International Commission of Jurists, an allegedly CIA funded alternative to the banned International Association of Democratic Lawyers (IADL).[25] The USSR objected to American Jewish organizations composed of dissident exiles protesting on behalf of Soviet Jewry.[26]

Additional NAM members with a new voting majority on ECOSOC's NGO committee initiated a thorough review for 1967, culminating in a resolution providing the criteria for suspension and withdrawal of consultative status:

> (a) If there exists substantiated evidence of secret governmental financial influence to induce an organization to undertake acts contrary to the purposes and principles of the Charter of the United Nations; (b) If the organization clearly abuses its consultative status by systematically engaging in unsubstantiated or politically motivated acts against States Members of the United Nations . . . ; (c) If, within the preceding three years, an organization had not made any positive or effective contribution to the work of the Council or its commissions or other subsidiary organs.[27]

In order to retain consultative status NGOs were expected to file responses to a Secretariat questionnaire every four years indicating their funding sources.

Ultimately, the new criteria had minimal impact on the NGOs in 1968–1969. ECOSOC delayed approval of the Coordinating Board of Jewish organizations for two years, but it recommended continued recognition for all others. Two states voted against The International Commission of Jurists[28] and four abstained in the vote on Amnesty International. ECOSOC restored consultative status to the IADL and Women's International Democratic Federation (WIDF), groups which had lost their privileges in the 1950s for their attacks on Western imperialism.

In the 1970s ECOSOC issued general reprimands to human rights NGOs for violation of confidential procedures and for politically motivated acts in the Commission and Sub-Commission. After an American representing the World Council of Religion and Peace accused several states of religious persecution in 1975, ECOSOC warned against unfounded and slanderous accusations. A new resolution threatened to withdraw consultative status from NGOs disregarding the ban on unsubstantiated allegations or other politically motivated acts against states members.[29]    The Soviet Union, which had supported the right of communist NGOs to attack the U.N. intervention in Korea, denounced Jewish NGOs for challenging the General Assembly declaration that Zionism is a form of racism. The British and Americans in turn found that their 1950s efforts to exclude communist propaganda from Commission deliberations established a precedent that was used against Western NGOs charged with making "'slanderous and tendentious political attacks'."[30]    Argentina inspired a 1978 ECOSOC review in an effort to have the U.N.'s Joint Inspection unit investigate five human rights NGOs that had submitted documents or made statements to the Commission and Sub-Commission alleging violations by member states.[31] The Soviet representative alleged abuse of consultative status by three other Western groups.[32]    The targets of these NGO reports—Chile, Brazil, Iran,

Bolivia, and Venezuela—sought to discipline the NGOs over objections by Western members who praised their contributions. Argentina particularly objected to the appointment of political exiles, "terrorists," to speak as representatives of private organizations attacking member states and to the release of confidential communications submitted under the 1503 procedure.

As in 1969, ECOSOC ultimately sustained the consultative status of all the challenged NGOs. Interrogation of NGO representatives by the Committee apparently had no greater intimidating effect than general ECOSOC resolutions warning against unsubstantiated political attacks and breach of the confidential procedures. NGOs became increasingly bold in naming offenders, although their charges usually supplemented prior allegations made with growing frequency by state members. The International Commission of Jurists published all its confidential communications concerning Uganda when the Commission failed to act on them[33] Other NGOs sponsored a presentation by Mrs. Salvador Allende against Chile's military rulers after her husband's overthrow.

### Target Situations Recognized as Gross Violations

At the outset, the NAM majority made self-determination, South African *apartheid*, and Israeli violations the exclusive enforcement priority. Members occasionally criticized in debate individual rights violations by Haiti, Greece, and other governments, but the Commission only acted on "gross" violations defined as racial and colonial domination. Government representatives charged a violation of both individual rights and the right to self-determination for subject groups in Portugal's African territories, Southwest Africa (Namibia), Southern Rhodesia (Zimbabwe), and in the Arab lands occupied by Israel.

A potentially significant change came in 1974 when the Commission recognized that something other than racism or foreign conquest amounted to a gross violation of human rights. The military junta which overthrew Chile's Salvador Allende employed means common to other totalitarian regimes—mass detention, torture, and killing. The Marxist Allende, however, had just brought Chile into the NAM; its members and the Soviet bloc particularly objected to United States opposition to Allende. Both the Sub-Commission and the General Assembly referred the situation to the Commission, and Mrs. Salvador Allende spoke as an NGO representative. For the first time, Eastern bloc and Afro-Asian members condemned a government's non-racial civil rights violations against its own citizens. They rejected appeals to domestic jurisdiction and nonintervention while revealing in public debate evidence from confidential communications. European governments also raised principled objections to the violations, despite the partisan anti-Western ideology motivating many complainants.

In the late 1970s human rights violations by other Latin American regimes outside the NAM, Nicaragua and Guatemala, also prompted a Commission response. The Commission asked the Secretariat to obtain information about the Somoza regime in Nicaragua, and in 1979 sent a telegram to the Guatemalan government expressing concern about the assassination of Dr. Alberto Fuentes Mohr, a former Secretariat employee.[34]

In contrast to the Commission's willingness to shift Chile's study from confidential to public proceedings, the members objected to a Sub-Commission resolution calling for public debate on the confidential situation in Uganda. In 1977 Britain and Canada supported a Sub-Commission resolution on Uganda in a public meeting, only to lose on a procedural vote that Idi Amin's offenses could not be reconsidered following the confidential deliberations.[35] Other NAM members such as Burundi, the Central African Empire, Equatorial Guinea, Ethiopia, Indonesia, and Kampuchea similarly escaped public review under an obvious double standard. Despite numerous credible allegations of massive, state-sponsored killing, the Commission would only review those gross violations via the Resolution 1503 confidential procedure. Once debated in private, members could not refer to the same situation in public session.

For the three pariah regimes the Commission designated separate "priority" agenda headings to facilitate lengthy public castigation. For the first half of each four-week session members denounced South Africa, Israel, and Chile. Then the members proceeded to another new agenda topic—self-determination— and condemned white minority rule in Rhodesia/Zimbabwe and Portuguese colonialism in Angola and Mozambique. The lone agenda item for alleging new violations came up at the end of each session, allowing little opportunity for complaints about other gross violations.

*Investigating Alleged Violations*

Members initially disagreed over whether the Commission should condemn a violation before studies had been completed and whether the investigators should report exculpatory evidence or only those facts which reveal gross violations. Proponents of a due process model wanted the United Nations to conduct impartial fact-finding of allegations before resolving that a government committed a gross violation. Richard Lillich analogized the Commission to a grand jury, which would report indictments to an independent group for "trial."[36] The Sub-Commission recommended that its experts be used as independent fact finders authorized to conduct missions of inquiry; alternately, the Commission could have appointed its own standing committee to screen allegations and make recommendations for action.

In practice, the Commission developed a different model, improvising separate *ad hoc* inquiry procedures for the different governments subject to ongoing review. Rather than impartial fact-finding, these procedures have generally sought "to amass whatever evidence there may be—even of doubtful probity—to reinforce predetermined political conclusions."[37] The NAM and Soviet bloc had little confidence that investigators would be impartial and recognized that even if they were, their embarrassing inquiries would be perceived as a sign of wrongdoing.[38]

To conduct its first "thorough study," the Commission appointed an *ad hoc* group on torture and ill treatment of South African political prisoners.[39] ECOSOC enlarged the mandate to include trade union rights and later extended the focus to all of Southern Africa (and, for 1969 only, to the Middle East as well).[40] The thorough study initiated presumed the target's culpability and sought facts to verify that conclusion. Before soliciting testimony from the first witness, the Commission had condemned the practices described and had sent a critical telegram to the South African government.[41] In addition to university professors, the Chairman appointed to the group representatives from Senegal, Tanzania, and India whose governments had previously condemned South Africa. The enabling resolution authorized the group "to receive communications . . . hear witnesses and use modalities it deems appropriate.[42] Thomas Franck characterized the procedural principles they adopted as "trivial."[43]

South Africa protested that the Commission had predetermined the result, objected to the group's political makeup, and would not allow an onsite visit. The group in turn rejected a Red Cross report prepared by a physician that South Africa had admitted to its prisons. The group conducted 44 hearings, some in closed session, in New York, London, Dar Es Salaam, and Geneva. Witnesses represented individuals, organizations, and national liberation movements. After pledging to testify truthfully,[44] witnesses faced friendly leading questions and were not cross examined. The group taped witnesses, published a transcript, and prepared a 435-page report finding serious violations of the U.N. Standard Minimum Rules for the Treatment of prisoners and suggesting the possibility of genocide. Sub-Commission expert John Carey concluded that the group's political composition and procedural bias precluded the appearance of impartiality.[45] In its determination to combat *apartheid*, the Commission pre-judged the South African regime without reference to an impartial, independent investigation.

After prompting by the 1968 Teheran International Conference on Human Rights and by ECOSOC, the Commission spent five years fruitlessly debating "model rules of procedure" for United Nations investigations. Austria and Finland proposed the project, and the Secretariat prepared a first draft based on a due process model; accused states would be presumed innocent while impartial fact-finders investigated *alleged* gross violations. The NAM and Soviet bloc insisted that studies could only be made "where *reliable* evidence exists of a consistent pattern of gross and massive violations." Where the Secretariat text referred simply to "particular situations," opponents favored language emphasizing investigations of race discrimination and colonialism. Five Commission representatives chaired by the Netherlands' Theo van Boven attempted to rework the provisions into a politically acceptable procedure. After three years of consultation,[46] the members could not agree on a consensus text.[47]

The Secretariat had proposed five detailed rules covering the admissibility and relevance of evidence, oral and written testimony, anonymous communications, and a solemn declaration by witnesses and their questioning. The group could not agree on any of the provisions, and particularly objected to authorizing an *ad hoc* investigatory body to make direct contacts with a target state. The Commission resolved that the political organ creating the *ad hoc* body would retain responsibility for contacting states under investigation. Ultimately, the Commission and ECOSOC simply "took note" of the incomplete draft rules, calling them to the attention of United Nations organs responsible for investigations. Since no group is thereby bound to follow the Commission's severely flawed model procedure, each *ad hoc* body operates with *ad hoc* methods controlled by the parent organ.[48]

Undaunted by criticism of its fact-finding methods, the Commission repeatedly renewed the South African group's mandate and adopted resolutions based on its recommendations. In form and substance the condemnations of *apartheid* resembled the harsh criticisms made annually by the General Assembly. The group did not, however, continue to investigate the Middle East, as the Commission received and acted on reports of the General Assembly's Special Committee to Investigate Israeli Practices Affecting the Human Rights of the Population of the Occupied Territories.

When the members resolved to study Chile's human rights violations, the Commission created a new *ad hoc* group. Although a public study under Resolution 1235 does not require a target state's consent, the Commission deferred to the junta's objection to Eastern bloc representation; the chair appointed members from Austria, Pakistan, Senegal, Sierra Leone and Ecuador. As in the South African situation, the Commission sent a telegram to the government expressing its deep concern about reported violations before the group even convened. The telegram named five individuals deemed in particular danger.[49] For several years the junta refused to admit the group to Chile, despite the exclusion of a Soviet bloc member, the high caliber of the individuals appointed, and their commitment to impartial procedures. Prior to their only visit in 1978, the group had interviewed exiles at hearings conducted outside Chile. The investigation continued after Chile refused further cooperation, but the Commission replaced the five-member group with a single rapporteur from Senegal.

Israel's representative to the Commission, and observers from Chile and South Africa raised similar legal objections to the Commission's jurisdiction and competence; first, that a Commission study violates Charter Article 2(7) by intervening in matters essentially within the state's domestic jurisdiction; and second, that states are not bound by United Nations declarations or international human rights instruments they never ratified. In responding to the first objection, Austrian law professor Felix Ermacora noted that the Charter expressly authorizes the Assembly and its subsidiary organs to promote human rights and to make recommendations. Thus the Commission asserted an "absolutely incontestable" right to study and recommendation that "does not constitute an intervention" prohibited by Article 2(7).[50] Even though South Africa abstained when the General Assembly approved the Universal Declaration and never ratified the convention on race discrimination, certain fundamental principles have become so widely accepted that governments are bound to respect them as rules of customary international law.

*Enforcement Tools*

There were no formally proscribed penalties or remedies to apply once a Commission majority found a human rights violation. In order to stop ongoing violations and to deter future offenses the Commission pressed governments with various measures that can be categorized according to three levels of severity. As a minimal first step, the Commission used exhortation, mediation, and conciliation. The resolutions adopted spared the alleged offender from reproach while professing a humanitarian spirit pitched to elicit cooperation. On a second level the Commission conducted ongoing investigations leading to repeated public condemnations. Finally, when the defiant governments of Israel and South Africa could not be shamed into compliance, the NAM and Soviet bloc members, determined to destroy *apartheid* and to liberate Namibia and occupied Arab lands, fashioned the most coercive measures to compel change and ultimately to remove the target regime. The Commission did not become involved in the comprehensive United Nations campaign against South Africa until long after the Assembly began combating *apartheid*, and the Commission's efforts cannot compare to the arms embargo imposed by the Security Council. Despite its limitations, the Afro-Asian and Soviet bloc members have enlisted the Commission in the larger attack on Israel and South Africa, and the results illustrate the most severe remedies employed to enforce international human rights norms.

Initially, the sponsors exhausted all possibilities for persuasion and public humiliation. Manouchehr Ganji, a Commission member from Iran, prepared a 1970 report in United Nations enforcement action and described how *apartheid* legislation worked in practice.[51] The *"ad hoc"* working group of experts became a permanently established public relations tool.[52] The appointees serve in their personal capacity; Ermacora is the only one to serve as a government representative and two others come from countries with Commission membership. The group's tasks grew steadily larger and came to include seminars, conferences, and studies on *apartheid's* effect on women and children, slavery, genocide, and criminal proceedings against individual offenders.[53] Until 1971 the group held hearings annually, recording testimony from 25 to 146 witnesses in each annual report. After 1972 the Commission has regularly granted two-year extensions of the group's mandate, with the experts filing an interim report in even numbered years and conclusions based on hearings in the second year. Despite South Africa's longstanding refusal to cooperate, the group continued to write diplomatically proper requests for permission to visit detention centers.

The Commission annually debated the group's report while considering four related agenda items on South Africa that take a full week of the six-week session.[54] For its public exposure of Israeli violations, the Commission has no working group of its own, but relies on the Assembly's Special Committee to Investigate Israeli Practices Affecting the Human Rights of the Population of the Occupied Territories. Debating that topic takes most of the session's first week.[55] Resolutions of exhortation and condemnation, combined with maximum public exposure through Commission debate, seminars, and publications failed to achieve any observable result in either South Africa or Israel. The Commission then joined in a comprehensive United Nations program to apply more effective and coercive measures.

The resulting campaign to delegitimize and ultimately overthrow human rights offenders appears to violate cardinal Charter principles prohibiting intervention and resort to force.[56] Sponsors proposing extreme remedies initially had to establish a conceptual framework and legal foundation. Those favoring coercive measures relied for precedent on the allied military response to Nazi crimes against humanity. The United Nations began as a military alliance fighting to overthrow a regime that could not be changed by peaceful means. The Charter allows membership to "peace loving states"[57] and authorizes a military response to aggression; human rights violations such as the holocaust may endanger international peace and security justifying collective action under the Charter.

Over strong Western objections, the Assembly created the conceptual basis for delegitimizing the Israeli and South African governments. In order to invoke against Israel Charter guarantees of equal rights and the convention against race discrimination, the Assembly resolved that Zionism was a form of racism.[58] South Africa became subject to a specially drafted treaty, The International Convention on the Suppression and Punishment of the Crime of Apartheid which makes *apartheid* a "crime against humanity" that constitutes "a serious threat to international peace and security."[59] The Commission's working group on South Africa has also concluded that *apartheid* constitutes genocide; its report on the effects of *apartheid* on black women and children[60] supported the thesis by presenting evidence about infant mortality, malnutrition, inadequate health care, and the killing of youthful demonstrators. A Sub-Commission working group equated *apartheid* with slavery.[61] Such crimes against humanity justify isolation, criminal prosecution, and ultimately removal of the responsible government.

*Isolation.* The first step taken was to attack a regime's supporters for collaborating in human rights violations. The Commission repudiated Western efforts to negotiate a Namibian settlement and rejected the Camp David framework for the Middle East. After 1974 a Sub-Commission rapporteur from Egypt, A. Khalifa, has prepared lists of corporations doing business with or investing in South Africa. The rapporteur simply listed thousands of company names in long lists without detail or analysis. As recommended by the Sub-Commission, the Commission added an agenda item on the adverse consequences of military and economic assistance to racist regimes. In order to isolate South Africa, the NAM sought to pressure the multinational corporations identified from continuing business operations in South Africa.

Western members with the most extensive trading relationships faulted the rapporteur for assuming without proving that non-racial business transactions strengthen the apartheid system. They also objected to the rapporteur's anti-Western, anti-capitalist approach, and cautioned that disinvestment would cause more suffering to *apartheid's* black victims than to the Afrikaaner government. Citing budgetary deficits the Western critics sought unsuccessfully to terminate the rapporteur's mandate. Amazingly, the United Nations Secretariat did not divest $250 million in pension fund investments in companies doing business with South Africa until 1985.[62] Despite persistent exhortation by both the Commission and the Assembly, the International Monetary Fund (IMF), French and German banks all granted additional credits to South Africa in the early 1980s.

Resolutions on Israel and South Africa typically urged all governments to stop nuclear collaboration with those states and criticized the United States and other Western powers for collaborating with human rights offenders. The Commission routinely endorsed economic sanctions, protesting great power vetoes in the Security Council. The United Nations applied economic sanctions against Southern Rhodesia/Zimbabwe. Sub-Commission expert Antonio Cassesse prepared a far more scholarly and persuasive analysis of how foreign investment sustained the military junta in Chile. His study effectively exposed how the regime's domestic policies increased economic hardship for the poor.[63] Even Chile's harshest critics were unwilling to extend Cassesse's mandate for ongoing review of sensitive national decision making.

*Prosecution.* In 1977 the Commission directed the six member working group on South Africa to identify individuals in Namibia suspected of committing a serious violation of human rights.[64] A World Court decision rejecting South Africa's claim to the territory gives the United Nations criminal jurisdiction in the territory. South Africa's government representatives have been denied credentials to the General Assembly since 1974; but continued United States support shielded Israel from expulsion, if not from the most virulent attacks on its military occupation and treatment of Palestinian detainees. Israel's observer participates actively, provoked by radical Arab attacks on "the Zionist entity."

The world organization also treats target regimes as outlaws by granting participant observer status to military organizations seeking their overthrow—the Palestine Liberation Organization (PLO), the Southwest African Peoples Organization, the Zimbabwe African National Union, and the African National Congress (ANC). In order to protect freedom figthers captured in the liberation struggle, the Commission relied on the 1977 protocols to the 1949 Geneva Conventions on the laws of war. Israel and South Africa treat PLO and ANC operatives as terrorists, denying the international safeguards granted to prisoners of a formally declared war. The Commission insisted that the 1977 protocols now require a government under seige to honor the Third Geneva Convention on Prisoners of War when holding national liberation combatants. Israel claimed that the conventions do not apply, in part because PLO terrorists attacked civilian targets, did not wear uniforms, and were not parties to the treaties. In any event, critics objected that the Red Cross, not the Commission, had the responsibility for monitoring and enforcing the agreements.

The extensive campaigns against South Africa, Israel and Chile became increasingly unpopular in the West as the Commission refused to deal similarly with other gross violations in Uganda and Kampuchea. Toward the end of the 1970s the Commission did begin responding to violations in Khartoum, Cyprus, Nicaragua, and Guatemala but only with quite conciliatory approaches. Rather than harsh criticism and public inquiry, the members addressed telegrams of concern exhorting the governments to respect human rights. Those infrequent, diplomatically phrased public resolutions resembled the far more extensive confidential good offices which had been separately developed in response to the individual communications screened under the Resolution 1503 procedure.

### Implementing Confidential Procedures

ECOSOC Resolution 1503 provided for a two-step screening process in the Sub-Commission before the Commission would receive confidential communications for review. After preparing rules of admissibility, the Sub-Commission would designate a five-member working group representing different geographical regions to identify communications "which appear to reveal a consistent pattern of gross and reliably attested violations."[65] Based on those recommendations, the full Sub-Commission must then select situations for referral to the Commission. Following its confidential review, the Commission could undertake either a study of the situation or, with the consent of the government concerned, an *ad hoc* committee investigation.

## Sub-Commission Screening

*Rules of Admissibility.* In 1971 the Sub-Commission drafted rules of admissibility to aid its working group decide which of the 20,000 communications under review merited consideration.[66] Communications are only admissible if they

> reveal a consistent pattern of gross and reliably attested violations of human rights and fundamental freedoms, including policies of racial discrimination and segregation and of *apartheid* in any country, including colonial and other dependent countries and peoples.

Communications revealing individual injuries are not considered unless they suggest a pattern or situation of gross violations. Anonymous resolutions are inadmissible.

The author need not be a victim to obtain review. Communications may originate from a person or a group of victims, as well as from other individuals and organizations with either direct and reliable knowledge or secondhand information accompanied by clear evidence. The victim must first exhaust any reasonably effective domestic remedies and then communicate with the United Nations within a reasonable time.[68] There is no requirement of prior recourse to regional human rights bodies, but communications are inadmissible "if their admission would prejudice the functions of the specialized agencies of the United Nations system."[69] The admissibility rules repeatedly disallow "politically motivated stands contrary to the provisions of the Charter" and make inadmissible communications based exclusively on news media reports. Communications with insulting references to a state may only be considered after deletion of the abusive language.

Western activists hailed the passage of Resolution 1503 as a major initiative creating an individual right of petition to the United Nations. Petitioners could attack human rights violations by any government, even states which did not belong to the United Nations. The procedure encompassed all human rights and fundamental freedoms, political and civil as well as economic and social. A brief reference to racism and colonialism was illustrative, not restrictive.[70] Both individual victims and organizations with second-hand evidence of violations could submit communications. In order to maximize Resolution 1503's potential impact, nongovernmental organizations published directions on how to file admissible communications.[71] In practice, the activists soon criticized the Resolution 1503 procedures as so politicized, secretive, and slow that offending governments escaped meaningful scrutiny.[72]

*Form and Sources of Communications.* Communications alleging widespread violations resembled class action complaints seeking the equivalent of an injunction from a national court. Resolution 1503 submissions did not seek monetary damages as individual compensation for injuries suffered.[73] No legal aid program offered assistance preparing communications, but the United Nations did not require a formal complaint drafted by a lawyer. Nor did the United Nations ever assess costs against those bringing complaints. Although violations of economic and social rights, such as forced labor, were occasionally alleged, most complaints involved civil and political rights.

Communications ranged in length from form post cards submitted by the thousands on a single issue, through more detailed personal letters, to thoroughly documented NGO submissions running to hundreds of pages. The "Model Communication" recommended in a practitioner's handbook includes:

1. Name of the country considered responsible,
2. Information identifying the alleged victim(s),
3. Information identifying the author, if not the same as the victim,
4. Human rights allegedly violated, with specific reference to an international instrument,
5. Statement of the facts identifying precisely events, government officials, witnesses, etc.,
6. Means of redress attempted, or explanation of why domestic remedies would be futile,
7. Purpose of the communication, relief sought,
8. Confidentiality of the communication, whether the author's identity may be disclosed, and
9. Signature and date.[74]

Nongovernmental organizations had the necessary resources to document the most informative complaints.[75] Organizations, even those without U.N. consultative status or an office in the country charged, may submit information. NGOs have an advantage over individual petitioners in the Resolution 1503 procedure, since their staff can document enough different violations by a government to establish a consistent pattern or situation.[76] NGOs simplify the Sub-Commission's task by aggregating individual cases, and help the Secretariat by identifying which international instruments apply, by submitting twelve copies of their work, and by preparing brief summaries suitable for referral to Commission members.[77]

Numerous different NGOs filed communications. Complaints about political killings, a mass exodus, and forced labor in Equatorial Guinea came from the Union Belge pour la défense de la paix, the International Federation for the Rights of Man, the Unión Bubi de Fernando Pó, the International University Exchange Fund, and from Swiss individuals with detailed knowledge.[78] Professor Frank Newman of the University of California Law School at Berkeley supplied evidence about torture and political persecution by the Greek military as volunteer counsel for Amnesty International, the International Commission of Jurists, the International Federation for the Rights of Man and the International League for the Rights of Man.[79] Amnesty International documented torture of prisoners by the British in Northern Ireland, torture and murder of 1081 individuals by 472 Brazilian officials, and the political detention of thousands in Indonesia.[80] ICJ submissions detailed the horror of mass killings under Idi Amin in Uganda. The International League estimated that over 100,000 were killed in Burundi during tribal warfare between Hutus and Tutsis[81] and charged the German Democratic Republic with denying citizens a right to leave.

Petitioners must mail or deliver their written complaints to United Nations headquarters in New York or to the Centre for Human Rights in Geneva. Prior to 1969 the 51 United Nations Information Centers in member countries had the discretion to accept and to transmit complaints. Shortly after the Commission obtained authority to review the communications, the U.S.S.R. protested when citizens in Moscow attempted to deliver a petition to the U.N. Information Center. After the Center's Soviet director refused to forward the complaint, Secretary-General U Thant directed all United Nations Centers not to receive or to forward communications concerning human rights;[82] he expressed concern that host governments would close down Centers used to transmit human rights complaints.[83] The Netherlands Government suggested that governments which prevent their citizens from communicating with the United Nations violate two articles of the Universal Declaration on interference with correspondence and the freedom to impart information.[84] Governments which block letters to the United Nations might construe the Declaration differently or simply ignore its provisions.

*Secretariat Processing.* A Communications Unit in the Division of Human Rights processed all requests for assistance. Complaints involving South Africa, Israel, or Chile could be directed to Commission rapporteurs and committees with specific assignments in those areas. The Division directed communications about trade unions and worker's rights to the ILO.[85] Letters raising general principles without reference to an offending government were made public and the author identified. The remaining communications alleging violations by a government began the lengthy 1503 review procedure.

First the staff edited out abusive language and removed information which identified authors who expressed no desire to be identified. Then the Division sent a copy to the government charged. The Secretariat acknowledged receipt to the author with a general explanation of the procedure and copies of the resolutions, but provided no further indication of the government or Commission response. If the same individual sent any supplemental information, the staff treated the material like a new communication. The Communications Unit prepared and distributed to Commission and Sub-Commission members a monthly summary of the communications and any replies from governments. As a result of delays in processing and translation, the Sub-Commission did not consider communications received in the three months preceding the annual session. The Sub-Commission Working Group could request the original text of any communication, but those dated materials normally involved situations which occurred at least six months earlier.

*Sub-Commission Working Group.* Since the Sub-Commission Working Group had total discretion about which situations to identify as gross violations, political considerations dictated its composition. Resolution 1503 requires appointment of five experts with "due regard for geographical distribution."[86] The Sub-Commission has specified one member each from the African, Asian, Latin American, Eastern European and Western European and other groups.[87] Despite the potential conflict of interest, government officials elected as "independent" experts to the Sub-Commission frequently served on the Working Group and on occasion constituted a majority.

The Sub-Commission reportedly received 35,000 communications in its first three-year period.[88] In 1979 the Group reviewed 13,124 communications made against 61 governments.[89] Prior to their arrival in Geneva, the Working Group members received monthly summaries from the Secretariat and may have divided the preliminary preparation based on different types of allegations.[90] The Working Group convened two full weeks before the Sub-Commission sessions. In ten days of meetings the Group determined the admissibility of new communications, decided whether the communications revealed any consistent patterns of gross violations, and reviewed cases previously referred to the Commission.

When following up situations referred in prior years, the Group had access to records of the Commission's confidential meetings.[91] The members had summary records of oral interventions made by state observers as well as government replies to the communications. The Group's Chairman-Rapporteur reported on his personal observation of the Commission's 1503 deliberations. In evaluating new situations, the members could obtain from the Secretariat originals of any communications summarized in the monthly digest. The Secretariat also made available any replies received from governments. A simple majority was required to refer a situation to the Sub-Commission. Although the Group met in closed session and submitted a confidential report, the members did not cast secret ballots. United Kingdom expert Benjamin Whitaker proposed that government employees not vote on situations involving their state, and that the Working Group meet twice a year and take decisions by secret ballot.[92] The parent organs disregarded the proposals.

Despite firm political opposition, a Working Group majority consistently referred situations to the full Sub-Commission each year after 1972. In that first year of substantive deliberation, the Working Group could not complete its review of 20,000 communications in the two weeks allotted. Unofficial reports indicated that the Group identified situations in Greece, Iran and Portugal's overseas territories.[93] The Sub-Commission reportedly referred the situations back to the Working Group for further consideration in 1973, thus allowing the governments more time to reply.[94] The Working Group had an additional 7,000 communications to review in 1973 when it referred several more situations to the Sub-Commission. The Working Group reportedly had no official replies to communications alleging violations by Guyana and by the United Kingdom in Northern Ireland. In 1974 and 1976 the Working Group reportedly identified situations in South Vietnam and the Republic of Korea, although those states did not belong to the United Nations. Press accounts in 1974 indicated that the Working Group also referred a situation in Cuba to the Sub-Commission, which took no further action.[95]

According to a 1978 article in *Le Monde* the Soviet and Pakistani experts prevented referral of the situation in Argentina.[96] NGO critics identified an "unholy alliance" of Argentina's military rulers and the communist governments fashioned to block meaningful enforcement procedures.[97] Notwithstanding the political and procedural obstacles, the Working Group apparently forwarded about eight to ten situations annually to the full Sub-Commission.

*Sub-Commission Review.* After the Working Group identified situations for consideration by the Sub-Commission, the Secretariat translated the original communications referred into the U.N. working languages: English, French, and Spanish. Starting in 1979 the Sub-Commission has taken up the 1503 communications after the general public debate on violations, as a separate agenda item during two to three days of private meetings. In addition to the Working Group's documentation, the experts also considered other available information on the situations identified. Current press accounts, NGO country studies, and global surveys, such as Amnesty's annual report, provide additional material. The experts also had access to records of the Commission's confidential deliberations on prior referrals, including written replies and oral interventions by government representatives. It is conceivable, though not very likely, that the full Sub-Commission might also have identified a situation and reviewed the originals of communications not referred by its Working Group.

Recurrent procedural disputes over secret voting, conflicts of interest, and duplication of public and confidential deliberations reflected the political interests at stake. While government observers cannot attend the private meetings, they can learn from confidential summary records and their own nationals what the experts said and how they voted. Secret voting might provide greater protection against intimidation, but only a few experts believed the Sub-Commission could make that procedural change unilaterally.[98] Despite obvious conflicts of interest, "independent" experts participated in decisions affecting their own countries. In 1978 Halima Warzazi answered at great length a complaint against Morocco; to block action against their governments, H. W. Jawardene of Sri Lanka and Mario Amadeo of Argentina successfully moved to postpone a decision. U.S. Ambassador Beverly Carter actually favored action on communications from the United States in the Working Group, but then changed his decisive vote in the full Sub-Commission; he explained that a late government reply had resolved his concerns.[99] Finally, the experts have repeatedly addressed without resolving the procedural confusion created by simultaneous public and confidential review of the same situations. Normally the Sub-Commission completes the public agenda item on violations before conducting confidential deliberations; after several years of confidential referral under Resolution 1503, at least seven situations have become subject to public recommendations.[100]

In 1979 the twenty-six experts discussed procedure first before reviewing all the situations and accompanying recommendations from the Working Group. The experts concluded by voting on each situation taken in alphabetical order.[101] In addition to referring cases to the Commission, the Sub-Commission may refer situations back to its Working Group, allowing governments an additional year to answer the allegations.[102] The experts may also defer consideration by the full body until the next session, as it did for several years on Sri Lanka.[103]

Neither the Sub-Commission nor the Commission could deal with urgent situations or communications received between sessions. That institutional deficiency contributed to the Sub-Commission's 1973 failure to refer violations by the Greek junta. On August 20, President George Papadopoulos proclaimed an amnesty and released hundreds of political prisoners.[104] While meeting that month in Geneva, the Sub-Commission discontinued its consideration of the Greek situation. Two months later another military coup ended the Papadopoulos regime and reinstituted repressive measures.[105] Despite Sub-Commission concern over the Greek situation dating to 1967,[106] the experts had no opportunity to refer confidential communications in time for the Commission's February 1974 session.

By the time the Sub-Commission reconvened in August 1974, the Greek military's intervention on Cyprus had triggered a confrontation with Turkey. That crisis, rather than United Nations action, brought a return to constitutional government in August 1974. Disappointed NGO observers released their evidence of torture and arbitrary killings by the Greek colonels to expose the Sub-Commission policy of "hear no evil, see no evil, speak no evil." "The complexity of your procedures results in victims of repression receiving less protection than the sensibilities of governments."[107] The Greek situation revealed anew the link between human rights violations and international conflict. Despite, or perhaps because of its failure to refer the Greek situation to the Commission, the Sub-Commission has subsequently identified numerous instances of gross violations that received more serious consideration.

From 1973 to 1979 the Sub-Commission referred to the Commission at least 20 situations, including two complaints against governments not belonging to the United Nations.[108] Unofficial sources identified 18 referrals made before 1978,[109] and starting in that year the Commission Chair has announced the names of governments subject to confidential decisions. Table 4.2, drawn from both official and unofficial sources, while somewhat speculative and incomplete, presents a reasonably accurate overview of the Sub-

TABLE 4.2
Situations Reportedly Referred to the Commission, 1973–1979

| Region | Country | Years |
|---|---|---|
| Africa (6) | | |
| | Burundi | 1973 |
| | Equatorial Guinea | 1975, 1976 |
| | Ethiopia | 1977 |
| | Malawi | 1976 |
| | Tanzania (Zanzibar) | 1973 |
| | Uganda | 1974, 1976, 1977 |
| Asia (6) | | |
| | Burma | 1979 |
| | Indonesia | 1973, 1974, 1977 |
| | Iran | 1973 |
| | Israel | 1974 |
| | Korea | 1976, 1978 |
| | South Vietnam | 1974 |
| Latin America (6) | | |
| | Bolivia | 1976 |
| | Brazil | 1973, 1974 |
| | Chile | 1974, 1976, 1977 |
| | Guyana | 1973 |
| | Paraguay | 1977 |
| | Uruguay | 1977 |
| Eastern Europe (0) | | |
| Western Europe and other (2) | | |
| | Portugal (Territories) | 1973 |
| | United Kingdom (Northern Ireland) | 1973 |

Commission's referrals.  The comparable totals for Africa, Asia, and Latin America support complaints that regional balance has been sought.  Over half the referrals involve NAM members, indicating that the non-aligned majority controlling U.N. policy organs did not block Sub-Commission experts from confidential review of NAM members.

*Commission Review*

*Information Forwarded.*  When the Sub-Commission referred a documented situation to the Commission, the Secretariat notified the government of its right to make written observations and to appoint a representative.  The individual petitioner, however, was never notified of any disposition. The complainant had no opportunity to refute the government response. The Commission, not the victim, had the responsiblity to enforce international norms in the *ex parte* proceedings. The policy of nondisclosure made the Resolution 1503 procedure more of a "petition-information" than a "petition-recourse" system.[110] The ostensible purpose was not to remedy individuals' injuries but to reveal and to stop patterns of gross violations.

That rationale does not explain why supplementary communications from the complaining individual were routed through the Sub-Commission Working Group to be treated like a new situation. Situations referred by the Sub-Commission did not reach the Commission until at least a year after the events reported. Supplemental information sent to the Secretariat after the Sub-Commission's confidential recommendation did not ordinarily become part of the record sent to the Commission. Although the type of situations identified involved ongoing violations, the Commission received only the first materials presented to the Sub-Commission working group.

The prolonged consideration of communications about Equatorial Guinea illustrates the delay.[111] The first complaint of November 14, 1974, detailed atrocities which had begun with Macías Nguema's accession to power in 1968. In August 1975, the Sub-Commission reviewed additional allegations from the International Federation for the Rights of Man in letters dated March 28 and April 11, 1975. At its 1976 session, the Commission considered a thirteen-page reply and an oral intervention from the government's representative. The Commission concluded that the evidence forwarded from the Sub-Commission did not reveal systematic and flagrant violations. As a result of procedural obstacles, that decision was taken in March 1976 without knowledge of letters submitted between June 1975 and January 1976. The Commission did not receive those letters from the Sub-Commission until 1977, a full year later,when the members did find a pattern of gross violations.[112]

NGO representatives urged that the Commission allow petitioners the same opportunity afforded governments to update the information submitted.[113] The United States supported that procedural reform in 1976,[114] and in 1977 the Commission reportedly decided to "receive and consider recent communications relating to situations referred by the Sub-Commission."[115] It appears that a December 1978 communication on Equatorial Guinea from the University Exchange Fund did go directly to the Commission's 1979 session without prior consideration by the Sub-Commission. NGO observers, however, continued to object that the Secretariat only provided inadequate summaries of supplemental communications, when the Commission should have received detailed extracts containing additional information.[116]

*Working Group.* The Commission designated its own five member, regionally balanced Working Group to make recommendations involving the communications forwarded by the Sub-Commission.[117] The Group met for five days before the Commission convened and considered as many as 17 situations at one session.[118] Normally the Commission received only two to three new referrals in a year and continued review of four to six situations previously identified. Resolution 1503 does not call for a Commission Working Group, and its members apparently do not screen out any cases referred by the Sub-Commission. The Group makes one of the following recommendations:

1. to take no action on a new referral;
2. to continue confidential review at the next session, allowing the government time to report developments;
3. to initiate direct contacts with the government charged for discussions prior to the next session;
4. to appoint a rapporteur or investigatory committee to report on the situation;
5. to discontinue confidential review and undertake a public inquiry;
6. to take no further action on a situation previously identified.

The Secretariat promptly forwards the group's recommendation to the government affected so that an informed representative may be sent for the full Commission's deliberations.[119]

*Deliberations.* Several weeks after the Working Group notified the target governments, the Commission spent three to six days in closed session to review the Group's recommendations. Unlike the Sub-Commission, the Commission began with private deliberations and decisions before a general public debate under the same agenda item on violations. Secretariat staff and the Chairman of the Commission and Sub-Commission Working Groups introduced the item noting any procedural problems. In 1979 Human Rights Division Director Theo van Boven unsuccessfully sought Commission authorization for the Secretariat to direct confidential communications to public procedures whenever possible.[120] The Soviet representative regularly objected for the record, challenging the confidential procedure as a violation of Charter Article 2(7), but he then participated in the decisions. Peru's representative candidly explained that he wanted to delay voting until after discussing all cases "with the specific purpose of ensuring a balance between . . . various decisions."[121]

Following procedural remarks, the Commission took up each situation separately, scheduled either in alphabetical order or for the convenience of government representatives dispatched to Geneva. Commission members being reviewed under the 1503 procedure such as Ethiopia, Uganda, and Uruguay both discussed and voted on their own situations. Nonmember governmental respondents from Bolivia, Equatorial Guinea, Indonesia, Korea, and Paraguay appeared separately and could remain until the final vote on their situation. When a government such as Burma or Malawi failed to appear, the Working

Group chairman or an individual designated to contact the government opened the discussion.

When the government charged was represented or was a member of the Commission, the 1503 deliberations resembled a legislative inquiry. The delegate's official response began the discussion. After enumerating statutory rights guarantees, the more persuasive representatives described government justification for and responses to the violations alleged. Commission questioners, both principled members and political antagonists, closely interrogated the representatives about detailed NGO reports of torture, disappearances, and executions. In defense, respondents questioned human rights practices of the critical government and attacked the NGO's partiality. Since complainants do not attend, NGOs cannot respond and remain uninformed of the exchange. Friendly members have sought to protect clients or allies by objecting to probing questions more appropriate for a judicial tribunal than for an intergovernmental Commission.[122] The same rules govern voting in both private and public sessions, except that every situation identified is put to the vote in the confidential proceedings. When a cooperative target acknowledged a problem, the Commission decided by consensus to continue review. When a Soviet bloc client such as Ethiopia was the target, roll call votes revealed predictable cold war competition for the decisive non-aligned vote.[123]

*Decisions and Responses.* In responding to the confidential communications, the Commission followed Resolution 1503 when it decided to reject some complaints, to treat situations in Chile and Equatorial Guinea under public procedures, and to conduct a confidential study on Uganda. In most of the situations, however, the Commission departed from procedures authorized by Resolution 1503. The Commission requested the Secretary General to designate a representative to visit Equatorial Guinea, Ethiopia, Paraguay, and Uruguay to provide good offices and to obtain information required for future decisions. In many other cases the Commission merely decided to continue reviewing the allegations in confidential sessions year after year.

Even though Burma failed to send a representative, the Commission effectively rejected the complaint against that government by deciding not to respond. The Commission's 1976 resolution on Equatorial Guinea illustrates that type of non-decision:

> the Commission endorsed the conclusions reached by its Working Group . . . that the information submitted to the Commission did not seem sufficient to justify the conclusion that flagrant and systematic violations had been committed in the situation concerned. The Commission therefore decided that there was no need to take action under Council Resolution 1503 (XLVIII) on the basis of the documents before it.[124]

Subsequent referrals from the Sub-Commission led to further confidential review of Equatorial Guinea, but the government refused to cooperate with the confidential monitoring. The Commission gave the Macías regime a year to accept the Secretary-General's good offices or to face public disclosure of the confidential communications. Equatorial Guinea's recalcitrance provoked the Commission to recommend that ECOSOC authorize disclosure of the 1503 materials.[125] Subsequently, a special rapporteur on Equatorial Guinea appointed under Resolution 1235 prepared a report making other recommendations approved by ECOSOC.

Malawi also refused to cooperate with the confidential procedures. In a 1980 recommendation to ECOSOC the Commission noted Malawi's failure to respond to allegations concerning abuse of Jehovah's Witnesses between 1972–1975, publicly deplored the violations, and urged the government to provide remedies. Since there had been no further reports of violations for several years, the members discontinued consideration under Resolution 1503.[126] As Chile's case revealed, noncooperation was not the only reason for publicizing alleged violations. The Commission immediately took up the complaints about Chile in public proceedings without first undertaking any confidential review.

In other situations, the Commission initiated a more conciliatory response which deferred to cooperative target governments' preference for confidential review. The Commission requested the Secretary-General to designate a representative to establish direct contacts with the target government for discussions between sessions. As a result, Davidson Nicol visited Ethiopia, Javier Perez de Cuellar conducted a mission to Paraguay, and Rivas Poseda met with Uruguayan officials. The appointees conducted discreet missions and then reported to the Commission on their prison visits, official interviews, and general observations. The appointees are expected to provide good offices to mediate a human rights dispute and to obtain information required by the Commission for future decisions. After Ethiopia barred the Secretary-General's representative from visiting an overcrowded prison, cold war partisans disputed whether to discontinue review based on his partial report. Although there is little to report, the Secretariat is expected to inform Commission members each quarter about developments in situations where he has been requested to obtain information or to use his good offices.[127]

Other cooperative governments such as South Korea have simply been requested to return to future sessions as the members keep the situation under review. Three operative paragraphs from the Commission's 1981 confidential resolution on Afghanistan reveal the scope of confidential monitoring.

The Commission on Human Rights,
1. *Decides* to keep the alleged human rights violations in Afghanistan under review within the framework of Economic and Social Council resolution 1503 (XLVIII), in the light of any official observations received from Afghanistan or information from other sources, without prejudice to resolution 10 (XXXVII) of the Commission on Human Rights;

2. *Urges* the Afghanistan authorities to co-operate with the Commission;
3. *Requests* the Secretary-General to communicate this decision to the Government of Afghanistan.[128]

By deciding to keep a situation "under review," the Commission allowed a government an additional year to respond to the complaint and to report any improvements. After the Commission Chair began announcing the names of governments subject to decisions in 1978, complainants could tell whether to submit additional information during the interval.

In only one case, Uganda, did the Commission approve the type of confidential investigation authorized by Resolution 1503. Before the designated rapporteur, Justice Onyeama of Nigeria, could begin the the study, Idi Amin had been overthrown. The successor government argued that the study was no longer required, and the Commission obliged by discontinuing consideration. Five other governments made subject to confidential monitoring in the late 1970s (Ethiopia, Indonesia, Korea, Paraguay, and Uruguay) remained under prolonged review as new complaints documented ongoing violations.

## Conclusion

The protection activities authorized by Resolutions 1235 and 1503 dominated Commission deliberations after 1967, but the members also continued to draft standards and to promote human rights. The NAM majority which made enforcement the Commission's top priority after 1967 also recognized that standard setting and promotion could help achieve the Third World's paramount human rights goals of racial equality, self-determination, and economic development. The following chapter shows how the Commission responded by giving priority to norms and values which frequently clashed with Western preferences.

# 5

## Promoting Third World Norms, 1967–1979

The Afro-Asian members who initiated the Commission's protection activities, also reoriented the standard-setting and promotional programs after 1967. The new majority drafted a convention against *apartheid*, promoted a decade to combat racism, and proclaimed a right to economic development. The Western minority sought a declaration against torture, and resisted efforts to give economic rights priority over civil liberties. The non-aligned members effectively used the Commission agenda as part of a larger campaign for racial and economic equality waged throughout the United Nations system.

### Standard-Setting

#### The Crime of Apartheid

No additional instruments were required to establish that *apartheid* violated international law. If the general nondiscrimination provisions of the International Bill of Rights were not clear enough, Article 3 of the International Convention on the Elimination of All Forms of Racial Discrimination expressly condemned *apartheid*. What sponsors wanted from the Commission was stronger enforcement measures that would more effectively protect the victims and punish those guilty of *apartheid*. Codifying *apartheid* as a crime against humanity became the vehicle for bringing to justice individuals responsible for racially motivated murder and torture. Establishing universal jurisdiction for national courts was intended as a deterrent for South African officials desiring to travel abroad.

The concept of criminal-type proceedings to enforce international law did not originate with South Africa's adversaries. In the 19th century, the international community had punished the crime of piracy and slave trading through national courts with universal jurisdiction over offenses committed on the high seas. The Nuremburg Charter created an international tribunal to prosecute Nazi war criminals. For defendants such as Martin Bormann, the Nuremburg judges held trial and determined guilt in the absence of the accused. [1] After the Nuremburg precedent, the General Assembly drafted a statute for a permanent international criminal court.[2]   The 1948 Genocide Convention anticipated the possibility of proceedings in "such international penal tribunal as may have jurisdiction with respect to those Contracting Parties which shall have accepted its jurisdiction."[3] In the decade following World War II, The International Law Commission, the General Assembly, and legal scholars gave serious consideration to establishing a world criminal court as well as to codifying an international criminal code.[4]

Although the General Assembly stopped work on the international criminal court after 1957, different treaties have granted national courts universal jurisdiction over international crimes.  The 1949 Geneva Convention for the Protection of Civilian Persons in Time of War requires "each High Contracting Party . . . to search for persons alleged to have committed, or to have ordered to be committed, such grave offenses . . . and [to] bring such persons, regardless of their nationality, before its own courts."[5] The 1958 Convention on the High Seas applies similar enforcement provisions to pirates.  The Hague Convention for the Suppression of Unlawful Seizure of Aircraft,[6] The Montreal Convention for the Suppression of Unlawful Acts Against the Safety of Civil Aviation, [7] and the UN Convention on the Prevention and Punishment of Crimes Against Internationally Protected Persons Including Diplomatic Agents[8] obligate states parties to enact domestic legislation criminalizing the international offense.[9]

After 1967 when the enlarged Commission shifted priorities, members and nongovernmental officials proposed comparable legal remedies for human rights violations in Southern Africa.  Sean MacBride, Secretary-General of the Inter - national Commission of Jurists, proposed an International Tribunal to punish crimes against humanity and a United Nations register for complaints of brutality.  The Commission's special rapporteur on *apartheid*  recommended declaring responsible South African officials "criminals at large who could be apprehended and tried by the courts of any state under the charge of the commission of crimes against humanity."[10]   When the General Assembly decided to impose direct United Nations administration on South West Africa,[11] the special rapporteur proposed a grand jury of legal experts for the territory. The U.N. tribunal would have firmer ground for *in personam* jurisdiction in South West Africa than in the Republic proper.  "It could be given a variety of police powers including the powers to issue arrest warrants, lists of wanted men and requests that they be brought to justice by Member States of the United Nations."[12] Even if the accused was unavailable, grand jury type proceedings could bring indictments to mobilize public opinion and to deter others.

Sponsors presented a draft convention embodying the criminal law approach to the Third Committee in 1971.[13]   After referral to the Commission for comment, the Third Committee drafted a final text. The General Assembly adopted the International Convention of the Suppression and Punishment of the Crime of *Apartheid* in November 1973.[14] Many Third World governments promptly ratified the convention and it entered into force in 1976. Eastern bloc supporters also became states parties, despite their longstanding opposition to international enforcement measures that compromised domestic jurisdiction. Communist representatives have consistently argued that South Africa's gross violations justify the most stringent Commission review. Moreover, the convention's provisions for consideration of interstate disputes by the International Court of Justice and for individual proceedings by an international penal court both stipulate that the affected states must first consent to such jurisdiction.[15] Not one Western state ratified the *apartheid* convention. Their representatives explained that the definition of *apartheid* was too vague to allow fair enforcement.

Despite objections by Western states that an offense must be precisely defined to justify criminal penalties, the sponsors drafted broad language. The convention declares that *apartheid* is a crime against humanity that constitutes a serious threat to international peace and security.[16] *Apartheid* includes the following conduct:

acts committed for the purpose of establishing and maintaining domination by one racial group of persons over any other racial group of persons . . .

(a) Denial to a member or members of a racial group or groups of the right to life and liberty of person: (i) By murder of members of a racial group or groups; (ii) By the infliction upon the members of a racial group or groups of serious bodily or mental harm, by the infringement of their freedom or dignity, or by subjecting them to torture or to cruel, inhuman or degrading treatment or punishment; (iii) By arbitrary arrest and illegal imprisonment of the members of a racial group or groups;

(b) Deliberate imposition on a racial group or groups of living conditions calculated to cause its or their physical destruction in whole or in part;

(c) Any legislative measures and other measures calculated to prevent a racial group or groups from participation in the political, social, economic and cultural life of the country . . . ;

(d) Any measures, including legislative measures, designed to divide the population along racial lines by the creation of special reserves and ghettos . . . ;

(e) Exploitation of the labour of the members of a racial group or groups, in particular . . . forced labour;

(f) Persecution of organizations and persons . . . because they oppose *apartheid*.[17]

In addition, international criminal responsibility applies irrespective of motive whenever individuals "[c]ommit, participate in, directly incite or conspire, . . . abet, encourage or co-operate in commission of the crime of *apartheid.*"[18]

The *apartheid* convention borrows from the Genocide Convention language on extradition and the provision cited above conferring jurisdiction on any international penal tribunal that may be created.[19] Unlike the territorial restriction on prosecution for genocide, the *apartheid* convention creates universal jurisdiction in all national courts. States undertake to enact legislation to prosecute and punish offenders. In addition, the Commission on Human Rights has implementation responsibility through the Group of Three members representing states parties.[20] Since 1978 the Group has met for up to five days before each Commission session to review periodic reports from the signatories.[21] The Commission is also authorized to prepare "a list of individuals, organizations, institutions and representatives of States which are alleged to be responsible for the crimes enumerated in article II of the Convention."[22] Chapter 6 describes the group's enforcement activities after 1979.

## Torture

Third World efforts to prevent and punish *apartheid* set a precedent for Western activists desiring stronger human rights norms against torture. The torture of South African political dissidents had already led to Commission appointment of an *ad hoc* investigating group in 1967. Similar abuse of prisoners in Chile, Argentina, and Northern Ireland stimulated highly effective nongovernmental lobbying efforts. In 1973 Amnesty International began a Nobel Prize winning campaign against torture on behalf of prisoners of conscience everywhere.[23] The International Commission of Jurists, the International Red Cross, the Swiss Committee Against Torture, and the Commission of the Churches on International Affairs all contributed to increased public awareness that generated pressure and proposals for more effective action.[24]

In 1975 the Fifth United Nations Congress on the Prevention of Crime and the Treatment of Offenders recommended a Declaration on the Protection of All Persons from Being Subjected to Torture and Other Cruel, Inhuman or Degrading Treatment or Punishment; it was approved by the General Assembly.[25] Two years later the Assembly adopted a Swedish proposal requesting the Commission to draw up a torture convention. A Commission working group decided to refer two draft conventions prepared by Sweden and the International Association of Penal Law to governments for comment. In 1979 an open ended working group met both prior to and during the Commission session to begin drafting the torture convention described below in Chapter 7. Western sponsors had less success in moving the Commission to draft a Declaration on Religious Intolerance, although a working group met regularly after 1974 to consider proposed articles.

## Promotion

Just as NAM priorities dictated a new response to violations after 1967, the Commission's new majority also promoted significantly different human rights ideals with advisory services and global studies. The Commission sponsored six seminars on discrimination[26] and four studies on *apartheid* in part during a United Nations Decade on Race Discrimination begun in 1973. Four other seminars[27] and one study dealt with economic rights before the Commission directed research leading to recognition of a newly conceived human right to development. Three regional seminars in Africa[28] laid the groundwork for an African Charter and Commission on Human Rights.[29]

The first seminars had been limited to participants from member states of the regional economic commission. Under its new leadership the Commission sponsored more worldwide seminars, seventeen in a twelve year period; thirty-two invitations to each meeting were allocated by region in accord with the Commission's 1967 membership base: African states—8; Asian and Latin American states—6 each; Eastern European states—4; Western European states and others—8. Eligible governments could nominate one expert and up to three alternates to attend; participants were confirmed by the Secretary-General but did not speak for their governments. The Secretariat also invited observers from other states, the specialized agencies, regional intergovernmental organizations, and NGOs. NGO representatives took part with fewer restrictions than in deliberations of United Nations policy organs.

Although studies and seminars increased in frequency, two other elements of the "Action Plan" oriented toward civil and political rights barely survived the 1970s. Fewer than half the United Nations members submitted periodic reports, and no governments asked for technical assistance from human rights expert advisers. The members gave increasingly sporadic and perfunctory review to the reports and repeatedly postponed consideration after the covenants' reporting requirements took effect in 1976.

### Apartheid, *Racial Discrimination, and Self-Determination*

After 1967 members from Africa, Asia, and Latin America collaborated in a systematic assault on white racism which, to the dismay of Western observers, often dominated Commission debates and programming. The Commission first appointed Manouchehr Ganji of Iran as a Special Rapporteur to study racial discrimination and *apartheid* in Southern Africa[30] and them directed the Working Group of Experts on South Africa to prepare studies on how international law penalized *apartheid* as a crime against humanity.[31] The Working Group also did a second study on implementation of the Apartheid Convention.[32] In order to pressure South Africa's trading partners, the Commission approved a study on assistance to racist regimes by Sub-Commission expert Ahmad Khalifa.[33]

After the 1968 International Year for Human Rights, the General Assembly designated 1971 as the "International Year for Action to Combat Racism and Racial Discrimination." Cameroon sponsored an international seminar on the evils of racial discrimination.[34] The Secretary-General prepared a program of action which targeted *apartheid*, nazism, and other forms of racism. At the end of the year, the Assembly directed the Commission to propose further actions in a "Decade for vigorous and continued mobilization against racism. . . ."[35] The Commission requested the Sub-Commission to prepare a draft programme of a "Decade for Action to Combat Racism and Racial Discrimination." The Assembly reviewed the Sub-Commission draft and launched the decade on 10 December 1973.

The comprehensive action programme called for both national and international measures to:

> promote human rights and fundamental freedoms for all, without distinction of any kind on grounds of race, colour, descent or national or ethnic origin . . . to eliminate the persistence of racist policies . . . to resist any policy and practices which lead to the strengthening of the racist regimes . . . ; to identify, isolate and dispel the fallacious and mythical beliefs, policies and practices that contribute to racism . . . and to put an end to racist regimes.

Implementation measures would include support for all peoples struggling for racial equality, a worldwide information campaign to dispel racial prejudice, the education of youth, and the full involvement of women. ECOSOC coordinated the program, and the Division of Human Rights added three professionals to staff a task force for the decade. The Commission directed the Sub-Commission to conduct studies on racial discrimination and instructed the Secretariat to convene a worldwide seminar in Geneva in 1978.

As the decade progressed, Third World and Eastern bloc sponsors succeeded not only in isolating South Africa, but also the Commission's Western members. Soviet bloc members have regularly sponsored anti-colonial resolutions calling for measures to prevent the resurgence of nazism and fascism, which the West accepted with slight modification. Western members withdrew support from the decade, however, when Arab representatives succeeded in obtaining an Assembly resolution in 1975 that Zionism was a form of racism. Several Western speakers objected that Zionism could not be equated with *apartheid*, and that the Palestinians, despite legitimate grievances, were not victims of racial persecution. Since that time, the United States has not participated in any of the Commission votes on the decade, and other members of the Western group have generally abstained. A solid majority of NAM and Eastern bloc members nevertheless continued the Commission's active support for the decade, appointing representatives to attend the first World Conference to Combat Racism and Racial Discrimination held in 1978.

Studies promoting the ideal of self-determination complemented the Commission's efforts to combat *apartheid* and race discrimination. Well before the Commission took up the colonial issue, the General Assembly had adopted sweeping declarations on granting independence to subject peoples, nonintervention, and national sovereignty over natural resources. The Commission repeatedly reaffirmed those principles by adopting general resolutions urging governments to promote political self rule and economic sovereignty. Two Sub-Commission rapporteurs undertook self-determination studies—Héctor Gros Espiell on the implementation of United Nations resolutions on the right of peoples under colonial and alien domination to self-determination,[36] and Aureliu Cristescu on the historical and current development of the right to self-determination.[37]

## Civil Rights and Individual Liberties

*Minorities.* The Commission's government representatives chosen by dominant ethnic groups have shown far less interest in promoting the rights of minorities than in assuring their own national sovereignty. A genuine commitment to cultural equality would require preservation of distinct language groups through separate public schools and related state sponsored programs. Third World governments determined to establish national unity often favor assimilation rather than special treatment for minorities. The United States created a "melting pot" ideal which threatened old world cultural identity. When the Commission first examined minority concerns, black American civil rights leaders fighting segregation repudiated the concept of "separate but equal." The Commission could not agree on a minority rights provision in the Universal Declaration, and the Sub-Commission had never been able to fashion a politically acceptable definition of minority rights.[38]

Despite the difficulty, Yugoslavia consistently championed minority rights based on its national experience in balancing the interests of competing ethnic groups. In 1965 Yugoslavia convened a meeting on the multinational society, the first worldwide seminar in the advisory services program.[39] A decade later Yugoslavia hosted another international seminar on the promotion and protection of human rights of national, ethnic and other minorities.[40] Yugoslavia's representatives subsequently initiated efforts to draft a declaration on the rights of minorities.

In the early 1960s the Sub-Commission requested the Secretary-General to list, classify, and compile the texts of special international protective measures for ethnic, religious, or linguistic groups. ECOSOC subsequently approved publication of the compilation.[41] In the 1970s Sub-Commission rapporteur Francesco Capotorti (Italy) completed a study on the rights of persons belonging to ethnic, religious, and linguistic minorities which has also been published.[42]

*Aliens.* The Commission also promoted rights for resident aliens—migrant workers and noncitizens—when their countries of origin protested discrimination. After press accounts described abuse of North African workers in Europe, Sub-Commission rapporteur Halima Warzazi (Morocco) reported on the "Exploitation of labour through illicit and clandestine trafficking."[43] Tunisia hosted a seminar on the human rights of migrant workers.[44] Led by Colombia, Yugoslavia, and Turkey, a Commission working group meeting in 1978 expressed particular concern about separation of migrant families and inadequate health care provided by employers. The Commission requested member states to insure the welfare of migrant children and the Secretary-General to prepare proposals for action.[45] ECOSOC opened the working group to all United Nations members, and the group supported firmer action. The Commission's 1979 resolution invited host governments to assure equal treatment of migrants, to adopt measures assuring civil, economic and social rights and to provide training, health, housing, and educational benefits similar to those enjoyed by other citizens.[46] Since the General Assembly assumed responsibility for the working groups in 1979, the Commission has approved Algerian sponsored resolutions endorsing the efforts to draft a migrant worker's convention to protect migrant workers from illicit trafficking and arbitrary expulsion.

Uganda's expulsion of Indian nationals eligible for admission to the United Kingdom led to a separate effort to promote the rights of noncitizens. Sub-Commission rapporteur Baroness Elles (U.K.) completed a study on applying international provisions for the protection of human rights to individuals who are not citizens of the country in which they live.[47] The Commission referred draft principles for a new instrument to the Assembly, where the Sixth Committee has given prolonged consideration without result.

*Individual Liberties and Due Process.* Prior to 1967 the advisory services program had relied on studies and seminars to promote improved criminal justice programs. In the 1970s the Commission relied instead on individual fellowships and on regional training courses for government officials. In 1967, the Secretariat in cooperation with the Japanese government organized a pilot project at the United Nations Asia and Far East Institute for the Prevention of Crime and Treatment of Offenders. After a second pilot project on children's rights in Poland, the Commission subsequently requested the Secretary General to organize one regional training course a year after 1969.[48]

Funds have never allowed annual courses, but the courses have become well established. The first five training courses brought together judges, public prosecutors, police officials, and jurists for sessions on criminal justice administration lasting from two weeks to a month. The participants heard lectures, visited local institutions, and exchanged views on criminal law and procedures. Japan hosted training courses in 1972 and 1977 for participants from Asia, the Far East, and English speaking African countries. Participants from countries belonging to the Economic Commission for Africa also attended courses in Egypt in 1973 and Costa Rica in 1975. Australia invited participants from members of the Economic and Social Commission for Asia and the Pacific to a 1976 course at the Australian Institute of Criminology.[49]

After the Commission and ECOSOC recommended adequate funding, the number of fellowships awarded annually ranged from 21 to 63. In 1978 the Commission recommended granting 25 Fellowships each year. Recipients do not work toward a degree, but rather spend two to three months observing procedures or studying laws in a host country. Over 100 governments nominated candidates, usually officials in the criminal justice field between 25 and 50 years of age—prosecutors, senior police officials and instructors, attorneys, university faculty, and departmental officials from justice, interior, labor, and social affairs. Women have received about 20 percent of the awards, and candidates from developing countries have priority.[50] Host government officials from the appropriate department or university supervised and directed the fellows' training. Fellows most often studied topics in criminal justice administration while observing legislative and judicial practice in the host country. Despite some interest in the rights of minorities, migrants, and indigenous peoples, a majority of the fellowships granted concerned topics in criminal justice.[51]

*Economic Rights and Development*

Prior to 1977 the Commission gave only sporadic attention to promoting economic rights. A variety of other United Nations bodies became increasingly preoccupied with economic development, but paid little heed to human rights. The General Assembly designated the 1960s as a "Development Decade" without asserting any significant link between economic growth and human rights.[52] When the Commission first attempted to promote human rights in less developed countries, members debated whether economic growth required sacrifice of personal liberty. The advisory services program arranged four regional seminars on "human rights in developing countries" in Afghanistan (1964), Senegal (1966), Cyprus (1969), and Zambia (1970). At Kabul and Dakar, participants considered the difficulty of reconciling national development plans with individual rights. Although the Eastern bloc consistently advocated giving priority to economic rights, there was only one seminar devoted to the Universal Declaration's economic and social provisions, a 1967 meeting in Poland.[53]

Proponents of economic rights contend that extreme poverty creates greater suffering and loss of life than torture or genocide. The World Bank has estimated that over 800 million people live in absolute poverty—malnourished, illiterate, and ill. Feudal agricultural systems bind peasant farmers in oppressive service to wealthy absentee landlords. Urban masses concentrated in makeshift shanty towns survive under subhuman conditions without sanitary facilities or fresh water. Two of five children born in Africa die before reaching age five. The life expectancy in Third World countries is barely 50 years, 24 years less than in industrialized nations.[54] As a result of those realities, Third World leaders have resisted Western oriented human rights principles that give civil liberties priority over economic rights. Economic destitution creates inhuman conditions which must be recognized as violations of fundamental human rights.

After obtaining a majority on the Commission, non-aligned representatives advanced new concepts of human rights. Kéba M'Baye of Senegal first proposed a right to development in 1972. Since poor countries lacked the resources to feed, clothe, and house their citizens, their peoples had a collective right to economic assistance from developed nations and former colonial powers. Studies indicate that in 1976 the most privileged 20 percent of the world's population disposed of 66 percent of the world GNP, while the bottom 35 percent of the world's population disposed of only 4 percent of the world GNP.[55] Economic progress and justice could only be achieved through international cooperation or solidarity.

Karel Vasak theorized that new concepts of collective, solidarity rights constituted a third generation of human rights. The West had advanced first generation political and civil liberties, while the Eastern bloc had promoted second generation economic, social and cultural rights. Third World representatives insisted that the time had come to develop a third generation of solidarity rights. They argued that peoples in former colonies had a collective right to development that had been violated by metropolitan powers responsible for centuries of economic and political exploitation. Industrialized nations which had acquired vast wealth at the expense of subsistence societies owed reparations to Third World peoples committed to a more equitable New International Economic Order. International solidarity and cooperation would ensure wider realization of fundamental rights.

The 1968 Proclamation of Teheran noted the "profound interconnexion between the realization of human rights and economic development" and asserted that "the full realization of civil and political rights without the enjoyment of economic, social and cultural rights, is impossible."[56] The Commission subsequently appointed Manouchehr Ganji of Iran to study the realization of economic, social and cultural rights. His 1973 report identified the special needs of developing countries and stressed the importance of independence, territorial integrity, and full sovereignty.[57]

Ganji's analysis led the Commission to reexamine the relationship between economic and political rights just as Third World states began pressing for an Assembly Declaration on a New International Economic Order. Iran's representative to the Commission advocated a "hierarchy or rights" claiming that respect for "psychological and political rights was frequently almost unattainable as long as the realization of material rights was not guaranteed."[58] Speakers from the U.S.S.R., Egypt, Ecuador, and India agreed that economic rights deserved priority over civil liberties. Although the economic covenant provides for progressive realization of the benefits promised, Argentina's representative argued instead that *political* rights were "long term objectives."[59] In response, speakers from the United States and Sweden argued that civil and political rights did not depend on the level of development.[60] By 1975 proponents of economic rights added a standing "high priority" item to the Commission's agenda:

> Question of the realization of the economic, social and cultural rights contained in the Universal Declaration of Human Rights and in the International Covenant on Economic, Social and Cultural Rights, and study of special problems relating to human rights in developing countries.

Additions to that unwieldy heading in later years created three sub-items: (a) the right to development; (b) the new international economic order; and (c) the right of popular participation.

Resolutions adopted by the General Assembly and the Commission in 1977 signaled a decisive reexamination of human rights priorities. In thirty years the United Nations membership had nearly tripled, calling into question the universality of the human rights declaration adopted by the founders. The newest members set out to reformulate basic principles and priorities. Earlier Commission debates had revealed profound ideological differences between proponents of political and economic rights, as well as between advocates of individual and collective rights. A strident debate about which political-economic structures cause gross violations became part of the North-South dispute over the right to development and the New International Economic Order. Not surprisingly, Western members attribute gross violations to immature economic and political systems in developing countries, while the non-aligned blame their plight on neocolonial economic domination by the industrial powers. In formulating the International Bill of Rights the Commission reached fragile compromises on property and minority rights, separate covenants for political and economic rights, and the collective right of political and economic self-determination. Until 1977 the Commission could promote human rights principles proclaimed in the International Bill of Rights as consensus formulations of the world community. After that point, to the consternation of Western critics, the Commission recognized a new right to development, and the Assembly directed that future human rights activity stress critical economic rights.

In 1977 Third World leaders also sponsored General Assembly resolution 32/130 declaring that economic and development priorities should guide further United Nations human rights activities. Western members negotiated several changes in the original draft, so that the final text would also support future promotion of individual civil and political rights. As a result, the compromise adopted lists eight somewhat inconsistent concepts which Commission partisans could cite to support contrary principles. Despite the rhetoric of Eastern bloc supporters, Resolution 32/130 does not expressly make economic rights a prerequisite for realization of individual civil and political liberties. The Resolution affirms that:

> (a) all human rights and fundamental freedoms are indivisible and interdependent; equal attention and urgent consideration should be given to the implementation, promotion and protection of both civil and political, and economic, social, and cultural rights;

Subsequent provisions nevertheless offer considerable support for proponents of an economic rights priority:

> (b) The full realization of civil and political rights without the enjoyment of economic, social and cultural rights is impossible; the achievement of lasting progress in the implementation of human rights is dependent upon sound and effective national and international policies of economic and social development, . . .
> (f)    The realization of the new international economic order is an essential element for the effective promotion of human rights and fundamental freedoms and should also be accorded priority.

The original draft addressed the rights of "peoples" but not individuals; the amended text refers to mass and flagrant violations of human rights of peoples or persons

> (e) . . . affected by situations such as those resulting from apartheid, from all forms of racial discrimination, from colonialism, from foreign domination and occupation, from aggression and threats against national sovereignty, national unity and territorial integrity, as well as from the refusal to recognize the fundamental rights of peoples to self-determination and of every nation to the exercise of full sovereignty over its wealth and natural resources.

Another amendment balancing individual and collective rights provides that:

> (c) All human rights and fundamental freedoms of the human person and of peoples are inalienable;

The following provision, however, appears to make individual human rights dependent on cultural, religious, social and economic conditions of different societies:

> (d) . . . human rights questions should be examined globally, taking into account the overall context of the various societies in which they present themselves, as well as the need for the promotion of the full dignity of the human person and the development and well-being of the society.

The overwhelming Assembly vote of 123 nations in favor of Resolution 32/130 indicates the extent of commitment to principles many perceived as a shift in United Nations human rights priorities. No member voted against the resolution, but eleven members of the Western group, joined by Chad, Israel, the Ivory Coast, and Paraguay abstained.

*The Right to Development.* The Commission's first formal recognition of a right to development appears in a resolution requesting the Secretary-General to study its international dimensions. The resolution's preambular paragraphs identified the obstacles to development as colonialism, aggression, foreign occupation, *apartheid*, all forms of discrimination and domination, and the refusal to recognize the fundamental right of every nation to exercise full sovereignty over its natural wealth and resources. The resolution further deplored the increasing disparity between developed and developing countries, asserted that the international community had a duty to end the disparity, and proposed that resources from general and complete disarmament be used for economic and social development. In stressing the "international" dimensions of the right, the framers wanted the study to highlight people's collective rights against developed nations. The study's cumbersome title also directed attention to the effect of international conflict on individuals' basic needs:

> The international dimensions of the right to development as a human right in relation with other human rights based on international co-operation, including the right to peace, taking into account the requirements of the New International Economic Order and the fundamental human needs.[61]

In defining and promoting the right to development, the Commission has relied heavily on the Secretary-General's 161 page report on its international dimensions.[62] The 1979 study reasoned that individuals as well as collectives had a right to develop, and that successful development required an opportunity for full participation and collective self reliance. Theo van Boven, Director of the United Nations Division of Human Rights, used the study to advocate a synthesis of political and economic, individual and collective rights in the development ideal. The arms race, colonialism, and trading practices by transnational corporations violated the rights of the destitute unable to live in human dignity. The right to development imposes duties on the international community, former colonial powers, transnational corporations, and national governments to make human rights an integral component in all development projects.

Western critics resisted the efforts to realign the Commission's promotional priorities and sought to sustain programs on fundamental civil and political rights. As a result, the Commission had a relatively balanced selection of topics for seminar and training courses conducted between 1967 and 1979, as displayed in Table 5.1.

TABLE 5.1
Subjects of Advisory Services Seminars and Training Courses, 1967–1979

| Topic Area | Regional | International | Total |
|---|---|---|---|
| Due Process | 6 | 0 | 6 |
| Individual Rights | 1 | 2 | 3 |
| Women's Rights | 3 | 3 | 6 |
| Minorities and Youth | 0 | 4 | 4 |
| Racial Discrimination | 1 | 5 | 6 |
| Institution Building | 3 | 1 | 4 |
| Economic Rights/Development | 2 | 2 | 4 |
| Total | 16 | 17 | 33 |

## Institutional Change

In addition to its standard-setting, promotional, and implementation activities, the Commission also dealt sporadically with both its own decision making procedures and broader organizational problems of the United Nations human rights system. In 1963 the Commission had added an agenda item entitled "Further promotion and encouragement of human rights," under which members worked primarily to create regional and national institutions. Following preliminary review by an *ad hoc* study group,[63] the Secretariat convened three advisory services seminars that led the Organization of African Unity to adopt the African Charter of Human and Peoples' Rights in 1981.[64] The African Commission on Human and People's Rights to be established under the Charter is only authorized to prepare confidential reports about complaints and does not have the judicial functions entrusted to the European and Inter-American regional bodies.[65]

The General Assembly and the Commission have both promoted national institutions even more than regional arrangements. Initially the Commission recommended that governments establish national advisory committees responsible both for public education and for reviewing national conditions. An advisory services seminar in 1978 recommended guidelines for local human rights commissions.[66] The Assembly has directed the Secretary-General to survey governments and to report on how they have developed and utilized local institutions. During its first three decades the Commission contributed to and witnessed the proliferation of new global and regional human rights bodies. The Political Covenant drafted by the Commission took effect in 1976 establishing an 18 member Human Rights Committee to review government reports and to receive petitions from individuals in states which had ratified the optional protocol. States parties to the Economic and Social Covenant began reporting to ECOSOC. In drafting the treaty on race discrimination the Commission had created another new United Nations implementation committee. The Apartheid Convention directed the parties to report to a committee appointed from Commission members. The ILO, UNESCO, and other specialized agencies had expanded their human rights programs in areas addressed by the Commission, as had the United Nations Commission on the Status of Women. The Convention on the Elimination of All Forms of Discrimination against Women created an implementation committee, even though the Political Covenant bars sex discrimination. Regional human rights bodies in Europe and Latin America heard some of the same complaints brought to the Commission. Theodor Meron noted the growing possibility of conflict between norms, such as standards against sex discrimination and the rights of religious groups to operate free of government regulation.[67] Uruguay and Chile objected to multiple proceedings before the Inter-American Commission, the Human Rights Committee, and the Commission. Louis Sohn advocated consolidating the reporting procedures to rationalize and simplify procedures which impose unnecessary burdens on states party to different conventions.[68] Meron concludes that

> [e]ventually, the international community will have to . . . ['legislate'] the consolidation of supervisory systems into one or two organs, instead of maintaining the present multitude of organs. Such a consolidation would solve or reduce conflicts in supervision. It would also reduce normative conflicts through a more consistent and rational application and interpretation of human rights instruments.[69]

As United Nations norms and institutions proliferated, the Secretariat's Division of Human Rights assumed extensive new responsibilities without receiving sufficient additional resources. Marc Schreiber, a Belgian, served as director during ten years in which the Commission's increased membership demanded support for major investigations of South Africa and Israel as well as thorough screening of individual communications. In addition the Division began providing services to the Human Rights and Race Discrimination Committees as well as to an enlarged Sub-Commission. Secretariat staff had great difficulty defending the Commission's budgetary requests in the General Assembly's cost conscious Advisory Committee on Administrative and Budgetary Questions (ACABQ). Governments more favorably disposed to the human rights program on the Assembly's Fifth Committee frequently restored cuts made by the ACABQ, but the Division was merely sustained, never expanded.

The Division organized its forty professionals into sections with subordinate units for communications, special procedures, research and studies, prevention of discrimination, advisory services, women's rights, and documentation and publications. The Commission's parent organs transferred the unit on Women's

Rights to another division and added three staff members for a new task force on the race decade in 1973. The Secretariat moved the Division of Human Rights form New York to Geneva in 1973, and thereafter the Commission convened its annual meetings at the Palais des Nations. As a result, European based human rights NGOs had greater opportunities for pressing the Commission and the Division to respond to serious violations.

Dissatisfaction with institutional deficiencies increased steadily during the 1970s, as the Commission failed to realize its members' goals and repeatedly postponed consideration of many agenda items. Representatives of opposing blocs increasingly stressed the need to improve the Commission's decision making procedures and to enhance its effectiveness. The NAM majority became frustrated at the United Nation's inability to change conditions in South Africa and Israel and also wanted to give greater attention to economic rights. After the Political Covenant's optional protocol allowing individual petitions entered into force, the Soviet Union attempted to terminate the Resolution 1503 complaint system. Western members led by Australia, Ireland, and France proposed significant changes that would enable the Commission to respond promptly to serious violations such as those in Uganda, Kampuchea, and Burundi—twice yearly Commission meetings, an inter-sessional role for the bureau, and additional funds and staff for the Secretariat.

United States Ambassador Patrick Moynihan castigated the totalitarian regimes at the United Nations for using the human rights agenda to flail more democratic states.[70] The Western press harshly denounced the Commission's double standard and failure to address the genocidal butchery in Kampuchea and Uganda.[71] Western scholars condemned the preoccupation with collective economic rights and self-determination and protested the Commission's willingness to sacrifice traditional individual liberties.[72] NGOs compiled and published persuasive evidence of widespread torture, kidnapping, and killings by government agents immune from United Nations inquiry.[73] NGO representatives complained that the Resolution 1503 procedures effectively shielded repressive regimes in Argentina, Uruguay, and Paraguay from public exposure. Several reformers pressed for the appointment of a United Nations Commissioner for Human Rights.

New personnel who joined the Secretariat and the Commission after 1976 pressed for institutional reform. Theo van Boven became Director of the Division of Human Rights in 1978. His prior experience representing Netherlands on the Commission complemented a strong personal commitment to take effective initiatives on behalf of victims. Representatives from Senegal, Ghana, Egypt, Panama, and Jordan also demonstrated independence and courage in identifying new violations for public investigation. A Senegalese chairman, Kéba M'Baye, first announced the names of countries subject to resolution 1503 decisions. The Third World chairmen who followed warned against statements revealing confidential 1503 materials or decisions, but allowed other allegations against the same countries. NGOs were not only allowed but encouraged to name offending governments when members suspected that their complaints against unnamed offenders drew on confidential materials.[74] As chairman in 1980, Jordan's Waleed Sadi ruled that NGO speakers could identify by name states charged with human rights violations.[75] After Kwadwo Nyamekye joined the Human Rights Division as van Boven's assistant, Jonas Foli continued Ghana's constructive work on the Commission.[76]

Several key Western democracies sought a more comprehensive and effective application of human rights norms as they became members—Canada in 1976, Australia in 1978, the Netherlands and Costa Rica in 1980. Yvon Beaulne of Canada and Peter Kooijmans of the Netherlands provided strong leadership for the Western bloc and initiated significant procedural reforms and substantive inquiries. Small Western democracies overshadowed by the military super powers fashioned internationalist foreign policies which satisfied their constituents' human rights concerns while offering opportunities for United Nations leadership. With Jimmy Carter's election in 1976, the United States changed both personnel and its human rights policy. After 1977 the Carter administration supported a stronger Commission and began pressing even friendly governments to improve their human rights practices. Jerome Shestack, President of the International League for Human Rights, headed the United States delegation in 1980, when the most significant changes culminated.[77]

Sustained efforts to improve the Commission's performance began when the Assembly's NAM majority directed the members to explore alternative approaches, ways and means and to give priority to economic rights, development, and the New International Economic Order. A pre-sessional, open ended working group chaired by India's representative began meeting in 1978 to negotiate competing bloc proposals for improving both the United Nations system and the Commission's work methods. Since the working group made decisions only by consensus, the profoundly divided members only recommended a few minor changes.

In the second year of negotiation the group agreed to enlarge the Commission to 43 members, to extend the meeting time from four to six weeks, and to alter the terms of reference to include responsibility for coordinating United Nations activities.[78] At the same time the Sub-Commission obtained authorization to increase its session from three to four weeks.[79] The revised terms of reference did not mention Assembly Resolution 32/130, although the resolution drafted for ECOSOC separately noted that the Commission should take those concepts into account. The group also noted and ECOSOC approved the possibility of special sessions for unfinished business, such as standard setting. The resolution's requests for suggestions on intersessional Bureau meetings and increased Secretariat staffing revealed unresolved differences on those Western proposals.[80] (See Appendix A for the full text of ECOSOC Resolution 1979/36.)

The changes approved in 1979 concluded the third stage of the Commission's development. Beginning in 1980 the Commission would have eleven additional members, two extra weeks for deliberation, and new authority to coordinate United Nations human rights activities. Western governments and NGO representatives would initiate the greatest changes as they sought Commission action on mass disappearances, killings, and torture.

# 6

# Global Protection, 1980–1986

The enlarged Commission on Human Rights that convened in 1980 appeared quite unlike the small Western controlled body of 1947, and it also differed considerably from the Third World dominated enterprise initiated in 1967. The significant changes introduced in 1980 resulted from several years of growing pressure for reform stimulated by widespread dissatisfaction with the Commission's performance. The Commission session was extended from four to six weeks, allowing more time to consider additional situations without curtailing debate on South Africa, Israel, and Chile. Enlarging the membership from 32 to 43 brought to Geneva new representatives with a broader substantive perspective and a commitment to improved procedures. The Netherlands, Ghana, and Costa Rica all began three year terms, and Jordan's Waleed Sadi presided as Chairman.[1] Table 6.1 identifies Commission members from 1980–1987.

The enlarged Western group formed an effective caucus that began meeting daily during the 1980 session.[2] With 10 of the 43 seats, the Western group commanded a proportionately larger voting bloc in the Commission than in the General Assembly. The Non-aligned Movement (NAM) controls 63 percent of the Assembly votes, but only half in the Commission. Thus with occasional support from a few moderate NAM members and from Latin American and Asian governments outside the NAM, a more disciplined Western bloc succeeded in opening the Commission to new complaints and in drafting new standards on torture and religious intolerance.

NAM solidarity also weakened. Cuba brought a radical pro-Soviet approach to the NAM Presidency at the 1979 Havana summit, alarming the more moderate members.[3] Following independence for Portugal's colonies and Zimbabwe, the Soviet Union invaded Afghanistan, and Vietnam occupied Kampuchea. Most NAM members condemned the violations of self-determination by Soviet bloc forces.[4] At least in some situations, moderate NAM members began to apply human rights principles against Soviet bloc and

TABLE 6.1
Commission Membership, 1980–1987 (42 members)

| Year 19–<br>Session | 80<br>36 | 81<br>37 | 82<br>38 | 83<br>39 | 84<br>40 | 85<br>41 | 86<br>42 | 87<br>43 |
|---|---|---|---|---|---|---|---|---|
| **Africa (11)** | | | | | | | | |
| Algeria | XX | XX | XX | | | | XX | XX |
| Benin | XX | XX | | | | | | |
| Burundi | XX | XX | | | | | | |
| Cameroon | | | | | XX | XX | XX | |
| Congo | | | | | | XX | XX | XX |
| Egypt | XX | | | | | | | |
| Ethiopia | XX | XX | XX | | | | XX | XX |
| Gambia | | | XX | XX | XX | XX | XX | XX |
| Ghana | XX | XX | XX | XX | | | | |
| Ivory Coast | XX | | | | | | | |
| Kenya | | | | | XX | XX | XX | |
| Lesotho | | | | | | XX | XX | XX |
| Liberia | | | | | | XX | XX | XX |
| Libya | | | | XX | XX | XX | | |
| Mauritania | | | | | XX | XX | XX | |
| Morocco | XX | XX | | | | | | |
| Mozambizue | | | | XX | XX | XX | XX | XX |
| Nigeria | XX | XX | | | | | | |
| Rwanda | | | XX | XX | XX | | | XX |
| Senegal | XX | XX | XX | XX | XX | XX | XX | XX |
| Somalia | | | | | | | | XX |
| Tanzania | | | | | XX | XX | XX | |
| Togo | | | XX | XX | XX | | | XX |
| Uganda | | XX | XX | CH | | | | |
| Zaire | | XX | XX | XX | | | | |
| Zambia | XX | XX | XX | | | | | |
| Zimbabwe | | | XX | XX | XX | | | |
| **Asia (9)** | | | | | | | | |
| Bangladesh | | | | XX | XX | CH | XX | XX |
| China | | | XX | XX | XX | XX | XX | XX |
| Cyprus | XX | XX | XX | XX | XX | XX | XX | XX |
| Fiji | | XX | XX | XX | | | | |
| India | XX | XX | XX | XX | XX | XX | XX | XX |
| Iran | XX | | | | | | | |
| Iraq | XX | XX | | | | | | XX |
| Japan | | | XX | XX | XX | XX | XX | XX |
| Jordan | CH | XX | XX | XX | XX | XX | XX | |
| Mongolia | XX | XX | | | | | | |
| Pakistan | XX | XX | XX | XX | XX | | | XX |
| Philippines | XX | XX | XX | XX | XX | XX | XX | XX |
| Sri Lanka | | | | | | XX | XX | XX |
| Syria | XX | XX | XX | | XX | XX | XX | |

(cont.)

TABLE 6.1 cont.

| Year 19–<br>Session | 80<br>36 | 81<br>37 | 82<br>38 | 83<br>39 | 84<br>40 | 85<br>41 | 86<br>42 | 87<br>43 |
|---|---|---|---|---|---|---|---|---|
| **Eastern Europe (5)** | | | | | | | | |
| Bulgaria | XX | XX | CH | XX | XX | XX | XX | XX |
| Byelorussia | XX | XX | XX | | | | XX | XX |
| German Dem. Rep. | | | | | XX | XX | XX | XX |
| Poland | XX | XX | XX | XX | | | | |
| Ukraine | | | | XX | XX | XX | | |
| USSR | XX | XX | XX | XX | XX | XX | XX | XX |
| Yugoslavia | XX | XX | XX | XX | XX | XX | XX | XX |
| | | | | | | | | |
| **Latin America (8)** | | | | | | | | |
| Argentina | XX | XX | XX | XX | XX | XX | XX | XX |
| Brazil | XX | CH | XX | XX | XX | XX | XX | XX |
| Colombia | XX | | | XX | XX | XX | CH | XX |
| Costa Rica | XX | XX | XX | XX | XX | XX | XX | XX |
| Cuba | XX | XX | XX | XX | XX | | | |
| Mexico | XX | XX | XX | XX | XX | XX | XX | |
| Nicaragua | | | | XX | XX | XX | XX | XX |
| Panama | XX | XX | XX | | | XX | XX | XX |
| Peru | XX | XX | XX | | | | | |
| Uruguay | XX | XX | XX | XX | XX | | | |
| Venezuela | | | | | | XX | XX | XX |
| | | | | | | | | |
| **W. Eur. + Other (10)** | | | | | | | | |
| Australia | XX | XX | XX | XX | | XX | XX | XX |
| Austria | | | | | | XX | XX | XX |
| Belgium | | | | | | | XX | XX |
| Canada | XX | XX | XX | XX | XX | | | |
| Denmark | XX | XX | XX | | | | | |
| Finland | | | | XX | XX | XX | | |
| France | XX | XX | XX | XX | XX | XX | XX | XX |
| Fed. Rep. of Germany | XX | XX | XX | XX | XX | XX | XX | XX |
| Greece | XX | XX | XX | | | | | |
| Ireland | | | | XX | XX | XX | XX | XX |
| Italy | | | | XX | XX | XX | | XX |
| Netherlands | XX | XX | XX | XX | CH | XX | | |
| Norway | | | | | | | XX | XX |
| Portugal | XX | XX | | | | | | |
| Spain | | | | | XX | XX | XX | |
| United Kingdom | XX | XX | XX | XX | XX | XX | XX | XX |
| United States | XX | XX | XX | XX | XX | XX | XX | XX |

CH  designates Chairman

selected Third World offenders. Third World preoccupation with racism, South Africa, Israel, and Chile continued to dominate the Commission agenda, but no longer to the exclusion of other concerns.

As in 1967, the altered political balance of 1980 made possible the approval of a new procedure for dealing with violations. The Commission instituted a thematic or global approach by appointing a five member working group authorized to investigate involuntary disappearances in any country. The group developed urgent action responses that became a model for separate rapporteurs subsequently appointed to deal with summary executions, torture, and religious intolerance. In addition the Commission identified new offenders for investigation, engaged in five standard setting projects, and extended its promotional program. Those efforts after 1980 incorporated initiatives sponsored by competing blocs, no one of which enjoyed the degree of control that had previously been enjoyed first by the West and later by the Third World majority.

## Thematic Approaches to Violations

In thirteen years of public debate on violations the Commission had only found the political will to apply special fact finding procedures to three pariah regimes. Complaints about similar violations by other governments triggered political divisions based on ideological alliances and bloc antagonisms that blocked meaningful scrutiny. Since the Commission appeared unlikely to undertake many country-based investigations, reformers proposed a new thematic procedure to investigate one type of violation wherever it occurred. The problem of greatest concern in 1980 was involuntary disappearances, political abductions sponsored by several dictatorships, primarily in Latin America.

### Enforced or Involuntary Disappearances

When the Commission replaced the five member Working Group on Chile, one rapporteur was appointed to examine the problem of the disappeared in that country. He reported to the General Assembly in late 1979.[5] At ECOSOC's request the Sub-Commission recommended that the Commission fashion an emergency remedy for the general problem of disappearances.[6] NGOs such as Amnesty International and the International Commission of Jurists (ICJ) were actively supported by Theo van Boven in their campaign to persuade the Commission to act. Van Boven and Neill MacDermot of the ICJ co-hosted a program on disappearances attended by nineteen Commission members during the first week of the 1980 session.[7]

France proposed a draft resolution in the Western contact group; despite general support, the bloc members disagreed on the precise details and wording, and none joined as cosponsors. Kramer and Weissbrodt report that the Western members favored non-aligned sponsorship to assure adoption by consensus. As delegates lobbied in the corridors, NGO representatives had the unusual opportunity to speak first on the agenda item in the general debate. Iraq's delegate Mohamed Redha Al-Jabiri actively organized non-aligned support. Yugoslavia and Senegal joined as cosponsors for amendments which replaced the operative paragraphs of the French draft. The United States insisted that the proposed five member working group be authorized to investigate actual cases of violations. Argentina's delegate sought to avoid scrutiny of disappearances attributed to his government by cabling protests to the home capitals of the most active delegations and by lobbying for a group limited to theoretical study. Although Brazil and Uruguay supported Argentina's efforts, the non-aligned sponsors led the Commission to adopt without a vote a resolution setting up a group for one year with authority to consider "questions relevant to enforced or involuntary disappearances of persons."[8] The Commission chair then appointed as working group members representatives from Iraq, Costa Rica, the United Kingdom, Ghana, and Yugoslavia.[9] The Division of Human Rights hired temporary staff in the Special Procedures Unit to service the group, which met for the first time in June 1980. Whatever the ambiguities in the authorizing resolution, the disappearances Working Group proceeded to institute a form of international *habeas corpus*.[10]

NGOs and organizations representing relatives of those who had disappeared lodged complaints that the Secretariat screened.[11] Most complaints involved South American countries where government sponsored abductions became a popular counter terrorist tool in the 1960s. The group met three times a year to decide which materials were sufficiently reliable to justify contacting the government charged. The group's chairman was authorized to contact governments immediately when reliable information about very recent events called for urgent action. The urgent action procedure clarified 216 of the 1,121 cases transmitted between 1981 and 1984.[12] Communications requesting government cooperation were highly conciliatory and deferential in tone, with no hint of blame or reproach. The Working Group simply asked governments to investigate reported disappearances so that anxious relatives could learn for certain what had happened to victims. In order to obtain first hand information, the members met once each year in South America, sent representatives to conferences sponsored by relatives of the missing, and sent missions to Cyprus, Bolivia, and Mexico. At a 1984 meeting in Costa Rica relatives of the disappeared conducted a hunger strike to press for more effective action.[13] In response the Group annexed to its report a statement and draft convention prepared by FEDEFAM, a federation of family organizations.[14]

By 1985 the group had contacted 38 governments with details about individuals and the alleged time and place of their abduction. The governments' replies have clarified only about six percent of the more than 10,000 cases identified. Those responding denied knowledge of the incidents, disclaimed responsibility, blamed terrorist groups or previous regimes, and/or pledged to investigate. Two have expressed a preference for dealing with the International Committee for the Red Cross, and in the cases of Cyprus, Chile, and South Africa the group has deferred to other United Nations procedures. Only 6 governments altogether refused to respond, but Argentina's representatives in Geneva never forwarded the inquiries to Buenos Aires.[15]

The Group's annual reports did not find particular governments guilty of any international law violations. The Group merely summarized evidence supporting different allegations and recounted its largely futile efforts to obtain information about individual victims. The members have resisted NGO pressure to recommend Commission action against responsible offenders. After complaints that the group's purely humanitarian appeals had little impact, a new chairman/rapporteur acknowledged that the group had often been satisfied with official explanations which victims found evasive. The group then asked six governments for permission to conduct missions of inquiry.

Only Peru had accepted by 1986. Two members assisted by two Secretariat officials interviewed government officials and held several hearings in villages where peasants related first hand accounts of abductions. In drafting a report, the authors had to determine whether to give a complete account or selectively to identify material that Peru's cooperative new civilian President could use to curb violations by military authorities. A special appendix to the Working Group's 1986 report summarized evidence obtained on the Peruvian mission and offered concrete recommendations for curtailing further disappearances.[16] The team then returned for a follow-up mission in October 1986. Thus, a procedure which originated as a thematic alternative produced its first country-specific investigation.

The Commission accepted the report on Peru without objection and for the first time extended the Working Group's authorization for a two year period.[17] Even before the United Nations budget crisis of 1986 the appointments of the temporary Secretariat staff serving the group were occasionally interrupted. With a freeze in hiring, the Centre reduced staff for the group from five to three, and members worried that further retrenchment would curtail meetings, missions, and reports.

## Mass Exodus

Canada attempted to fashion a second thematic procedure to prevent human rights violations resulting from mass exoduses. Agencies such as the Red Cross and the U.N. High Commissioner for Refugees merely helped victims, without correcting the situations which caused mass migrations. Canada's first proposal to appoint a special rapporteur in 1979 did not pass, but the General Assembly requested that Commission make recommendations after reviewing a report on the problem by the Secretary-General.[18] In 1981 the Commission proposed the appointment of a special rapporteur.[19] The former U.N. High Commissioner for Refugees, Prince Sadruddin Aga Khan, then prepared a comprehensive report containing several annexes with specific details about situations involving many countries, as well as case studies on Afghanistan, Ethiopia, Indochina, and Mexico.[20] Governments troubled by such detail succeeded in having the report reissued for "technical reasons" without the offending annexes.[21] The Commission forwarded the report to the General Assembly which had already established a Group of Governmental Experts on International Cooperation to Avert New Flows of Refugees. That effectively concluded the Commission's second thematic initiative.

*Summary or Arbitrary Executions*

Once the disappearances working group had successfully instituted a procedure for threats to liberty, reformers sought a parallel thematic mechanism for wrongful taking of life. The General Assembly had already expressed concern about summary capital punishment without adequate procedural safeguards, and the Sixth U.N. Congress on the Prevention of Crime and the Treatment of Offenders had deplored murder committed or tolerated by governments. Director Theo van Boven welcomed delegates to the 1982 Commission meeting with an impassioned appeal for some response to the flagrant killings by certain governments, such as Iran, which he identified by name. Photograph 6.1 shows the first meeting of that 38th session. Van Boven's bold initiative may have cost him his job, as the new Secretary-General Javier Perez de Cuellar had advised him not to name offenders and then declined to renew his appointment.[22] NGOs publicly documented widespread extra-legal killing by governments and lobbied forcefully for a special rapporteur.

Denmark sponsored a resolution proposing the appointment for one year of a special rapporteur responsible for investigating both arbitrary and summary executions. The text authorized the rapporteur to seek information from governments as well as nongovernmental organizations with consultative status and called for a report on the occurrence and extent of executions. The Soviet Union won only six votes for its motion opposing the procedure, and thirty-three members voted in favor of the final draft.[23] The Commission Chair appointed as rapporteur S. Amos Wako, Kenyan Secretary-General of the Inter-African Union of Lawyers.

Temporary Secretariat staff promptly began screening information from NGOs in order to brief the rapporteur during his three trips a year to Geneva and to convey urgent communications to him. Wako's first report defined summary killing as executions authorized without the due process guarantees required by the Universal Declaration and the International Covenant on Civil and Political Rights.[24] Arbitrary execution was defined to include extra-legal killing. The rapporteur then sought clarification from 39 governments, exclusively Third World states. His report summarized information about alleged executions occurring after 1980 in eighteen different countries; for twenty-one situations that reportedly occurred before 1980 the report merely named the country

Officers, Secretariat staff, members, and observers at the first meeting of the 38th session in the Palais des Nations, Geneva, on February 1, 1982. (U.N. Photo 149, 369)

without giving details. Fifteen governments responded to Wako's inquiries, five held personal conversations, and twenty-four made no response. Wako reported the governments' assorted denials and explanations either by summarizing their replies or by reproducing correspondence.

Critics found the unsubstantiated allegations about killings far more objectionable than the Disappearances Working Group's reports about alleged abductions. Wako's mandate was renewed on an annual basis, but the official displeasure convinced him to eliminate specific references and supporting detail from his next two reports. The rapporteur continued to relay information to governments for clarification, but his second report merely identified the factors causing arbitrary killings and referred generally to situations A, B, C, etc.[25] Wako's third report identified only three states which had refused all cooperation.[26]

For cases of impending summary executions, Wako immediately sent telegrams urging ten governments to respect the criminal procedures embodied in the Universal Declaration and Articles 6 and 14 of the International Covenant on Civil and Political Rights. Wako noted in the text of the five telegrams that the government was a party to the covenant, but sought to hold five other states which had not ratified to the same standard. The four governments responding made no objection to being judged by the Covenant, and most defended their criminal procedures as eminently fair. Wako reproduced the text of all the urgent telegrams in his second report. The Commission endorsed his urgent action initiative and added to the resolution reauthorizing his mandate a request that he "respond effectively . . . when a summary or arbitrary execution is imminent or threatened."[27] The rapporteur sent thirteen telegrams in 1985. Only two governments responded, one stating that the death sentence challenged had been commuted.[28] In two other cases the government commuted the sentence without acknowledging that Wako's intervention influenced the decision.[29] Eleven governments made no response. When Wako objected to the United States that forthcoming executions in Texas and South Carolina violated the international covenant's proscription of capital punishment for youthful offenders, the United States strongly questioned his authority. Wako's report did not mention the United States, although he had earlier noted that Bangladesh intended to execute individuals convicted for crimes committed as juveniles.[30]

In its latest addition to his mandate, the Commission has asked Wako to consider drafting standards for autopsies in cases of suspicious deaths. While welcoming the rapporteur's attention to imminent executions, Amnesty Inter - national criticized his failure to respond effectively when governments com - mitted extensive extra-legal killings. Government sponsored para-military hit squads which routinely eliminate political opponents justify United Nations attention and action. Libyan officials have publicly proclaimed their right to liquidate "running dogs" of imperialism, and the press has reported several assassination attempts in Egypt, Greece, and the United Kingdom.[31] The rapporteur and the Commission have not responded. More than a year after an Inter-American Human Rights Commission inquiry,[32] rapporteur Wako did visit Suriname at the government's invitation to investigate a single mass killing; his report found government officials responsible.[33]

### Torture

The Commission's response to the global evil of torture has included drafting a convention completed in 1984, medical assistance for victims, as well as a third thematic procedure authorizing a timely response to reported violations. Like his predecessor Theo van Boven, Kurt Herndl urged the Commission to initiate a special procedure. After the members completed work on the draft Torture Convention in 1984 Herndl, as Assistant-Secretary General and Director of the Secretariat's renamed Centre for Human Rights, pointed out the need for a mechanism on torture comparable to the procedures for disappearances and executions.[34] At the 1985 session, outgoing chair Peter Kooijmans of the Netherlands called for new machinery to monitor complaints of torture, and Herndl repeated his recommendation.

The representative of Argentina's newly elected democratic government introduced a resolution authorizing appointment of a special rapporteur. Western governments and NGOs wanted a special rapporteur on torture, ostensibly to monitor compliance until sufficient ratifications brought the new convention's own enforcement provisions into effect. Past practice with the covenants indicates that even after the Torture Committee begins operations, the Commission's rapporteur can be expected to fault nonratifying states for violating the convention. Even with a mandate limited to one year, twelve Soviet bloc and NAM members abstained in the vote on the authorizing resolution.[35] That resolution directs the rapporteur to seek information and to respond effectively "with discretion."[36] The Secretariat estimated that the rapporteur would require one temporary professional assistant for six months and would make three trips to Geneva and one field mission.[37] The U.S.S.R. reportedly objected to Peter Kooijmans as rapporteur and sought appointment for a Soviet national; the chairman appointed Kooijmans, the Netherlands' repre - sentative who had effectively chaired the Commission and had pushed the draft - ing sessions on the torture convention to fruition. NGOs hoped that an assertive, independent rapporteur would extend the global procedures beyond humanitarian intervention when oppressive governments reject the cooperative approach. In preparing his first report,[38] Kooijmans reviewed extensive evidence of torture supplied by nongovernmental organizations. He contacted eight gov - ernments with requests for urgent action. Three did not respond, while the others denied the allegations; the Soviet Union responded by protesting that the rap - porteur had no authority to issue such appeals. Despite Soviet objections to the first report, the Commission extended the rapporteur's mandate for a second year.

*Religious Intolerance*

The United States took a lead at the Commission's 1986 session in lobbying for a special rapporteur to investigate complaints of religious intolerance. Opponents noted that a Sub-Commission rapporteur was already preparing an analytic study of the problem, but sponsors wanted an individual authorized to contact governments in response to complaints.[39] Twenty-six members voted for the proposal, the fewest to approve any thematic procedure; five Soviet bloc supporters voted against, and twelve Third World governments abstained. The Commission chair appointed Portugal's Angelo Vidal D'Almeida Ribeiro as the rapporteur. Opponents who suspected the Western sponsors of cold war motivations will most certainly question the rapporteur's political bias against any communist or non-Christian governments subjected to criticism. Such objections, if successful, would undermine the basic nonpolitical premise of thematic approaches: that the problems addressed are global and not limited to a single country, region, or ideological bloc. After the first report described recent atrocities without identifying any countries, the Commission without vote in 1987 renewed the rapporteur's mandate to "respond effectively to credible and reliable information." As reported in the Afterword, the Commission approved a new thematic procedure on mercenaries for the 1987 session.

## Public, Country-Specific Responses

*Decision Making Procedures*

The membership and organizational changes of 1980 that resulted in new thematic procedures also brought important changes to the Commission's Resolution 1235 public debate on violations. The well organized Western contact group lodged complaints against Soviet bloc members and client states. The West could not get the Commission to act on behalf of Soviet dissident Andrei Sakharov, but did succeed in obtaining review of Poland, Afghanistan, and Kampuchea. Anti-communist South American regimes also became targets of Commission inquiry when Western democracies, NGOs, and anti-American members jointly condemned the violations. In addition, Third World states charged not only the major powers, but also some aggressive non-aligned governments with self-determination violations. As a result, after 1980 the Commission applied some enforcement tools honed on South Africa, Israel, and Chile against many additional offending governments.

About half of the more than 20 items on the Commission agenda provide opportunities for complaints about violations. South Africa, Israel, and Chile are the only situations which have separate agenda items. The largest number of other cases is considered under the general item on gross violations added to the agenda in 1967. The Commission has also charged specific governments with violations under the agenda item on self-determination. Complaints have also attacked governments when debating items on the rights of detainees, and Arab members once introduced a resolution condemning Israel under the item on science and technology. The United States and the Netherlands proposed a new agenda item on religious intolerance in 1985, presumably seeking new country-specific protection as well as promotional activities. Western representatives have been unable, however, to merge consideration of the Chilean situation with similarly treated cases under the general item on violations.

Since the Commission has normally been unable to complete its long agenda, the order in which items are debated has more than symbolic value. After the first public meeting, the new officers meet privately with Secretariat staff to group agenda items and to schedule them for consideration in order of priority. In a six-week session, the Commission usually meets twice each weekday, morning and afternoon, in sixty separately numbered meetings. The members routinely request a supplementary budgetary appropriation for evening debates when the Commission falls behind schedule. Since 1967 the Commission has given top priority to debate on the Middle East and South Africa, spending the first two full weeks on five related agenda items. Lengthy speeches generally repeat familiar arguments from debates of the General Assembly or prior Commission meetings. Standard resolutions with minor changes and additions are adopted each year. In 1980 the Western bloc attempted without success to make the detention of Andrei Sakharov in the U.S.S.R. the first topic of discussion. Instead the Commission dealt with that situation, along with allegations of most other violations, under a general agenda item scheduled for the final two weeks of the session.

Discussion on agenda items begins with an introductory statement by Secretariat staff from the Centre for Human Rights, by an appointed expert, or by the chair of a working group submitting a report.[40] The speaker summarizes past U.N. action on the topic and describes the available documents received from states, the General Assembly, ECOSOC, specialized agencies, the Secretary-General, and NGOs. The chair first enrolls members on a speakers list in the order names are received, and subsequently adds other government observers, representatives of specialized agencies, and finally NGO spokesmen who wish to address the topic. NGOs capitalize on the opportunity to the distress of many embarrassed government officials who often seek to cut short critical statements.

The general debate appears disjointed because speakers limited to one principal statement on an agenda item such as self-determination may refer to five different situations (Namibia, Palestine, Western Sahara, Kampuchea, Afghanistan) rather than to only one. The next speaker may or may not refer to the same situations; nonmember observers far down the speaker list respond to attack long after the event. Polemics directed at "fascist oppressors," "hypocrites," and "terrorists" prompt state representatives to insist on their right to reply. Representatives may use the right of reply once for ten minutes and a second time for five minutes, but must wait to do so until the end of the meeting or possibly the end of the agenda item. If a representative needs authorization or guidance from the foreign ministry, cabled instructions may further delay a response.

The chair declares the speakers list and general debate closed "with the consent to the Commission"[41] and also announces the deadline for members to submit proposed resolutions. Protracted discussion often, however, prevents conclusion of debate within the time allotted on the work schedule. Meetings run late into the night toward the end of each session, and the Commission still neglects the final items on its work schedule. The Commission spent an estimated two-thirds of the 1982 session considering alleged violations.[42] Table 6.2 provides data about the participants in different agenda items on violations debated at the 1985 session. Following completion of the general debate on an agenda item, the Commission considers at a later meeting the resolutions proposed to address different situations. Only a select few of the violations condemned in general debate become subjects of resolutions, and only Commission members can speak for and against. Sponsors develop ideas for draft resolutions and contact potential supporters long before arriving in Geneva.[43] States often introduce resolutions in the Commission similar to drafts already approved by the General Assembly. An Assembly resolution on Kampuchea or Afghanistan does not resolve the matter for subordinate bodies. Affected members seek continual publicity and maximum exposure in all United Nations political organs. The Commission can address condemnations or recommendations directly to governments, and can react to developments occurring after the Assembly adjourns. Sponsors may, however, need to adhere closely to the specific terms of an Assembly resolution to retain majority support. The Commission also regularly reenacts resolutions of its own that have not resolved violations of longstanding concern. After decades of repeated

TABLE 6.2
1985 Debate: Length, Speakers, and New Situations

| Agenda Item | Hours of Debate | No. of Speakers | | | NGOs | Total | | Cases | |
|---|---|---|---|---|---|---|---|---|---|
| | | Memb. | Observ. | Reply | | Oral | Written | New | Old |
| Israel | 23 | 25 | 19 | 1 | 4 | 50 | 2 | | 1 |
| S. Africa | 30 | 40 | 21 | 1 | 10 | 71 | 4 | | 1 |
| Chile | 4 | 10 | 6 | 0 | 7 | 23 | 13 | | 1 |
| Self Determination | 14 | 22 | 20 | 18 | 9 | 53 | 18 | 1 | 6 |
| Violations | 25 | 26 | 18 | 22 | 28 | 73 | 22 | 0 | 9 |

pronouncements, systematic investigations, and extensive debate on Israel and South Africa, the same resolutions are addressed to those governments each year with only modest revisions needed to update the text. In a few situations, prior Commission resolutions have prompted the Assembly to examine new violations, and in other cases the Commission has acted alone without further review by its parent organ.

Certain states regularly take the lead in drafting resolutions on situations of particular concern—Mexico on El Salvador, Syria on Palestinian rights, Canada on Bolivia. On sensitive political questions involving Poland and Iran, Western states have jointly sponsored resolutions that create less risk for one complaining government. All resolutions begin with a series of preambular paragraphs "noting," "recognizing," or "recalling" that summarize prior United Nations action on the subject and describe the alleged violations which prompted action by the Commission. The concluding operational paragraphs "urge," "condemn," or "recommend" and may denounce offenders, create investigative bodies, or direct an appeal for restraint during emergency conditions. When resolutions identify an offending state by name, members differ on the use of "condemn" rather than "deplore," dispute whether to "urge" or to "demand" and negotiate over the authority and mandate of investigatory bodies. If the resolution proposes a fact-finding inquiry or other procedure requiring financial expenditure, the Secretariat prepares a statement on financial implications involving extra budgetary resources.

Opponents may seek to weaken proposed resolutions by amendment, to postpone consideration, or to force withdrawal. Amendments can soften the preambular paragraphs by toning down harsh accusations of violations and can weaken the operative paragraphs by substituting general exhortations to comply for provisions creating investigatory procedures. Members can offer short amendments orally, but sponsors submit written drafts for more substantive proposals or alternative resolutions.

The procedural maneuvering over a Western resolution denouncing martial law in Poland illustrates tactics used in 1982. The U.S.S.R. proposed major amendments to be voted on before a decision was taken regarding the Western sponsored draft resolution. The Byelorussian S.S.R. then introduced a separate alternative draft resolution which could only be voted on after the Western proposal.[44] The Zambian representative moved to adjourn debate on all three proposals until the next session of the Commission. The Commission voted first on the motion to adjourn, which failed. Next, the Commission voted that the Soviet proposals were so comprehensive that they did not qualify as amendments and could not be put to a vote before the Western resolution. After the sponsors had accepted an oral amendment offered by Cuba, the Commission voted to approve the Western proposal. No further discussion of the Soviet amendment was then required, and the Byelorussian S.S.R. withdrew its resolution.[45]

The U.S.S.R. and others have been more successful in defeating resolutions by introducing counter charges against the complaining government. For several years supporters of opposing forces in the Western Sahara sponsored competing resolutions that were both withdrawn. The U.S.S.R. successfully thwarted a vote on Sakharov's internal exile by means of Eastern bloc resolutions deploring the treatment of prisoners in Northern Ireland and blacks in the United States. In 1980 neither the United Kingdom nor the Soviet Union called for a vote on their resolutions directed at each other. In 1981 a majority voted to postpone consideration of resolutions involving United States blacks and Sakharov[46] as well as two resolutions introduced by Syria and Jordan charging each other with human rights violations.

Unless it "decides otherwise," the Commission will not vote until at least twenty-four hours after a proposal has been submitted in writing and circulated to all members.[47] In 1979 the Commission waived that rule to send an immediate telegram to Israel expressing concern over reports of torture and bulldozing of Palestinian homes. Without allowing the Israeli observer an opportunity to respond, the Commission called on the government to cease practices that violated the 1949 Geneva Convention and "to inform the Commission urgently of this matter."[48]

Rarely can the Commission decide by consensus on a resolution identifying a violation, and often the members vote separately on critical provisions before a roll call vote on the full text. States may demand a recorded vote in order to reassure their allies or to embarrass their adversaries. Pakistan requested a roll call on the Western proposed investigation of Iran to show that Muslim state it had supporters outside the Eastern bloc.[49] Representatives may vote "yes," "no," or "abstain." The truly cautious, such as China in 1982, do not even abstain, but rather state for the record that they did not participate. On highly controversial situations many representatives explain their vote, either before or after the roll call, to put in the record their state's policy rationale. Only a simple majority of those casting affirmative or negative votes is needed for passage.[50] Resolutions on Iran and Poland passed with only nineteen affirmative votes of the forty-three members participating in 1982.[51]

The small Eastern European bloc has shown the greatest voting cohesion, although Yugoslavia does not caucus with or always support the bloc. Pro-Soviet governments in Cuba, Ethiopia, Syria, and Mongolia routinely join with the Eastern bloc. Although generally united, Western members do not always vote as a bloc, as illustrated by the occasional differences between Greece and the United States after 1980. While frequently outvoted, the West has become increasingly successful. In 1980 the Commission for the first time indirectly condemned an Eastern bloc ally by passing a resolution calling for withdrawal of foreign forces from Kampuchea. In the following two sessions, the Commission denounced foreign intervention in Afghanistan. The West also succeeded in getting Commission action on Poland and Iran in 1982. The third world states have the votes to dominate the Commission and uniformly prevail when united. Ideological divisions, however, have repeatedly emerged as some Latin American and moderate non-aligned members concurred with Western views in certain situations. Table 9.4 in chapter 9 displays regional voting patterns in order to assess charges of partisanship in Commission decision making.

### Exhortation, Conciliation, and Restoration

Chapter 4 explained how after 1967 the Commission developed three types of response to violations—(a) conciliation, exhortation, (b) investigation, and (c) prosecution, removal. Since 1980 the members have significantly increased the number of governments dealt with under the first two approaches. By way of exhortation, the Commission has sent telegrams urging Guatemala to solve a murder and Malawi to spare the life of a political dissident.[52] The Commission's 1985 resolution on Grenada simply reaffirmed the principles of nonintervention and urged all governments to respect the island's territorial integrity.[53] The Commission often urges disputing parties to engage in good faith negotiations or to cooperate with external mediators. Resolutions on the Western Sahara have endorsed OAU mediation efforts between Morocco and the Polisario.[54] The Commission urged Portugal and Indonesia to cooperate in resolving the dispute over East Timor.[55] A decision on Sri Lanka commended the government's plan to confer with Tamil separatists.[56]

Beyond moralistic pronouncements, the Commission has attempted to provide political or technical assistance. The Commission has requested the Secretary-General to use his good offices in situations such as Afghanistan, with little apparent result.[57] In situations where governments have professed a willingness to reform, as in Bolivia, the commission has directed a special rapporteur to recommend appropriate aid.[58] Where a new government has acknowledged past violations and indicated a desire to respect human rights, the Commission has expressed support without condemnation. Despite the cooperative approach, governments such as Equatorial Guinea and the Central African Empire did not respond favorably to the Commission's overtures. Equatorial Guinea's President received two constitutional law advisers, but disregarded their most important suggestions.[59] Uganda and Bolivia, though professing great interest, found that the United Nations had no resources for meaningful aid. Following Commission review, Western governments did contribute for a new law library and for training legal professionals in Uganda.[60]

### Investigation

The Commission's progressive response to developments in Guatemala illustrates how unrequited conciliatory exhortation may lead to formal investigation. First in 1979 the Commission sent a conciliatory telegram to the government requesting information about the assassination of Dr. Alberto Fuentes Mohr, a former Secretariat employee.[61] The following year's resolution noted the government's reply, but expressed profound concern at the deteriorating situation and directed the Secretary-General to contact the government. The government refused to deal with the Secretary-General's emissary for two years and then objected when the Chairman appointed as rapporteur a Costa Rican delegate who had participated in the debate. After a one year delay, Guatemala in 1983 approved the Chairman's second appointee as special rapporteur, the United Kingdom's Viscount Colville of Culross. The rapporteur visited Guatemala in 1983 and 1984 and prepared annual reports to both the General Assembly and the Commission.[62] Before or in lieu of undertaking an original investigation, the Commission has often requested the Secretary-General to seek secondary source material and to obtain from the government a response to the allegations. In five situations, the Secretariat or a Sub-Commission expert have been directed to solicit information from governments, NGOs, specialized agencies, the press, and other public sources.[63] In six other cases the Commission has designated its own rapporteur to make an original study, including onsite investigation.[64] For the most egregious cases, South Africa and Israel, the Commission and the Assembly appointed a full working group of experts. Table 6.3 identifies the country specific fact-finding inquiries approved by the Commission.

The different country reports have varied widely based on the author chosen. Secretariat employees naturally hesitate to give offense to governments which run the organization. A highly critical report provokes the most threatening reaction, while an inadequate study merely causes disappointment. Yielding to extreme Soviet bloc pressure, the Secretary-General's report on Poland ignored serious violations.[65] Secretariat reports on Iran have also been most inadequate and superficial.[66] Commission and Sub-Commission experts can be expected to show more independence as investigators, and to be less acceptable to target governments.

Resolutions authorizing Commission rapporteurs typically direct the Chairman to appoint an individual of "recognized international standing" after consultation with the bureau. While only two other regional representatives need to concur, a cautious Chairman may seek consensus, allowing any one officer to veto an appointment. Although not required, the Chairman may also consult the target government to assure cooperation in allowing an onsite visit. Some targets prefer a rapporteur from a neighboring or friendly state, preferably fluent in the national language. El Salvador refused to recognize Professor José Antonio Pastor Ridruejo as a Commission rapporteur, but has allowed him to visit in his "personal capacity" as a Spanish national.[67] Chile refused to cooperate with any Eastern bloc representative, and the Chair has appointed rapporteurs from Senegal, Mauritius, and Costa Rica. Guatemala successfully objected to a Costa Rican appointee who had participated in the Commission

TABLE 6.3
Governments Subject to Public Inquiry

| Target State | Initiated Complaint | Type of Violation | Commission Action | Government Response | Dates of Resolutions |
|---|---|---|---|---|---|
| South Africa | GA Committee 3rd World | Apartheid Prisons Workers | Telegrams Committee Isolation | Rejection | 1967–198_ |
| Israel | Arab | Prisons | Telegrams Committee | Debate | 1968–198_ |
| Chile | Sub–Comm. | Detention | Telegrams Committee Rapporteur | Allow 1 visit | 1975–198_ |
| Kampuchea | United Kingdom | Killing | Sub Comm. S.G. | Rejection | 1978–198_ |
| Nicaragua | Cuba | Killing | S.G. | | 1979 |
| Bolivia | G.A. Sub–Comm. | Detention | Special Rep. Gros Espiell | Cooperate | 1981–1983 |
| Guatemala | Cuba | Killing | Telegram S.G. Rapporteur Culross | Cooperate | 1979–1986 |
| El Salvador | Conference G.A. | Killing | Representative Ridruejo | Cooperate | 1981–198_ |
| Equatorial Guinea | NGO Sub–Comm. | Repression | Expert Volio | Cooperate | 1980–198_ |
| Poland | West, U.S. | Workers | S.G. | Debate | 1982–1983 |
| Iran | Sub–Comm. | Killings | S.G. Rapporteur Aguilar | Debate | 1982–198_ |
| Afghanistan | Sub–Comm. | Killings | Rapporteur Ermacora | Debate | 1984–198_ |

NOTE: As noted above the Working Group on Disappearances conducted a mission to Peru which resulted in a separate report to the Commission. With Commission approval the Sub–Commission has also undertaken an investigation, a 1984 mission to examine slavery in Mauritania. In other cases the Sub–Commission has forwarded detailed NGO reports of violations to the responsible governments with a request for comment and has sent cables to South Africa, Israel, Malawi and Uruguay.

debate and accepted a British rapporteur who could not speak Spanish.[68] Afghanistan, Iran, and Poland have so categorically rejected the Commission's "intervention" that no individual, whether Secretariat officer or independent rapporteur, would have been accepted. A few of the most frequently selected rapporteurs are international law professors and jurists from Europe, South America, and Africa with long experience in United Nations and human rights activities. Professors Felix Ermacora of Austria and Fernando Volio Jiménez of Costa Rica, for example, have carried out several different Commission assignments in Africa and Latin America.

Once approved by the Commission for an initial one year term, a rapporteur must wait several months for ECOSOC authorization. Following budgetary approval, the Secretariat can pay the rapporteur's expenses (but no honorarium) and can employ temporary professionals to staff the inquiry. Several rapporteurs have complained that the annual reauthorization procedure creates unnecessary disruption and takes so long that there is insufficient time to complete a thorough study.[69]

The rapporteurs have received ill-defined, general mandates to study or investigate, which they have interpreted to authorize (a) fact-finding, (b) legal analysis, and (c) broad recommendations. For fact-finding all have depended heavily on second hand accounts from the press, Amnesty International and other NGO materials, reports by regional inquiry commissions, specialized agencies, and U.S. State Department country studies,[70] or *ad hoc* groups. Rapporteurs barred from South Africa, Chile, and Afghanistan have also interviewed exiles in refugee centers to obtain first hand accounts. Investigators granted admission by target governments have traveled with two Secretariat assistants on missions lasting one to two weeks. They have typically interviewed top government officials and visited several population centers to conduct interviews with local leaders, detainees, and other grievants.

Viscount Colville of Culross has frankly acknowledged his inability to verify facts alleged by NGOs; he felt that Guatemala's military conflict precluded a proper inquiry.[71] Unsettled conditions as well as inadequate time and resources have also hampered missions to Equatorial Guinea and El Salvador. When confronting wildly conflicting claims by a target government and its critics, the rapporteurs can at best generalize about the scope of the problem and whether conditions have recently improved or deteriorated.

On legal questions, the rapporteurs have adopted a common approach to the three jurisdictional defenses raised by target governments—first, that a Commission study violates Charter Article 2(7) by intervening in matters essentially within the state's domestic jurisdiction; second, that states are not bound by international human rights instruments they have not ratified; and third, that the Commission has no authority to enforce compliance with international treaties which provide their own implementation measures. Austrian law professor Felix Ermacora summarized the United Nations response to the first objection in his 1985 report on Afghanistan. The Charter expressly authorizes the Assembly and its subsidiary organs to promote human rights and to make recommendations, so the United Nations has not only a right but a duty to examine reports of extensive violations. Adopting the response given to South Africa, Ermacora asserts that the organization has an "absolutely incontestable" right of study and recommendation that "does not constitute an intervention" prohibited by Article 2(7).[72]

The rapporteurs typically introduce their legal analysis by listing the international instruments which the target government has and has not ratified. They most frequently seek to apply the International Covenants and the Geneva Conventions, treaties that most target governments have not ratified. States accepting those treaty obligations submit to separate compliance procedures unrelated to the Commission. The International Covenant on Civil and Political Rights obliges state parties to report to a Human Rights Committee, and its optional protocol grants individuals the right to submit complaints against their government. The International Red Cross monitors compliance with the 1949 Geneva Conventions and supplemental 1977 Protocols protecting civilians in war. The Inter-American Commission on Human Rights and the International Labor Organization investigate violations of their conventions.

Professor Héctor Gros Espiell has explained why he judged Bolivia by treaties which the government had never ratified. The Universal Declaration of Human Rights, the International Covenants, the Geneva Conventions, and other widely accepted instruments have become illegally binding in his view, because they provide an authoritative interpretation of the obligations United Nations members accept in their Charter pledge to cooperate with the organization in achieving objectives such as universal respect for human rights.[73] Although Guatemala never ratified the covenants, Viscount Colville concurred with Gros Espiell, concluding ". . . there has been no disagreement with the proposition that standards set by the covenants are a proper foundation for this report."[74] Ermacora made the most forthright admission of the rapporteurs' purpose: "Unless these human rights instruments are implemented they will become valueless, serving purely propaganda purposes, and will make no contribution to the promotion of human rights in a difficult situation."[75]

That policy objective, rather than any strict legal analysis, best explains why the rapporteurs have asserted Commission jurisdiction over states which have consented at most to alternative compliance procedures. Poland for example notified the Secretary-General under Article 4 of the International Covenant on Civil and Political Rights that it was derogating from certain treaty obligations during a state of emergency.[76] Although the Covenant grants to the Human Rights Committee responsibility for reviewing state reports, the Commission began an independent study. In their zeal to protect victims, the rapporteurs have also duplicated the jurisdiction of national courts. In his report on Bolivia, Gros Espiell cited that state's constitutional and statutory provisions which correspond to guarantees contained in international human rights instruments. Through frequent repetition and consistent practice, the rapporteurs seek to create enduring precedent supporting an international enforcement regime. The many states which have challenged rapporteurs on the merits without questioning the Commission's jurisdiction have, as hoped, created increasingly specific customary obligations under the United Nations Charter.

Ranging in length from ten to fifty pages, the final reports have made findings and recommendations of uneven quality. Too often a report's legal section consists primarily of lengthy excerpts from relevant international and domestic laws without significant legal analysis. The factual findings contain little original information, and the stencilled Commission documents lack both the substance and polished form of more widely circulated publications by NGOs and the Inter-American Commission on Human Rights dealing with the same situations.[77] As an economy measure in 1986 the Secretariat only translated the reports' introductory and concluding sections for distribution; the evidentiary portions of the full report were only available in the original language. Ermacora strongly objected when the General Assembly did not receive a full account of his reports on atrocities in Afghanistan. In reaching factual conclusions, the rapporteurs on Afghanistan, Chile, and El Salvador have been considerably more independent than those on Guatemala and Equatorial Guinea. A harshly critical report, however justified, might be softened in hopes of securing cooperation from the government. Without clear guidance from the Commission, some rapporteurs avoided criticism in order to mediate, while others felt a responsibility to perform rigorous fact-finding and to expose violations.[78] After Chile indicated a willingness to permit a new rapporteur's visit, the following report for the first time neglected to mention Chile's secret police.[79] When Iran would not allow him to conduct an onsite mission, Rapporteur Reynaldo Galindo Pohl, a lawyer from El Salvador, failed to include any facts or conclusions in a severely criticized ten page report to the General Assembly in 1986. Rapporteurs visiting Equatorial Guinea and Guatemala have been criticized for their generosity to government officials who extended minimal assistance. A government military escort accompanied Viscount Colville during his visit to Guatemala. Disregarding a provision in the resolution authorizing his mission, he unilaterally decided in 1985 to make no further comments about disappearances in Guatemala, because such incidents were subject to investigation by the Disappearances Working Group.[80] After Guatemala's 1985 elections, the Commission gradually switched from special reporting to expert advising for the restoration of rights. El Salvador admitted a special rapporteur in his "personal capacity," but has not been spared from criticism.[81] Afghanistan refused to admit the Commission rapporteur, so the author could be critical without jeopardizing any government contacts.

The Commission receives the rapporteur's recommendations while considering the general agenda item on violations. Reports on different situations are all presented together at the beginning of an unstructured debate ill-suited for the target government's response. Any speaker can refer to one or all of the situations studied, answer allegations, or raise new complaints. Partisan speakers subject target regimes to general vilification, while more principled participants use detailed public exposure to press for specific reforms.[82]

Target governments have participated in varying degrees. The three most responsive Latin American governments have formally denied the allegations at the Commission and have invited or allowed rapporteurs to visit.[83] Those who have cooperated ask in return for relief from further review and threaten noncooperation if the Commission persists with unreasonable demands. Afghanistan, Iran, Israel, and Poland have defended themselves at the Commission but refused to cooperate with the investigatory procedures. They have challenged the Commission's power to intervene in their domestic affairs and rejected the procedures as unfair. For a time Chile appeared at the Commission, but initially refused to allow an onsite visit. After an onsite mission in 1978 resulted in a critical report and further scrutiny, the junta refused all further cooperation until the appointment of a more acceptable rapporteur in 1984.[84] Apart from an occasional letter of rejection, South Africa has not responded at all. When South African observers reportedly appeared at the Commission in 1985, NAM and Soviet members rebuked the Secretariat for a breach in security.[85] Following the general debate, the Commission conducts case by case deliberations on the different resolutions introduced. The resolution may express appreciation to the rapporteur or simply "take note" of a less acceptable report. Sponsors dissatisfied with Viscount Colville's findings relied on NGO and other materials to denounce Guatemala. In ensuing years the resolution's basic text is readopted with slight modifications in both the Assembly and the Commission. The more detailed resolutions mention specific violations, invoke the Charter and Universal Declaration, and condemn target governments. Not surprisingly, some resolutions have proclaimed as true findings for which there is no evidentiary support, while others have repeated ritualistic condemnations of an "alarming increase in executions" despite a report showing a decrease.[86]

To keep a situation under review, the Commission typically renews the rapporteur's mandate, authorizing further inquiry missions and public reports. The resolutions, while urging the government to cooperate with the inquiry, may at the same time deplore its conduct. Members seeking to distance themselves from harsh denunciations or desiring to support the rapporteur's mandate request separate roll call votes on the relevant operative paragraphs. Target governments and their supporters lobby for votes to soften the criticism and if possible to terminate the inquiry. Iran reportedly took economic reprisals against the Netherlands for sponsoring a critical inquiry, and Argentina's military made similar threats against Senegal.

By 1985 the Commission had discontinued five of the twelve public inquiries, but no government had obtained a formal resolution of absolution. The Commission discontinued action on Poland by voting to postpone consideration of a proposal to continue review. A favorable report by the Secretary-General's emissary undermined the effort to extend the inquiry. In two other cases, the Commission terminated inquiries after target regimes were forcibly overthrown, despite reports of excesses by the new rulers. Following Somoza's overthrow and liberation of Portugal's African colonies the Commission ignored allegations made against Nicaragua's Sandinistas and the new governments of Southern Africa, Zimbabwe, and Mozambique. In Equatorial Guinea and Kampuchea, however, violations by new regimes have remained under review. The Commission has also offered technical aid to help restore democracy in Bolivia and Uganda. Presumably even the most obliging governments will not cooperate to the point of surrendering power to escape further scrutiny.

The remaining seven governments subject to ongoing review include the most cooperative and the most recalcitrant targets. In order to increase public exposure the Commission has directed rapporteurs on Chile, Bolivia, El Salvador, Guatemala, Iran, and Afghanistan to make interim reports to the General Assembly each fall.

*Isolation, Prosecution, Removal*

As noted in Chapter 4, the Commission progressed beyond fact-finding inquiries with more severe measures designed to isolate, to prosecute, and ultimately to remove human rights offenders in Israel and South Africa. Commission resolutions strongly urge states to disregard Israeli claims to occupied Arab territory[87] and condemn "certain Western states, Israel and other States" for nuclear as well as other forms of collaboration with the racist regime of South Africa.[88] Speeches denouncing Israel take most of the session's first week,[89] and the Israeli observer responds to radical Arab attacks on "the Zionist entity" with comparable vitriolic fervor. At least in part as a result of United States support, the harsh resolutions condemning Israel had not by 1986 reached the extremes of prosecution or removal sought for South Africa.

The general debate on four agenda items related to South Africa takes several days, and the Commission regularly adopts five or more resolutions dealing with different aspects of violations in Namibia and the Republic.[90] By 1984 the Working Group of Experts had named over two hundred South African police and prison officials charged with assorted acts of torture and killing in Namibia.[91] In each case the report identified the victim, date, and circumstances.[92] Since South Africa has effectively blocked United Nations entry to Namibia, individuals charged will only be prosecuted in the unlikely event that they visit one of the eighty-three states ratifying the *apartheid* convention.

The Commission appointed Group of Three under that convention[93] recommended a convention for the establishment of an international criminal court and an additional protocol for the suppression and punishment of the crime of *apartheid*.[94] The Commission has also requested the Group of Three to examine "whether the actions of transnational corporations which operate in South Africa come under the definition of the crime of *apartheid*, and whether or not some legal action could be taken under the Convention."[95] The Commission routinely endorses economic sanctions, protesting great power vetoes in the Security Council.

Commission challenges to the South African government's legitimacy represent the ultimate enforcement tool. Tanzania's representative declared that since the apartheid system could not be reformed, it must be destroyed.[96] The Commission has suggested that the Assembly invite the International Court of Justice to decide whether South Africa "may lawfully continue to hold a place in the international community."[97] Denying the regime's authority to amend its own constitution, the Commission resolved that a limited power sharing arrangement introduced in 1984 was "null and void."[98] Commission resolutions endorse the use of any means necessary, including armed struggle, to achieve national liberation or self-determination. The Commission welcomes liberation movements to its deliberations and sponsors seminars on international support for their just cause.[99]

The response to violations by South Africa indicates the most severe protection measures available to the Commission, the culmination of procedures that begin with confidential monitoring and proceed through public censure invoked by a fact-finding inquiry. However limited the Commission's resources to impose effective sanctions, target governments would obviously prefer confidential monitoring to the embarrassment of public procedures. After dramatically expanding its caseload under Resolution 1503 in the early 1980s, the Commission kept only four situations under confidential review in 1986.

## Confidential Procedures

*Secretariat and Sub-Commission Screening*

In addition to its responsibility to the Sub-Commission Working Group on Communications, in the 1980s the Secretariat's renamed Centre for Human Rights had to screen petitions to the Human Rights Committee established under the Political Covenant and to staff the Commission's newly appointed rapporteurs making country reports and global, thematic inquiries. Nine professionals in the Human Rights Centre's Communications Unit receive any submission, however addressed, provided it is intended for the United Nations and alleges some violation.[100] At that point, the staff may have some discretion in deciding whether to refer the communication to a special procedure that results in a public report or to send the communication for confidential screening by the Sub-Commission Working Group. In its confidential resolution to monitor Afghanistan, the Commission provided that information obtained from other sources is "without prejudice" to the resolution on disappearances, thus allowing some communications about that country to be publicly cited. The Secretariat unit refers as many petitions as possible to the Human Rights Committee, which reviews communications about states party to the Optional Protocol of the International Covenant of Civil and Political Rights.[101]

For the 1984–1985 biennium, the United Nations budgeted funds to process 40,000 to 50,000 communications received each year outside the Covenant's optional protocol.[102] The Secretariat referred 25,196 communications concerning 76 countries to the Sub-Commission Working Group in 1980.[103] Communications exceeded 26,000 in each of the following two years, with mass mailings of 10,000 in 1981 and 13,000 in 1982 concerning a single situation.[104] The Working Group could not review any communications in 1986 when the U.N. budgetary crisis forced postponement of the annual Sub-Commission session.

In their attempts to influence the five member Sub-Commission Working Group, some governments have compromised the experts' independence. Beverly Carter of the United States, Sergey Smirnov and Vsevolod Sofinsky of the Soviet Union, Ibrahim Jimeta of Nigeria, and Fisseha Yimer of Ethiopia all held posts in their state's foreign service while "expert" members of the Sub-Commission and its Communications Working Group. Others such as S. Shariffuddin Pirzada of Pakistan and Syed Masud of India came from the legal ministry or the courts. Most of the government officials elected as Sub-Commission experts come from the African, Asian, and Eastern European regions. By contrast, the British expert Benjamin Whitaker directs the Minority Rights Group, an NGO which has frequently exposed government violations.

Each year the Chairman of the Sub-Commission announces which five experts will participate at the next pre-sessional Working Group meetings. In practice, experts from the different regions determine which representative of their group will serve. A Soviet official has consistently represented the Eastern bloc, even in 1980 when the Chairman had designated a Bulgarian alternate for Smirnov. Smirnov was absent, but was replaced on the Working Group by his Soviet foreign ministry colleague Sofinsky, rather than by the Bulgarian Yuli Bahnev.[105] By contrast, when the United States expert Carter died before the 1982 session, his U.S. alternate John Carey did not replace him on the Working Group. Instead, the Western group's previously designated alternate, an expert from Belgium, assumed the post. Whitaker represented the Western group in 1980. Pirzada apparently found the Working Group's meetings more important than the Sub-Commission session. For several years he attended the pre-sessional Working Group meetings but was then reported as "not present" at the

Sub-Commission.[105]    The African and Latin American regions were unrepresented at two of the three working group sessions between 1979 and 1981.[107]

Conflicting proposals to reform the Sub-Commission's screening process reveal the sponsors' disagreement over whether independent experts can make neutral, principled judgments.  Whitaker has unsuccessfully sought to take decisions by secret ballot and to prohibit government officials from voting on situations in their own country.[108]  Sub-Commission experts from Pakistan and Morocco, Munir Akram and Halima Warzazi, have proposed increasing the membership to eight, "taking account of the larger number of States Members of the United Nations from Asia, Africa, and Latin America."[109]  The Soviet expert Sofinsky proposed that the Working Group take its decisions by consensus, instead of by majority vote.  The draft resolution lost by 15 votes to 2 with 5 abstentions.[110]  A draft resolution introduced by Akram and Warzazi recognizes the importance of allowing governments a reasonable time to reply and underlines the need for strict confidentiality.[111]  Whatever procedural changes the Sub-Commission might ultimately propose would require Commission and ECOSOC approval to take effect.  The Commission has never approved the experts' request for authorization to conduct independent fact-finding.[112]

## Commission Deliberations

Between 1978 and 1986 the Commission's reports have identified 30 governments subject to decisions under the 1503 procedure.  A five member Commission Working Group[113] reviews the Sub-Commission referrals, prepares a recommendation for the Commission, and invites each government reviewed to send a representative.  Under traditional concepts of national sovereignty, a state could not be hailed before an international tribunal without giving prior consent.  None of the twenty-one governments offering a defense in the Commission's confidential 1503 deliberations consented in advance to answer complaints under that procedure.  Only nine of the target states had ever ratified the International Covenants, and only four had ratified the optional protocol allowing individual petitions to the Human Rights Committee.[114]  Twenty of its targets have not ratified the International Convenants, yet the Commission proceeds as though all are bound by those norms.

By their regular participation, target governments tacitly acknowledge that emerging customary human rights norms require some response.  Soviet bloc members and clients have repeatedly challenged the Commission's jurisdiction over their internal affairs, but they have also denied particular allegations and noted remedial measures taken.  Equatorial Guinea similarly cited Charter Article 2(7) to challenge interference in its domestic affairs.  After that protest, however, the government generally denied that any human rights violation occurred.  Two-thirds of the situations referred have elicited government participation in Commission review proceedings.[115]  Over half the governments referred had a representative at the first confidential deliberation, and only eight failed to send representatives in succeeding years.[116]

Half the states subject to decision have had observers (or members) at every Commission session their governments were under review. Indonesia for example, had observers present from 1980 to 1984 with the exception of 1982, the only year it was not subject to a Resolution 1503 decision. One-fourth have never had observers, but only four appear to have missed two consecutive sessions of confidential review.[117] Members subject to review, such as Argentina and Uruguay, have sent large delegations with more than ten members to Commission sessions. Nonmember target governments have had up to six observers in Geneva.[118] Their participation supports claims that international human rights norms have become customary rules acknowledged by governments. Table 6.4 identifies the fifteen governments that had observers at sessions when the Commission reviewed their situations in confidential meetings. Presumably those government observers appeared at the private sessions where they could comment and answer questions. The table also lists the states which have ratified the covenant and optional protocol.

The Commission's annual Resolution 1503 deliberations have made routine a practice where previously nonconsenting governments respond to complaints against them. Their apparent participation in the procedure legitimizes the Commission's authority to hold sovereign nations accountable under international instruments they have never ratified. In defending themselves against human rights complaints, governments have tacitly acknowledged the Commission's power to enforce international norms. The summary data in Table 6.5 reveals that governments which never ratified the covenants are as likely to respond as states parties, and that only eight of the thirty governments referred have failed to answer complaints.

## Selecting Situations for Review

Between 1978 and 1986 the Sub-Commission referred thirty situations to the Commission under the Resolution 1503 procedure. In seven cases the Commission decided not to keep the case under review; the Commission kept most of the remaining twenty-three situations under confidential review for at least a year, initiated private contacts with five governments, and transferred eight cases to the public procedures. By 1986, when the budgetary crisis delayed further Sub-Commission screening, the Commission had discontinued review of twelve situations, and only four governments remained subject to confidential review.[119]

Without access to the confidential communications, it is difficult to tell what differentiates the seven referrals disregarded by the Commission from the twenty-three situations kept under review. Allegations of arbitrary detention, abductions, and extra-legal killings result in such imprecise and unverifiable

TABLE 6.4
Thirty Governments Subject to Commission Review
Under Resolution 1503 from 1978 to 1986

| Commission Decisions | Years | Total Years | Years Observe | Ratified Coven. | Protoc. |
|---|---|---|---|---|---|
| **Africa (9)** | | | | | |
| Benin | 1984,1985 | 2 | 0 | | |
| Central African Republic | 1980,1981 | 2 | 1 | Y | Y |
| Equatorial Guinea | 1976–1979 | 4 | 2 | | |
| Ethiopia | 1978–1981 | 4 | 4(M) | | |
| Gabon | 1986 | 1 | 1 | | |
| Malawi | 1977–1979 | 3 | 0 | | |
| Mozambique | 1981 | 1 | 0 | | |
| Uganda | 1978–1981 | 4 | 2(M) | | |
| Zaire | 1985–1986 | 2 | 1 | Y | Y |
| **Asia (8)** | | | | | |
| Afghanistan | 1981–1983 | 4 | 4 | | |
| Burma | 1979 | 1 | 0 | | |
| Indonesia | 1978–1981,1983–1985 | 7 | 6 | | |
| Iran | 1973,1983 | 1 | 1 | Y | |
| Japan | 1981 | 1 | 1 | Y | |
| Republic of Korea | 1978–1982 | 5 | 3 | Y | |
| Malaysia | 1984 | 1 | 1 | | |
| Pakistan | 1984,1985 | 2 | 2(M) | | |
| Philippines | 1984–1986 | 3 | 3(M) | S | S |
| Vietnam | 1974 | | | | |
| **Latin America (10)** | | | | | |
| Argentina | 1980–1984 | 5 | 5(M) | S | |
| Bolivia | 1978–1981 | 4 | 4 | | |
| Brazil | 1973,1974 | | | | |
| Chile | 1974,1976,1977,1981 | 1 | 0 | Y | |
| El Salvador | 1981 | 1 | 0 | Y | S |
| Guatemala | 1981 | 1 | 1 | | |
| Haiti | 1981–1986 | 6 | 5 | | |
| Paraguay | 1978–1986 | 9 | 8 | | |
| Uruguay | 1978–1984 | 7 | 7(M) | Y | Y |
| Venezuela | 1982 | 1 | 1 | Y | Y |
| **Eastern Europe (2)** | | | | | |
| Albania | 1984–1986 | 3 | 0 | | |
| German Democratic Republic | 1981–1983 | 3 | 3 | Y | |
| **Western Europe and Other (1)** | | | | | |
| Turkey | 1983–1986 | 4 | 4 | | |

(M) denotes member      Y = yes      S = signed but not ratified

TABLE 6.5
Government Responses to Commission Review Under Resolution 1503

| Representatives | Covenants Non–Parties | Parties | Total |
|---|---|---|---|
| Present at first referral | 11 | 5 | 16 |
| First attended later sessions | 4 | 1 | 5 |
| Never responded | 5 | 3 | 8 |
| Total | 20 | 9 | 29 |

tallies that efforts to rank order offending regimes are of dubious value.[120]  With the possible exception of Pakistan, the other six situations disregarded appear to have attracted less press and NGO attention than the cases kept under review.

A government's failure to answer the allegations has not uniformly provoked scrutiny.[121]  Although Mozambique and Burma failed to send any representative, the Commission rejected those Sub-Commission's referrals after some members supported the governments and criticized the complaints as without foundation. The Commission has kept under review six other governments which failed to send representatives and publicly criticized two regimes for noncooperation.[122] Governments sending representatives, however, have been subjected to review in about the same proportion as nonparticipants, with three Sub-Commission referrals accepted for each one disregarded.  Nor has membership resulted in more lenient treatment; four governments represented on the Commission became subjects of review, and Pakistan was the only member referred by the Sub-Commission to escape ongoing scrutiny (despite separate recommendations in two succeeding years).[123]

By deciding to keep a situation under review, the Commission requests the government charged to report at the next session.  In most cases, confidential monitoring has never gone beyond annual reports in the closed meetings.  In five cases where reports of serious violations continued, the Commission arranged for Secretariat staff or one of its own members to make direct contacts with the accused regime.  Some favorable reports from the appointees have sparked skeptical questions and partisan squabbling in the closed sessions. Theo van Boven reportedly challenged then Under Secretary-General Perez de Cuellar's account of an interview conducted with an Argentinian detainee.[124]  Skeptical members wondered how Jonas K. D. Foli could conclude after two visits to Haiti that conditions were so much better than those described by a mission from the Inter-American Commission for Human Rights.[125]  After Ethiopia barred Davidson Nicol from visiting an overcrowded prison, Western members objected to discontinuing review based on his partial report. Since the "thorough study" authorized for Uganda was never completed, it is unclear how such a report would have differed from the reports of those making direct contacts.

As long as the target government cooperates by responding to the complaint, by accepting direct contacts, and by sending representatives to answer member's questions, the confidential review may continue indefinitely with no apparent deadline for action or a recommendation to ECOSOC. The Commission has monitored the situations in Paraguay for over nine years without a thorough study, investigation, or public disclosure of the evidence presented. The Commission twice discontinued review of Paraguay, but the Sub-Commission referred more communications. Prior to restoration of democratic rule, Uruguay's military cooperated in seven years of confidential review by allowing the de Cuellar visit described above and by releasing a long-term detainee just prior to the Commission's 1984 discussion of its situation. On August 31, 1983 the Sub-Commission had cabled the government urging clemency for Professor José Luis Massera Lerena, a mathematics professor and parliamentary deputy.[126] Uruguay's regime appears to have timed the release to influence the Commission's seventh year of deliberation on its situation. Situations in Haiti and Indonesia also remained on the Commission's confidential agenda for over four years. The Commission has publicly disclosed its recommendation that ECOSOC request assistance for Haiti "to facilitate the realization of full enjoyment of human rights."[127] Indonesia, initially charged with torture and murder of political detainees, has more recently been scrutinized for repression on East Timor.

NGO observers have urged the Commission to assume the truth of unrebutted allegations in order to make a timely decision on the merits.[128] Governments have several months to reply after the Sub-Commission has referred communications and should not require any more time. The NGO proposal notes that The Inter-American Commission on Human Rights and the Human Rights Committee do not defer their decisions to benefit governments which fail to respond.

For the most recalcitrant and politically disfavored offenders, confidential review has merely been the initial stage of a process leading to more embarrassing public scrutiny. In four cases, the Commission never acted on Sub-Commission confidential referrals because public review was already underway. In four other situations several years of confidential review preceded public deliberations or disclosure. A 1980 Bolivian coup d'etat aggravated a situation that had been under confidential review for several years. At the urging of the Sub-Commission and the General Assembly, the Commission appointed a Special Envoy to prepare a report.[129] After four years of monitoring, the Commission discontinued confidential review of Afghanistan in 1984, because a Special Rapporteur had been authorized to study that situation under Resolution

TABLE 6.6
Speculative Overview of the Types of Confidential Decisions Taken
with Illustrative Examples of Governments Possibly Affected

---

I. No action on a new referral. The situation referred need not
   be subjected to confidential review: (7)
   A. The communications do not reveal a sufficient violation
      Burma 1979          Mozambique 1981
   B. The Government's response to the communications was adequate
      Gabon 1986          Pakistan 1984, 1985
      Japan 1981          Venezuela 1982
      Malaysia 1984

II. The situation should be confidentially monitored    (14)
      Afghanistan 1980-83              Indonesia 1978-81, 1983-84
      Albania 1984-198_               Paraguay 1978-198_
      Argentina 1980-83               Republic of Korea 1978-81
      Benin 1984                      Philippines 1984-1985
      Bolivia 1978-83                 Turkey 1983--1985
      Central African Republic 1980   Uruguay 1978-1984
      German Democratic Rep. 1980-82  Zaire 1985-198_

III. The Violations require a confidential Resolution 1503 inquiry: (6)
     A. Direct contacts by the Secretary-General or a rapporteur
           Equatorial Guinea (Secretary-General)
           Ethiopia (Davidson Nicol)      Paraguay (Perez de Cuellar)
           Haiti (Jonas K.D. Foli)        Uruguay (Rivas Poseda)
     B. A confidential "thorough study"
           Uganda 1978  (Judge Onyeama)
     C. A confidential ad hoc committee investigation
           subject to approval    (None ever conducted)

IV. The situation is subject to public procedures  (7)
      Afghanistan 1984        El Salvador 1981
      Bolivia 1981            Guatemala 1981
      Chile 1981              Iran 1983
      Equatorial Guinea 1979

V. Confidential review should be discontinued  (12)
      Argentina 1984                    Republic of (South) Korea 1980
      Benin 1985                        Malawi 1980
      Central African Republic 1981     Paraguay 1981
      Ethiopia 1981                     Philippines 1986
      German Democratic Republic 1983   Turkey 1986
      Haiti 1987                        Uruguay 1985
      Indonesia 1981, 1985

---

1235.[130] Paraguay, by contrast, came under both procedures—confidential monitoring for the massacre and enslavement of tribal Indians, and a 1984 public resolution concerning a twenty year state of siege.[131]

The Commission has discontinued confidential proceedings against twelve other states without public explanation. In four cases new regimes repudiated past violations. After Tanzania helped overthrow Uganda's Idi Amin and France intervened to topple Bokassa of the Central African Empire, the Commission discontinued review of those situations without any public report.[132] Argentina's new foreign minister reported to the Commission after his democratically elected government began prosecution of past human rights offenders. Uruguay made a similar presentation after a democratically elected government replaced the military. Both Argentina and Uruguay have requested and ECOSOC has agreed to release the confidential materials about the prior violations.[133]

In several other cases, the Commission apparently discontinued confidential review because there had been no recurrence of violations after the offense which gave rise to the initial allegation. The closely contested decisions to end monitoring of Ethiopia and the German Democratic Republic revealed partisan East-West calculations, while the political factions on Indonesia departed from the normal alignments. The Sub-Commission's more independent experts have found ongoing violations in several situations found acceptable by the Commission. When the Commission discontinued review of Indonesia and Paraguay, the Sub-Commission referred further complaints against those governments. NGOs have also continued to publicize violations by other governments relieved of confidential scrutiny by the Commission. Table 6.6 presents a speculative overview of decisions that have been taken on the 30 states named since 1978 presented in a context which outlines the range of options employed by the Commission.[134]

TABLE 6.7
Number of Countries Mentioned
in Commission Resolutions and Procedures, 1978-1986

| Region | Total | 1503 | Public Reso- lutions | Theme Report | Investi- gations |
|---|---|---|---|---|---|
| Africa | 25 | 9 | 6 | 16 | 2 |
| Asia | 21 | 8 | 7 | 16 | 4 |
| E. Europe | 4 | 2 | 1 | 1 | 1 |
| Latin America | 20 | 10 | 7 | 14 | 5 |
| W. Europe+Other | 1 | 1 | 0 | 0 | 0 |
| Total | 71 | 30 | 21 | 45 | 12 |

## Summary

Beginning in 1980 the Commission significantly expanded the protection activities initiated in 1967. Western representatives and moderate third world members fashioned four thematic approaches which publicly reported complaints against over forty governments. Those global procedures resulted in public reporting about situations which had previously been limited to confidential monitoring. The Commission undertook country specific fact-finding missions in twelve situations, and adopted general resolutions of exhortation and conciliation in many more. Table 6.7 identifies the number of governments affected by the different protection activities according to region.

The table demonstrates that Commission procedures have touched about half of the United Nations members, but does not reveal whether any qualitative improvements matched the quantitative increase. Chapter 9 below evaluates the impact and effectiveness of the Commission's growing protection activities, and that conclusion also assesses the post 1980 standard setting and promotional and institutional changes described in the following chapter.

# 7

# New Standards, Promotion, and Institutional Adjustment, 1980–1986

After 1980 the resurgent Western bloc brought greater political balance not only to the Commission's enforcement agenda, but also to its important standard-setting and promotional programs. Expanded monitoring of violations did not prevent the successful drafting of a torture convention and a declaration on religious intolerance. While unable to complete their proposed conventions and declarations prior to 1986, Eastern bloc and Third World members organized seminars to promote disarmament, self-determination, and economic rights. Difficulties in coping with and coordinating numerous standards, programs, committees, and procedures generated proposals to rationalize the Commission's agenda and for institutional reform.

## Standard-Setting

*Overview*

Despite the priority given to protection activities, between 1980 and 1986 the Commission worked on two conventions and four declarations, more norms than had been considered in any previous period. In addition, the Commission either approved or requested work by the Sub-Commission on six other norms. Western members and NGOs proposed all but three of the projects initiated. Governments have become associated with specific proposals: Scandinavian representatives on torture, Canada on human rights defenders, Poland on children, Yugoslavia on minorities, Cuba and Senegal on development. Amnesty International and the International Commission of Jurists lobbied effectively for new standards on torture and the rights of detainees. Apart from the torture convention referred by the Assembly, the other projects originated in the Commission or Sub-Commission.

If the particular right to be elaborated, such as development, was not expressly provided in the Universal Declaration or covenants, the first proposed resolutions pronounced a new right and requested a Sub-Commission or Secretariat study of its dimensions. Based on such research, state sponsors or the Sub-Commission then recommended drafting a set of principles, a declaration, or a convention.[1] The Commission has recently worked on more declarations than conventions. Declarations have been recommended either as preliminaries to the preparation of a binding convention or because there was insufficient support for a formal treaty. Sponsors unable to win support for a convention on religious liberty for example, instead proposed a declaration that would add to customary law, provide a preliminary to drafting a convention, and support promotional and implementation measures. Short of a declaration, the Commission has also approved statements of general principle offered as a model to governments.

In order to work simultaneously on several different standards without interrupting other business, the members convened open ended working groups one week before or during the annual sessions. *Ad hoc* Working Groups to draft norms have varied considerably in size and operation. To prepare a declaration on the right to development, the Commission created a group of fifteen experts, three from each regional caucusing group, and funded three meetings per year in Geneva. For norms on torture, religious intolerance, minorities, and children, the working groups have been open to any United Nations member and have met the week prior to and/or during the Commission session. Perhaps because they had less interest or expectation of adoption, the government representatives have referred proposed norms on detainees, indigenous peoples, and capital punishment to the Sub-Commission for drafting. Sponsors frustrated at the Commission's inability to draft norms on migrants and development referred those drafting projects directly to the Assembly.

Consumers of national legislation have been warned that the production process appears as unpalatable as the manufacture of salami. Commission working groups' requirement of consensus has made the drafting task even more difficult than the confusing political turmoil of national legislatures. International legislators must show far greater deference to minority interests, because they cannot impose new human rights standards on sovereign nations without their consent. Treaties and conventions under international law bind only states parties who have ratified their terms. The Commission invariably asks the Secretariat to solicit government comments on draft standards before approving the final text. Frequently states acceding to multilateral conventions make express reservations to objectionable provisions they refuse to accept. Thus a dominant majority wins a dubious political victory by enacting United Nations standards that have no legal consequence for opponents who refuse to ratify their terms. As a result, drafting effective international norms requires extensive negotiation to find compromise terms acceptable to all. Normally the drafters have avoided contested votes and required unanimity on each provision.

By granting each participant an effective veto, consensus decision-making resulted in considerable delay and weaker enforcement provisions. The Torture Convention, for example, allows a state party to block investigations by the implementation committee. The Commission took twenty years to agree on a declaration against religious intolerance; after similarly protracted negotiations, the members had still not completed a convention on children's rights or a declaration on minorities by 1986. Review by committees of the General Assembly led to swift adoption of the Torture Convention drafted by the Commission but has caused continuing delay for principles recommended by the Sub-Commission.

Following adoption by the General Assembly, conventions take effect only after ratification by the minimum number of states specified in the instrument. In order to complete the legislative process, the Commission has then urged governments to ratify and has requested periodic reports from the Secretary-General about the latest status of United Nations human rights instruments. In the case of general declarations, sponsors have proposed implementation without further attempts at codification. As noted in the preceding chapter, the Commission has held states accountable despite their objections that they were not bound by the international covenants. Western members who sponsored the Declaration on Religious Intolerance treat it as a norm of customary international law that should guide state conduct. Table 7.1 presents an overview of the Commission's major drafting projects, conventions, and declarations approved by the General Assembly that have come into force, as well as work underway in 1986.

*Conventions*

*Torture.* Following the 1975 United Nations Declaration Against Torture, Amnesty International (AI) pressed for a binding convention to prevent the widespread practice. Estimating that more than a third of the world's governments used or permitted the use of torture, AI published evidence of torture committed in 90 countries from all regions.[2] After joining the Commission for the first time in 1977, Sweden chose that forum rather than the Assembly to introduce a draft proposal. Niall MacDermot of the International Commission of Jurists presented a separate proposal of the International Association of Penal Law. An open-ended Working Group chaired by India convened for the first time during the 1978 session, but made little progress. Over Soviet bloc objections, the group then began meeting one week prior to each annual session.

MacDermot, counsel from AI, and experts of the International Committee of the Red Cross provided substantial technical advice and substantive proposals as

TABLE 7.1
Commission and Sub-Commission Standard-Setting, 1980-1986

| Sub-Commission | Commission | General Assembly |
|---|---|---|
| **Conventions:** | | |
| 1 Optional Protocol on Capital Punishment | | |
| 2 | Rights of the Child | |
| 3 | Torture | Adopted 1984 |
| 4 | | Migrant Workers |
| **Declarations:** | | |
| 1 Indigenous Peoples | | |
| 2 Impartiality and Independence of Judiciary | | |
| 3 Non-Citizens | | |
| 4 Right to Leave | | |
| 5 | Religious Intolerance | Adopted 1981 |
| 6 | Right to Development | Adopted 1986 |
| 7 | Minorities | |
| 8 | Rights of Defenders | |
| 9 | | Medical Ethics |
| **Principles and Guidelines:** | | |
| 1 Detainees 1979 | | Under Review 1987 |
| 2 Mental Detainees | | |
| 3 Unacknowledged Detention 1985 | | |
| 4 Computerized Personnel Files 1983 | | |

active participants in the drafting process.[3] MacDermot attempted to extend the reach of the convention to prohibit other acts of cruel, inhuman, or degrading treatment that do not amount to torture and to secure a right to compensation for victims of such abuse.[4] In 1980 Costa Rica introduced a draft optional protocol of implementation measures recommended by the International Commission of Jurists and the Swiss Committee Against Torture.[5]

After early agreement on a definition of torture and the need for domestic legislation prohibiting it, disputes over universal jurisdiction, extradition, and implementation delayed consensus on a final text. In accord with procedures under the *Apartheid* Convention, a majority favored granting jurisdiction over offenses committed outside their territory to any government which obtained custody of an alleged torturer. The minority wanted trials to be conducted in the territory where the alleged offense occurred.[6] Other states indicated they would not be bound by an article barring extradition of persons in danger of being tortured, if that obligation contravened treaty obligations incurred before the convention.

Proponents seeking to consolidate implementation procedures proposed that the Human Rights Committee created by the Political Covenant also serve as the supervisory body under the Torture Convention. When the United Nations Legal Office advised that the proposal would require amending the covenant, a new Torture Committee was proposed. Western delegations pressed for committee powers like those granted to the Committee on the Elimination of Racial Discrimination: to receive state complaints, to initiate mandatory conciliation procedures, and, at the request of any party, to refer interstate disputes to the International Court of Justice. The communist bloc objected that the implementation procedures should be optional and that the International Court should take jurisdiction only when both parties agreed.[7]

J. H. Burgers of the Netherlands as Chairman-Rapporteur of the Working Group in 1982 and 1983 worked effectively to narrow the areas of disagreement by formulating revised proposals. When the members could not obtain consensus on the final items in 1984, the Commission forwarded a draft to the General Assembly with contested provisions delineated by brackets.[8] Negotiations in the Third Committee produced agreement in time for adoption on December 10.[9] By February 1987, 49 governments had signed, and 15 had ratified;[10] ratification by twenty would bring the convention into force. As explained in the preceding chapter, the Commission promptly appointed its own torture rapporteur in 1985 before any states had ratified the convention.

The convention's definition of torture does not include pain or suffering arising only from "lawful sanctions," and its most important provisions do not encompass less severe punishments deemed "cruel, inhuman, or degrading."[11] Some states indicated that they would interpret "lawful" in accord with international norms in order to prosecute brutal sanctions authorized by national law. The convention provides for a ten member implementation committee authorized to receive government reports and to conduct confidential inquiries if reliable information suggests systematic torture.[12] At the time of ratification a state may declare that it does not accept the committee's jurisdiction to investigate.[13] States may expressly allow the committee to hear complaints against them made by other governments or by individuals.[14] All states parties agree to make torture an extraditable offense, and to refuse extradition of individuals believed to be in danger of being subjected to torture.[15] The convention obliges states to investigate reliable complaints and invalidates any defense claim of compliance with superior orders.

In addition to its campaign against torture, AI has firmly opposed all capital punishment. Since such punishment is widely accepted and increasingly used in the 1980s, few governments would accept prohibition in a new convention. West Germany proposed a second optional protocol to the International Covenant on Civil and Political Rights that would prohibit executions.[16] The Commission referred the matter for study to a Sub-Commission expert, Marc Bossuyt of Belgium.[17]

*Rights of the Child.* Chapter 3 described the Commission's contribution to a Declaration on the Rights of the Child adopted by the General Assembly in 1959.[18] Hoping to have a convention approved as part of the International Year of the Child in 1979, Poland introduced a draft in the Commission the preceding year. Polish representatives chaired a pre-sessional Working Group each year, even when they attended as observers rather than Commission members. As in the Torture Working Group, members used consensus procedures that prolonged deliberations. The issues were in any event extremely difficult to resolve: "adoption, children of separated parents of different nationalities, children kidnapped and taken across frontiers, children temporarily or permanently deprived of parental care owing to imprisonment, exile, deportation or other judicial or administrative sanctions."[19]

Opportunities for scoring cherished political debating points abounded. The United States representative introduced extensively detailed provisions on religious liberty that were considered obstructive delays.[20] One nongovernmental observer suggested that the United States was responding to communist obstruction of drafting by the Torture Working Group. Eastern European representatives, in turn, proposed state regulation of the broadcast media to prevent injury to young viewers. Third World participants demanded technology transfers from the developed states to aid the handicapped. The Soviet delegate objected to a United States proposal that a child and his parents have a right to leave any country, including their own, and that request for permission to leave shall have no adverse consequences for the persons concerned. Delegates from Finland and Poland joined the cold war adversaries on a working party to resolve the dispute.[21]

By 1986 the group had agreed on nearly twenty articles, but remained divided on several provisions and had not yet considered implementation proposals.[22] The convention would apply to individuals under age 18 and provide nationality in the territory of birth. Several draft articles reaffirm the basic civil liberties and economic rights provided for in other instruments. States parties would refrain from recruiting children under age 15 into their armed forces and would see that no child takes a direct part in hostilities.

The Islamic states may reject several key provisions previously approved in the working group. The Bangladesh delegate has suggested that the provisions on free choice of religion and adoption are incompatible with Islamic law and has proposed language barring improper proselytization. In addition, the Bangladesh representative objected to the clause on nationality and noted that the least developed countries could not afford to provide compulsory free education, health care, and economic security. Considering the profound social, cultural, economic and legal differences in approach to families and minors, the Commission is likely to require considerable time to achieve consensus on a binding convention. Poland and Canada want a Group of Experts to implement the convention by reviewing state reports. NGOs have advocated more extensive monitoring, so that the implementation group can receive information about violations from other sources and make follow up inquiries to governments. UNICEF would be enlisted to provide its expertise in implementation.[23]

*Promoting Ratifications.* Since a convention adopted by the United Nations only becomes law when states ratify the agreement, Commission standard-setting has entailed frequent requests that governments accede to international norms. One year after adopting the Torture Convention, the Commission approved a Norwegian resolution requesting all states to sign and ratify and inviting those doing so to "consider the possibility" of allowing interstate and individual complaints.[24] The Commission established a separate agenda item on the status of the International Covenants and receives annual reports from the Secretary-General on new ratifications. Twenty years after the General Assembly approved the two human rights covenants and a decade after they came into force, only half of the members of the United Nations had ratified—85 the Economic and 81 the Political Covenant.[25] Roughly one-third of the African and Asian states had ratified, approximately two-thirds of the European and Latin American governments acceded, and, with the exception of Albania, all the Eastern European members had become states parties.[26] By 1986 only eighteen states had made the declaration under Article 41 of the Political Covenant allowing interstate complaints; thirty-eight governments had ratified the optional protocol authorizing individual petitions by their own nationals.[27] The Commission has appealed "strongly" to states not yet parties to ratify so that the Covenants acquire genuine universality, but simply "invites" governments to "consider" allowing individual and state complaints. The same Western sponsored resolution directed the Secretary-General to use the advisory services program to encourage and assist states to become parties.[28] On the Genocide Convention's thirty-fifth anniversary, the Commission approved an Eastern bloc resolution urging states not yet parties to ratify without further delay.[29]

Encouraged by NGOs eager to pressure the United States, among others, the Sub-Commission has assertively asked governments to explain why they have not acceded to the covenants as well as to several other conventions. France's representative to the Commission protested that the Sub-Commission had no authority to demand such explanation, and the Brazilian delegate also complained that the experts had exceeded their mandate.[30] Assistant Secretary-General Herndl assured the experts that the Secretary-General when making official visits to states routinely encouraged ratifications where appropriate.[31] After receiving only five replies in 1985, the Sub-Commission resolved to discontinue its Working Group on the Encouragement of Universal Acceptance of Human Rights Instruments and to consider the topic thereafter in alternate sessions.[32]

*Declarations*

*Religious Intolerance.* Following adoption of the Declaration and Convention on Racial Discrimination in the mid-1960s, Sub-Commission proposals for a similar declaration on religious intolerance were never approved. Between 1974 and 1978 the Commission's group drafting a declaration on religious liberties could only agree on a preamble. In 1979 the Working Group shut off an Eastern bloc filibuster to approve three substantive articles by vote. The majority reasoned that consensus did not require unanimity and advised dissenters to file a minority report. A Senegalese Chair of the working group, Abdoulaye Dièye, forced agreement on all but two clauses of four remaining substantive articles in 1981. Dièye concluded deliberations by the working group so that the full Commission could resolve the disputes. Oddly, the Arab members raised no objection to language affirming the right to change religion. The communists by contrast objected that the Declaration gave too much attention to individuals with religious beliefs and too little to atheists. Five states abstained as the proposed Declaration passed the Commission with 33 votes in favor.[33]

The Commission urged Assembly "adoption" of the Religious Declaration at its next session. The Assembly did so without a vote, after the Western members negotiated a compromise with Arab representatives in the Third Committee. In return for giving up preambular statements on the right to change religion, the West insisted on a new substantive article providing: "Nothing in the present Declaration shall be construed as restricting or derogating from any right defined in the Universal Declaration on Human Rights and the International Covenants on Human Rights."[34] In addition, the first article implies a right of choice: "This right shall include freedom to have a religion or whatever belief of his choice."[35]

The Declaration on the Elimination of All Forms of Intolerance and of Discrimination Based on Religion or Belief has ten preambular paragraphs and eight substantive articles.[36] It directs all states to "take effective measures to prevent and eliminate discrimination on the grounds of religion or belief . . . and to make all efforts to enact or rescind legislation where necessary to prohibit any such discrimination. . . ."[37] Parents may determine the religious training of their children, who are to be protected from discrimination and compulsory instruction from others.[38] The Declaration lists nine specific freedoms including the right to assemble for worship, to publish, to maintain institutions, to solicit contributions, to train leaders, to celebrate holidays, and to maintain international contacts.[39] Finally, "The rights and freedoms set forth . . . shall be accorded in national legislations in such a manner that everyone shall be able to avail himself of such rights and freedoms in practice."[40]

In an effort to give the nonbinding declaration effect, the Netherlands and the United States added an item on implementation to the Commission's agenda in 1983. When communist members objected to annual review of states' compliance with the Declaration, Western representatives replied that the United Nations had performed similar oversight for the Declaration on the Granting of Independence to Colonial Countries and Peoples. Just as the Commission had promoted implementation of the Declaration on Race Discrimination prior to adoption of the Race Convention, so the members could monitor compliance with the declaration on religious intolerance.[41] In the 1983 debate on the implementation item, speakers charged that North Korea, Czechoslovakia, Poland, Guatemala, Iran, and others had violated the religious freedoms of their people.[42] The Netherlands' representative objected that the United Nations pamphlet on the Declaration had not been published in Chinese, Arabic, or Russian.[43] The communist members abstained from a resolution calling for a worldwide seminar on religious liberty and directing the Sub-Commission to update its study on religious discrimination.[44] In 1986 the Commission's special rapporteur on religious intolerance began responding to complaints of discrimination.

*The Right to Development.* In contrast to the familiar civil liberties norms favored by Western representatives, Third World governments wanted to codify the right to development first proclaimed in the 1970s. Demands for a New International Economic Order have accompanied claims for a "third generation of 'solidarity' rights." Developing states insist on a right to development unlike the first and second generation political liberties and economic rights advanced by the West and East. For some, the collective need for national progress has priority over individual rights.

In 1981 the Commission gave high priority to drafting an international instrument on the right to development by creating a fifteen member Working Group on Development, composed of governmental experts to make recommendations. For the first time since preparation of the Universal Declaration, a Commission drafting committee would meet between regular sessions. Three representatives each from the five geographic regions would meet three times each year, making the project one of the Commission's most costly undertakings. After the group decided that a declaration would be more appropriate than a convention, the experts could agree on little else.

Third World representatives have sought to proclaim that realization of a New International Economic Order is essential for assuring other rights and that peoples have a collective right to control their resources. Third World members give priority to the collective rather than to the individual dimensions of the right to development. According to their majority view, the holders of the right are peoples and states; its objective is the democratization of international relations; and its basis is the principles of self-determination, nonintervention, peaceful coexistence, sovereignty, territorial integrity, and economic cooperation. Western representatives stress that individuals rather than states have a right to development which encompasses all the civil, political, economic, social and cultural rights. Western experts have proposed language guaranteeing individuals a right to development which includes full political participation. Soviet proposals advocate disarmament and nationalization as means to development.[45]

The non-aligned experts submitted one draft, and the experts from France and the Netherlands submitted a second.[46] Alioune Sène of Senegal presided as Chair and G. Chouraqui of France as rapporteur. The Working Group met three times during its first year of operation,[47] held two sessions of two weeks each in 1982[48] and met again for two sessions in 1983.[49] The Working Group's 1983 Report lists 17 pages of principles suggested by the members, none of which had been accepted. The group appointed a smaller drafting committee of five to speed its work. The experts produced a "Technical Consolidated Text" of sixteen preambular paragraphs and thirteen articles, but had only reached general agreement on the preambular material by 1985.[50] Once the rights to be included within the concept of development have been accepted, the text will undoubtedly provide that they are interdependent and indivisible. Despite the high priority and expense, in four years the members could not resolve their profound differences.

Over Senegal's objections, more radical NAM members from Cuba and Tanzania abruptly terminated further negotiations with Western representatives at the Commission in 1985. With 25 votes in favor, the Commission resolved to forward the group's partial draft to the Assembly for completion of a declaration.[51] After the Assembly failed to adopt a compromise draft declaration in 1985;[52] the Commission directed the Working Group to meet for three weeks and to recommend measures for promoting the right.[53] After the Assembly adopted the Declaration in 1986, the group recommended activities to promote the right and a restructuring of international economic relations. The United States voted against the Declaration and announced plans to withdraw from the group in 1987.

*Minorities and Indigenous Peoples.* Futile attempts to fashion rights for minority groups began at the Sub-Commission's 1947 session and have continued in a Commission Working Group since 1978. After eight years, the members had agreed on ten preambular paragraphs for a declaration; work on substantive articles had only begun.[54] Yugoslavia introduced a draft text in 1980, and its representative served as Chair of the Working Group each year. After thirty-five years, the Commission could still not agree on a definition of "minority." Deliberation on substantive rights proceeded without prior agreement on whether national minorities would be protected along with ethnic, religious, and linguistic groups.[55] Still unable to agree in 1985, the Commission once again requested the Sub-Commission to undertake the impossible task of preparing a politically acceptable definition. Undaunted, expert Jules Deschênes prepared a conceptual study,[56] but his formulation was not accepted.[57]

Familiar disputes about free speech and propaganda advocating discrimination, assimilation, and state support for distinct cultures, individual and group rights, domestic jurisdiction, and international protection have all frustrated agreement. Although it has continued the open-ended Working Group, the Commission appears unlikely to go beyond the limited protection already granted. Under the Political Covenant, states must allow a minority group to enjoy its culture, religion, and language, but they have no affirmative duty to protect or to preserve distinct peoples from assimilation.[58]

At the urging of Theo van Boven, Director of the Human Rights Division, the Commission in 1981 authorized a pre-sessional Working Group of the Sub-Commission to consider the problems of minorities belonging to indigenous populations.[59] Indigenous leaders and their supporters sought to use the group as a platform to demand political self-determination and economic control of mineral wealth on their lands. They wanted the group to expose and to investigate specific violations, rather then to draft norms or to promote general principles.[60] The Commission and Assembly approved the experts' proposal for a United Nations fund to support travel of indigenous peoples to attend Working Group sessions.[61] Despite its repeated frustration in fashioning politically acceptable norms for other minority rights, the Sub-Commission resolved that its Working Group should prepare a Declaration on Indigenous Rights for the Assembly.[62]

*Defenders' Rights.* The inadequacy of international enforcement has made self-protection essential. Local human rights activists, particularly lawyers, have represented victims, demanding that repressive governments honor international norms. Soviet dissidents, for example, sought to monitor their government's compliance with the Helsinki Agreement. Such human rights defenders often themselves become victims of violations by the public officials they charge with wrongdoing. Under the general agenda item on violations, Canada pressed the Commission to prepare a declaration affirming the rights and responsibility of individuals to promote and protect fundamental rights without government persecution or punishment.

Once the Commission had approved in principle that defenders had such rights,[63] the Canadian draft resolutions requested the Secretary-General to draft principles and the Sub-Commission to study and prepare recommendations for a declaration.[64] Following completion of a report by expert Erica-Irene A. Daes, the Commission resolved to convene an open-ended Working Group to prepare a declaration during the 1985 session.[65] Canada left the Commission, Australia took responsibility for the project, and the group never met in 1985. The Soviet bloc abstained on a resolution providing for a one week pre-sessional meeting in 1986.[66]

At that meeting, Soviet representatives predictably stressed that human rights activists should give priority to *apartheid*, colonialism, foreign intervention, self-determination, world peace, and disarmament. Eastern European delegates routinely stressed that states rather than individuals had the responsibility for protecting human rights and objected that the Sub-Commission proposal improperly sought to create new rights for individuals. Western sponsors and NGOs who considered states the cause rather than the cure of human rights violations proposed a radically different norm affirming an individual's right and responsibility to defend other citizens abused by their governments.[67] The group planned to continue drafting prior to the 1987 meeting,[68] but swift progress appears highly unlikely. At the same time, a Sub-Commission expert from India, L. M. Singhvi, had just completed a related declaration affirming the importance of independent lawyers and an impartial judiciary.[69]

*Migrants' Rights.* The Commission has become indirectly involved in drafting three proposed standards affirming rights to travel, to work, and to enjoy equal rights abroad. Rather than undertake a comprehensive declaration encompassing the related issues, the Commission has dealt piecemeal with separate aspects as different blocs responded to different problems. After Idi Amin expelled Indian nationals from Uganda, a United Kingdom expert, Baroness Elles, began to prepare a declaration on the rights of non-citizens.[70] The text recommends standards for naturalization, identifies rights which citizens and aliens should share equally, and provides for compensation to be paid aliens for seized property. Neither the Sub-Commission nor the Commission approved the proposed declaration before forwarding the draft for "consideration" by a General Assembly working group.[71] The Assembly appears unlikely to approve a draft prepared by Sub-Commission experts which the Commission's government representatives have neither negotiated nor approved.

A second Western-initiated declaration with little prospect of success would bar limitations on emigration imposed by Eastern bloc governments and Third World countries concerned about a "brain drain." Principles in a 1960s Sub-Commission study of the problem were never approved,[72] and Western members revived the project in the 1980s. Sub-Commission expert Mubanga-Chipoya of Zambia was directed to complete as soon as possible a draft declaration on the right of everyone to leave any country, including his own, and to return to his country.[73]

For their part, Third World members have sought a convention to protect migrant workers reportedly mistreated in Western Europe. A Sub-Commission expert from Morocco, Halima Warzazi, studied the illicit, clandestine traffic in workers as well as discriminatory treatment of migrants in host countries. Her report recommended severe penalties for employers and traffickers who exploited unlawful immigrants.[74] Algeria pressed for a United Nations convention to supplement the Migrant Workers Conventions of the International Labor Organization. The Commission repeatedly discussed the issue, but appeared a less attractive forum than the Assembly, where a Working Group chaired by Mexico began drafting an instrument in 1980.[75] The sixty-four draft articles under review are comprehensive in scope and extend far beyond the employment relationship.[76]

*Principles and Guidelines*

When the Commission started drafting the Torture Convention, it directed the Sub-Commission to prepare draft principles on the rights of detainees.[77] The United Nations Standard Minimum Rules for the Treatment of Prisoners illustrate how such nonbinding principles may provide a model for national legislative action.[78] In the 1960s the Commission committee studying arrest, detention, and exile had proposed a body of principles that was referred to governments, and the Sub-Commission proposed urgent consideration of draft principles in 1975. An Austrian expert, Eric Nettel, completed a set of thirty-five principles on detainees that the Sub-Commission unanimously approved in 1978.[79] Without reviewing them, the Commission asked ECOSOC to forward the proposals to the Assembly for consideration along with government comments.[80] The Assembly's Sixth Committee has discussed the draft principles for years without completing its review. The Sub-Commission has also drafted for adoption a one paragraph declaration on unacknowledged detention,[81] which the Commission returned for further consideration.

Sub-Commission expert Erica-Irene Daes prepared a second set of principles specifically to protect persons detained on grounds of mental ill-health.[82] When a Sub-Commission Working Group failed to complete the recommended guidelines, the United Kingdom won Commission approval of a resolution urging the experts to give high priority to the task.[83] Language expressing concern at "the misuse of psychiatry to detain persons on non-medical grounds"[84] suggest the possibility of opposition by the Soviet Union when the Commission reviews the draft. In receiving recommended guidelines for computerized personnel files, the Commission, which has never formulated a set of principles, merely "welcomed" without adopting the Sub-Commission report.[85] The Commission's disregard for norms either initiated by or solicited from Sub-Commission experts indicates that the Assembly is unlikely to approve, unless government representatives are thoroughly involved in the preparation or re-drafting.

## Promotional Activities

By 1981 the Commission had discontinued two and radically changed the third promotional method initiated as the United States' sponsored Action Plan of the 1950s. First, the Assembly and the Commission approved a Secretariat recommendation to terminate the system of periodic reports.[86] The Commission had postponed consideration of the reports for three years after the Covenants created a separate reporting system, even though fewer than half the United Nations members had ratified those standards. Second, Commission members no longer prepared their own global studies. During the 1970s the Working Group of Experts on Southern Africa had completed two studies on criminal penalties for *apartheid*,[87] and thereafter the Commission requested the Secretariat or Sub-Commission to conduct research. Third, Western members enlisted advisory services experts and courses to assist new governments which replaced offending regimes and to train officials responsible for implementing human rights norms.

The Commission promoted a comprehensive array of human rights values with advisory services seminars and public information activities designed to satisfy different ideological blocs. Afro-Asian states followed up the first Decade to Combat Racial Discrimination with a second. Third World members organized seminars on the New International Economic Order and the Right to Development. The Soviets favored seminars and research on disarmament, while Western members sponsored a seminar on religious freedom.

*Expert Services to Restore Rights*

Canada led Western members of the Commission in proposing country-specific use for expert consultants in the advisory services program. Normally, a government would not seek public assistance that would publicize a human rights problem. When new leaders repudiate violations by their discredited predecessors, however, a request for advice might help establish international respectability. Even if new rulers fail to take the initiative, they might find it hard to refuse a specific offer from the Commission. New regimes in Uganda, Equatorial Guinea, Bolivia, and Haiti allowed human rights experts to visit in the 1980s. Commission resolutions typically (a) request the Secretary-General to provide advisory services and other appropriate assistance and (b) invite all States, specialized agencies and other United Nations organs, and nongovernmental organizations to lend their support in reconstruction and development.[88]

Following Idi Amin's overthrow, Canada introduced a resolution cosponsored by Ghana, Senegal, and Gambia. The Commission unanimously requested the Secretary-General to provide needed assistance.[89] The following year, at Uganda's request, the Commission authorized aid for: rebuilding a law library for the Ministry of Justice and High Court; a consultant for codification and publication of revised laws; training for prison officers and police officials.[90] The Secretariat reported on the multilateral and bilateral assistance provided,[91] and Uganda solicited continued aid. NGOs, however, reported serious violations during a protracted civil war that brought another change of government in 1986.

In his eight year reign of terror, Francisco Macías Nguema destroyed both the political and economic system of Equatorial Guinea. The Commission appointed a Special Rapporteur, Professor Fernando Volio Jiménez of Costa Rica, to investigate the gross violations which drove an estimated one-fourth of the population into exile. Following Nguema's overthrow, trial, and execution in 1979, the new military government allowed the Special Rapporteur to visit. He recommended that the Commission appoint an expert to advise on the drafting of a new Constitution. The Commission then named Professor Volio Jiménez as the expert.

After reviewing materials supplied by the government, the rapporteur submitted a comprehensive report to the Commission identifying the need for both political/legal reforms and measures to protect the rights of workers.[92] The Commission then requested the Secretary-General to draft a plan of action for the restoration of human rights in Equatorial Guinea based on the expert's recommendations.[93] The resulting draft offered United Nations assistance over three years in eight areas. The plan called for adoption of a new Constitution incorporating the Universal Declaration, ratification of the International Covenants, new penal, civil and electoral codes, creation of a law school, training courses for judges and public officials, labor inspectors and cooperatives, and development of a free press.[94]

Equatorial Guinea's President, Colonel Obiang Nguema Mbasogo, made no response to the offer of assistance until after a National Commission had nearly completed drafting of a new constitution. Following meetings in New York wih Equatorial Guinea's permanent representative to the United Nations, the Secretariat was asked to provide two constitutional experts. On the recommendation of Professor Volio Jiménez, Dr. Ruben Hernandez-Valle (Costa Rica) and Dr. Jorge Mario Laguardia (Guatemala) spent two weeks in Equatorial Guinea advising government officials. They recommended several changes in the text, and Professor Volio concluded "that the mission was well accomplished.[95] Reports to the Commission fail to indicate any implementa-tion of the labor reforms proposed in the draft plan. The new constitution was approved in an August 1982 referendum.

In a formal submission to the Commission, The International Commission of Jurists documented serious shortcomings of the reform.[96] The ICJ complained that a twenty-member Commission designated by Equatorial Guinea's Supreme Military Council had drafted the new constitution without representation of political, trade union, social or community-based organiza-tions. Opposition leaders driven into exile by the Macías regime had not returned, and a government ban on political parties remained in effect. The new President won a seven year term of office with the referendum approval of a Constitution that gave him emergency powers to suspend both the legislature and constitutional guarantees of due process. Contrary to the official report received by the Commission, the government did not accept the experts' recommendation to abolish the death penalty. The ICJ concluded that Colonel Obiang Nguema designed the constitution to perpetuate indefinite control of the country for himself and members of his ethnic group. The Commission adopted a resolution which encouraged the government of Equatorial Guinea to cooperate "in implementing the plan of action prepared by the Secretary General at the request of the Government of Equatorial Guinea." [97]   Two Costa Rican specialists visited Equatorial Guinea in January 1986 to assist in drafting penal, civil, commercial, and procedural codes.[98]   The government discussed its needs with the expert adviser in New York, but despite annual review by the Commission did not send observers to the annual session in Geneva.

As described in Chapter 5, the Commission had appointed a special envoy to investigate gross violations of human rights by the Bolivian military prior to a 1981 change of regime.   A cooperative response by the new government led the Commission to discontinue its investigation and to offer expert advisory services instead.   In 1982 and 1983 Canada introduced resolutions adopted unanimously, that directed the Secretary-General to provide appropriate advisory services as requested by the new government.[99]   The Centre for Human Rights sent two consultants to La Paz to discuss possible forms of aid.[100]   An expert previously responsible for Resolution 1503 good offices, Jonas K. Foli, made an advisory services mission to Haiti in October 1984, even before the flight of Jean Claude Duvalier.   The Commission urged United Nations members to increase their bilateral foreign aid to Haiti and Bolivia, the poorest Latin American countries.   In recommending special advisory services for another impoverished country in 1981, West Germany introduced a resolution "[n]oting with satisfaction that human rights and fundamental freedoms have been restored in the Central African Republic in spite of that country's economic and financial difficulties."[101]

*Voluntary Fund for Victims.*   Although not part of the advisory services program, The United Nations Voluntary Fund for Victims of Torture offers a related type of assistance.   The Fund solicits contributions from governments in order to relieve victims of abuse by their own governments.   The process promotes greater public awareness.   The voluntary fund originated in 1978 as a narrowly designed program for victims of Chile's military dictatorship.   The Pinochet regime had tortured, imprisoned, detained, and driven into exile thousands of political dissidents.   When several years of investigation and condemnation failed to change the government, the Sub-Commission proposed financial relief to individual victims.[102]   Sweden introduced the proposal to the Commission, and it was approved 21-3-6;[103] in 1978 the General Assembly established the United Nations Trust Fund for Chile.[104]   A five member board, selected on the basis of geographical distribution, was authorized to receive voluntary contributions to provide "legal and financial aid to persons whose human rights have been violated by detention or imprisonment in Chile, to those forced to leave the country," and to their relatives.

In 1981 four Scandinavian governments, responding to a request from the Assembly, sponsored a resolution in the Commission to make the Trust Fund for Chile a Trust Fund for Victims of Torture generally.   Amendments proposed by the U.S.S.R. lost 15-12-14, and the Commission adopted the proposed change 22-7-14.[105] The authorizing resolution approved by the Assembly directs the Board of Trustees to give priority "to victims of violations by States in which the human rights situation has been the subject of resolutions or decisions by either the General Assembly, the Economic and Social Council, or the Commission on Human Rights."[106] The Secretary-General, in consultation with their governments, selects five trustees who serve in their personal capacity. The Commission regularly appeals for contributions which the Fund then distributes through established channels of humanitarian assistance. At the 1983 session, Finland's representative expressed regret that only six countries had contributed to the fund.[107]

*Training to Implement Conventions*

West Germany introduced resolutions in 1985 and 1986 which significantly reoriented the advisory services program to provide practical assistance for implementing human rights conventions. The Commission directed the Secretary-General to facilitate bilateral aid, to seek voluntary contributions for program activities, to organize training courses for government personnel, to award fellowships to persons directly involved in implementation, and to coordinate activities with U.N. Development Program officers.[108] In conjunction with the United Nations Institute for Training and Research (UNITAR), the Centre planned three regional pilot training courses for persons responsible for preparing reports required by the conventions. In addition, the Secretariat notified the governments of Uganda, Equatorial Guinea, Bolivia, and Haiti that United Nations experts would conduct training courses for their officials and that two of their nationals could obtain individual fellowships.[109] The programs were designed primarily for individuals who would draft national legislation giving effect to international conventions. The Secretariat convened the first regional training course in Barbados, and Bolivia agreed to a national course. Voluntary contributions made possible the regional training courses, but the Commission deferred consideration of a Secretariat request for a new Trust Fund on Advisory Services.[110]

The Western members responsible for reorienting the advisory services program sponsored only two seminars in the 1980s and provided minimal support for fellowships. In 1980 the Netherlands organized a symposium at the Hague for the Western European region on the "Role of the Police in the Protection of Human Rights."[111] A 1984 Western initiated seminar on religion encouraged understanding, tolerance, and respect for different faiths.[112] When the Soviets proposed a seminar on world peace, Western members successfully objected that the Secretariat could not afford the estimated $250,000 cost of such a conference in light of the new priorities for advisory services.[113] In 1985 the Secretariat awarded thirty-three Fellowships to individuals from thirty countries.[114] The 1986 financial crisis prevented further fellowship awards.

In addition to advisory services, Western states have sought to improve United Nations public education activities. Amnesty International effectively prodded the delegates by reporting that U.N. Information centers could not provide the most important declarations and conventions, and that the Division of Public Information had not published texts in several of the working languages.[115] Australia introduced a resolution directing the Secretariat to prepare an inventory of available materials, to stock basic references at the information centers, to prepare a draft teaching booklet, and to issue a personalized version of the Universal Declaration in all six working languages.[116] The resulting inventory revealed that twelve of the sixty-two information centers had no copies of the Universal Declaration in stock, and that the international covenants were virtually unavailable in Arabic, Russian, and Chinese or at United Nations centers in countries where those languages were spoken.[117] Commission resolutions have repeatedly stressed the need for mass education, but have only recently monitored the Secretariat's performance and given specific direction to public information activities.

*Racism,* Apartheid, *and Fascism*

Rather than expert advisers, training courses, and public education, non-aligned and Eastern bloc members relied on seminars, studies, and hortatory resolutions for campaigns against racism, *apartheid*, and fascism. For its annual review of the first decade to combat race discrimination, the Commission considered reports from the Secretariat and the specialized agencies. The Commission made four requests for a study on ways and means to implement United Nations resolutions and decisions on discrimination and *apartheid* before the Sub-Commission finally designated Asbjørn Eide as a rapporteur.[118] Sub-Commission rapporteur Abu Sayeed Chowdhury examined discriminatory treatment of members of racial, ethnic, religious or linguistic groups in the administration of criminal justice,[119] and Ahmed Khalifa prepared an annually updated list of transnational corporations doing business with South Africa.[120] An international seminar considered ways to prevent transnational businesses from collaborating with the racist regime of South Africa.[121] Of the nine seminars on *apartheid* and discrimination held before 1986, the Commission specifically proposed the five designated by asterisks in Table 7.2.

In promoting the decade's goals, Third World members have denounced racism with the harshest polemics in lengthy speeches which took a substantial part of the Commission's meeting time. Beyond the attacks on South Africa, speakers complained of discrimination against Indians in the United Kingdom, exploitation of nonwhite migrant laborers in Western Europe, minority rule in Zimbabwe, Portuguese colonialism in Africa, and corporations doing business with South Africa. Western members took particular exception to Commission resolutions reaffirming "the legitimacy of the peoples' struggle for independence, . . . by all available means, including armed struggle."[122] The United States

TABLE 7.2
Seminars on Apartheid and Discrimination, 1973-1986

| Host State | Year | Type | Topic |
|---|---|---|---|
| Lesotho | 1978 | I | Exploitation + Prison Conditions in South Africa |
| *Geneva | 1979 | R | Remedies for Victims of Race Discrimination |
| Nicaragua | 1981 | R | Remedies for Victims of Race Discrimination |
| *Geneva | 1979 | I | Teaching About Race Discrimination |
| *Nairobi | 1980 | R | Factors Underlying Racism |
| *Geneva | 1981 | I | Measures to prevent corporate aid to S. Africa |
| Bangkok | 1982 | R | Remedies for Victims of Race Discrimination |
| Geneva | 1985 | I | Community Relations Commissions |
| *Cameroon | 1986 | I | Assistance to Peoples fighting Apartheid |

* Seminars proposed by the Commission
I World-Wide Seminars
R Regional Seminars

also raised free speech objections to proposals that governments censor racist propaganda and ban organizations advocating racial hatred. Following a second world conference on the theme, the General Assembly approved a Second Decade to Combat Racism and Racial Discrimination beginning in 1983.[123] The Commission resolved to take up a different theme in each year of the decade. For the first topic the members arranged a 1986 seminar in Cameroon on: "International assistance and support to peoples and movements struggling against colonialism, racism, racial discrimination and *apartheid.*"[124] An earlier seminar of the second decade brought representatives from twenty-eight states to Geneva to discuss community relations commissions and their functions.[125] Another seminar on the rights of Palestinians to a homeland further illustrates how Third World members have adapted promotional activities to address a specific violation.[126]

*Economic Rights and Development*

Even while a Working Group of experts negotiated provisions for a declaration on the right to development, Third World members assiduously promoted the concept. After the Secretary-General's first report in 1979, proponents adopted a variety of theoretical research and promotional activities designed to popularize economic rights: additional studies by the Secretary-General, two Sub-Commission studies, three seminars in the advisory services program, and a fifteen member Commission Working Group of experts on development. As a sequel to his report on its international dimensions, the Commission requested the Secretary-General to study the Regional and National Dimensions of the Right to Development.[127] Third World representatives have argued that human rights practices may vary depending on the level of development or cultural differences. Western critics respond that the Universal Declaration affirms inalienable rights which must be respected in all societies.

As part of the Universal Declaration's 35th Anniversary observance in 1983, the Assembly called for an international seminar to consider the experience of different countries in the implementation of international human rights standards.[128]

The Secretary-General's third study on development examines the right to participation.[129] The Report stresses that individuals should be the subjects who make development happen, not the objects receiving benefits conferred by others. Yugoslavia has championed participatory rights, particularly in the local workplace. The United Kingdom representative to the Commission, while agreeing that participation is an important factor in development, objected that no such right had ever been formulated.[130]

Two international seminars requested by the Commission have treated international structures as the cause of human rights problems in the Third World. In 1980 the advisory services program arranged a seminar in Geneva on the Effects of the Existing Unjust International Economic Order on the Economies of the Developing Countries and the Obstacle that this Represents for the Implementation of Human Rights and Fundamental Freedoms.[131] The other seminar, on the Relations between Human Rights, Peace and Development, met in New York in 1981.[132] On the Sub-Commission, Raul Ferrero (Peru) prepared a report on the New International Economic Order and the promotion of human rights, and Asbjørn Eide (Norway) undertook a study on the right to food. The Sub-Commission disregarded the Commission's requests for two other studies, one on how science and technology ensures the right to work and development and a second on the consequences of an arms race on the observance of human rights.[133]

For several sessions Commission members debated the scope and content of the right to development before adopting general resolutions approving the ill-defined concept. The Commission passed by consensus a Senegalese draft that called for both personal and collective advancement.[134] More nationalistic Third World states, however, have rejected Western attempts to tie development assistance to human rights progress. Cuba sponsored a 1979 resolution adopted 23-1-7 reiterating "that the right to development is a human right and that equality of opportunity for development is as much a prerogative of nations as of individuals within nations."[135] The Commission further expressed its concern that bilateral and multilateral trade policies affected human rights and called for the seminar on the unjust international economic order.[136] Western members resisted the effort to reorient the human rights program from promotion of individual's rights against the state, to a campaign of developing against developed states.

## Principle and Propaganda

Propaganda competes with principled promotion under Commission agenda items on Science and Technology, Youth, Religious Intolerance, and Nazi and

Fascist Ideology. Without identifying specific wrongdoers, politically motivated delegates sponsor hortatory resolutions condemning practices associated with their adversaries. The Eastern bloc denounces Nazi and fascist ideologies, advocates disarmament, and promotes world peace as the paramount end. Western members condemn religious persecution, encourage free speech, and oppose limits on individual travel. Third World delegates inveigh against transnational corporations and propose a new world information order.

Occasionally, the debates reveal a genuine effort to educate rather then to embarrass those professing different values. The Netherlands, for example, unsuccessfully attempted to persuade non-Western delegates to affirm a right of conscientious objection to military service.[137] Often the sponsors propose special years, such as the 1985 International Youth Year, or commemorative anniversary celebrations, marking the second world war's end or adoption of the international covenants. Time pressures and an overcrowded agenda led the Commission to schedule the two agenda items on youth and science and technology for alternate years rather than annually.[138]

## Institutional Change

In addition to standard-setting and promotion, the Commission has continued its largely futile efforts at institutional reform. Attempts at institutional development have floundered because of irreconcilable differences between the blocs about both means and ends. No one group has had sufficient control to push through its preferred reforms, and outvoted minorities typically prefer weaker rather than stronger international organizations.

Most Western and several Latin American and Asian members currently advocate independent, impartial, quasi-judicial mechanisms capable of protecting individual civil and political rights. The regional human rights treaties and commissions in Western Europe and Latin America suggest the models favored for the United Nations system. The Soviet bloc insists that sovereign nations are responsible both for protecting their own citizens and for exerting diplomatic pressure on wrongdoers. The Eastern states have no regional human rights treaty or commission, and universally reject individual petition procedures. Non-aligned states give highest priority to international measures for realizing self-determination, racial equality, and economic development. The Organiza - tion of African Unity has established a weak human rights commission, and the Asian states have no regional treaty or agency. Very few non-aligned states have accepted individual petition procedures. Like the Soviet bloc, they prefer promotion (propaganda to Western cynics) to enforcement mechanisms for individual civil and political rights. While all members proclaim their support for institutional improvement, their conflicting goals have spawned uncoordinated bodies that do not function as a coherent system.[139]

The sessional Working Group on Alternative Means which had recommended the 1980 increases in Commission membership and meeting time reconvened from 1981–1984 to decide further institutional reforms. The group sought not only to improve the Commission's performance but also to develop a more coherent international human rights regime. The group made no progress on either front, and discontented Western members opposed further meetings.

*Commission Practice, Procedure, and Planning*

The Commission's annual six week session now appears like a meeting of the General Assembly more than it resembles the original Commission which convened in 1947. The forty-three member governments send not simply one representative, but delegations lead by career diplomats with as many as fifteen alternates and advisers. As many as sixty nonmember government observers participate in regional caucuses, take part in debate, and co-sponsor resolutions. Unlike the Assembly, NGO representatives sit in the meeting hall (in the back row), circulate short written papers, and give brief speeches. Five major geopolitical groups determine which states ECOSOC elects as members, nominate candidates for Commission office, and coordinate strategy. The Eastern group strongly objected when Israel and then the United States criticized its nomination for vice-chairman of a reputed former Nazi from the German Democratic Republic. After Hermann Klenner served as Vice-Chairman at the 1986 session, American officials began diplomatic efforts to block his 1987 election as chairman representing the Eastern group.[140] In 1986 the Commission covered a twenty-five item agenda, received more than fifty reports from various rapporteurs, committees, specialized agencies and Secretariat staff, convened several major working groups, and adopted 63 public resolutions. Table 7.3 lists the 1982 agenda items in the order considered, and Table 7.4 estimates the amount of meeting time and resolutions adopted in the Commission's four main activity areas.

Participation by the eleven additional members who joined the Commission in 1980 consumed much of the extra meeting time authorized. The Commission resolved that time limits on statements would be useful,[141] but the chairman normally calls time only on NGO speakers. Members can make two statements, first of twenty and then of ten minutes on each agenda item; observers are allowed one fifteen minute statement, and NGO speakers can make ten minute presentations. In addition, governments are entitled to one ten minute and one five minute right of reply whenever attacked, as well as a separate opportunity to explain their vote.[142] At each session, additional night meetings are required, and a few agenda items are still postponed when time runs out. The lengthy, repetitive speeches delivered in time consuming general debate create significant administrative costs in translation and documentation with no observable impact on the resolutions adopted. Whatever the reason, many capable, busy individuals have become inured to intolerably protracted

TABLE 7.3
Order of Initial Consideration of Agenda Items in 1982

| Order of Debate | Subject | Agenda Item Number |
|---|---|---|
| 1 | Electing Officers, Agenda, Schedule | 1--3 |
| 2 | Israeli Occupied Arab Territories | 4, 9 |
| 3 | Science and Technology | 15 |
| 4 | Future Work Program of the Commission | 11 |
| 5 | South Africa and Apartheid | 6,7,16,18 |
| 6 | Self Determination | 9 |
| 7 | Right to Development, NIEO | 8 |
| 8 | Report of the Sub-Commission | 20 |
| 9 | Detention and Disappearances | 10 (a) (b) |
| 10 | Chile | 5 |
| 11 | Confidential Communications on Violations | 12(b) |
| 12 | Publicly alleged violations | 12(b) |
| 13 | Other and Postponed (Minorities, Migrants Youth, Advisory Services) | 13,14,17,21--23 |

Source: CHR 1982 Report, p. 167, par. 144.

general debates and have not considered the possibility of proceeding directly to arguments for and against draft resolutions.

A ten member informal working group met in 1983 to rationalize the agenda, but could only agree to eliminate one redundant item on communications and to schedule two others for biennial rather than annual review.[143] Even though the Commission regularly considers four related agenda items on South Africa together, NAM members rejected Australia's proposal to consolidate those topics and to combine the item on Chile with other violations. Nor could the carefully negotiated diplomatic compromises embodied in overlong agenda headings be simplified into concise titles like "Self-Determination" or "Detention and Torture." The title for the agenda item on the Commission's work methods and alternative approaches for improving the system now exceeds forty words and takes five lines of print. The agenda group also rejected proposals to shift some business to the Sub-Commission with triennial review by the parent organ. The Commission has never prepared the type of long range work plan it has required from the Sub-Commission experts. When Secretariat staff presented a 1984–1989 Medium Term plan, few members commented and there were no substantive changes.

Competing proposals for alternative approaches to violations and communications all failed. Western members could not obtain authorization for the Commission's five member bureau to meet between sessions whenever an emergency situation required an immediate response. ECOSOC rejected a Japanese initiated proposal for the annual calendar that would have permitted a

TABLE 7.4
Number of 1982 Meetings and Resolutions by Agenda Item

| Subject | Working Group Meetings | Full Commission Meetings | Resolutions Approved |
|---|---|---|---|
| **Violations** | | | |
| Israel and Arab Lands | | 8 | 4 |
| South Africa and Namibia | | 6 | 5 |
| Self Determination | | | |
| Afghanistan, Kampuchea, Western Sahara | | 6 | 3 |
| Disappearances[1] | | 3 | 1 |
| Other Violations—Bolivia, Iran | | | |
| El Salvador, Poland, Guatemala | | 7 | 9 |
| Chile | | 2 | 1 |
| Confidential Communications | 10 | 9 | 8 |
| Sub-Total | 10 | 41 | 31 |
| | | | |
| **Standard-Setting** | | | |
| Torture Convention | 17 | | 1 |
| Rights of the Child | 16 | | 1 |
| Declaration on Minorities | 4 | | 1 |
| Human Rights Defenders | | | 1 |
| Migrants | | | 1 |
| Status of Covenants | | | 1 |
| Sub-Total | 33 | | 6 |
| | | | |
| **Promotion** | | | |
| Race Decade | | | 1 |
| Right to Development[1] | | 3 | 1 |
| Science and Technology | | 3 | 3 |
| Youth | | | 1 |
| Advisory Services | | 1 | 1 |
| Public Information Activities | | | 2 |
| Sub-Total | | 7 | 9 |
| | | | |
| **Organization and Procedures** | | | |
| Sub-Commissin Report | | 4 | 4 |
| Officers, Agenda, Schedule | | 3 | |
| Program Planning | 5 | | 2 |
| Sub-Total | 5 | 7 | 6 |

[1] Does not include meetings of Working Groups on Disappearances and the Right to Development conducted between sessions.
Source: U.N. Doc. E/CN.4/1982/SR. 1-61.

logical progression of business from meetings first by the Sub-Commission, then the Commission, and finally ECOSOC before the fall Assembly session.[145] Instead, the Sub-Commission continues to meet between sessions of ECOSOC and the Assembly, six months after the Commission. The Soviet Union, which opposes international oversight, argued without effect that the covenant's petition procedure under the optional protocol eliminated the need for the Commission's 1503 communication procedure. Non-aligned and Eastern bloc states favored a restatement of the Commission's terms of reference that would assign greater importance to economic rights and development.[146]

*Fostering Institutional Growth*

The Commission has done very little with ECOSOC's 1979 authorization to coordinate and to improve United Nations human rights activities. The members continued their longstanding support for national and regional institutions, resurrected a doomed proposal for a United Nations High Commissioner for Human Rights, offered ineffective recommendations for strengthening the Secretariat, and generally disregarded the growing duplication among United Nations human rights agencies. The Commission has been no more effective in bringing coherence to the larger United Nations system than it has been in rationalizing its own agenda.

Proponents of regional institutions sought to replicate in Asia the successful regional seminars which led to an African Human Rights Charter. However, only one-third of the Asian governments attended a 1982 seminar on national, local, and regional arrangements in Sri Lanka.[147] India expressed its preference for global rather than regional approaches, and even opposed attempts to give a special role to the U.N. Economic and Social Council for Asia and the Pacific.[148]

To foster national organizations, the Assembly has directed the Secretary-General to survey governments and to report on how they have developed and utilized local institutions. The Commission has reviewed the Secretariat reports at three year intervals.[149] The Secretariat's 1986 consolidated report was to be published as a United Nations handbook on national institutions, informing governments about various types and models in different social and legal systems.[150] The Secretariat reports distinguish judicial institutions protecting human rights from educational agencies undertaking promotional activity. Press reports from the war zones of El Salvador and Nicaragua indicate that local human rights commissions may be co-opted by either government officials or rebel groups for political propaganda against their adversaries. Government programs like the Scandinavian ombudsman appear more genuinely oriented to protecting citizens rather than public officials. The Secretariat reports rely primarily on sporadic government responses and give little specific detail that would show whether United Nations efforts have produced effective, independent local institutions.

Proposals for a United Nations High Commissioner for Human Rights regularly reappear at the Commission. In 1967, the International Commission of Jurists and other NGOs, Costa Rica, and several Western members developed specific plans for a High Commissioner.[151] The most recent draft approved by the Sub-Commission in 1982 provided for elections by the Assembly to a five year term and authorized direct contacts with governments in urgent situations.[152] The proposal is anathema to the Soviet bloc; India and Brazil expressed Third World opposition in the Commission. Unlike one earlier effort, the recommendation was not forwarded to the Assembly. Opponents argued that elevating the Director of the Human Rights Division to the rank of Assistant Secretary-General in 1983 satisfied any need for a High Commissioner. The potential threat to national sovereignty remained the critical concern, a fear that any further Sub-Commission study requested will not allay. In practice the theme rapporteurs using urgent action procedures have performed overlapping responsibilities that would be centralized in a High Commissioner for Human Rights.[153]

The Commission working group on alternative approaches has claimed credit for the Assembly resolutions redesignating the Division of Human Rights as a Centre and reclassifying the post of Director to the level of Assistant Secretary-General.[154] The Commission, however, has not made staffing decisions; its requests for additional funding have not brought increased appropriations, and the change in titles appears more symbolic than substantive. The Netherlands' former representative to the Commission, Theo van Boven, served just one term as director. To the dismay of NGO and some government representatives attending the 1982 session, Secretary-General Perez de Cuellar unexpectedly denied him reappointment. Van Boven attributed his own termination to a campaign launched by Argentina, but the Secretary-General is in theory free to make his own choice.[155] Although some Third World governments wanted an African director, the post remained a Western preserve when Austria's Kurt Herndl became the division's fourth head. Commission resolutions have urged that staff appointments be based on geographic representation; the selection of lower ranking human rights officials reflects such balance, although critics note a Western orientation in their education or outlook.[156]

## Coordinating Agencies in the U.N. System

As the Commission has expanded its role to assert universal jurisdiction over all human rights violations, specialized agencies like UNESCO have also proceeded from standard-setting and promotion to enforcement activities. United Nations policy making organs have drafted both global and issue specific norms, most of which are stated in slightly different terms in regional treaties. Empire builders in new international bureaucracies jealously guard their institutional turf as responsibilities overlap. Ideologically divided on institutional objectives, the

TABLE 7.5
Human Rights Activities and the United Nations System, 1986

U.N. Principal Organs

General Assembly
    Subsidiary Committees and Working Groups
        Granting Independence to Colonial Countries
        UN Council for Namibia
        Special Committee Against Apartheid
        Palestinian Rights
        Working Group for Relief for Palestine Refugees
        Israeli Practices in the Occupied Territories
        Drafting Committee for convention on mercenaries
        Drafting Committee for convention on migrant workers
    Trust Funds
        South Africa
        Namibia
        Victims of Torture
        Indigenous Populations
    Related Organs
        UN High Commissioner for Refugees  (UNHCR)
        UN Children's Fund  (UNICEF)
    International Convention Committees--Treaty Bodies
        Elimination of Racial Discrimination
        Human Rights (Civil and Political Rights)
        Elimination of Discrimination Against Women
        Torture (Proposed)
    Specialized Agencies Affiliated with ECOSOC
        International Labor Organization (ILO)
        UN Educational, Scientific, and Cultural Organization (UNESCO)
        Food and Agriculture Organization (FAO)
        World Health Organization (WHO)

Secretariat
        Centre for Human Rights
        Centre for Social Development and Humanitarian Affairs
            Advancement for Women Branch
    Department of Political and Social Security Affairs
        Centre Against Apartheid
        Division for Palestinian Rights
        UN Commissioner for Namibia

Economic and Social Council
        Committee on Economic, Social and Cultural Rights
        Social Committee
        Committee on Non-governmental Organizations
    Commission on the Status of Women
            Working Group on the Status of Women

    Commission on Human Rights
            Sub-Commission on Prevention of Discrimination and
            Protection of Minorities

(cont.)

TABLE 7.5 cont.

---

Commission and Sub-Commission Groups and Rapporteurs

Commission on Human Rights

| Working Groups | Rapporteurs |
|---|---|
| Group of Three on Apartheid Convention | Summary or Arbitrary Execution |
| Group on South Africa | Torture |
| Screening communications on violations | Religious Intolerance |
| Enforced or involuntary disappearances | Chile |
| Right to Development | El Salvador |
| Human Rights Defenders | Iran |
| Drafting convention on rights of child | Equatorial Guinea |
| Drafting declaration on rights of minorities | Guatemala |
| Drafting declaration on rights of defenders | Afghanistan |

Sub-Commission on Prevention of Discrimination and Protection of Minorities

| Working Groups | Rapporteurs |
|---|---|
| Communications | Leaving and Returning to Countries |
| Slavery | Religious Intolerance |
| Indigenous Populations | Drafting optional protocol on the death penalty |
| | Economic and military assistance to South Africa |
| | States of Seige, Emergency |
| | Independence and Impartiality of Jurists |
| | Mauritania |
| | Computerized Personnel Files |
| | Individual and International Law |
| | Race Decade |
| | Right to Food |
| | Detainees    Disability    Youth |

Regional Human Rights Organs Outside the U.N. System

Committee of Ministers of the Council of Europe
European Commission of Human Rights
European Court of Human Rights

General Assembly, Organization of American States
Inter-American Commission on Human Rights
Inter-American Court of Human Rights

Assembly of Heads of State of the Organization of African Unity
Proposed African Commission of Human and Peoples' Rights

Selected Global Nongovernmental Human Rights Organizations

International Committee of the Red Cross
Amnesty International
International Commission of Jurists
Commission of the Churches for International Affairs

---

Commission has not yet considered duplication a problem or attempted to coordinate a coherent international system. Members who advocate even more supra-national enforcement measures apparently view the proliferating bodies as a sign of vitality, rather than as a cause for administrative concern.

The Commission's innovative Resolution 1235 and 1503 procedures anticipated the Political Covenant's interstate complaint and the optional protocol's individual petition procedures. Even after the Political Covenant took effect and its Human Rights Committee began to function, the Commission continued to make ad hoc responses without regard for possible duplication. United Nations Legal Counsel questioned the legal validity of proposals to make the Human Rights Committee the implementation organ for the draft torture convention.[157] Since it appeared unworkable to amend the Political Covenant, a new torture committee was created. Instead of rationalizing procedures, the Commission has contributed further to the haphazard proliferation of human rights institutions by creating new procedures for torture and religious intolerance. Table 7.5 lists United Nations human rights bodies operating in 1986 as well as several groups with related missions outside the U.N. system.

The Commission has repeatedly failed to provide institutional leadership in the United Nations system, or even to reconcile inconsistencies in its own public and private procedures. Rarely has the Commission attempted to coordinate United Nations' bodies. ECOSOC approved a proposal to grant the Commission on the Status of Women authority to review confidential communications alleging sex discrimination. The members have recommended technical assistance to governments unable to comply with onerous reporting obligations, but have also made repeated requests for additional information without attempting to simplify or to consolidate the requirements. The General Assembly directed the Secretary-General to convene a meeting of the chairmen of the Commission on Human Rights, the Human Rights Committee, the Sessional Working Group of Governmental Experts on the Implementation of the Economic Covenant, and the Committee on the Elimination of Racial Discrimination. Among other proposals, the four chairmen suggested that reports to the different bodies have a common format for the country description.[158]

The Commission's often stormy relationship with its own Sub-Commission illustrates how little the members have cared about institutional collaboration and how difficult coordination can be, even when dealing with a theoretically subordinate body. The following chapter describes the Sub-Commission's forty year development in relation to its inattentive parent.

# 8

# The Commission's Independent
# Sub-Commission

When it established the Commission on Human Rights, ECOSOC authorized the creation of three sub-commissions. The United States initially proposed a Sub-Commission on Freedom of Information and the Press. The Soviet Union insisted on two additional sub-commissions, one for the prevention of discrimination and another for the protection of minorities. The Sub-Commission on Freedom of Information and the Press met for only three years, 1947–1950; ECOSOC decided that a proposed Sub-Commission for women ought to be established as a full Commission in its own right. As a result, the Commission's only enduring Sub-Commission has been the body initially assigned responsibility for both discrimination and minorities.[1]

The U.N. Sub-Commission on Prevention of Discrimination and Protection of Minorities which the Commission created at its first session in 1947 is a subsidiary organ that member governments have alternatively regarded as a blessing and a curse. Despite its subordinate status and precise title the Sub-Commission has taken initiatives concerning the full range of human rights with minimal supervision by the Commission. NGO activists have used the Sub-Commission to propose new standards and to identify violations which the Commission might not otherwise consider. Although they are theoretically "independent" experts, Sub-Commission members have often been political appointees instructed by their governments. Over forty years, the Sub-Commission has both served the Commission and challenged it with independent initiatives that prompted attempts to curtail the experts.

## Composition

The Commission resolved to establish a Sub-Commission of independent experts serving in an individual capacity rather than as government representatives.[2] In practice, political considerations have influenced the selection, expertise, and independence of Sub-Commission members. In theory governments were to nominate candidates after consultation with the Secretary-General. In practice, governments have controlled selection of their nationals for Sub-Commission membership without objection from the Secretary-General. The Indian government, for example, replaced Minoo R. Masani on the Sub-Commission, even though he had been reelected after a six year term.[3]

*Size and Regional Balance.* Political factors have also determined the size and regional balance of the Sub-Commission's membership. In 1959 the Commission increased the membership from twelve to fourteen.[4] African and Asian members held only five of the Sub-Commission's fourteen seats in 1962. In order to provide greater representation for the U.N.'s new members from Africa and Asia the Sub-Commission was enlarged to eighteen in 1965 and twenty-six in 1968.[5] After 1968 twelve experts would come from African and Asian states, six from Western Europe and other states, five from Latin America, and three from Eastern Europe.[6] A gentlemen's agreement that seven Africans would be elected broke down during the Commission's secret balloting in 1978 when only five nominees form continental Africa, including just two from sub-Saharan Africa, were elected.[7] In response to African protests, the Commission subsequently established a fixed allocation of seven African members and five from Asia. Table 8.1 details the changes in membership of the Sub-Commission over a twenty year period.

Since 1968, regional balance has determined rotation of officers on the Sub-Commission bureau and composition of each five member working group. The Sub-Commission elects five officers for each annual session, one from each region—a chairman, three vice-chairmen, and a rapporteur. Members caucus by region before a session to agree on a nominee but do not thereafter hold regional meetings. When two Western members competed for the position in 1985, the divided regional group accepted the candidate preferred by a majority of the full membership. As on the Commission, the position of chair rotates among the

TABLE 8.1
Number of Sub-Commission Experts by Region

| Region | 1952 | 1962 | 1972 | 1982 |
|---|---|---|---|---|
| Africa | 0 | 2 | 7 | 7 |
| Asia | 3 | 3 | 5 | 5 |
| Eastern Europe | 2 | 2 | 3 | 3 |
| Latin America | 2 | 2 | 5 | 5 |
| West Europe and Other | 5 | 5 | 6 | 6 |
| Total | 12 | 14 | 26 | 26 |

five established regions, and the members conduct nominations, elections, and salutations with all the diplomatic niceties of U.N. government representatives.

*Elections.* Prior to 1987 the Commission elected all the Sub-Commission experts for simultaneous three year terms. In future, the Commission plans to provide greater continuity by having staggered four year terms, with half the membership elected every two years.[8] Governments nominate candidates, and the Secretariat circulates a brief biographical sketch for each. Governments from the Eastern European group nominate only three candidates for the three positions available, so that part of the election offers the Commission no real choice. In the 1984 election, there were thirty-nine nominees for the twenty-three positions allocated to the four other regional groups.

Sponsoring governments lobby actively on behalf of their nationals, and Commission members make political calculations when casting their twenty-six votes by a secret ballot. Candidates from the Soviet Union and Rumania, for example, received only thirty-nine votes each in 1984, indicating that four of the Commission's forty-three members withheld approval, even though there were no alternative nominees from the Eastern European region. Strategic abstentions exceeded 12% of the votes allocated for the contested positions from the Latin American and Western European regions. Norway's highly respected and effective expert Asbjørn Eide, whose initiatives on Afghanistan offended the Soviet bloc, lost by four votes.[9] Observer governments like Norway are obviously handicapped in winning election for their nationals when competing against candidates nominated by Commission members. In 1981 twenty of the twenty-six Sub-Commission members came from states represented on the Commission which elected them. The Tunisian expert Abdelwahab Boudhiba, rapporteur for a highly praised Sub-Commission study on child labor, lost his seat to African nominees who lobbied for their own election to the Sub-Commission while serving as government representatives on the Commission. Altogether, seven of the Sub-Commission experts elected for the 1981–83 term also served as government representatives or advisers to the Commission.[10] Nominees of the permanent members of the U.N. Security Council routinely win approval.[11] Governments such as Argentina have sought representation on the Sub-Commission in order to defend against criticism of human rights violations. Two former directors of the Human Rights Division, John Humphrey and Theo van Boven, have been elected.

Until 1983, election by the Commission did not always mean that the individuals elected actually participated in Sub-Commission meetings. From the outset, Sub-Commission members that were unable to attend all or part of a session designated alternates to replace them. As this practice became more frequent, the Commission repeatedly warned that "permitting alternates to represent members . . . might not on occasion be in keeping with the character of that body."[12] The United Nations Legal Office construed the rules of procedure to permit designation of alternates, and up to half the Sub-

Commission members used alternates approved by their governments. In 1981 alternates replaced ten of the twenty-six members; the elected expert from Pakistan failed to attend five of the twelve Sub-Commission sessions held during his tenure.

Western representatives on the Commission protested the practice of governments dispatching members of their U.N. missions to replace experts elected to the Sub-Commission. The Commission resolved that after 1983 only one alternate designated for and elected with each expert by the Commission would be authorized to participate in Sub-Commission meetings.[13]  In the first election under the new rules, the Commission elected seven experts without designated alternates, and nineteen with alternates of the same nationality. Since over half the experts elected in 1984 held foreign service or other government posts, the new selection procedure has simply reduced the number of alternates without improving the expertise members bring to the Sub-Commission. In fact the 1984 selection appears to have removed some of the more independent experts, as only eleven of twenty-six incumbents won a new term: eleven governments with incumbent experts nominated different individuals, and three other incumbents renominated by their governments also lost their positions.[14]

*Independence and Expertise.* Sub-Commission "experts" have shown varying degrees of expertise and independence. Several distinguished jurists, lawyers, and professors have had the technical expertise indicated by the official job description. Governments occasionally have nominated genuinely independent activists, such as Benjamin Whitaker, director of the London-based Minority Rights Group. The first members of the Sub-Commission included Belgian and Soviet diplomats who had also served on the Commission, a newspaper editor and former administrative aid to President Roosevelt, as well as a number of private citizens.

In 1982, over half of the members held government posts; three were cabinet ministers, two were sitting judges, and five belonged to national delegations to the Commission. Nicole Questiaux, an exception, resigned from the Sub-Commission after joining the French government. Eastern bloc states categorically reject the principle of "independent" experts and regularly assign diplomats to the Sub-Commission. In 1950, the two communist members protested participation by the "Kuomintang" representative and walked out of the Sub-Commission's session in accord with their governments' policy. During the same period, officials of the United States and the United Kingdom inadvertently described their nationals as "representatives" of the government.[15] For nearly a decade the United States sent private citizens to head its delegation to the Commission, a body of government representatives, and nominated a career foreign service officer as an independent expert for the Sub-Commission. A 1979 State Department press release clarified that one of Ambassador Beverly Carter's Sub-Commission votes had been made in an individual capacity and did not signal a change in U.S. policy toward the Palestine Liberation Organiza -

tion.[16] With the possible exception of Carter, a comparison of roll call votes cast at the Commission's 1982 session with positions taken on related resolutions by members at the previous Sub-Commission session revealed little disagreement between the independent experts and their governments. Inis Claude's analysis of the members' "independence" in 1951 remains valid today:

> It is difficult to draw conclusions from the substantive views expressed in the meetings of the Subcommission as to the actual freedom from govern - mental instructions enjoyed by its members, and it would be invidious to suggest that they are acting as governmental delegates disguised as independent experts whenever they take positions which are typical of the predilections and policies of their governments. . . . However, it may be suggested that the lay visitor . . . would probably not be aware that he had discovered a special and distinctive sort of United Nations organ if he should inadvertently stumble into a meeting of the Subcommission. . . . The critical fact is that the Subcommission has the responsibility of dealing with problems which are political in every sense of the word. . . . When experts have to deal with problems in which political considerations are deeply embedded, it is quixotic to suppose that their views will not be tinged with attitudes which reflect their national affiliations more than their technical qualifications.[17]

Since 1947, the Sub-Commission's hybrid membership has included independent private citizens and instructed government representatives, qualified experts and political appointees. Consequently, its operations have differed somewhat from those of the Commission. The Sub-Commission has fewer members than the Commission and meets for a shorter time. Although often supported by an alternate, the individual experts do not have a national delegation of advisers and deputies. States with experts on the Sub-Commission often assign separate observers to participate as official representatives. Place markers identify the members by name, rather than by country. The United Nations provides the individual members with a travel and a per diem allowance, but they receive no honoraria. Four weeks of daily meetings in Geneva appears more than some private members can afford; absenteeism toward the end of session may leave a bare quorum to decide important resolutions.[18] Although governed by the same rules of procedure as the Commission, the Sub-Commission operates with less formality. When unable to obtain a consensus, members vote by show of hands rather than by roll call; they rarely offer an official "explanation of vote." Nongovernmental organizations have greater access to the Sub-Commission than to the Com - mission. Sub-Commission members frequently proclaim their independence and remind each other that all serve in an individual capacity.[19] While never completely realizing that ideal, Sub-Commission members have been sufficiently independent to provoke efforts by some Commission members to curtail or abolish the subsidiary organ. Throughout their difficult relationship, the Commission has contributed to the Sub-Commission's defiance by drafting ambiguous directives and ignoring the response.

## Terms of Reference

Deciding what the Sub-Commission should do has been as difficult for the Commission as determining who should serve as experts. Over a period of four decades the Commission has formulated and amended the Sub-Commission's official terms of reference in several general authorizations. In addition, the Sub-Commission has engaged in practices beyond its established mandate occasionally without obtaining approval from the Commission. As a result, The Sub-Commission on Prevention of Discrimination and Protection of Minorities has become a *de facto* Sub-Commission on Human Rights, despite the Commission's refusal to change its name. More importantly, new terms of reference added in 1967 shifted the Sub-Commission's primary emphasis from research to the monitoring of human rights violations.

In the beginning, the Commission had a very different purpose in mind. The Eastern bloc representatives from multi-national states wanted a U.N. body that would both affirm minority rights and criticize their cold war adversaries who practiced discrimination. Latin American representatives, by contrast, asserted that national minorities should be assimilated.[20] Western Europeans had fashioned an elaborate system of minorities treaties through the League of Nations, but were uncertain what device to adopt after Hitler exploited the interests of German minorities for national expansion. Clearly the Nazi doctrine of racial supremacy and religious persecution demanded some response from the United Nations. The 1947 compromise formulation which resulted directed the Sub-Commission members

(a) to examine what provisions should be adopted in the definition of the principles which are to be applied in the field of the prevention of discrimination on grounds of race, sex, language or religion, and in the field of the protection of minorities, and to make recommendations to the commission on urgent problems in these fields;
(b) to perform any other functions which may be entrusted to it by the Economic and Social Council or the Commission on Human Rights.[21]

Those terms of reference provided for a research function as well as for active consideration of pressing human rights problems. At their first two-week session, the new Sub-Commission members drafted a provision for the Universal Declaration of Human Rights on discrimination that proved more acceptable to the Commission than their formulation on minority rights.[22] Uncertain whether they also had authority to forward "urgent proposals" to parent organs, the experts requested clarification from the Commission.

In 1949 the Commission reformulated the Sub-Commission's terms of reference, eliminating its mandate to consider "urgent problems" and directing the experts to "undertake studies, particularly in the light of the Universal Declaration of Human Rights."[23] As a result, the Sub-Commission functioned primarily as a research organ until 1967, giving only indirect attention to reported violations of human rights. The members drafted an article for the International Covenant on Civil and Political Rights which provided that "minorities shall not be denied the right, in community with other members of their group, to enjoy their own culture, to profess and practice their own religion, or to use their own language."[24] Proponents of stronger language argued that states with minority populations had an affirmative obligation to provide separate schools and language instruction that would preserve distinct cultures.[25]

The Sub-Commission spent five years in a futile effort to carry out its mandate on behalf of minorities before abandoning that task to focus exclusively on discrimination. Ultimately the members must have realized that the Commission simply buried the politically divisive minorities issue in the Sub-Commission with no expectation of action.[26] The General Assembly's refusal to include a Soviet sponsored provision on minorities in the Universal Declaration of Human Rights was an early indication that the United Nations would not carry forward the League's program.[27] At its second session in 1949, the Sub-Commission recommended interim measures for the protection of minorities, and the following year proposed a definition of "minority."[28] The Commission referred both proposals back to the Sub-Commission for further study without guidance or direction. Government representatives had charged Sub-Commission experts with the politically impossible task of protecting minorities in states committed to national sovereignty and to the inviolability of domestic jurisdiction. Even Eastern bloc governments, in spite of their avowed commitment to minority rights, opposed international interference in national affairs and used the Sub-Commission as a symbol to embarrass political adversaries.[29]

After the Sub-Commission's third session, government representatives attacked the experts for failing to fulfill their mandate.[30] When the Secretariat complained of budgetary constraints, the Commission and ECOSOC willingly sacrificed both the overly independent Sub-Commission on Information and the Sub-Commission on Discrimination and Minorities. The Western majority saw no further need for the Sub-Commissions, concluding that the Secretariat and the Commission itself could perform their functions. A General Assembly majority of socialist and nonwhite states intervened to save the Sub-Commission on Discrimination and Minorities, although the Sub-Commission on Information was abolished. When the Commission continued to reject the Sub-Commission's recommendations on minorities, and would not even authorize a study of the problem, the experts wisely narrowed their terms of reference to concentrate solely on discrimination. Not until the 1970s did the Sub-Commission resume serious consideration of international norms to protect the rights of minorities. Between 1954 and 1966 the Sub-Commission designated rapporteurs to begin seven studies on discrimination which the Commission approved but largely ignored.

The Commission showed greater interest when the Sub-Commission condemned a resurgence of anti-semitism and neo-Nazi slogans in several European cities. With the approval of the Commission and the General Assembly, the Secretariat supplied the Sub-Commission with material that led to the drafting of the U.N. Declaration Against Racial Discrimination in 1963. The Sub-Commission then completed the text for the International Convention for the Elimination of All Forms of Racial Discrimination that was approved by the General Assembly in 1965.[31] By contrast, Sub-Commission recommenda - tions for a declaration on religious discrimination met objections that were not overcome for twenty years. Apart from principles on discrimination in education embodied in a 1960 UNESCO convention, principles recommended in other Sub-Commission studies have not been enacted as United Nations declarations or conventions.

After nearly twenty years of work on minorities and discrimination, the Sub-Commission received less specialized assignments after 1965. First, the Commission invited the experts to review and comment on the periodic reports submitted by member nations. Previously the Sub-Commission had received only Secretariat summaries of those reports and had had limited authority to comment on minority concerns and problems of discrimination. Second, the Commission directed the Sub-Commission to undertake regular consideration of the problem of slavery and to advise ECOSOC's Special Rapporteur on *Apartheid*. Third and most important, the Commission, with ECOSOC approval, authorized the Sub-Commission to submit annual reports on violations of human rights as well as to review confidential communications in order to identify patterns of violations. In conjunction with its enlarged mandate, the Sub-Commission's membership was enlarged to 26, an increase that brought marked political and procedural changes to its deliberations.

*Periodic Reports.* Following ECOSOC approval of the American sponsored "Action Plan" in 1956, the Commission had requested governments to submit periodic reports on the state of human rights in their countries. Proponents of the procedure had hopes to subject the country reports to the same type of scrutiny given to materials submitted to the International Labor Organization staff.[32] Government representatives on the Commission, however, had never critically reviewed the reports nor questioned the government officials responsible for their preparation. Nongovernmental organizations often submitted critical commentary which the Commission ignored. In 1964 the Commission appointed a committee of eight members to review approximately sixty-four reports covering the 1960–1962 period.[33] The following year the

Commission, over the objection of the Soviet Union, decided to ask Sub-Commission experts to analyze the periodic reports.[34]

While recognizing that the opportunity to consider the full range of human rights issues detailed in the reports presented the Sub-Commission with a new frontier, the experts nevertheless postponed effective action. The Soviet expert proposed a resolution seeking clarification from the Commission that delayed the first meaningful review until 1967. In that year the Sub-Commission's rapporteur, Judge Zeev Zeltner of Israel, prepared a review of the reports with an annex summarizing NGO commentary. Observers from Arab states criticized by the NGOs vehemently protested reference to human rights violations in their countries. The Soviet expert moved to have the annex destroyed, and the Sub-Commission voted eight to six with four abstentions to withdraw the study.[35] On learning that the Sub-Commission had taken no action on the reports again in 1967, the Commission withdrew its authorization for further consideration by the experts.

*Slavery.* The Sub-Commission responded with far greater zeal and effectiveness to the Commission's 1967 assignment that it take up the problem of slavery on a regular basis.[36] The sponsors expressly included in the Sub-Commission mandate the "slavery like practices of *apartheid* and colonialism" and directed the experts to collaborate with the ECOSOC Special Rapporteur on *Apartheid.* This new responsibility entailed far more than an expanded decolonization campaign, however. The Commission also directed the experts to review country reports submitted under the 1926 Supplementary Convention on the Abolition of Slavery. The London based Anti-Slavery Society thereafter regularly reported to the Sub-Commission its findings on forced labor, debt bondage, and related slavery-like practices. With strong encouragement from the General Assembly, the Sub-Commission created a permanent working group of five experts which has met before the regular session since 1975. This Slavery Working Group has extended its inquiries far beyond slavery-like practices to consider prostitution, female circumcision, and many other human rights violations alleged by a variety of nongovernmental organizations.

*Violations.* The Commission's most important assignments to the Sub-Commission in 1967 ultimately transformed it from a research body into a quasi-judicial forum investigating human rights violations. Chapter 4 explained how the impetus for those assignments came form the United Nations' new African members supported by the Soviet bloc. The Western experts on the Sub-Commission insisted that the new procedures have universal application.[37] Although the Sub-Commission continued to conduct studies and renewed its concern for minorities, after 1967 the experts became increasingly preoccupied with actual violations of human rights and the investigatory procedures authorized by Resolutions 1235 and 1503. Heightened interest in the Sub-Commission's new powers and expanded mandate led to a substantial increase in membership and significantly greater participation in its sessions. Before considering the resulting conflict and recent decisions affecting the scope of the experts' mandate, it is necessary to examine in greater detail the Sub-Commission's long established and extensive research studies.

## Studies and Standards

*Purpose and Method.* By the mid-1980s the Sub-Commission had under - taken fifteen studies on discrimination, fifteen on individual rights, and eight on economic rights. The research was designed to educate world opinion, to prepare draft principles for declarations or conventions, and to press governments for reform. Studies have originated in various ways: with rapporteurs anxious to explore a personal concern, with Secretariat officials seeking a vehicle for influence, or with political rivals bent on embarrassing their adversaries. The selection of a subject may indicate the economic philosophy of a sponsor; it may represent a rapporteur's response to current events, or be an effort to advance the political ideology of one group. Whether proposed by the Sub-Commission or assigned by the Commission, official studies require formal approval by ECOSOC.

The research methodology adopted by the Sub-Commission for its first study in 1954 was used in many of its early reports.[38] The rapporteur prepared country reports based on information from governments, the Secretary-General, specialized agencies, nongovernmental organizations, and published writings. These summaries of material from and about each country detailed the extent of human rights violations and national protection measures. The rapporteur then shared country reports with the governments studied to obtain comments and supplementary information. Without publishing the separate country reports supporting his conclusions, the rapporteur then drafted a final global report describing both *de facto* conditions and *de jure* situations. Those seeking to press governments to make reforms had hoped the Secretariat would also translate and publish the rapporteur's country reports, but they were never circulated.[39]

More recent reports have varied considerably in scope, quality, and distribution. Truly independent Sub-Commission rapporteurs have done largely original research and authored their own reports. Others have simply reviewed work done by Secretariat staff of the Centre for Human Rights, contributing little to the text. Five staff members of the Centre's Research and Studies Unit are responsible for most Sub-Commission reports, but the Centre's Prevention of Discrimination Unit supports rapporteurs investigating racial discrimination. The most efficient rapporteurs have taken two years to complete their projects, while the slowest experts prolonged their research for over a decade. Starting in the 1980s, all studies were to be completed within three years.

The Sub-Commission has reviewed annual progress reports before receiving the final study. For less satisfactory or more politically controversial work, about one study in five, the Sub-Commission merely notes the report or refers it to the Commission without recommendation. Sub-Commission approval brings a recommendation for publication, and in the most favored cases a request for "the widest possible distribution." Whatever the form of publication, ECOSOC must approve the expense. Initially the Secretariat prints a total of only 3,320 copies in six languages based on the normal demand by governments, missions, and staff.[40] When requested to give the widest distribution to a publication, the Secretariat lists the title in a monthly listing of sales publications sent to specialized agencies, bookshops, NGOs, libraries, universities, and others.[41] The Sub-Commission and Commission have also taken recommended principles from several studies as the basis for proposed standards defining human rights.

*Discrimination Studies.* Frustrated by the futility of their work on behalf of minorities, Sub-Commission members welcomed Secretariat proposals for a program of studies on discrimination.[42] The Sub-Commission decided to undertake a series of studies on the types of discrimination proscribed by the Universal Declaration of Human Rights. For its first study on education, the Sub-Commission selected Charles Ammoun of Lebanon as rapporteur. John Humphrey, Director of the Division of Human Rights, preferred Ammoun for the task since that expert also served on the board of UNESCO (which had shown no interest in the project).[43] The Commission approved the education study in 1954, although it refused to authorize a study on discrimination against minorities proposed at the same time. Ammoun spent over three years on the project which culminated in the submission of ten draft principles to the Commission and UNESCO in 1957.[44] UNESCO used the Sub-Commmision proposals as the basis of a 1960 Convention on Discrimination in Education. Neither Ammoun nor Humphrey, however, could overcome objections by budget-conscious Secretariat officals and Soviet representatives to translation and publication of the country monographs. As a result, those unofficial "conference room documents" had minimal impact on governments charged with discrimination.[45]

Budgetary and political considerations also affected the timing and scope of other studies. The Commission initially insisted that the Sub-Commission complete work on its first project before beginning a second study. The Sub-Commission nevertheless persisted and won approval for studies on religious discrimination and political rights to begin in 1956.[46] Cold war disputes gave some of the research a partisan slant. When the Sub-Commission proposed a study on emigration and immigration, Western members of the Commission eliminated rights of immigration from the terms of reference. Judge José Ingles thus had to limit his report to the right of individuals to leave and return to their own countries.[47] In 1982 Western members on the Sub-Commission critical of continuing restrictions on emigration from the Soviet Union sponsored an analysis of "current trends and developments" by C. L. C. Mubanga-Chipoya.[48]

The original series of discrimination studies begun before 1967 also included research on the rights of children born out of wedlock,[49] equality in the administration of justice,[50] and race discrimination.[51]

Although no longer restricted to problems involving minorities and discrimination after the 1967 expansion of its mandate, the Sub-Commission did complete four additional studies in those areas. In 1971 the Sub-Commission initiated two studies on the rights of minorities and indigenous populations and one on genocide. The minorities study by Francesco Capotorti of Italy raised anew the intractable issues the Sub-Commission confronted in its first years.[52] Despite approval of the rapporteur's final report, the Commission still could not agree on a definition of "minority" for a convention proposed by Yugoslavia. After five years of debate, the members could only agree that minority individuals rather than minority groups should enjoy rights. For the third time in forty years, the Commission requested the Sub-Commission to prepare an acceptable definition of minority; in 1985 a Canadian expert offered a revised definition for consideration.[53]

José Martínez Cobo's report on Indigenous Populations took twelve years to complete.[54] Impatient with the slow progress, the Sub-Commission obtained approval in 1982 for a permanent working group on the rights of indigenous peoples which convened before completion of the Martínez Cobo study. Following Idi Amin's abrupt expulsion of aliens from Uganda, the Sub-Commission in 1974 named Baroness Elles from the United Kingdom as rapporteur for a study on the rights of noncitizens.[55] Although the Western sponsors had sufficient votes to get the final report published, the recommended principles affirming rights of noncitizens have never been enacted as a United Nations declaration. Justice A. S. Chowdhury completed the fourth study on race discrimination in criminal justice in conjunction with activities of the Decade to Combat Race Discrimination.[56] Table 8.2 lists discrimination studies completed by the Sub-Commission before 1983.

*Economic Rights.* In the 1970s after the Commission had enlarged the Sub-Commission's membership and responsibilities, the experts moved from research limited to discrimination to questions of civil liberties, economic, and collective rights. As might be expected, new Third World members on the Commission and Sub-Commission sponsored studies that addressed their primary human rights concerns for decolonization and economic rights. Two Sub-Commission studies, on self-determination by Héctor Gros Espiell[57] and Aureliu Cristescu[58] and a second that analyzed foreign economic aid to South Africa by Ahmed M. Khalifa were favorably received and widely distributed.[59] Khalifa continues to supply the Sub-Commission with an annual update of banks and firms dealing with South Africa.

In 1973, Halima Warzazi of Morocco began a study on the exploitation of labor, after press accounts described North African workers packed in cattle cars en route to jobs in Europe.[60] Like other Sub-Commission studies unsupported

TABLE 8.2
Discrimination Studies by Sub-Commission Rapporteurs

| Subject | Rapporteur | Dates of Preparation |
|---|---|---|
| Education | C. Ammoun | 1954–57 |
| Religion | A. Krishnaswami | 1956–60 |
| Religious Intolerance | O. Benito | 1983–8 |
| Political Rights | H. Santa Cruz | 1956–62 |
| Emigration | J. Ingles | 1960–63 |
| Persons Born out of Wedlock | V. Saario | 1962–67 |
| Equality in Administration of Justice | A. Rannat | 1963–67 |
| Racial Discrimination | H. Santa Cruz | 1966–70 |
| Decade | A. Eide | 1984– |
| Minorities | F. Capotorti | 1971–77 |
| Noncitizens | B. Elles | 1974–79 |
| Criminal Justice Administration | A.S. Chowdhury | 1980–82 |
| Indigenous Populations | J. Martínez–Cobo | 1971–83 |
| Disabilities | L. Despouy | 1984– |
| Youth | D. Mazilu | 1985– |

by evidence from NGOs about *de facto* conditions, the report was based primarily on government sources that claimed *de jure* compliance with international norms.[61] The Commission did not accept a 1975 recommendation for publication, but approved a second request in 1984, long after the General Assembly had begun work on a migrants convention.[62] In the 1980s Warzazi collaborated with an expert from India and representatives of UNICEF, UNESCO, and WHO on how traditional practices, such as female circumcision, affected the health of women and children. A study by Abdelwahab Boudhiba on exploitation of child labor set forth such alarming data that the Commission approved immediate publication as well as further work on an action program to attack the abuses detailed.[63] The Commission, however, took no action on the proposals after approval by the Sub-Commission, and Boudhiba did not win reelection as an expert in 1980.

The most radical economic analysis appeared in a report on aid to the Chilean junta prepared by Antonio Cassesse of Italy in 1978. Cassesse examined how the military regime had deliberately created unemployment in an attempt to curb inflation. The study demonstrated that private banks had disregarded sanctions by international lending institutions in order to further import policies that favored foreign luxury goods over basic necessities.[64] Although U.N. human rights organs had increasingly disregarded claims of national sovereignty to attack *political* repression, particularly in Chile, Cassesse's analysis advocated international monitoring of government *economic* policies that affected human rights. Even the most independent experts on the Sub-Commission found that prospect too alarming. The United States and Austrian members viewed the report as an attack on free market economies. Members from Morocco, Colombia, and Egypt also objected to the innovative analysis, but gave different reasons. The Bulgarian and Soviet members expressed approval. The Sub-Commission merely referred the report to the Commission without recommendation, and it has never been printed.[65] Cassesse's work in completing the four-volume study in one year established a Sub-Commission record, but he was not reelected to that body after completing his three year term. Table 8.3 lists Sub-Commission studies on collective and economic rights including a 1983 study on the New International Economic Order[66] and a report in preparation on the right to food by Asbjørn Eide of Norway.

*Individual Rights.* Western experts and nongovernmental organizations have typically favored studies affirming the rights of individuals against the state. Erica-Irene Daes of Greece completed three reports on the individual and the community,[67] the individual and international law,[68] and the rights of mental health detainees.[69] Western members of the Commission and NGOs attempted to use those studies as vehicles for declaring new principles of international law protecting individual liberty. Nicole Questiaux of France was rapporteur for a study on states of siege or emergency[70] that recommended principles to protect detainees. The Sub-Commission then appointed a special rapporteur to prepare an annual information report on compliance with rules governing a state of emergency and adopted a resolution criticizing Paraguay's thirty year state of siege.[71] Eide of Norway has joined with Mubanga-Chipoya of Zambia to examine conscientious objection to military service.[72] Joinet of France reported on computerized personnel files, examined amnesty laws, and studied detention without trial. John Carey of the United States proposed a one paragraph Declaration Against Unacknowledged Detention of Persons.[73]

Rapporteurs from Third World states have also conducted research on

TABLE 8.3
Sub-Commission Studies on Collective and Economic Rights

| Topic | Rapporteur | Dates of Preparation |
|---|---|---|
| Self Determination--History | A. Cristescu | 1974-78 |
| Self Determination--Implementation | H. Gros Espiell | 1974-78 |
| Aid to Southern Africa (Annual Update) | A. Khalifa | 1974-79 |
| Aid to Chile | A. Cassesse | 1977-78 |
| Exploitation of Labor | H. Warzazi | 1973-75 |
| Exploitation of Child Labor | A. Boudhiba | 1980-81 |
| Female Circumcision | H. Warzazi | 1983-86 |
| New International Economic Order | R. Ferrero | 1980-82 |
| Right to Food | A. Eide | 1983- |

fundamental rights of life, liberty, and due process of law. Mohammed Awad of Egypt carried out an early study on slavery.[74] Renewed concern about slavery and slavery-like practices resulted in a 1982 supplement by Benjamin Whitaker to the original report.[75] A jurist from India, L. Singvhi, prepared a report on the independence of the judiciary which included a draft Declaration on the Independence of the Judiciary.[76]

When Nicodeme Ruhashyankiko of Rwanda included the 1915–18 massacre of Armenians by the Ottoman Empire in the Sub-Commission's genocide study, Turkey prevailed on the rapporteur to revise the text. Dissatisfied with the expurgated version, neither the Sub-Commission nor the Commission recommended publication.[77] In 1983 the Sub-Commission appointed Benjamin Whitaker to update the genocide study.[78] His revised text mentioned not only genocide of the Armenians but also mass killings in Burundi, Germany, Iran, Kampuchea, Paraguay, and Ukrania.[79] Whitaker proposed major strengthening of the genocide convention to include political groups, to establish universal jurisdiction, to provide an early warning system, and to create a new implementation body. The report's specific references provoked substantial objections, and the Sub-Commission merely took note of the sweeping recommendations without referring them to the Commission. Table 8.4 lists the Sub-Commission studies relating to civil liberties.

*Evaluation.* After thirty years of studies, recurring problems of coordination continue to mar research efforts. Although instrumental in selecting the first

TABLE 8.4
Civil Liberties Research by Sub-Commission Rapporteurs

| Topic | Rapporteur | Dates of Preparation |
|---|---|---|
| Slavery | M. Awad | 1964–71 |
| Update | B. Whitaker | 1981–82 |
| Genocide | N. Ruhashyankiko | 1971–78 |
| Update | B. Whitaker | 1983–85 |
| Independence of Judiciary | L. Singvhi | 1980–8_ |
| Individual and Community | E. I. Daes | 1974–81 |
| States of Seige or Emergency | N. Questiaux | 1979–82 |
| Individual and International Law | E. I. Daes | 1981–8_ |
| Mental Health Detainees | E. I. Daes | 1981–83 |
| Conscientious Objection | Eide, Mubanga-Chipoya | 1981–83 |
| Right to Leave | | |
| Update | Mubanga Chipoya | 1983–198_ |
| Amnesty Laws | L. Joinet | 1983–1985 |
| Computerized Personnel Files | L. Joinet | 1984–1985 |
| Administrative Detention | L. Joinet | 1985– |

topics for study, the Commission paid little attention to the results. The Commission promptly approved principles against discrimination in education, but became deadlocked on the recommendations of the religion study in 1960. Thereafter, the Commission postponed consideration of later studies for years, until by 1968 it confronted a backlog of five Sub-Commission reports. General approval of the Sub-Commission's work might be inferred from the Commission's use of similar methods for its own studies on arbitrary arrest and the right to counsel,[80] although consideration of those reports was also delayed for several years.

Sub-Commission experts have occasionally disregarded express directives from the Commission to undertake particular studies. Eastern bloc members seeking a study on "the negative consequences of the arms race" sponsored a Commission resolution in 1982 that brought no response from the Sub-Commission.[81]  The Commission adopted resolutions in three consecutive years[82] requesting the experts to study how science and technology could ensure the right to work.  Instead, the Sub-Commission has initiated research of concern to its own members without formal authorization.  Commission members have expressed dissatisfaction at the proliferation of studies and have directed the experts to prepare as part of their annual report a comprehensive listing of work in progress.  The Sub-Commission which has had as many as six special rapporteurs reporting at one session, listed a total of eleven studies in progress in its 1982 report.

Sub-Commission rapporteurs for their part have repeatedly complained that their work merely gathers dust on the shelves of United Nations archives. The Commission rarely has time to give more than a perfunctory review to the material submitted.  Rapporteurs nevertheless must be careful not to offend governmental representatives who ultimately control the decision to publish. In its programme budget, the Secretariat's Centre for Human Rights has assigned lowest priority to research.  As a result, studies may not be completed until years after the needs which prompted their preparation have passed. Nongovernmental organizations publish timely reports on similar subjects that suffer fewer political constraints and enjoy wider distribution. The experts' recent efforts to revive and update several studies indicates, however, that the Sub-Commission remains convinced of their utility,.  Financial restrictions, however, could result in strict enforcement of a previously ignored thirty-two page limit for reports.

Ultimately the Sub-Commission studies have done more to educate world opinion and to expose violations than to lay the groundwork for new international norms. The Sub-Commission's most important drafting project, the Declaration and Convention on Race Discrimination, for example, preceded the official study on the subject. When standard-setting is the primary goal, the Sub-Commission's process of preparing country surveys and summaries is too cumbersome for effective legislative preparation. Moreover, studies limited to the preparation of guidelines and principles do not need to be published if the main objective is fulfilled by sending draft proposals to the Commission. Sponsors promoting a convention on the rights of detainees, for example, might prefer swift approval of draft principles without awaiting completion of a global study written to promote public understanding. Published Sub-Commission studies have most often led to draft principles with limited force rather than to United Nations declarations or conventions.

## Violations

Although research has remained an important priority for the Sub-Commission, its most controversial contributions to the Commission program have been its efforts to investigate human rights violations. The 1967 Commission decision authorizing the Sub-Commission to give annual consideration to violations of human rights profoundly changed the nature of its work. The experts immediately began public debate on government abuse of individual rights and by 1985 had made confidential recommendations involving over thirty countries. In the process, the Sub-Commission generated increased participation by nongovernmental organizations anxious to expose violations and by government observers determined to defend their records. Table 8.5 illustrates the increase in state observers and nongovernmental participants since 1952.

*Confidential Communications.* The Sub-Commission considers violations through several different procedures and under a variety of agenda headings. The review of confidential communications authorized by Resolution 1503 begins with a five-member Working Group that convenes two weeks before the annual session. The group presents its recommendations in several days of closed meetings when the experts decide which target countries to refer for further review by the Commission. Nongovernmental and press interest in which states are suspected of gross violations led to a series of dramatic leaks and harsh warnings during the initial years of the new procedure. When Secretariat staff

TABLE 8.5
Increase in Participation at Sub-Commission Meetings

|                                | 1952 | 1962 | 1972 | 1982 |
|--------------------------------|------|------|------|------|
| State Observers                | 1    | 4    | 18   | 45   |
| Nongovernmental organizations  | 12   | 34   | 28   | 45   |
| Specialized Agencies           | 2    | 2    | 4    | 2    |
| Regional Organizations         | 0    | 0    | 0    | 4    |

neglected to turn off earphones in the pressroom, one reporter learned which countries the Working Group had referred to the Sub-Commission in 1976.[83] Two years later the Sub-Commission demanded an inquiry when a *Le Monde* correspondent reported that the Soviets had opposed further confidential hearings on Argentina.[84] Sub-Commission members feel considerable political pressure, and have repeatedly sought authority for secret voting.[85] The Commission has ignored those requests.

*Slavery.* A second pre-sessional Working Group on slavery has met since 1975. A week before the Sub-Commission meets the five members convene to hear reports by nongovernmental organizations such as the Minority Rights Group and the Anti-Slavery Society. Minority Rights Group Director Benjamin Whitaker's membership on the Working Group partially accounts for the NGO's success in influencing the group's program. After conducting their own investigations, NGOs document for the Working Group various forms of exploitation and violation of individual rights. The Working Group report then invites the Sub-Commission to request that the Secretariat provide the damaging information to the government concerned and to solicit a response. In 1981 Mauritania replied to Anti-Slavery Society charges by inviting two Sub-Commission observers to visit the country. Over two years later one expert accompanied by the Anti-Slavery Society Director conducted an eleven day mission to Mauritania and reported on the government's efforts to end traditional forced labor practices.[86]

The slavery Working Group's precise title misstates the comprehensive scope of its agenda. The group solicits and welcomes evidence on a great range of human rights violations including prostitution, bonded labor, female circumcision, child labor, colonialism, and the plight of the Biharis in Bangladesh.[87] Eastern bloc members of the Sub-Commission have challenged the group for exceeding its mandate, and the Soviet expert once disassociated himself from its report.[88] Although the group has gone far beyond the Third World concerns over *apartheid* that brought the slavery item to the Sub-Commission, a sympathetic majority has supported its work.

*Indigenous Populations.* In 1982 the Sub-Commission created a third permanent pre-sessional Working Group. The five members initially construed their mandate on indigenous populations broadly in order to provide a forum for those with grievances to raise complaints against governments. Representatives of several Indian organizations from the Americas attended the group's week-long meeting to argue that their peoples remained subject to colonial rule.[89] The Sub-Commission subsequently recommended, and ECOSOC approved, a United Nations Voluntary Fund for Indigenous Populations to fund travel by their representatives to the Working Group's meetings in Geneva.[90] Four of the group's five members, including its activist Chair Asbjørn Eide lost their seats on the Sub-Commission in 1984. Thereafter a reconstituted group chaired by expert Erica-Irene Daes determined that its mandate from ECOSOC was to draft a declaration on indigenous rights rather than to review specific complaints and allegations made against particular governments.[91]

With the creation of the third pre-sessional Working Group, fifteen of the Sub-Commission's twenty-six members (or their alternates) are scheduled for meetings in Geneva at least a week before the regular four-week session. For the Eastern European bloc, all three Sub-Commission experts must accept a working group assignment to achieve the necessary geographical balance. Some members served double duty at the 1982 session, and as a result of simultaneous Working Group meetings, the slavery Working Group often proceeded without a quorum.

*Rights of Detainees.* Since 1974 the full Sub-Commission has annually examined problems related to detention by reviewing materials compiled by the Secretariat from governments and NGOs. The agenda item on detainees has provided the full Sub-Commission with an opportunity to hear allegations of mistreatment by public officials and to draft standards to protect the imprisoned. On several occasions the experts have sent telegrams on behalf of individual detainees in Southern Africa. On the recommendation of the International Commission of Jurists the experts drafted a telegram to the government of Malawi in 1982 on behalf of a couple detained on charges of treason.[92]

In 1980 the Sub-Commission sought authorization for a pre-sessional Working Group to examine the rights of persons subjected to detention or imprisonment.[93] When the Commission failed to act, the Sub-Commission created a five member group to meet during the session. In 1983 the group had planned to conduct hearings on torture and to receive information directly from nongovernmental organizations,[94] but the Commission requested the members to await its approval. The Soviet member has challenged the very legality of the working group, a position supported by an ECOSOC procedural rule that prohibits the creation of intersessional bodies without prior Council approval.[95]

Notwithstanding the Commission's hesitations, the sessional Working Group on Detention, chaired by United States alternate John Carey, proceeded boldly in 1985. NGO representatives complained to the group that the Secretariat's synopsis of their complaints was meaningless, because the governments charged with abusing detainees were not identified. At the Chair's suggestion, the group decided that the original NGO materials would be available for their consideration. The group has proposed a declaration on unacknowledged detention calling on all governments to disclose the identity, location, and condition of all persons in custody. The French expert prepared a paper on administrative detention without charge or trial, and the chair made recommendations for preventing excessive use of force by law enforcement and military personnel.[96]

*Country-Specific Violations.* The agenda item on violations of human rights has become the primary vehicle for exposing human rights offenses. Unlike the Commission, the Sub-Commission has no separate agenda item on self-determination, so the members hear charges of colonialism and foreign intervention in conjunction with claims of individual rights violations. Resolution 1235 authorizes the Sub-Commission to "examine information relevant to gross violations of human rights" and permits the Commission to "make a thorough study of situations which reveal a consistent pattern of violations of human rights."[97]   The Sub-Commission's annual review of violations has taken between four and ten of the annual session's forty meetings. After NGO representatives, government observers and the members themselves publicly identify a large number of offending states, the Sub-Commission enacts resolutions involving the most serious cases.

During the first year of public debate on violations, Western experts sought to refer the cases of Greece and Haiti to the Commission. The non-aligned and Eastern bloc representatives on the Commission, however, opposed extending United Nations monitoring activity beyond the situations in Southern Africa and Israel. Only after the Commission took up the case of Chile in 1974 could the Sub-Commission begin meaningful review of situations in "all countries." By 1985 the Sub-Commission had enacted public resolutions naming twelve governments—Afghanistan, Albania, Argentina, Bolivia, El Salvador, Iran, Israel, Kampuchea, Malawi, Paraguay, South Africa, and Uganda. These Sub-Commission resolutions generally have included the same forms of condemnation and exhortation to reform that appear in Commission resolutions. In urgent situations the Sub-Commission has directed the Secretariat to telegraph objections to the governments of South Africa[98] and Iran.[99] When members of the Commission complained that the Sub-Commission had exceeded its mandate, the Sub-Commission asked the Commission's Chairman to send telegrams to South Africa[100] and to Israel[101] on its behalf. At other times the Sub-Commission designated special rapporteurs[102] to compile information about the situations in Kampuchea and Bolivia for presentation to the Commission. In 1985 the experts resolved to appoint a special rapporteur authorized to prepare annual lists of countries declaring, maintaining, or terminating states of emergency with an evaluation of whether any declarations violate international standards.[103]

Critics have complained that the Sub-Commission's proper function is to refer problems to others for resolution, rather than to replicate debates of the General Assembly and Commission. Observers form target states such as Argentina have accused the experts of partiality and have condemned Sub-Commission procedures. In response, the Sub-Commission convened in private session to draft a statement affirming the members' independence and rejecting efforts at intimidation.[104]   After Argentina won election for one of its own experts to the Sub-Commission, the views of its government were heard in both public and private sessions. Other Third World members such as Munir Akram of Pakistan have joined the Eastern bloc in opposing self-proclaimed independent experts from scrutinizing matters subject to domestic jurisdiction.

The Soviets profess a commitment to national sovereignty and a skepticism about "impartial" international tribunals and have repeatedly opposed efforts to invest the Sub-Commission with greater authority for enforcement.

## Relations with the Commission

Undissuaded by such opposition or by the Soviet expert's refusal to participate, in 1980 a large Sub-Commission majority proposed significant reforms of its procedures in order to improve monitoring of human rights violations. The members sought permission to meet twice a year in two week sessions, once in Geneva and one in New York.[105] They also sought authorization to vote by secret ballot and to be renamed "The Sub-Commission of the Commission on Human Rights."[106] In order to obtain material needed for their consideration of specific violations, the members proposed the establishment of an information-gathering service within the Secretariat.[107] They suggested various ways the members could assist the Commission and the General Assembly in responding to emergency situations that occurred between regular sessions.[108] John Carey of the United States authored a resolution that would have empowered the Chairman with the consent of the government charged, to select experts for country visits.[109]

In response to the Sub-Commission's sweeping proposals, some members of the Commission have sought to curtail the experts' growing independence. Carlos Calero Rodriques of Brazil insisted that his fellow government representatives devote several meetings of each Commission session to detailed consideration of the Sub-Commission report. His own thorough, critical analysis of the Sub-Commission's 1980 report identified practices and proposals that went beyond the established terms of reference.[110] He challenged the experts' authority to contact governments directly, to criticize their policies, and to impose costly research tasks on the Secretariat. He categorically rejected the Sub-Commission's unauthorized appointment of a rapporteur to brief the Commission on developments in Bolivia, although noting that similar briefings on Kampuchea by a Sub-Commission member had been approved by the General Assembly. The French government protested that the Sub-Commission had no right to demand explanations of why states had not ratified particular international human rights instruments. Other Western members criticized the appointment of government-designated alternates from the permanent missions to replace elected experts.[111] The Commission refused permission for a proposed visit by Sub-Commission members to Israeli prisons and ignored the experts' request for general authority to conduct visits. Nor has the Commission acted on the Sub-Commission's proposals for a new name, two meetings per year, secret voting procedures, fact-finding capability for the Secretariat, or two intersessional meetings of its bureau.

Despite its reluctance to support an expanded role for the Sub-Commission in 1981, the Commission did not at that time take any effective measures to restrict the experts. In a most gentle reprimand, the Commission resolution reminded the experts to recall their terms of reference and to take note of the comments of government representatives. The resolution expressed doubts about the participation of alternates and requested improvements in the Sub-Commission report to help the Commission to recognize priorities for action.[112] When selecting new members for the Sub-Commission in 1981 and 1984 the Commission has reelected several of the most independent members while removing several other activitists.

The ten new experts who joined the Sub-Commission in 1981 may have felt uncertain of their role and intimidated by criticism voiced in the Commission. Yet by the end of the newcomers' first session, the Sub-Commission had added a new item to its agenda: a review of its status and relationship with the Commission and other United Nations bodies. The following year the experts went into closed session to discuss their plans without intimidation by government observers. The summary records, later made public, indicate that the most ambitious members, such as Ahmed M. Khalifa of Egypt, wanted complete independence from the Commission. Nine members introduced a draft resolution that would have provided for direct reporting to ECOSOC.[113] Opponents argued that no matter what body served as parent, the experts would be subject to political control, and that in any event the Commission would never sanction an attempted divorce by its subsidiary organ. Another draft resolution introduced by five Western experts would have restricted the designation of alternates and required preparation of a five year work program.[114] The Sub-Commission voted thirteen to two with one abstention not to decide on either resolution. The Commission, however, later adopted the major provisions of the Western experts' resolution.[115]

Munir Akram and Halima Warzazi introduced a draft resolution to enlarge the communications working group to eight by adding Third World members.[116] A counter amendment proposed by Benjamin Whitaker to recommend secret votes by the working group led to a decision to defer consideration of both recommendations until the next session.[117] When John Carey reintroduced his proposal that the Sub-Commission be authorized to conduct country visits, Akram successfully amended the text to require Commission approval of each planned investigation.[118] The Sub-Commission's boldest resolution in 1982 proposed terms of reference that would have authorized a United Nations High Commissioner for Human Rights to collect information and respond to urgent situations.[119]

In response, the Commission returned the High Commissioner proposal for further study and enacted unusually decisive measures to control the Sub-Commission. In addition to restricting the designation of alternates to individuals elected with the experts, the Commission "discouraged" the Sub-

Commission from taking decisions affecting its status, role, and competence. That compromise provision represented a defeat for the Soviet Union which had introduced a resolution stripping the Sub-Commission of authority to consider its status.[120] The Eastern bloc also unsuccessfully opposed the new procedure limiting states' power to name alternates. The Soviets have favored decision-making by consensus to protect their minority interests, but were able to obtain only weak language urging the members to reach decisions by "the widest possible agreement."[121]

By 1983 the Western states which in 1950 had sought to abolish the Sub-Commission, had reversed roles with the Soviet Union by becoming its principal defender. Western members of the Commission sponsored language inviting the Sub-Commission to improve its effectiveness by adopting a five-year work programme that would establish clear priorities and rationalize its work methods.[122] Several Sub-Commission members, including the previous session's chairman A. S. Chowdhury, participated in the Commission debate as government representatives. Despite their presence, the Commission took no action on the recommendation for fact-finding missions, the proposed action program on child labor, or the proposed studies on female circumcision and updating of the emigration report. The Commission did request that rapporteurs limit the body of future studies to thirty-two pages and that the experts discontinue making requests to introduce the reports personally.[123]

When the General Assembly approved the Secretary-General's recommendation to postpone the Sub-Commission's 1986 meeting as an economy measure, NGO activists feared that the financial crisis would give governments an excuse to shut down the overly independent body. Brazil was reportedly advocating that a Commission working group or its bureau take over the screening of Resolution 1503 communications from the Sub-Commission.[124] At about the time the Sub-Commission would have held its late summer 1986 session, fifteen experts attended a privately funded three day meeting at the ILO offices convened by the NGO Special Committee on Human Rights in Geneva. The Working Group on Indigenous Populations had an unoffical session, and another working group discussed relations between the Sub-Commission and the Commission. The World Council on Indigenous Populations and the Anti-Slavery Society intended to submit the results of the unofficial meetings as NGO documents when the Sub-Commission convened its next regular session.[125] As the General Assembly considered recommendations for major retrenchment in the fall of 1986, NGO representatives feared that the Sub-Commission would be a casualty. A group of 18 experts considered reducing the number of ECOSOC meetings from three to one per year, and scheduling subsidiary bodies on a biennial basis.[126]

"Harmonization, complementarity and co-ordination" were the key terms of one Commission invitation to the Sub-Commission to recommend ways to improve their relationship. The disharmony dates back to the Sub-

Commission's birth and appears inevitable given the composition of the two bodies. Genuinely independent experts with aspirations to construct a supra-national mechanism for the enforcement of human rights norms will seek to make the Sub-Commission an impartial forum for investigating violations. Government representatives just as certainly will protect their national interests by circumscribing the independence of experts who scrutinize state policies. A representative of the United Kingdom aptly characterized the relationship from his governmental perspective:

> States [are] understandably jealous of their autonomy and consequently insistent on the primacy of intergovernmental organs. The Sub-Commission and the Commission must build a mutually sympathetic and supportive relationship, with the Sub-Commission as the prized, spirited, independent and perhaps occasionally recalcitrant first child of the Commission. The Commission would be a poor parent if it expected that first child to be consistently obsequious and never to try to stretch its license. And the Sub-Commission would, in turn, be ill-advised if it sought to renounce its benevolent and sympathetic natural parent, the Commission, and to put itself up for adoption by that relatively obscure and money-minded body, the Economic and Social Council.[127]

Given the existing United Nations hierarchy, those experts seeking meaningful independence from political control have little chance of success. They have nevertheless pushed the capacity of the Sub-Commission far beyond the narrow confines of its original mandate. In doing so they have provided a valuable forum for nongovernmental organizations and have compelled governments to respond to human rights complaints. Apparently Eastern bloc officials considered Sub-Commission deliberation so threatening that they arranged to have all criticisms of two countries deleted from the Summary Records of meetings in 1977.[128] For nearly forty years significant political divisions have prevented the Commission from dominating the Sub-Commission. Perhaps the financial emergency will either make the Sub-Commission expendable or preclude the type of independence previously enjoyed. If allowed to do so, the Sub-Commission will undoubtedly strive to remain a quasi-independent agent with some ability to shape its own agenda.

# 9

# Politics, Impact, and
# Future Prospects

Commentary assessing the Commission on Human Rights is often as
intemperate as the rhetorical excesses made by its members in general debate.
American critics have made the sharpest attacks, venting their greatest anger
prior to 1980 and since then against the U.N. in general and the Assembly in
particular. The Commission's harshest critics claim that unfair procedures have
been manipulated to subvert democratic governments and fundamental rights.
The Commission's defenders lament its limited impact on government practice
and propose a variety of structural reforms. Commenting on the Commission's
credibility and authority, the Chair in 1986 warned of a "lack of confidence" and
"growing skepticism."[1] This final chapter separately addresses charges that the
Commission has been partisan and ineffective before drawing conclusions about
its future prospects.

## POLITICAL RESPONSIBILITIES AND PARTISAN EVILS

### Political Eras

Three of the four periods in the Commission's growth described in the
preceding chapters are differentiated by a distinctive political balance. Western
members dominated in the first two stages prior to 1967. A United States
delegate served as Chair for six consecutive sessions, and no Eastern bloc
member ever held that office. The Soviets were excluded from the initial three-
member drafting committee for the Universal Declaration, and two anti-
American NGOs were stripped of their consultative status. The Peoples
Republic of China was blocked from membership, the Asian region was
generally underrepresented, and there was no black African representative before
1964. The Commission adopted and followed the United States sponsored
"Action Plan" giving top priority to political and civil rights.

The increase to thirty-two members in 1967 entailed membershp quotas for five geo-political regions and systematic rotation of officers. The dominant Afro-Asian members initiated new protection measures, made self-determination and racial equality priority agenda items, and systematically attacked Western colonialism. Eastern bloc client states in the Third World influenced the non-aligned coalition to attack anticommunist regimes in Latin America. Relegated to minority status, Western members suffered systematic attacks on multi - national corporations and European-based NGOs. Prior to 1978 Daniel Moynihan characterized the U.N. as a tool manipulated by totalitarian regimes to undermine Western democracies.[2]

The political balance tipped once again, however, when the membership increased to forty-three in 1980, and a more complex voting pattern emerged. Bloc voting at the United Nations has never corresponded perfectly with the many regional and other caucusing groups. Within the Western group, the Benelux and Scandinavian countries have had separate caucuses, as have NATO members. Within the African regional caucus, the former Brazzaville group of primarily French speaking countries has a distinctive voting pattern, as have several conservative Arab governments. Former colonial links appear in the Commonwealth caucus and occasional voting agreement among Spanish-speaking members. Voting studies in the General Assembly have generally found the folllowing eight overlapping blocs with degrees of agreement ranging from 75 to 100 percent: Old Europeans, Latin, Soviet, Arab, Casablanca group, Brazzaville group, Africans, and Asians.[2] Although the same bloc alignments appear in Commission votes, the Western members have a higher and the African and Asian members a lower proportion of the total than in the Assembly.

Despite the changes begun after 1980, Western critics continued to indict the United Nations human rights program on several counts. Jack Donnelly asserted that it has twisted basic concepts beyond comprehension by giving priority to economic and collective rights over individual civil liberties.[4] By contrast, Third World observers note a preoccupation with Western civil liberties concerns. United States Ambassador Jeane Kirkpatrick denounced the partisan, anti-American approach dictated by Soviet bloc and radical Third World states hostile to Western concepts of individual civil and political rights.[5] The Reagan administration shared Moynihan's view that an anti-democratic, anti-Western majority of human rights offenders perversely attacks governments whose citizens enjoy greater freedom. Academic observers complained of selective enforcement and double standards. Thomas Franck contrasted the Commission's severe attack on Chile's violations with its innocuous response to similar abuses in Poland.[6]

In the period after 1980, has the Commission improperly subordinated individual to collective rights, political and civil to economic and social rights? Have the members demonstrated a consistent anti-democratic, anti-Western bias?

Has a partisan double standard corrupted the Commission's enforcement program?  Several objective, quantitative measures are available to answer these questions, but in each case it is necessary to make separate calculations about the Commission's distinct activities in standard-setting, in promotion, and in enforcement.

## Responsible    Political    Policymaking

*Standard-Setting and Promotion*

Judging by the time spent in drafting and the norms adopted, the Commission appears to have given higher priority to Western sponsored political and civil than to Third World initiated economic and social standards. The Universal Declaration and the two Covenants give nearly equal consideration to economic rights, but create more effective enforcement procedures for civil liberties.  The conventions on race discrimination and *apartheid* affirm the rights of groups as well as individuals, but give no special priority to economic concerns.  The most recently adopted norms on torture and religious intolerance were primarily Western initiatives, while standard-setting efforts by Poland and Yugoslavia on children and minorities had not been successful by 1986.  The consensus decision-making procedure delayed and weakened the 1986 Declaration on Development.  If any standard-setting priority exists, the Commission has given the greatest attention to individual civil and political rights.

Promotional activities most easily quantified include: seminars, fellowships, advisory services, publications, studies, and resolutions of exhortation.  Much of the Commission's general debate, several priority agenda headings, and many of its hortatory resolutions stress the primacy of economic and collective rights. After the 1950s seminars on criminal procedure and women's rights, the most recent conferences have supported self-determination, economic development, and the two decades against race discrimination.  Special units in the Secretariat deal with *apartheid*, Palestinians, and transnational corporations.  United Nations publications campaign against South Africa and Israel.  Judging by the disproportionate meeting time devoted to economic and collective rights, proponents of civil liberties dismiss as empty rhetoric resolutions proclaiming the interdependence and indivisibility of all rights.

United Nations promotional activities are not, however, exclusively devoted to economic and collective issues.  Perhaps because other Secretariat operations have preempted those concerns, the Centre for Human Rights allocates more budgetary and staff resources to political and civil rights.  The legal experts dispatched to advise Third World governments have given top priority to legislation for democratic institutions and for impartial judicial procedures.  The planned training courses will provide similar instruction.  More fellowship recipients have studied political and civil than economic and social rights. Supplies of United Nations publications on the Universal Declaration and political and civil standards considerably exceed those on *apartheid* and the race decade, some of which are completely out of stock.[7] Although the Secretariat has followed Commission directives to prepare studies on economic rights, the Sub-Commission experts have often disregarded such requests and most of their research deals with political and individual rights.

*Enforcement Priorities*

Commission practice reveals several common features that distinguish situations identified as gross violations from other human rights offenses that have been disregarded. The Commission's top concerns have been colonialism, foreign domination, racism, *apartheid*, mass political detention, arbitrary execution, involuntary disappearances, and torture. The complaints most frequently rejected, and the reported violations least often presented to the Commission, involve minority groups seeking equal treatment or internal self-determination, economic suffering, and individual liberties—speech, press, religion, and assembly.

*Self-Determination and Minority Rights.* The members initially gave top priority to assuring the right of subject people's to self-determination. For the first five years, the Commission's resolutions on self-determination challenged only foreign occupation by Israel and alien domination in Southern Africa. Israel's settlements in the West Bank, annexation of Jerusalem, occupation of the Golan Heights, and 1982 intervention in Lebanon claimed even higher priority than South Africa's rule of Namibia. By 1984 the smaller non-aligned members' overriding commitment to territorial integrity and non-intervention prompted other challenges to foreign occupation by Third World and Eastern bloc states in Afghanistan, Kampuchea, Western Sahara, and East Timor.

While the Commission has fairly consistently supported freedom from external domination, the members have never recognized a right to internal self-determination. The United Nations law of self-determination elaborated by General Assembly resolutions  does not include a Western supported universal right of all peoples to internal, democratic self-government based on citizen consent. Rather, the Non-Aligned Movement (NAM) and Soviet bloc members have stressed freedom from external colonial or alien domination. United Nations resolutions require internal self-determination only when ruling European settler populations deny equal rights to indigenous racial groups.

Once colonial or alien domination has ended, the U.N. law of self-determination stresses non-intervention and territorial integrity. After independence, dissident or minority groups have no general right to self-determination against oppressive indigenous rulers. United Nations resolutions have consistently rejected the right of secession by minorities in newly independent countries. The new state, however, has full sovereign right to control its natrual resources and to determine its political system free of foreign interference.[8]  Secessionist groups—Eritreans in Ethiopia, Kurds in Iraq, Armenians in Turkey, Tamils in Sri Lanka, Ibos in Nigeria, Bengalis in East Pakistan—have had no recognized right of self-determination that would divide their countries.

As originally applied, gross violations of human rights meant the persecution of a particular racial, religious or nationality *group*, rather than denial of *individual* rights. The NAM would only approve United Nations scrutiny of domestic affairs when the political rights violations affected peoples subject to alien domination. Non-aligned and Soviet bloc members added the item on violations to the Commission agenda in order to protect nonwhites and Arabs from South African *apartheid* and Israeli practices in the occupied territories. Even after expanding its enforcement agenda, the Commission has not effectively responded to flagrant equal rights violations for the Hutus in Burundi, Jews in the U.S.S.R. and Syria, Armenians in Turkey, Kurds in Iraq, Jehovah's Witnesses in Malawi, Meskito Indians in Nicaragua, and Tamils in Sri Lanka. The Commission took no action against Japan when the Sub-Commission referred a complaint on behalf of Korean immigrants victimized by discrimination.  Public resolutions supporting the Baha'is of Iran and confidential intervention on behalf of Paraguay's Ache Indians are notable exceptions. Out of deference to national unity, the Commission appears as unlikely to assert collective group rights, especially for large minorities, as it has been to accept internal self-determination.

*Civil Liberties.* The freedoms of speech, press, religion, and assembly enshrined in the First Amendment to the United States Constitution also have a low priority in the Commission's enforcement program.  Third World states value collective economic growth ahead of individual liberties, and even Western European states curtail free speech and assembly in time of emergency. Muslim governments such as Morocco do not allow Christian proselytizing, and the Sudan has applied Koranic criminal penalties to non-Muslims. Religious persecution is condemned in principle, but in practice the Commission has not vigorously championed the free exercise of religion or separation of church and state.  Nor has the Commission considered press censorship, voting irregu - larities, property seizures, and restrictions on travel sufficient to warrant a United Nations response.[9]

Instead, the Commission has accorded top priority to the fundamental civil rights of life and freedom from detention and torture. Several common factors distinguish those situations that have prompted formal investigation from those violations occurring after 1980 that the Commission has treated briefly or ignored. While members and NGO representatives publicly denounce offenses as varied as religious discrimination and forced labor, those cases have not lead to formal investigation. To warrant sustained consideration by a designated investigator the situation must normally involve massive torture, kidnapping, and/or killing by government agents over a long period. The complaints formally reviewed have charged mistreatment of prisoners, arbitrary political detention, torture, summary execution, and related political and civil rights violations.

Three-fourths of the situations under confidential review involve political detention, half of which reach the extremes of torture, mass killing, and summary execution. In situations reviewed confidentially by the Commission thousands of victims have suffered barbarous atrocities. *Agence France Presse* reported 21,121 political prisoners in Turkey after the military coup.[10] Observers accused Paraguay of conducting genocide against a small Indian tribe.[11] Authorities of the Central African Empire killed over 100 children between the ages of eight and sixteen after a student demonstration.[12] Political dissidents in Argentina, Paraguay, and Uruguay disappeared by the thousands, and their families continue to search in vain. The Indonesian regime issued a manual instructing soldiers to conceal their acts of torture.[13] The governments of Haiti, Paraguay, and Equatorial Guinea have been charged with forcing workers to labor under slave-like conditions.

Publicly targeted regimes are ordinarily small, politically isolated governments charged with abuse of power against domestic adversaries who enjoy greater international support. Unpopular regimes that repeatedly suppress public demonstrations or rebellions with extreme measures are the most likely candidates for special investigatory procedures. Ironically, members who deny the existence of any internationally recognized right to internal self-determination most frequently protect individuals seeking more power in public affairs through enforcement of fundamental political rights. As public demonstrations have progressed to armed insurrection, the Commission has examined situations in Southern Africa, the Israeli occupied territories, Nicaragua, Equatorial Guinea, Guatemala, El Salvador, and Poland. When oppressive regimes lost power in Bolivia, Nicaragua, and Portugal's African colonies, the public investigation was normally concluded, despite some evidence of continued violations by Mozambique, Zimbabwe, and Sandinista officials. In Equatorial Guinea, Kampuchea, and Uganda, however, violations by the new regime have remained under review, as the Commission sought to assist in establishing rights guarantees.

Other investigations began when new rulers seized or consolidated power with brutal means; supporters of the former government then find political allies on the Commission, especially when cold war loyalties are involved. New governments in Chile, Kampuchea, Bolivia, Iran, and Afghanistan have been investigated for mistreating "counter revolutionaries" or others deemed a threat to their new repressive order.

Despite the strident rhetoric about balancing economic and political rights, the gross violations identified have involved considerably more political than economic injustice. The country rapporteurs deal in greatest depth with arbitrary arrest, detention, and mistreatment of political dissidents. Although the rapporteurs have scrutinized labor policies in South Africa, Chile, and Poland, the ILO handles most workers' complaints. All four global procedures initiated since 1980 deal with political and civil rights violations, and no thematic approaches to economic rights have even been proposed. Mass starvation in Africa has not sparked any measures to implement a right to food.[14] Instead, the United Nations responded to the emergency through traditional development and relief agencies rather then through the human rights program. Similarly, complaints about forced labor, particularly involving children, have not prompted a response unless the violation also involved mass killing or another top priority.

Staff assignments and expenditures in the Centre for Human Rights provide another measure of Commission priorities. In the 1980s the Centre employed forty-eight regular professional staff in three main sections whose functions roughly parallel the Commission's program areas: (a) Research, Studies and Prevention of Discrimination (Standard-Setting); (b) Advisory Services and Publications (Promotion); and (c) International Instruments and Procedures (Implementation and Protection). The sections not only managed Commission and Sub-Commission programs, but also served the Human Rights Committee, the Committee on the Elimination of Racial Discrimination and committees of ECOSOC and the General Assembly. Table 9.1 shows how the distribution of professional staff and budget allocations correspond to recent Commission priorities with the largest share going to implementation. The Centre had a $10.2 million biennial regular appropriation for 1982–83. In addition to the Centre's direct costs, the U.N. apportioned another $18 million of administrative overhead expenses to human rights activities for facilities, conference servicing, public information, management, etc., in the 1982–83 biennium.[15]

There are no separate line items in the Centre's regular budget to indicate the cost of different programs, nor does the Commission have its own budget. Commission requests that require supplemental appropriations do, however, allow comparison of relative expenditure levels for special projects. Table 9.2 presents Secretariat estimates of its supplemental budgetary requirements to satisfy Commission requests made for 1982. The raw estimates are based on the maximum foreseeable costs, and U.N. budget committees granted less than the $684,100 estimate. Revised appropriations added $540,600 in 1982 and $415,000 in 1983, increasing the Centre's $10.2 million budget for the biennium by about 10%.[16] The figures in Table 9.2 further illustrate the Centre's fiscal priorities in program management. Over eighty percent of the re - quested budget additions and all the temporary staff were sought for fact-finding and implementation efforts involving primarily civil and political rights.

TABLE 9.1
Personnel and Budget Priorities at the
U.N. Centre for Human Rights, August 1982

| Sections | Professional Posts Permanent | Temporary | Regular Budget Share 1982–83 |
|---|---|---|---|
| Office of the Director | 8 | | |
| International Instruments+Procedures  1 | 18 | | 40% |
| International Instruments Unit  6 | | | |
| Communications Unit  8 | | | |
| Special Procedures Unit  4 | | 5 | |
| Research, Studies + Discrimination  1 | 11 | | 24% |
| Research and Studies Unit  5 | | | |
| Prevention of Discrimination Unit  5 | | | |
| Advisory Services and Publications  1 | 7 | | 18% |
| Advisory Services Unit  3 | | | |
| Documentation + Publications Unit | | | |
| Task Force, Decade to Combat Racism  2 | 2 | 1 | 18% |
| Total | 48 | 6 | 100% |

Note: Figures do not include clerical staff (33), temporary professionals, and supplementary budget allocations not included in regular $10.2 million biennial budget.  See Table 9.2.

## Political Values and Policy Priorities

Western observers complain of imbalance, object to a preoccupation with racism, and lament the Commission's disregard for free speech.  Non-Western and some European critics, by contrast, object that the Commission deals with symptoms, disregarding the fundamental economic causes of torture, kidnapping, mass murder, and related civil liberties violations.  Impoverished nations want something more than a United Nations Commission on Civil Rights.  Their representatives fear that Western concern for violations of individual liberties and property rights in new states merely conceals new forms of economic control by former colonial powers.

Unequivocal evidence that the Commission has favored economic rights, or conversely has given priority to political rights, would not in any event discredit its program.  In any legal order, society must establish value priorities about which rights to protect by law and which violations to punish most severely.  The international community is even more ideologically divided than its constituent members, therefore attempts to enforce universal human rights exacerbate fundamental political differences.  The three main blocs profoundly disagree about which human rights violations should be the top enforcement priority.  Afro-Asians regard racism as the paramount evil and freedom from foreign occupation as the foremost goal.  Some Westerners, particularly in the

TABLE 9.2
Secretariat Estimates of Supplementary Expenditures
Required to Meet Commission Requests for 1982
(In thousands of U.S. dollars)

| Function | Centre | Conference Services |
|---|---|---|
| **Implementation and Protection** | | |
| Disappearances Working Group | 181.0 | 238.9 |
| South Africa Experts | 121.1 | 363.8 |
| Chile, Special Rapporteur | 101.0 | 390.8 |
| Poland | 29.9 | |
| El Salvador | 45.0 | |
| Guatemala | 44.5 | |
| Bolivia | 32.8 | |
| Summary Executions Rapporteur | 24.7 | |
| Mauritania (Sub-Commission) | 8.7 | |
| | | |
| **Standard Setting** | | |
| Right to Development, Working Group | | 191.2 |
| Rights of the Child, Working Group | | 35.4 |
| Torture Convention, Working Group | | 34.9 |
| Indigenous Peoples WG (Sub-Commission) | 2.6 | 38.8 |
| | | |
| **Promotion** | | |
| Seminar on Rights of Palestinians | 90.9 | 232.6 |
| Publishing Sub-Commission Study | 1.9 | 151.3 |
| Total | 684.1 | 1677.7 |

Source: P. Malone, Senior Administrative Officer, Centre for Human Rights

United States, consider atheistic communism the foremost threat to fundamental rights. The Soviet bloc perceives capitalist economies as the unparalleled injustice. Given those inconsistent social and economic perspectives, setting enforcement priorities inevitably requires political compromise.

Critics who object that the Commission is politicized disapprove when governments attempt to enhance national power without regard for human rights. While that form of politicized decision-making deserves reproach, the Commission cannot avoid other "political" decisions required for establishing enforcement criteria. By necessity, the Commission has made value judgments that certain rights, such as self-determination and the right to life, merit more protection than others. Indeed, all enforcement regimes are selective to some degree, and no national system has achieved perfectly even handed prosecution. As Republicans replaced Democrats in the United States Justice Department, for example, enforcement priorities changed; federal prosecutors discontinued some investigations while selecting a few different targets. The Commission's selective enforcement similarly reflects shifting political accommodations between East and West, North and South.

Those who strongly disagree with the resulting policy choices should not reproach the Commission for making political decisions establishing human rights priorities. That task is the organization's preeminent political responsibility. Critics should be able to favor and to campaign for an alternative set of priorities without insisting that the Commission maintain a nonpartisan balance which treats all rights equally. In a diverse world of competing ideologies, no conceivable balance would satisfy all; complaints of distorted priorities are unavoidable. Vocal dissatisfaction with the priorities established indicates that the Commission has performed its most important responsibility, not that it has violated some higher law against political decision-making.

Western indictments of the Commission, however, also allege political corruption of a different type. Even democratically governed organizations forfeit their legitimacy when an overbearing majority systematically disregards minority interests or when the standards proclaimed are selectively applied only to the politically weak and unpopular. Such political favoritism differs significantly from the legitimate political judgments about which rights deserve the most protection. Has a partisan majority spared its friends and skewered its foes under an egregious double standard?

## Partisan Political Favoritism

### Selective Enforcement and Disparate Treatment

Granting the propriety of favoring external self-determination over minority rights and the right to life over freedom of association, the Commission has been selective in enforcing its values. Characterizing "gross" violations, no less than judging "beauty," depends on the eye of the beholder. Has the Commission fairly distinguished those situations that merit United Nations action from violations that do not? When responding to similar violations, has the Commission been lenient with the politically favored while selectively penalizing others? Unlike a national court, the Commission does not fix prison sentences of varying length that would permit observers readily to identify disparate treatment for similar offenses. Instead, the Commission enhances penalties by:

- proceeding from confidential treatment to public resolutions of exhortation
- appointing an investigatory rapporteur and requesting extra-budgetary support for Secretariat staff
- creating a separate agenda item on the situation
- devoting more meeting time to speeches of condemnation
- adopting several resolutions denouncing the same government
- referring the situation to the Assembly for further action

TABLE 9.3
Varied Responses to Different Situations

| Type of Violation Alleged | |
|---|---|
| Self-Determination | Killing, Disappearances, Torture, Detention |

**Isolation**
South Africa--Namibia     South Africa
Israel--Arab lands        Israel

**Investigation/Condemnation**
Vietnam--Kampuchea     Chile, El Salvador, Guatemala, Bolivia,
USSR--Afghanistan           Nicaragua (1979)
                             Afghanistan, Iran
                             Poland
                             Equatorial Guinea

**Exhortation/Conciliation**
Public Resolution
    Morocco--West Sahara     Haiti, Paraguay
    Indonesia--East Timor    Sri Lanka
    Turkey--Cyprus           Malawi, Uganda
    U. S.--Grenada

Confidential Monitoring
                             Argentina, Uruguay
                             Benin, Central African Republic, Ethiopia,
                                 Gabon, Malawi, Mozambique, Uganda, Zaire,
                             Indonesia, Malaysia, Pakistan, Philippines,
                                 South Korea
                             Albania, German Democratic Republic
                             Greece, Turkey, United Kingdom

Thematic Reports
                             Angola, Cameroon, Chad, Comoros, Ghana,
                                 Guinea, Lesotho, Liberia, Libya,
                                 Mauritania,
                             Morocco, Nigeria, Somalia, Sudan, Togo
                             Bangladesh, Cyprus, India, Iraq, Kuwait,
                                 Lebanon, Syria, Thailand, Arab Emirates
                             Belize, Colombia, Ecuador, Honduras, Mexico,
                                 Nicaragua, Peru, Suriname,
                             U.S.S.R.

NOTE: Many states subject to several different procedures are listed only once, in the highest classification identifying the Commission's most severe level of response.

The sanctions identified above permit a rough three part classification of the Commission's varied responses to the more than seventy situations addressed between 1979 and 1986. Fifty-seven governments received the most lenient treatment—conciliatory review in confidential proceedings or exhortation in gently worded public resolutions. Eleven governments became subjects of public investigation and resolutions of condemnation. The Commission has applied its most severe penalties of isolation in only two cases. Table 9.3 differentiates the Commission's responses by degree of severity identifying at each level the countries charged either with denying self-determination or with committing torture, execution, and arbitrary detention.

The table display is designed to overcome the inadequacy of selective two state comparisons made by critics who contrast, for example, the Commission's lenient approach to Poland and severe reproach of Chile. The comprehensive classification presented permits a more systematic analysis of the relationship between the extent of a violation and the severity (or absence) of the Commission's response. The classifications made, however, remain imprecise, since the Commission has not treated similarly all situations grouped at the same level. At the investigatory level for example the Commission has had thoroughly critical reports on Afghanistan but no meaningful inquiry whatever from the first few rapporteurs in Iran. Despite that imprecision, the table display offers an improved tool to assess selective enforcement and disparate treatment.

The three distinct response levels identified reveal clearly unjustified disparities in treatment of similar situations. The Commission has most strongly condemned Israel's seizure of Arab lands and South Africa's retention of Namibia, but has barely reproached Indonesia and Morocco for their conquest of East Timor and Western Sahara. The Commission made no objection at all to interventions by Tanzania in Uganda and India in East Pakistan, in part because the military incursions did not lead to permanent occupation.

Extensive disappearances and mass killings elicited major public investigations of Chile, El Salvador, and Guatemala but only confidential monitoring of Argentina and Uganda. When Lebanese Christians attacked the Sabra and Shatila Palestinian refugee camps, the Commission denounced Israel's occupation forces. When Amal Shiite Muslims attacked the same camps, the Commission remained silent. The Commission exposed widespread detention and torture in Afghanistan, Chile, and Iran but gave minimal attention to similar situations in Paraguay, Ethiopia, Haiti, and Indonesia. The Commission has condemned to the utmost South Africa's forced relocation of blacks from urban shantytowns to segregated tribal "homelands." Forced relocation undertaken by Third World governments for urban renewal purposes has been ignored.

Selective enforcement appears less serious than disparate treatment, but the Commission has obviously disregarded several major situations in each category. The members have not, for example, addressed United States intervention in Nicaragua, killings in Syria and Zimbabwe, political detention in the Soviet Union, and widespread persecution in Iraq. Well publicized violations in Lebanon, Vietnam, and Pakistan have been largely disregarded, as have assassinations advocated by Libya. While the Commission has in one form or another now reviewed most of the truly egregious violations, a few offenders have still escaped scrutiny.

*East vs. West, North vs. South*

While NGO activitists count victims, most Commission members apparently count allies or trading partners. Political calculations by the non-aligned members largely explain the disparate treatment and selective enforcement. The loose coalition dominated by African and Asian governments has blocked serious criticism of its members, approved investigations of Latin American non-members, and subjected its adversaries to the most severe attack. Initially concerned solely with terminating foreign domination of Southern Africa and occupied Arab lands, the NAM attacked violations of life and liberty only when South Africa and Israel denied those rights along with self-determination. Suspected American intervention against a new NAM leader in Chile in part explains non-aligned support for the first investigation that became primarily concerned with disappearances, torture, and mass killing. An NAM majority severely condemned the Soviet intervention in Afghanistan, and expressed less objection to the United States brief intervention in Grenada and limited involvement in Nicaragua. When NAM members Morocco and Indonesia committed aggression, the Commission's response has been quite muted. What might be defended as humanitarian interventions by NAM members Tanzania in Uganda and India in East Pakistan, elicited no response whatever.

NAM solidarity helps but does not fully explain the Commission's double standard in responding to disappearances, torture, and killing. Western European governments pressed the Commission to investigate such situations, while the NAM and Soviet bloc shielded their members and allies but approved investigations of others. As a result, the Commission dealt most severely with Latin American regimes outside the NAM—Bolivia, El Salvador, Guatemala, Nicaragua, Paraguay, and Haiti. Equally serious allegations against NAM members Argentina, Ethiopia, Indonesia, Pakistan, and Uganda were considered only in confidential proceedings. NGO efforts to obtain Commission review of other NAM members such as Sri Lanka, Sudan, and Iraq have all been fruitless.[17] Afghanistan and Iran have been the only NAM members subjected to significant public scrutiny, as the members have not united to defend those regimes.

Neither the budget allocations shown in Table 9.3 nor an analysis of Commission voting confirms Western complaints that the non-aligned function in lock step with the Eastern bloc. East and South have combined against the West most dramatically on South Africa and the Middle East, virtually to the exclusion of other concerns prior to 1980. Since that date, however, the West has found Southern support against the East in some situations, and has even received Soviet support on Iran.[18] The Commission has challenged undemocratic practices by both pro- and anti-Western governments, and has reviewed both right-wing regimes (Turkey, The Republic of (South) Korea, the Philippines, Paraguay) and totalitarian, Marxist states (Ethiopia, Afghanistan,

German Democratic Republic). Of the governments reviewed in the 1503 procedure, it appears that about twice as many are anticommunist as pro-Soviet regimes. The Soviet bloc, however, has been unable to terminate the Resolution 1503 procedures, could not win approval for an advisory services seminar on peace, fruitlessly opposed new procedures on torture and religious intolerance, and regularly suffered defeats on Afghanistan and Kampuchea.

The Commission has criticized United States' policies on self-determination for Palestinians and Namibia, but not its interventions in Vietnam, Grenada, or Nicaragua. The United States nevertheless objects that its allies, especially in Latin America, suffer disproportionately harsh attack. However, other United States allies—Morocco, Indonesia, Pakistan, and Turkey—have largely been spared. Commission response to violations by Soviet clients has been similarly uneven. The situations in Afghanistan and Kampuchea have been among the most severely criticized, but the Commission did little about Ethiopia, East Germany, and Poland. Rapporteurs for two thematic procedures have shown somewhat greater deference to the United States than to the Soviet Union. The torture rapporteur noted that the U.S.S.R. disputed his authority when he had inquired about alleged abuse. Without mentioning that the United States had raised similar jurisdictional objections to his inquiry about two death sentences, the rapporteur on summary and arbitrary executions simply noted "several instances" where youths received capital punishment for crimes committed when they were under eighteen years of age, contrary to Political Covenant provisions.[19]

The United States applied its own double standard by leading the campaign against Poland and opposing the attack on Chile.[20] The NATO allies proposed resolutions on mistreatment of Andrei Sakharov by the Soviet Union, which countered with resolutions on Northern Ireland and the United States. In 1980 the Commission postponed a decision on the rival items.[21] In a notable exception, the Sub-Commission considered complaints agianst the United Kingdom's torture of prisoners in Northern Ireland.

Undoubtedly United States adversaries have viewed the inquiries on El Salvador, Bolivia, and Guatemala as political victories, but Western European members and NATO allies Canada and the Netherlands have both supported and co-sponsored the authorizing resolutions. In order to examine the regional balance in Commission enforcement decisions since 1980, roll call votes involving nine situations are examined. Table 9.4 illustrates that the Com-mission has investigated a balanced selection of targets, in each case with support drawn from competing regional or ideological blocs.

Four of the five Eastern European states[22] form the tightest voting bloc with the support of pro-Soviet governments in Cuba, Ethiopia, Mozambique, Nicaragua, and Syria. United by a radical socialist ideology and anti-Western animus, the bloc usually controls a solid seven to ten votes. Soviet representatives have asserted that all law must serve a political purpose; their

TABLE 9.4
Support for Review by Region

| Target State Resolution | Introduced By | Vote | Votes in Favor (Region Members) | | | | |
|---|---|---|---|---|---|---|---|
| | | | Africa *(11) | Asia (9) | East (5) | Latin (8) | West (10) |
| South Africa Res. 1982/8 | Zimbabwe | 42-0-1 | 11 | 9 | 5 | 8 | 9 |
| Israel Res. 1982/1 | Cuba | 32-1-9 | 10 | 8 | 5 | 8 | 1 |
| Latin-American Anti-Communist | | | | | | | |
| Chile Res. 1982/25 | Mexico | 28-6-8 | 10 | 2 | 5 | 2 | 9 |
| El Salvador Res. 1982/28 | Mexico | 25-5-13 | 10 | 3 | 5 | 2 | 5 |
| Guatemala Res. 1982/31 | Netherlands | 29-2-12 | 10 | 3 | 5 | 2 | 9 |
| Paraguay Conf. Res (1983) | 1503 Group | 34-3-5 | 9 | 5 | 5 | 5 | 10 |
| Non-Aligned | | | | | | | |
| Equatorial Guinea Conf. Res (1979) | | 20-6-6 | 5**(8) | 3(6) | 0(4) | 4(6) | 8(8) |
| Indonesia Conf. Res. (1983) | 1503 Group | 15-13-2 | 8 | 1 | 0 | 3 | 3 |
| Iran Res. 1982/27 | West | 19-9-15 | 4 | 2 | 0 | 3 | 10 |
| Eastern Pro-Soviet | | | | | | | |
| Afghanistan Res. 1984/55 | Sub-Comm. | 27-8-6 | 9 | 6 | 0 | 3 | 9 |
| E. Germany Conf. Res. (1981) | 1503 Group | 19-14-9 | 3 | 2 | 0 | 4 | 10 |
| Kampuchea Res. 29(XXXVI) (1980) | Australia | 20-9-6 | 6 | 3 | 0 | 3 | 8 |
| Poland Res. 1982/26 | West | 19-13-10 | 2 | 3 | 0 | 4 | 10 |
| Religion Rapp. Res. 1986/20 | U.S. | 26-5-12 | 7 | 3 | 0 | 6 | 10 |

NOTE: Numbers in ( ) indicate the total number of seats allocated to the regional group in the session adopting the resolution: *( ) after and **( ) before 1980.

voting record demonstrates an unswerving commitment to partisan advantage without regard for consistent application of neutral standards.

With twenty-three members in 1986, the non-aligned coalition is the largest, but also the least cohesive group; African, Asian, Arab, and Latin American states joined by Yugoslavia concur on decolonization and race discrimination issues but frequently split over investigations of torture, kidnapping, and mass killing in their different regions. Eleven non-aligned members voted for a rapporteur on religious intolerance, and an equal number abstained. The Western bloc of ten has united in support of anti-Soviet investigations and in opposition to the most extreme anti-Western resolutions. The group has initiated investigations of several Third World offenders, and has disagreed over other initiatives sponsored by the non-aligned. Several Latin American and Pacific countries outside the non-aligned movement, such as Costa Rica, Venezuela, and the Philippines, normally vote with the West, and Japan meets with the Western caucus.

Whatever their ideological persuasion, the most partisan members split predictably on East-West and North-South lines; with no regard for consistency, they favor investigation of their adversaries while defending their allies from inquiry. The same delegates alternately profess indignation at gross violations of human rights by their foes, and then defend allies by complaining of selective enforcement, double standards, and unlawful political intervention in domestic matters. None of the representatives have shown a consistent interpretation of Charter Article 2(7) by a principled opposition to all enforcement procedures.

If the Soviet view of national self-interest is correct, then no government would see any advantage in supporting investigations favored by an ideological foe. Nevertheless, a few governments' voting records do reflect an internationalist policy. The roll call votes displayed in Table 9.4 in 1984 reveal occasional departures form strict partisan voting that had decisive impact. Ideological considerations have not prevented France, the United Kingdom, and other Western governments form challenging violations by the anticommunist regimes of South Africa, Chile, Nicaragua, Bolivia, Guatemala, and El Salvador. Five of the ten Western members supported an investigation of El Salvador's anticommunist government, two Latin American members favored the inquiries on Chile and Guatemala, and eight non-aligned states voted to investigate Iran; African states allowed a consensus decision on Equatorial Guinea without a vote.

Four governments which supported all but one or two of the inquiries appeared the most genuinely nonpartisan—Canada, the Netherlands, Senegal, and Mexico. The same governments also introduced and sponsored the major resolutions creating investigatory procedures for target offenders. Argentina and Uruguay provided further evidence of an internationalist perspective by dramatically reversing their opposition to enforcement procedures following the restoration of democratic rule.

Despite their efforts, only a small minority votes with any regularity as though the national interest is best served by an impartial international regime uniformly enforcing universal principles of international law. The existing regional/ideological balance nevertheless frequently permits internationalist ideals to determine which partisan complaints are investigated on their merits. A Western sponsored investigation of Poland was approved only because nine non-aligned states voted in favor. When Costa Rica, Jordan, Mexico, and Senegal changed their votes in 1984, the inquiry concluded. While construed as a victory for the Soviet bloc, that same year the Commission also initiated a special investigation of Afghanistan over the strongest Soviet protest.

Only the NAM coalition has sufficient members to investigate a target regime without support from others. When the African, Arab, Asian, and Latin American members have concurred on South Africa, Israel, Kampuchea, and to a lesser extent Afghanistan, the Commission has undertaken an investigation. With ten to fifteen reliable votes, the West needs fewer allies than the smaller Eastern bloc to win approval for new initiatives. For most investigations no single voting bloc, whether principled or partisan, has decided which offending regimes to target for public investigations. Cohesive voting coalitions can block proposed initiatives, but adding a new situation to the Commission's list requires finding common cause with others. As a result of the occasional political equilibrium between East and West, North and South, the more internationalist members have occasionally been able to lead the Commission in targeting for investigation serious situations which genuinely merit review. Put another way, a few nonpartisan delegations will lend support to those partisan political complaints which reveal the most significant human rights violations. Nevertheless, the Commission has disregarded some serious violations, and regional political balance could still result in an improper double standard. Even if the least partisan members could totally disregard short term national political interests, they constitute a small minority, unable to win support for reviewing global or regional leaders.

### Consequences

Some critics have concluded that politically motivated double standards, selective enforcement, and disparate treatment totally discredit the Commission's enforcement program. When the Commission acts selectively, its exceptionally rare actions appear arbitrary and capricious. One dominant bloc continually manipulates the Commission to seek political advantage over its adversaries, and human rights offenders dominate the debate with lengthy tirades castigating governments with superior human rights practices. Target governments may legitimately disregard judgments so tainted by political bias.

While Commission supporters also complain that too many serious violations escape scrutiny, they favor imperfect enforcement to none at all. Theo van Boven has argued that even if some governments have been politically favored, other wrongdoers should not as a result be spared reproach.[23]   Criminal defendants in national courts cannot escape punishment by proving that some privileged citizens are above the law and that others get away with murder.   The Commission has not falsely charged innocent governments, but has pursued regimes that committed serious violations.

Thomas Franck contends that an intergovernmental organ should not be expected to function as an impartial arbiter.   Its members are not philosophers or judges, but government representatives with a political responsibility to promote the national interest.   The Commission's double standard is simply an aggregation of unavoidable partisan positions with minimal concern for ethics or objectivity.   Franck argues that United States observers demonstrate a theoretical commitment to equal protection and fairness not shared by others, including democratic allies.[24]   Most participants recognize what United States delegates acknowledge in practice—that national advantage takes priority over human rights when the two conflict.

The Commission is not a court and should not be judged by standards applied to judicial tribunals.   Despite some superficial parallels, the practice is quite unlike a judicial proceeding.   Without regard for separating legislative and judicial functions, the Commission both drafts and implements international standards. Complainants have standing to accuse a government, whether they are victims, other states, non-governmental organizations, or international agencies. The Commission has initiated most studies without prior screening by Sub-Commission experts.   Investigators apply human rights law never ratified by the accused government.   The charges are evaluated in a political forum dominated by partisan blocs where go ernments vote on their own cases.   The threshold decision to investigate is a judgment of culpability, and the public report a form of penalty.  Judgments are enforced largely by moral suasion and publicity, and there are no penal sanctions to assure compliance.  Petitioners seeking the assistance of an inter-governmental body in their quest for human rights must accept whatever advantages or disadvantages result from that body's political character.

Western democracies have national legislatures which, like the Commission, generate competition for group and regional advantage by politically selected representatives.   Pluralists in the United States contend that pressure between such conflicting political interests advances the larger public good.   Partisan competition by Commission members has produced inconsistency, but political compromise has also advanced the cause of international human rights.   The pursuit of national interest has frustrated uniform decision making, but the Commission as an entity has behaved with less bias than its individual members or the General Assembly.

The Commission's four thematic procedures have been considerably more even-handed and have thus far avoided charges of selective enforcement and disparate treatment.   Related improvements in the 1980s make the recent program defensible if not highly praiseworthy. The ultimate "fairness" test for either a national or an international enforcement system is the degree to which the results depart from uniform, impartial administration of the law. The Commission's record shows greater departures from the norm than national practice in some Western democracies, but its failures have moved within tolerable limits.

Naturally new procedures take time to implement; over time the Commission has improved the enforcement process. Gradually, the less punitive actions taken against South Africa and Israel have been applied to scores of other states, including governments which supported the initial campaigns against the first targets. The pariah regimes remain the only offenders subject to the most coercive penalties, and only a dozen states have undergone thorough public investigation. Nevertheless, the Commission has established precedents for more effective action and has steadily brought more offenders under review. While the enforcement program remains quite far from the ideal, current trends lead the Commission toward the norm. Ultimately what counts is whether the Commission's enforcement program can provide meaningful assistance to victims and can induce offending governments to respect human rights.

## EVALUATING EFFECTIVENESS AND IMPACT

### Protection

*Methodological Problems*

Before attempting to assess the Commission's impact, it is necessary to recognize four methodological problems that make reliable evaluation difficult if not impossible. First , it is difficult to judge the Commission's distinct impact in situations where numerous actors press for change. Superior United Nations organs, regional human rights bodies, NGOs, and specialized agencies have all made similar responses—fact-finding, exhortation, condemnation, public exposure, and coercive pressure. It is impossible to say with certainty whether the Commission's responses added anything to measures taken by other international enforcement agencies in the same situations. Second, those assessing the cumulative impact of international enforcement measures have no reliable data base to determine whether violations have increased or decreased. Increased reports about mass killings, torture, and political detainees might reveal a deteriorating human rights situation, or conversely a heightened public sensitivity to abuses previously ignored.[25]

Third, political scientists explaining government practice simply cannot isolate precise cause and effect. Governments confront so may different domestic and international pressures for change that observers subjectively attribute significance to causes which confirm their own theories. Who can weigh with scientific certainty the relative importance of domestic discontent, world public opinion, and the Falkland's war in bringing an end to Argentina's human rights abuses? Finally, there is no way to measure the Commission's deterrent effect. No one can tell how many additional or more serious violations, if any, might have occurred had it not been for international enforcement measures that failed to elicit direct compliance.[26] Despite the imponderables, observers frequently make sweeping generalizations that are somewhat easier to critique than the Commission's effectiveness.

## The Skeptics' Case

As evidence of the Commission's impotence, critics have repeatedly cited obvious failures to prevent the most extreme violations in Kampuchea and Uganda. In a speech to the General Assembly, the President who replaced Idi Amin complained about the United Nations failure to end the eight year nightmare: "For how long will the United Nations remain silent while governments represented within this organization continue to perpetrate atrocities against their own people?"[27] Citizens in Equatorial Guinea plaintively asked why the international community had not rescued them from Macías.[28] Equatorial Guinea's new rulers subsequently drafted a constitution with the assistance of United Nations legal consultants, but then breached an agreement to include recommended democratic guarantees. Less severe measures have clearly failed to arrest deteriorating situations in Afghanistan, Kampuchea, East Timor, Western Sahara, Guatemala, and Iran. Oppressive regimes did fall to opposition groups in Uganda, the Central African Republic, Bolivia, Greece, and Equatorial Guinea, but deliberations in Geneva contributed little if anything to those results.

Some commentators have concluded that the most severe Commission penalties provoke defiance rather than reform. Whites in South Africa and Rhodesia removed moderate leaders who had responded to United Nations complaints, replacing them with extreme racists from the Nationalist and United Front Parties. George Mudge argues that white rulers realized the United Nations would reject any reform short of capitulation and so used international condemnation to unify their constituencies behind a hard line nationalist position.[29] Israel's invasion of and subsequent withdrawal from Southern Lebanon, and South Africa's shifting policies on Namibia, appear unrelated to United Nations action. Officials responsible for the United Nations anti-*apartheid* campaign concede the limited impact of their efforts and make only fleeting reference to the extensive efforts by the Commission.[30] After years of obstruction, Chile admitted a Commission inquiry group, but then refused further cooperation. The Pinochet junta defied foreign critics by holding a national plebiscite to legitimize the regime. The junta has alternatively relaxed and reinstituted martial law with more regard for domestic than for international developments.

Idealists and skeptics have both attacked the United Nations' disappointing record. In his fourth pessimistic annual report to the General Assembly in 1985 Secretary-General Perez de Cuellar worried that "the promising foundations, established with so much thought and hard work, will end up surmounted by a rambling contentious slum, the breeding ground of endless new troubles and disasters."[31] By the 1980s nongovernmental activists who had advocated United Nations action to preserve peace and human rights had lost any illusions about the imminent arrival of a new international order.

A skeptical realist who rejects the possibility of an international human rights enforcement regime argued that failure was unavoidable.[32] J. S. Watson contends that human rights monistic idealists with impeccable intentions have unfortunately diminished the credibility of international law.[33] In their zeal to hold states accountable to supranational authority, idealists have confused states' rhetoric for practice. Despite frequent academic analysis showing that Charter Article 2(7) offers no legal defense to regimes violating human rights,[34] govern - ments customarily maim and kill their citizens with impunity. National sovereignty remains the harsh reality, and victims must rely on their own devices rather than international protection. International human rights obligations will only bind consenting states, and treaties subject to auto-interpretation by the parties can be casually disregarded. Unless a state's own nationals are victimized abroad, officials have no reciprocal interest in and so will not protest when governments abuse their own citizens. From that skeptical perspective the United Nations human rights standards are moral principles rather than law, and the Commission's enforcement measures are futile gestures without practical effect.

*Assessing Practical Consequences*

Has the Commission been a total failure at achieving its stated goal of stopping gross violations? Conditions in several countries have improved while other situations have deteriorated, but the causes are difficult to discern. Regimes subjected to public vilification have occasionally instituted modest reforms. Bolivia's military stepped aside to allow democratic elections. El Salvador has reduced extra-judicial killings and conducted several elections. Polish authorities replaced the most onerous emergency procedures with less obvious controls.

More coercive responses have accompanied if not produced decolonization in Portugal's territories and liberation for Zimbabwe. The prolonged struggles against Portuguese colonialism and Rhodesia's white minority regime appeared futile or counterproductive until their goals were realized. After decades of unsuccessful efforts to end *apartheid* and to secure Palestinian rights, it may still be too early to label those measures a failure. Certainly the economic sanctions against Southern Rhodesia, however imperfectly observed, did not prolong Ian Smith's tenure.  He and other South African whites would nevertheless dispute Africans' claims that self-determination improved the overall human rights situation.  In Angola, Mozambique, Zimbabwe, and other new states, strong rulers have suppressed political opponents; leaders in Uganda, Burundi, and the Central African "Empire" committed grave atrocities.

Although the Commission's stated goal is to stop gross violations, its conciliatory measures have brought the greatest benefit to selected individuals.  A procedure fashioned to redress massive violations in several cases has produced an isolated individual remedy granted for symbolic effect.  During a visit by the Secretary-General, Poland released a Secretariat official who had been imprisoned for three years as a spy.  The Secretary-General's favorable report to the Commission a month later was instrumental in the vote to postpone further action on Poland.  Three days before its situation came up for private discussion in 1984, the government of Uruguay released a dissident mathematician who had been imprisoned for nearly a decade.[35]  Equatorial Guinea and Chile have partially responded to international pressure, only to renege later.  The regimes most sensitive to international opinion have granted symbolic concessions that have benefited a limited few without redressing the most significant complaints.  By contrast, the worst offenders flatly refuse to be held accountable.

In two situations victims have praised the Commission for providing moral support.  While the peoples of Argentina and Uruguay suffered for years under brutal regimes the Commission made only conciliatory responses under confidential procedures.  Persecuted opposition politicians who took office in new civilian governments nevertheless expressed their personal gratitude to the Commission while expressly acknowledging their government's obligation to respect international human rights law.  Argentina's new foreign minister in 1984 repudiated the obstructionist policies of his predecessor and affirmed the legitimacy of the Commission's role:

> The preservation of human rights was a legitimate interest of individuals and groups that went beyond the sovereignties and powers of the States and was also of concern to the international community. . . . Argentina has received in recent years too many indications of solidarity to forget the incalculable value of co-operation in the human rights field through the United Nations, . . .[36]

In 1985, Senator Alberto Zumaran, a candidate defeated in the Uruguayan election which ended military rule, spoke to the Commission as his government's special representative:

> The Commission had handed down innumerable decisions on individual cases, all of which had been consistently disregarded by the dictatorship but had nevertheless greatly boosted the people's morale. . . . The work

accomplished by the UNCHR during those years had been simply stupendous; many Uruguayans owed their life and freedom to that agency. He recalled with particular gratitude the telegram sent by Mr. Kooijmans, Chairman of the Commission at its previous session. . . .

The understanding of all political parties in Uruguay was that human rights could not be considered a matter of domestic jurisdiction and that violations of human rights in any member State jeopardized the well-being of the entire international community. Uruguay . . . intended to repay its debt of gratitude to the international community for the assistance it had received during the years of darkness.[37]

Somewhat inconsistently Senator Zumaran also reported that because of the confidentiality, "In all likelihood, the Uruguayan people were unaware of the invaluable services rendered." He revealed that the Secretary-General's special representative to Uruguay, Rivas Poseda, had never met the Uruguayan Human Rights Commission. Disenchanted NGO activists had previously criticized the Commission for covering up abuses by keeping complaints about Uruguay confidential for seven years. Restricted summary records from the confidential meetings show that Uruguay replied specifically to 620 communications in 1981. Uruguay's representative, Carlos Gianbruno, specifically referred to complaints by Amnesty International, the Women's International Democratic Federation and the Inter-Parliamentary Union in his annual appearances before the Commission.[38] Uruguay has asked the United Nations to release the confidential materials which may reveal more impact than the occasional symbolic measures known publicly.

As in the case of Argentina, Commission scrutiny of complaints about Uruguay's government merely supplemented more significant public pressures by others. As a party to the International Covenants and the optional protocol, Uruguay was required to report to the Human Rights Committee and its nationals could file complaints. Many did so, and the Committee published ten case reports finding covenant violations involving the right to a fair trial, torture, and the right to life.[39] The Commission's seven years of confidential deliberations appear ineffective by comparison, notwithstanding the moving testimony by Senator Zumaran. When governments submit to other human rights procedures, the Commission would only make a difference if every little bit helps.

Duplication also frequently appears in Commission self-determination resolutions urging foreign powers to comply with demands previously made by the General Assembly. Conceivably a more weakly worded Commission resolution, as on East Timor, may detract from an Assembly measure extending the Secretary-General's good offices. Appeals urging the Security Council to impose economic sanctions expose the Commission's powerlessness to enforce maximum penalties. Nor does the Commission have the staff, resources, or political will to conduct plebiscites for determining the political preferences of a people alleging a denial of self-determination. The Inter-American Commission on Human Rights, the ILO, the Red Cross, and NGOs conduct more highly respected and thorough fact-finding missions.

The Commission has addressed a few situations that have never been acted on by other, more politicized United Nations organs—Poland, Iran, Equatorial Guinea. (The Sub-Commission has responded to still more—the Sudan, Suriname, Sri Lanka.) Meeting in mid-winter after the Assembly has adjourned, the Commission provides ongoing review and continuous pressure on regimes that might otherwise enjoy a year long respite. Condemnation by sovereign governments embarrasses in a way that exposure by nongovernmental critics cannot. The Geneva meetings provide a forum where human rights specialists can negotiate understandings that might not be obtainable in the larger, more heavily politicized New York headquarters. The Commission has also provided a needed forum for developing and debating new legal theories and implementation measures to enforce compliance.

In many cases beyond the jurisdiction of the Human Rights Committee and regional bodies, the Commission has had a unique and significant impact. Since 1970 the Commission has fashioned an international complaint procedure that has enabled individual petitioners and nongovernmental organizations to charge any state with violations of human rights. Conceivably, the broad provisions of Resolutions 1235 and 1503 might also support allegations against transnational corporations and other nongovernmental actors.[40] The Commission has successfully subjected to international scrutiny governments that never formally consented to United Nations jurisdiction over domestic human rights practices.

So many governments have now been reviewed under Resolutions 1235 and 1503, that ample precedent supports the Commission's quasi-judicial authority to receive complaints. Heeding Watson's admonition to examine state practice reveals that he misreads the significance of Article 2(7) and sovereign consent. Governments that rhetorically proclaim that the Charter forbids intervention in their domestic affairs have in practice cooperated with international enforcement measures. Target governments that never formally accepted the International Covenants have in practice responded to complaints alleging violations of those standards. The skeptics are undoubtedly correct that compliance remains an occasional and largely voluntary phenomenon, but by successfully asserting its jurisdiction the Commission has taken a vital first step toward enforcing international norms.

Fewer than half of the thirty states subject to decisions under Resolution 1503 have ratified the International Covenant on Civil and Political Rights, and only three that have ratified allowed an individual right of petition under the optional protocol.[41] When ratifying the covenants, neither Japan nor the German Democratic Republic accepted a right of individual petition under the optional protocol. Yet the Commission has effectively asserted the right to review complaints of covenant violations made against those two states. Target states such as South Korea have not even ratified the Charter. The Commission has for ten years claimed the authority to review communications charging thirty governments with violations of international human rights law. The governments charged have challenged the Commission's power to act, but have also responded to the allegations. Nineteen of the target governments have had representatives in Geneva the first year their states were subject to confidential decisions; only four states have failed to have observers at two consecutive sessions when their government was under Resolution 1503 review.[42]

Despite their unequivocal support for action on South Africa, Israel and Chile, Soviet representatives still object in principle that Charter Article 2(7) bars Commission intervention in the domestic relations between a government and its citizens. When the review has involved United States allies such as Greece and Paraguay, however, the U.S.S.R. representatives have supported the enforcement of international norms against nonconsenting states. The inconsistency appeared most striking in 1984 when the Soviet bloc members first opposed any public resolution on Paraguay because that government had been subject to a Resolution 1503 decision. After losing that procedural motion, the Eastern states then favored the broadest possible censure of Paraguay.[43]

However successful in creating the world's most comprehensive international complaint procedure, the Commission has failed to achieve its stated objective— to stop gross violations. At most, the procedures have benefited a few individuals released as a symbolic gesture in response to Commission pressure. Just as the Security Council has exercised jurisdiction over acts of war without maintaining peace, the Commission has taken only the first step toward enforcing international law. NGO activists who initially hoped the 1503 procedure would lead to meaningful international scrutiny have found the procedures manipulated to aid offending governments. Regimes use the process as a shield against public embarrassment and attempt to muzzle NGOs by using the confidentiality rule to prevent disclosure of documented atrocities. To the extent that an oppressive government feigns cooperation with the Commission's confidential scrutiny, it can escape public inquiry and political shame under the Resolution 1235 procedure. Communications showing government responsiblity for thousands of involuntary disappearances were not disclosed while Argentina's situation remained under confidential review; the Commission kept complaints about Paraguay and Uruguay confidential for over seven years.

The first twenty years of serious enforcement efforts have gravely disappointed those seeking effective implementation measures. Although its direct contributions have not been substantial, the Commission has nevertheless added an unquantifiable something to attempts to secure compliance.

## Standards and Promotion

*Standards*

Perhaps of greater long-term significance than its imperfect enforcement activities will be the Commission's standard-setting, promotion, and insititutional initiatives. While it is impossible to quantify how many people have greater respect for human rights because of the Commission's work, its norms have undoubtedly had widespread influence. By 1986, the General Assembly had adopted five Declarations as well as six conventions drafted in whole or in part by the Commission. Chapter 2 reported how many national constitutions included principles from the Universal Declaration. The 115 governments accepting the Race Discrimination Convention and over eighty states party to the covenants pledged to adopt necessary implementing legislation and to report to newly constituted committees. Ironically, the covenants may have the greatest impact on countries in Africa and Asia that have not ratified or accepted the complaint procedures. The Western European and Latin American governments with the highest proportion of ratifications were previously bound by similar provisions of regional agreements. Commission rapporteurs and NGO activists have insisted that nonparties, such as the United States, should respect the covenants' substantive guarantees as binding norms of customary law.

Standard-setting indirectly supports enforcement programs by establishing norms that inform public opinion. Peoples inspired by the ideals of the international bill of rights can more effectively protect their own freedoms when the Commission fulfills its responsibility to refine international human rights law. Lawmaking establishes aspirational goals frequently unrealized in practice that may nevertheless educate citizens as much as promotional campaigns. As the norms drafted by the Commission continue to find a place in national Constitutions and legislation, the impact will affect ever larger numbers unaware of where certain legal guarantees originated. The Commission's quasi-legislative promulgation of fundamental norms may impress the international consciousness more effectively than its failings as a quasi-judicial institution. As David Forsythe concludes, the United Nations may as a result have greater long-term than immediate effect.[44]

In 1947 the Commission elaborated broad, fundamental principles that many believed should have been incorporated in the United Nations Charter. By drafting an international bill of rights, the Commission gave human rights law a quasi-constitutional basis for continued development. Such development now requires precisely defined forms of international legislation addressing specific problems, rather than universal principles. The Commission has drafted comparatively few of those more narrowly drawn United Nations human rights standards, in part because of its shift into promotion and implementation activities. In addition, an uncoordinated array of United Nations organs, conferences, and specialized agencies has drafted human rights norms that might conceivably have remained a primary Commission responsibility. The General Assembly has a working group on a migrant workers convention, the Commission on the Status of Women has adopted four conventions, UNESCO drafted a convention on discrimination in education, etc. Conventions drafted by the Commission each create new implementation bodies and procedures. By contrast, The International Labour Office oversees implementation of all the ILO conventions. Unlike the Commission, the ILO has been able to update earlier conventions as events dictate the need for supplementary provisions.

In preparing the Draft Medium Term Plan for 1984–1989, Secretariat officials acknowledged shortcomings in the Commission's drafting performance:

> [S]tandard-setting activities have become somewhat unplanned and unco-
> ordinated in recent years. The decision to elaborate standards on a subject
> is heavily dependent upon initiatives by individual governments and, in
> many instances, not enough consideration is given to the relative priorities
> of different subjects proposed for standard-setting activities. The existing
> standards or fields of competence or specialized agencies have also not been
> taken sufficiently into account in some instances. Simultaneous standard-
> setting activities on too many subjects often pose difficulties for some
> governments and international organizations.[45]

*Promotion*

Measuring the effectiveness of Commission sponsored promotional activities is even more difficult than assessing the impact of its standards. Very few United Nations publications reach a mass audience, nor do Commission studies and reports appear in many libraries except for United Nations depositories. Reporters from only a few Western European countries cover Commission meetings, and no more than a few articles a year appear in the English language press. Professionals in government, law, and education constitute a small attentive public that has participated in seminars, received fellowships, and reviewed Commission sponsored research. Presumably those individuals have learned from their involvement and have influenced a wider audience. NGO publications and conferences, however, appear to be far more widely distributed and frequently cited.

The ideas and values promoted by the Commission have become so highly regarded internationally that governments found wanting occasionally undertake public relations efforts to defend their records. Polish and Sandinista officials have assiduously courted world public opinion in order to avert censure for human rights abuses. Even unrepentent South African officials wage a public relations campaign to counter United Nations reproaches.[46] Totalitarian rulers must view Commission advocacy of fundamental rights as subversive propaganda. Victimized individuals may be inspired to form opposition groups and to claim the rights promoted. When allowed by local officials, citizens in several Latin American countries have formed national commissions on human rights and then disappeared. Educating individual victims may ultimately stimulate self-protection initiatives of greater significance than international pressures. The Commission's weak and futile enforcement measures reinforce victims' moral convictions and provide legal authority for self-help initiatives.

Perhaps the rhetoric about human rights and fundamental freedoms may even have an impact on government officials who suffer through Commission debates. Some Western European members have gradually recognized the need for international protection of economic rights, while Third World representatives have acquired an enhanced respect for political and civil liberties. Former Commission representatives have occasionally obtained higher government posts where the human rights ideals they espoused in Geneva could benefit their societies. The 1983 Commission Chairman, Olara A. Otunnu, became Interior Minister in Uganda's 1985 military government.

United Nations development directors, however, have been criticized for their reluctance to integrate human rights considerations into technical assistance programs.[47] Research has shown that United States citizens who praise the Bill of Rights as a general abstraction do not in practice, endorse or even understand some of its most fundamental guarantees. Presumably the more recently adopted and imperfectly publicized Universal Declaration is similarly respected more in principle than in practice. That Declaration nevertheless embodies several powerful ideas whose time has arrived while the Commission engaged in a fitful but vital struggle to foster new attitudes and behavior.

## Institutional Effectiveness

### Commission Decision Making

As the Commission celebrates its fortieth anniversary, members frequently complain about institutional inadequacies—tedious, repetitive debate, excessive documentation, an irrational agenda, cumbersome decision-making procedures, and misallocation of time and money. Although the Commission completes most of its agenda while continuing to enlarge its caseload, gridlock threatens. NGO speakers are most likely to be curtailed first, although their participation adds a perspective that non-member governmental observers could never provide. Members of the United States legislature spare their colleagues time by having remarks never made orally printed in the Congressional Record. At the cost of adding further to the voluminous summary records, the members could appreciably shorten their plenary discussion on each agenda item and proceed directly to debate resolutions.

The agenda compounds the organizational disarray by failing to treat separately the Commission's distinct responsibilities for standard-setting, promotion, implementation, and institutional coordination. A lame duck chair appoints investigative rapporteurs, and the bureau of officers does not act between annual sessions. Proponents of twice yearly Commission sessions wanted timely responses to unanticipated emergency situations; in practice when the press reported massive killings during Commission sessions in 1983, the members did not even mention the situations arising in India and Zimbabwe. For governments previously under review—South Africa, Israel, and Malawi—the Commission has promptly responded to current developments by sending telegrams during a session.[48]

Despite members' increasing frustration, working groups could not agree on alternative arrangements. Perhaps the United Nations financial crisis will compel a major retrenchment that mandates more efficient procedures. A group of eighteen high-level experts reporting to the General Assembly in 1986 recommended that ECOSOC subsidiary bodies substantially reduce the frequency and duration of their meetings and proposed a 15 percent staff reduction over three years. Whatever the level of funding, a policy making organization of governmentally appointed experts should not be expected to operate in a businesslike fashion. Although considerable streamlining is clearly needed, the Commission, no less than democratic national legislatures, is bound to employ occasionally irrational procedures when resolving major political differences. Profound ideological disputes naturally cause procedural discord. While organizational disarray has occasionally impaired effective action, overly rigid procedures might close the Commission to some creative initiatives.

*Coordinating an International Human Rights Regime*

Although the Commission is the only global agency with comprehensive responsibility for all human rights, its members have never regarded institutional leadership as a primary responsibility. Secretariat staff prepare a five year work program for the Commission, but government representatives make *ad hoc* responses that create rather than coordinate new institutions. After forty years of haphazard expansion a variety of United Nations and regional agencies perform related responsibilities without reference to the Commission. (See Table 7.5) The Commission on the Status of Women in 1983 obtained authority to review some confidential 1503 communications. The U.N. High Commissioner for Refugees responds to emergency situations with staff resources that exceed the Commission's capabilities. The Commission defers to the ILO on key questions affecting workers' rights. Unlike staff at the Centre for Human Rights, NGO's have the resources and authority to respond to emergencies by sending observers or by issuing press releases. Regional commissions and the U.N. Human Rights Committee have assumed major responsibility for reviewing individual complaints. The General Assembly and ECOSOC address emergency situations and draft standards without reference to the Commission. Duplication is common, even within the Commission's own country investigations and thematic procedures.

Institutional tensions and rivalry both with its own Sub-Commission and with other agencies have stimulated ambitious proposals for more effective coordination. One visionary scheme would elevate the Commission to a Council parallel to ECOSOC and reporting directly to the Assembly. The United Nations needs a Human Rights Council far more than a Trusteeship Council, since there is only one remaining trust territory. ECOSOC has been simply a "post office" sending Commission recommendations to the Assembly, and its separate human rights responsibilities should be assigned to the proposed Council. If peace and human rights are inextricably linked, the United Nations should have a Human Rights Council as well as a Security Council. However appealing in theory, the political difficulty of amending the Charter makes serious consideration unlikely.

Advocates of a "structural approach" to achieving human rights, such as Theo van Boven, envision a unique coordinating responsibility for the Commission. *Ad hoc* responses to gross violations merely attack symptoms without correcting underlying structural causes. Conditions of forced labor result when severe declines in commodity prices disrupt international agricultural markets. Torture, political detention, and mass killing will recur as long as citizens remain subject to authoritarian political structures. Militarism, arms rivalries, and the nuclear peril pose the most significant threat to the right to life. In response, the Commission has a paramount responsibility to see that human rights concerns become an integral component of United Nations programs for technical assistance, disarmament, economic, and political development.[49] Human rights agencies alone can not remove the unjust societal structures that are the root cause of violations.[50] The studies on development and advisory services seminars on popular participation and peace and development have remained largely theoretical exercises without apparent effect on institutional arrangements.[51]

At a more basic level, the Commission has made ineffective attempts to strengthen the Centre for Human Rights as it steadily increased demands on Secretariat staff. The Commission has significantly expanded its activities beyond standard-setting into promotion and implementation programs during a period when membership increased from eighteen to forty-three. When the International Covenant on Political and Civil Rights took effect in 1976 the Division acquired only two additional permanent staff to service the newly created Human Rights Committee. From 1952 to 1982, total U.N. staff grew by more than 200 percent, but the human rights division grew by only 47 percent.[52] By contrast, the U.N. Division of Narcotic Drugs nearly doubled its professional staff to thirty-two in the same period, and the U.N. Centre for Social Development and Humanitarian Affairs employed sixty professionals in 1983, 25 percent more than the Centre for Human Rights.[53] Combining both direct and indirect costs, total human rights expenditures accounted for 1.8 per cent of all U.N. outlays. Excluding staff in conference services and other

Secretariat departments, Centre personnel made up .7 percent of the total U.N. payroll in 1983.

The Commission has no budgetary authority, and its hortatory resolutions urging more funds for human rights are of little value without member support in the Assembly. Clearly, the Assembly has kept Secretariat staff who are responsible for the protection of human rights on a tight budget leash. U.N. human rights officials have complained for years that staff and budget constraints preclude effective servicing of Commission requests. The Centre has no independent fact-finding capability, and Commission appointed rapporteurs visiting Peru relied on the NGO America's Watch for essential referrals.[54] Human rights officers at the Centre lack personal computers for rudimentary word and data processing. The political distrust which dominates Commission decision-making also accounts for the strict limitations on Secretariat human rights personnel. Even if the Commission had the authority to increase staff and budgetary resources, the members would be unlikely to spend money for staff that could challenge their national interests.

However uncoordinated, the proliferation of human rights agencies has heightened international concern for fundamental freedoms. Centralized direction, particularly by an inter-governmental body, could pose unacceptable risks of political control. Improved coordination, however, might reduce a wasteful duplication of scarce resources. The Commission has a sufficiently broad mandate, and no other regional body or U.N. organ appears to have the responsibility or capability for long term international planning. Decisive leadership by a cohesive, dominant group accomplished earlier organizational reforms, and the political balance of the 1980s impedes significant change. Preoccupied with urgent situations that demand immediate response, as well as its traditional tasks of standard-setting and promotion, the Commission appears unlikely to give serious consideration to institutional arrangements.

## PROSPECTS FOR THE FUTURE

After forty years of uneven performance, what lies ahead for the Commission? The short term goals pursued by the three main voting blocs are well-established and signal predictable division. A majority of the NAM members have the votes to disregard Western objections and to give the right to development top priority. Their effort recalls the 1950s Third World campaign to make reluctant Western governments respect a collective human right of self-determination. Three recently completed standards have been Western initiatives—a declaration on religious intolerance, the torture convention, and guidelines on the rights of detainees. The Declaration on Development would partially restore balance, and the NAM might also proceed without a consensus to adopt a convention assuring that right, however vaguely defined.

By defining development primarily as a collective right of nations, the NAM offends the basic Western premise that states are the principal violators not the beneficiaries of human rights. Saddled with impossible interest payments, NAM debtor governments encouraged by Cuba and the Soviet bloc will increasingly blame transnational corporations, multinational banks, and Western lenders for violating their fundamental right to economic justice. A confrontational approach appears likely to fragment the Commission without obtaining for the plaintiffs either debt relief or compensation for past exploitation. Western attempts to divide the NAM might succeed in attracting countries like Senegal on some issues, but are likely to be ineffective when basic economic interests are at stake. Arab governments might divide the NAM by demanding a greater number of the seats allocated for African and Asian members. South Africa, Israel, Afghanistan, and Kampuchea will remain paramount concerns for the foreseeable future, and the NAM appears unlikely to favor either East or West when either intervenes in the Third World.

The Western bloc has lost two effective leaders, the Netherlands and Canada, but remains actively represented and well organized to compete in Commission politics. More Western governments want representation on the Commission and Sub-Commission than can be accommodated, so increased competition for membership appears likely. The Western group will seek to extend and strengthen the global procedures for disappearances, summary executions, torture, and religious intolerance. Another major goal is to find means for protecting local human rights activists persecuted by government officials. Previously unsuccessful standard-setting efforts likely to be continued include an optional protocol to the Political Covenant renouncing capital punishment, standards of treatment for detainees, a declaration affirming rights of conscientious objectors to refuse military service, and principles for confining the mentally ill. While both East and West properly complain about wasteful spending, in practice each bloc seeks economies in programs favored by the opposing group. The West has enforcement aspirations far beyond the Secretariat's meager resources, but has never followed through with the needed budgetary support. The United States induced financial crisis of 1986 may expose the hypocrisy of human rights proponents who welcome a pretext for major retrenchment.

Stung by Commission action on East Germany, Poland, Kampuchea, and especially Afghanistan the Soviet Union can be expected to initiate counter measures. United States intervention in Nicaragua presents an immediately available, inviting target. Playing on the fears of the increasing number of states subjected to confidential review, the Soviets might build a majority prepared to terminate the procedure. Similar resentment at embarrassing revelations from the rapporteurs on summary execution, torture, and religious intolerance might, with Soviet encouragement, undermine the support needed for renewing their annual mandates. Instead of institutionalized enforcement measures for political and civil rights, the Soviets would greatly prefer opportunities to propagate their anti-Western views on Nazism, nuclear arms, youth and peace. By withholding votes in Sub-Commission elections the Eastern bloc can help defeat the more independent members nominated by the West.

The tenuous balance achieved between the blocs in the 1980s has created a fragile vitality which survived the deadening rhetoric. Reemergence of a single dominant bloc would destroy the healthy clash of philosophy so essential to fashioning universal human rights values. For most of its history the Commission has been dominated by one bloc with a consistent program. From 1946 to 1967 the West dominated, providing strong leadership on standard-setting until the early 1950s, but thereafter allowing the promotional program to drift with minimal effect. NAM control for a decade after 1967 stimulated procedural innovation, but resulted in a single-minded partisan campaign against selected adversaries. Coalition building is not a prerequisite for action, but the shared decision-making begun in the 1980s will have the greatest influence on those susceptible to the persuasive tools available.

The Commission's forty year development since 1946 provides further indication of its future prospects. Believing that the holocaust helped cause World War II, the founders created a Commission ostensibly to prevent a recurrence of human rights violations which might lead to war. In practice the Commission did not respond to abuses in East Pakistan, Uganda, and Kampuchea which led to international conflict. Instead, the Commission has sought to prevent violations after military conflict has begun and has promoted human rights for their own sake. The Commission has not controlled the United Nations human rights agenda, but has adapted its program to the prevailing issue of the time—first individual civil and political rights, then decolonization and racism, followed by disappearances and torture.

No one can predict with certainty what global issues will arise at the end of the century, but the military and economic trends of the 1980s are likely to create new crises which preoccupy the Commission. Local rivalries and arms expenditures strengthen military officers who seize power imposing authoritarian controls. The impoverished governments most frequently charged with violating political rights have been pressed to take austerity measures to repay overwhelming loan obligations. Latin American democracies have repeatedly failed when economic conditions deteriorated. Significant economic decline associated with unrepayable debt obligations could result in massive political upheaval accompanied by increased human rights abuses. The international debt crisis seems likely to exacerbate the tension between Commission members seeking economic justice and advocates of political rights.

The Commission is ill-equipped to cope with the underlying military and economic causes of the worst human rights violations. At best its measures temper and moderate the most extreme offenses. Once the killing has begun, human rights remedies, like United Nations relief for refugees, merely alleviates symptoms. Nevertheless, the United Nations Commission on Human Rights has had enough success and has sufficient potential to justify its continued existence. The standards drafted by the Commission have justifiably won high praise; the Universal Declaration in particular has influenced domestic legislation around the world. The Commission is still needed as a permanent forum for negotiating universal principles, however elusive and unattainable such norms might appear.

Equally important, the Commission has cracked the citadel of national sovereignty first by drafting standards and then by eliciting government responses to complaints about their misconduct. Human rights optimists foresee an ineluctable expansion of supranational authority over nonconsenting state actors. The Commission's complaint procedures in their eyes represent the first comprehensive opportunity for individuals to assert rights against their own governments. While there is little proof that victims have yet derived tangible benefit, the Commission has taken a significant first step toward protecting human rights. Whether or not an intergovernmental body will take further measures limiting national autonomy is far from certain. The first forty years of Commission practice confirms neither the faith of the true believer nor the cynical realism of skeptics who debate the future prospects for an effective international system.

# Afterword:
# Developments at the Commission's
# Forty-Third Session, 1987

At its forty-third session from February 2 to March 13, 1987, the Commission approved 61 resolutions and 11 decisions. In addition to 43 member states, 76 observer governments and 98 NGOs attended. The Eastern bloc's Leonid Evmenov of Byelorussia presided as chair.[1]

*Protection.* Thematic approaches: The Disappearances Working Group reported on its second mission to Peru and has another year remaining on its two year mandate.[2] The torture rapporteur recommended a system of periodic visits and independent local bodies which could receive individual complaints .[3]

Without vote the Commission renewed the mandates of the thematic rapporteurs on summary and arbitrary executions, torture, and religious intolerance for an additional year.

The non-aligned and Eastern bloc members overwhelmed Western objections to a new thematic procedure. Resolution 1986/27 had condemned the recruitment, financing, and training of mercenaries. The United States initially objected to Commission action which duplicated work by the Assembly's Ad Hoc Committee on Drafting of an International Convention Against the Recruitment, Use, Financing and Training of Mercenaries. ECOSOC subsequently urged the Commission to appoint a special rapporteur. At the 1987 session Congo introduced a draft resolution which noted the violations of self-determination caused by mercenaries particularly in Southern Africa, but which proposed a global mandate for a new rapporteur.[4] The United States and its Western allies then proposed amendments to focus attention primarily on Southern Africa and to assign responsibility to the existing Working Group of Experts rather than to a new rapporteur. Nicaragua vigorously opposed such attempts to divert attention from United States support for the contras. The proposed amendments were defeated and Resolution 1987/16 was adopted by the same 31-11-1 vote; the ten member Western group and Japan could not prevent the extension of a thematic procedure of their own invention.

Country Specific Procedures: The Group of Experts on South Africa reported,[5] and the Commission adopted resolutions condemning violations in the Republic and Namibia. At the General Assembly session in fall 1986, the

Secretariat had translated and distributed only the abridged introductory and concluding sections of reports by the Special Rapporteurs, purportedly for economic reasons. After sharp criticism, the Secretariat reissued them in all working languages with the complete text of reported violations in each country.

For the first time, the rapporteur on Iran included specific details of alleged atrocities in his report. A Pakistani resolution to postpone further consideration of the Iranian situation failed by the narrowest of margins, 16-16-10.[6] Chile authorized a special rapporteur to visit in March 1987, and the members renewed his mandate without a vote. On contested votes the Commission renewed for another year the mandates for country rapporteurs for Afghanistan, El Salvador, and Iran. After noting democratic progress in Guatemala, the Commission accepted a final report from the Special Representative and requested technical assistance to help restore human rights. A special resolution on Haiti called for an expert adviser, three fellowships and a training course to reestablish rights.

Resolutions of Condemnation and Concern: The United States sent a new ambassador to the Commission, E. Robert Wallach, a trial lawyer who initiated a "witness program." A former Cuban political prisoner, Armando Valladares, joined the U.S. delegation; Soviet exiles Anatoly Scharansky and Yuri Orlov gained accreditation as Jewish NGO representatives; and other released detainees became lobbyists. In addition, the U.S. U.N. ambassador addressed the Commission and campaigned for a resolution on political prisoners in Cuba.[7] That government countered with a draft on racism in the United States. India's motions to postpone consideration of the two resolutions passed by just one and two vote margins.[8] In reviewing confidential communications, the members discontinued review of Haiti following Duvalier's departure. Since the 1986 budget crisis prevented further confidential referrals by the Sub-Commission, only Albania, Paraguay, and Zaire remained subject to the Resolution 1503 procedure.

*Standard-Setting.* Drafting continued on the Convention on Children's Rights, and the Working Group will reconvene one week before the 1988 session. The protracted work on a declaration on minorities and the more recently begun but equally difficult effort on the rights of human rights defenders also continued. NGO critics urged the members to end the slow and costly drafting of repetitive new instruments by drafting amendments to previously adopted standards in the form of supplementary protocols to the International Covenants.[9] Some Western European delegates and NGOs supported a new protocol to the Political Covenant that would abolish capital punishment.

*Promotion.* Western delegates initiated a request to the Secretary-General to create a new voluntary fund for advisory services and technical assistance. Another resolution urged Equatorial Guinea to make use of recommendations made by expert legal advisers in January 1986. General hortatory resolutions sponsored by the Eastern bloc and non-aligned asserted property rights against transnational corporations, stressed the right to housing, and promoted the newly proclaimed right to development.

*Institutional Coordination and Change.* Despite forecasts of major financial retrenchment, the Commission gave even less attention than usual to organizational concerns. With little regard for program coherence or expense, the members assigned new tasks to the Secretariat; adopted several standard resolutions on public information activities, promotional undertakings in the Asian region, and national institutions; and did not reconvene their open ended working group on alternative approaches. The Commission established a new thematic procedure on mercenaries, urged full funding with summary records for the Sub-Commission in 1987, and requested funding for 20 extra meetings of their own in 1988. With ECOSOC approval the Commission postponed election of new Sub-Commission members to 1988 so that the experts forced by the financial emergency to miss the regularly scheduled meeting in 1986 could complete their terms at the 39th Session in 1987.

Other important decisions affecting the Commission's operation and future prospects are being made elsewhere. The nineteen member ECOSOC Committee on Nongovernmental Organizations deferred for two years applications for consultative status from several highly respected human rights groups. The Soviet Union challenged the International Human Rights Law Group, and the Lawyers Committee for International Human Rights in New York was rejected for the fourth time. Arab members blocked the Cairo based Arab Organization for Human Rights which had alarmed governments such as Syria, Iraq, and Algeria concerned about interference in their domestic affairs. The most influential, and most threatening, NGO activists in Commission deliberations won consultative status before 1977 when the ECOSOC committee began requiring approval by consensus.[10]

Pressed to economize by reducing highly paid top Secretariat staff, Secretary-General Javier Perez de Cuellar consolidated two posts when Kurt Herndl concluded his five year appointment as Assistant Secretary-General for Human Rights. Jan Martinson, Director of the U.N. Office at Geneva, was assigned additional duties as Director of the Centre for Human Rights. Kwadyo Nyamekye of Ghana, formerly Herndl's top assistant, will take on significant responsibility for the Centre's daily operation. The Secretariat has begun preparing the draft medium-term plan for 1990-1995, but the Commission has expressed no policy preferences and appears unlikely to offer substantive review.

A Special Commission of ECOSOC on the In-depth Study of the United Nations Intergovernmental Structure and Functions in the Economic and Social Fields is preparing a plan for completion in 1988 to rationalize and to simplify agendas, calendars, and work programs of subsidiary bodies. Chaired by Abdel Halim Badawi of Egypt, the Special Commission elected a twenty-five member regionally based Bureau that will propose economy measures with considerable potential impact on the frequency, scope, and duration of future Commission and Sub-Commission meetings.[11]

# Appendix A:
# ECOSOC Authorizing Resolutions

**ECOSOC Resolutions 5(I) February 16, 1946 and
9(II) June 21, 1946 Provided in Part:**

## 1. Functions

The work of the Commission shall be directed towards submitting proposals, recommendations and reports to the Council regarding:

(a) An international bill of rights;
(b) International declarations or conventions on civil liberties, the status of women, freedom of information an[d] similar matters;
(c) The protection of minorities;
(d) The prevention of discrimination on grounds of race, sex, language or religion;
(e) Any other matter concerning human rights not covered by items [(a)–(d)].

The Commission shall make studies and recommendations and provide information and other services at the request of the Economic and Social Council.

The Commission may propose to the Council any changes in its terms of reference.

The Commission may make recommendations to the Council concerning any sub-commission which it considers should be established.

## 2. Composition

(a) The Commission on Human Rights shall consist of one representative from each of eighteen members of the United Nations selected by the Council.

(b) With a view to securing a balanced representation in the various fields covered by the Commission, the Secretary-General shall consult with the Governments so selected before the representatives are finally nominated by these Governments and confirmed by the Council.

(c) Except for the initial period, the term of office shall be for three years. For the initial period, one-third of the members shall serve for two years, one-third for three years, and one-third for four years, the terms of each member to be determined by lot.

(d) Retiring members shall be eligible for re-election.

(e) In the event that a member of the Commission is unable to serve for the full three-year term, the vacancy thus arising shall be filled by a representative designated by the Member Government, subject to the provisions of paragraph (b) above.

### 3. Working Groups of Experts

The Commission is authorized to call in *ad hoc* working groups of non-governmental experts in specialized fields or individual experts, without further reference to the Council, but with the approval of the President of the Council and the Secretary-General.

## Communications Concerning Human Rights, ECOSOC Res. 728 (XXVIII)F

*adopted* July 30, 1959, 28 U.N. ESCOR, Supp. (No. 1) 19, U.N. Doc. E/3290 (1959)

*The Economic and Social Council,*

*Having considered* chapter V of the report of the Commission on Human Rights on its first session, concerning communications, and chapter IX of the report of the Commission on its fifteenth session,

1. *Approves* the statement that the Commission on Human Rights recognizes that it has no power to take any action in regard to any complaints concerning human rights;

2. *Requests* the Secretary-General:

(a) To compile and distribute to members of the Commission on Human Rights before each session a non-confidential list containing a brief indication of the substance of each communication, however addressed, which deals with the principles involved in the promotion of universal respect for, and observance of, human rights and to divulge the identity of the authors of such communications unless they indicate that they wish their names to remain confidential;

(b) To compile each session of the Commission a confidential list containing a brief indication of the substance of other communications concerning human rights, however addressed, and to furnish this list to members of the Commission, in private meeting, without divulging the identity of the authors of communications except in cases where the authors state that they have already divulged or intend to divulge the names or that they have no objection to their names being divulged;

(c) To enable the members of the Commission, upon request, to consult the originals of communications dealing with the principles, involved in the promotion of universal respect for, and observance of, human rights;

(d) To inform the writers of all communications concerning human rights, however addressed, that their communications will be handled in accordance with this resolution, indicating that the Commission has no power to take any action in regard to any complaint concerning human rights;

(e) To furnish each Member State concerned with a copy of any communication concerning human rights which refers explicitly to that State or to territories under its jurisdiction, without divulging the identity of the author, except as provided for in sub-paragraph (b) above;

(f) To ask Governments sending replies to communications brought to their attention in accordance with sub-paragraph (e) whether they wish their replies to be presented to the Commission in summary form or in full.

3. *Resolves* to give members of the Sub-Commission on Prevention of Discrimination and Protection of Minorities, with respect to communications dealing with discrimination and minorities, the same facilities as are enjoyed by members of the Commission on Human Rights under the present resolution;

4. *Suggests* to the Commission on Human Rights that it should at each session appoint an ad hoc committee to meet shortly before its next session for the purpose of reviewing the list of communications prepared by the Secretary-General under paragraph 2(a) above and of recommending which of these communications, in original, should, in accordance with paragraph 2(c) above, be made available to members of the Commission on request.

## ECOSOC Res. 1235(XLII)

*adopted* June 6, 1967, 42 U.N. ESCOR, Supp. (No. 1) 17, U.N. Doc. E/4393 (1967)

*The Economic and Social Council*

Noting resolutions 8 (XXIII) and 9 (XXIII) of the Commission on Human Rights,

1. *Welcomes* the decision of the Commission on Human Rights to give annual consideration to the item entitled "Question of the violation of human rights and fundamental freedoms, including policies of racial discrimination and segregation and of apartheid, in all countries, with particular reference to colonial and other dependent countries and territories," without prejudice to the functions and powers of organs already in existence or which may be established within the framework of measures of implementation included in international covenants and conventions on the protection of human rights and fundamental freedoms; and concurs with the requests for assistance addressed to the Sub-

Commission on Prevention of Discrimination and Protection of Minorities and to the Secretary-General;

2. *Authorizes* the Commission on Human Rights and the Sub-Commission on Prevention of Discrimination and Protection of Minorities, in conformity with the provisions of paragraph 1 of the Commission's resolution 8 (XXIII); to examine information relevant to gross violations of human rights and fundamental freedoms, as exemplified by the policy of apartheid as practised in the Republic of South Africa and in the Territory of South West Africa under the direct responsibility of the United Nations and now illegally occupied by the Government of the Republic of South Africa and to racial discrimination practised notably in Southern Rhodesia, contained in the communications listed by the Secretary-General pursuant to Economic and Social Council resolution 728 F (XXVIII) of 30 July 1959;

3. *Decides* that the Commission on Human Rights may, in appropriate cases, and after careful consideration of the information thus made available to it, in conformity with the provisions of paragraph 1 above, make a thorough study of situations which reveal a consistent pattern of violations of human rights, as exemplified by the policy of apartheid as practised in the Republic of South Africa in the Territory of South West Africa under the direct responsibility of the United Nations and now illegally occupied by the Government of the Republic of South Africa, and racial discrimination as practised notably in Southern Rhodesia, and report, with recommendations thereon, to the Economic and Social Council;

4. *Decides* to review the provisions of paragraph 2 and 3 of the present resolution after the entry into force of the International Covenants on Human Rights:

5. *Takes note* of the fact that the Commission on Human Rights, in its resolution 6 (XXIII), has instructed an ad hoc study group to study in all its aspects the question of the ways and means by which the Commission might be enabled or assisted to discharge functions in relation to violations of human rights and fundamental freedoms, whilst maintaining and fulfilling its other functions;

6. *Requests* the Commission on Human Rights to report to it on the result of this study after having given consideration to the conclusions of the ad hoc study group referred to in paragraph 5 above.

## Procedure for Dealing with Communications Relating to Violations of Human Rights and Fundamental Freedoms ECOSOC Res. 1503 (XLVIII)

*adopted* May 27, 1970, 48 U.N. ESCOR, Supp. (No. 1A)8, U.N. Doc. E/4832/Add. 1 (1970)

*The Economic and Social Council*

Noting resolutions 7 (XXVI) and 17 (XXV) of the Commission on Human Rights and resolution 2 (XXI) of the Sub-Commission on Prevention of Discrimination and Protection of Minorities,

1. *Authorizes* the Sub-Commission on Prevention of Discrimination and Protection of Minorities to appoint a working group consisting of not more than five of its members, with due regard to geographical distribution, to meet once a year in private meetings for a period not exceeding ten days immediately before the sessions of the Sub-Commission to consider all communications, including replies of Governments thereon, received by the Secretary-General under Council resolution 728 F (XXVIII) of 30 July 1959 with a view to bringing to the attention of the Sub-Commission those communications, together with replies of Governments, if any, which appear to reveal a consistent pattern of gross and reliably attested violations of human rights and fundamental freedoms within the terms of reference of the Sub-Commission.

2. *Decides* that the Sub-Commission on Prevention of Discrimination and Protection of Minorities should, as the first stage in the implementation of the present resolution, devise at its twenty-third session appropriate procedures for dealing with the question of admissibility of communications received by the Secretary-General under Council resolution 728 F (XXVIII) and in accordance with Council resolution 1235 (XLII) of 6 June 1967;

3. *Requests* the Secretary-General to prepare a document on the question of admissibility of communications for the Sub-Commission's consideration at its twenty-third session;

4. *Further requests* the Secretary-General:

(a) To furnish to the members of the Sub-Commission every month a list of communications prepared by him in accordance with Council resolution 728 F (XXVIII) and a brief description of them, together with the text of any replies received from Governments;

(b) To make available to the members of the working group at their meetings the originals of such communications listed as they may request, having due regard to the provisions of paragraph 2(b) of Council resolution 728 F (XXVIII) concerning the divulging of the identity of the authors of communications;

(c) To circulate to the members of the Sub-Commission, in the working languages, the originals of such communications as are referred to the Sub-Commission by the working group;

5. *Requests* the Sub-Commission on Prevention of Discrimination and Protection of Minorities to consider in private meetings in accordance with paragraph 1 above, the communications brought before it in accordance with the decision of a majority of the members of the working group and any replies of Governments relating thereto and other relevant information, with a view to determining whether to refer to the Commission on Human Rights particular

situations which appear to reveal a consistent pattern of gross and reliably attested violations of human rights requiring consideration by the Commission;

6. *Requests* the Commission on Human Rights after it has examined any situation referred to it by the Sub-Commission to determine:

(a) Whether it requires a thorough study by the Commission and a report and recommendations thereon to the Council in accordance with paragraph 3 of Council resolution 1235 (XLII);

(b) Whether it may be a subject of an investigation by an ad hoc committee to be appointed by the Commission which shall be undertaken only with the express consent of the State concerned and shall be conducted in constant co-operation with that State and under conditions determined by agreement with it. In any event, the investigation may be undertaken only if: (i) All available means at the national level have been resorted to and exhausted; (ii) The situation does not relate to a matter which is being dealt with under other procedures prescribed in the constituent instruments of, or conventions adopted by, the United Nations and the specialized agencies, or in regional conventions, or which the State concerned wishes to submit to other procedures in accordance with general or special international agreements to which it is a party.

7. *Decides* that if the Commission on Human Rights appoints an ad hoc committee to carry on an investigation with the consent of the State concerned:

(a) The composition of the committee shall be determined by the Commission. The members of the committee shall be independent persons whose competence and impartiality is beyond question. Their appointment shall be subject to the consent of the Government concerned;

(b) The committee shall establish its own rules of procedure. It shall be subject to the quorum rule. It shall have authority to receive communications and hear witnesses, as necessary. The investigation shall be conducted in co-operation with the Government concerned;

(c) The committee's procedure shall be confidential, its proceedings shall be conducted in private meetings and its communications shall not be publicized in any way;

(d) The committee shall strive for friendly solutions before, during and even after the investigation;

(e) The committee shall report to the Commission on Human Rights with such observations and suggestions as it may deem appropriate;

8. *Decides* that all actions envisaged in the implementation of the present resolution by the Sub-Commission on Prevention of Discrimination and Protection of Minorities or the Commission on Human Rights shall remain confidential until such time as the Commission may decide to make recommendations to the Economic and Social Council;

9. *Decides* to authorize the Secretary-General to provide all facilities which

may be required to carry out the present resolution, making use of the existing staff of the Division of Human Rights of the United Nations Secretariat;

10. *Decides* that the procedure set out in the present resolution for dealing with communications relating to violations of human rights and fundamental freedoms should be reviewed if any new organ entitled to deal with such communications should be established within the United Nations or by international agreement.

## ECOSOC Res. 1979/36

*adopted* May 10, 1979, 1979 U.N. ESCOR Supp. No. 1 U.N. Doc. E/1979/79

*The Economic and Social Council,*

*Recognizing* the responsibilities of the Commission on Human Rights under the Charter of the United Nations,

*In conformity* with General Assembly resolutions 32/130 of 16 December 1977, and 33/104 and 33/105 of 16 December 1978,

*Recalling* the importance of the Universal Declaration of Human Rights and of the International Covenants on Human Rights in further promoting international co-operation for respect for and observance of human rights and fundamental freedom, as required by the Charter,

1. *Notes* that, in conformity with the Charter of the United Nations, the Universal Declaration of Human Rights and the relevant international instruments, in fulfilling its tasks as laid down in Council resolution 5 (I) of 16 February 1946 and amended by Council resolution 9(II) of 21 June 1946, should take into account the concepts enumerated in General Assembly resolution 32/130;

2. *Reaffirms* that the Commission on Human Rights will be guided by the standards in the field of human rights as laid down in the various international instruments in that field;

3. *Decides*, further, to add the following provisions to the terms of reference of the Commission as contained in the Council's resolution 5 (I) of 16 February 1946 as amended by resolution 9 (II): "The Commission shall assist the Economic and Social Council in the co-ordination of activities concerning human rights in the United Nations system;"

4. *Authorizes*: (a) An increase in the membership of the Commission on Human Rights to forty-three members, equitable geographical distribution being maintained; (b) Regular meetings of the Commission for six weeks each year, with an additional week for meetings of working groups;

5. *Notes* that in certain circumstances the Commission may need to hold special sessions in order to complete unfinished business, including the drafting of human rights instruments;

6. *Requests* the Commission on Human Rights to prepare suggestions on the possibility of convening meetings of the officers of the Commission in intersessional periods in exceptional circumstances;

7. *Requests*, in order to enable the Commission on Human Rights to carry out the study requested by the General Assembly in its resolution 33/54 of 14 December 1978, those specialized agencies and other organs and bodies within and related to the United Nations system which are, according to their explicit mandates, concerned with the protection and promotion of human rights and fundamental freedoms, to provide the Secretary-General with a short survey of their human rights activities and programmes;

8. *Further requests* the Secretary-General to compile for the Commission on Human Rights at its thirty-seventh session an analytical presentation of the material submitted pursuant to paragraph 7 above;

9. *Notes* that the Commission on Human Rights, at its thirty-seventh session, may wish to set up a sessional working group to study the material compiled and to make proposals, if it deems it appropriate, for the co-ordination of specific human rights activities and programmes within the United Nations system;

10. *Requests* the Secretary-General, in the light of the increase in the workload of the Division of Human Rights, to examine the question of the staffing and other resources of the human rights sector of the Secretariat, bearing in mind that it should always be at a level, which will allow it to discharge its duties efficiently;

11. *Emphasizes* the value of the programme of advisory services in the field of human rights and reaffirms that this programme should be maintained and developed;

12. *Requests* the Sub-Commission on Prevention of Discrimination and Protection of Minorities, with a view to consolidating its effectiveness and resources, to examine its programme of work so as to identify specific areas for its concentrated attention of work so as to identify specific areas for its concentrated attention and to make recommendations thereon to the Commission on Human Rights;

13. *Decides* that the annual session of the Sub-Commission on Prevention of Discrimination and Protection of Minorities may be extended to four weeks;

14. *Expresses its appreciation* to the Secretary-General for his efforts to continue rendering the good offices envisaged in the Charter of the United Nations in the field of human rights;

15. *Takes note* of General Assembly resolution 33/105, in which the Assembly requested the Commission on Human Rights to take into account, in continuing its work on the over-all analysis of the alternative approaches and ways and means for improving the effective enjoyment of human rights and fundamental freedoms, the views expressed on the various proposals, including that for the establishment of a post of United Nations High Commissioner for

Human Rights, and notes that the Commission was unable to reach agreement on the latter proposal;

16. *Requests* the Commission on Human Rights to continue its work on the further promotion and encouragement of human rights and fundamental freedoms, including the question of the programme and methods of work of the Commission and the examination of the alternative approaches and ways and means for improving the effective enjoyment of human rights and fundamental freedoms;

17. *Requests* the Secretary-General to bring the present resolution and the relevant chapter of the report of the Commission on Human Rights on its thirty-fifth session to the attention of the General Assembly.

# Appendix B:
# Commission Membership, 1947–1987

TABLE B.1
Countries Elected as Commission Members by Region, 1947–1987

### Africa

Algeria 1980–82, 1986–88
Benin 1964–68, 1979–81
Burundi 1979–81
Cameroon 1984–86
Congo 1985–87
Egypt 1947–55, 1967–80 Ch 1953–54
Ethiopia 1980–82, 1986–88
Gambia 1982–87
Ghana 1970–75, 1980–83
Kenya 1984–86
Ivory Coast 1978–80
Lesotho 1976–78, 1985–87
Liberia 1963–65, 1985–87
Libya 1976–78, 1983–85
Madagascar 1968–70
Mauritania 1969–71, 1984–86
Mauritius 1971–73, Ch 1973

Morocco 1967–72, 1979–81
Mozambique 1983–88
Nigeria 1967–69, 1972–74, 1977–81
Rwanda 1976–78, 1982–84, 1987–89
Senegal 1966–89, Ch 1968, 1978
Sierra Leone 1974–76
Somalia 1987–89
Tanzania 1967–76, 1983–85
Togo 1982–84
Tunisia 1973–76
Uganda 1977–79, 1981–83, Ch 1983
Upper Volta 1975–77
Zaire 1967–75, 1981–83
Zambia 1980–82
Zimbabwe 1982–84

### Asia

Afghanistan 1961–63
Bangladesh 1983–88, Ch 1985
Ceylon 1957–59, Ch 1958–59
China 1947–64, 1982–87
Cyprus 1974–1988
Fiji 1981–83
India 1947–88, Ch 1961
Iran 1947–49, 1957–59, 1967–80, Ch 1970
Iraq 1956–61, 1965–67, 1970–75, 1979–81, 1987–89
Israel 1957–59,1965–70
Japan 1982–87
Jordan 1976–78, 1980–86, Ch 1980
Lebanon 1947–1960, 1962–64, 1968–76, Ch 1951, 1962
Mongolia 1980–81
Pakistan 1951–57, 1960–62, 1967–69, 1971–84, 1987–89, Ch 1965
Philippines 1947–49, 1953–73, 1980–89, Ch 1957, 1965
Sri Lanka 1985–87
Syria 1977–82, 1984–86

(cont.)

Eastern Europe

Bulgaria 1973-86, Ch 1982
Byelorussia 1947-48, 1972-77, 1980-82, 1986-88
German Democratic Republic 1984-88
Poland 1952-72, 1978-83 Ch 1972
Romania 1972-74
Ukraine 1947-71, 1983-85 Ch 1967
USSR 1947-88

Latin America

Argentina 1957-62, 1966-68, 1980-88 Ch 1960
Brazil 1979-87, Ch 1981
Chile 1947-56, 1963-74
Colombia 1978-80, 1983-88, Ch 1986
Costa Rica 1964-67, 1975-77, 1980-88, Ch 1966
Cuba 1976-84
Dominican Republic 1973-75
Ecuador 1963-65, 1972-77 Ch 1964, 1976
El Salvador 1962-64
Guatemala 1949-51, 1967-72
Jamaica 1965-70
Mexico 1955-60,1971-73,1981-89
Nicaragua 1973-75, 1983-88
Panama 1947-48,1961-63,1974-82
Peru 1967-72,1974-82, 1985-87
Uruguay 1947-54,1969-71,1976-84
Venezuela 1960-62,1968-73,1985-87

Western Europe and Other

Australia 1947-55, 1978-83, 1985-87
Austria 1960-62, 1964-75, 1977-79, 1985-87, Ch 1974
Belgium 1947-50, 1952-54, 1958-60, 1986-88
Canada 1963-65, 1976-84, Ch 1979
Denmark 1949-51, 1960-65, 1980-82
Finland 1970-72, 1983-85
France 1947-76, 1978-89, Ch 1955-56
Federal Republic of Germany 1975-77, 1979-87
Greece 1950-52, 1954-56, 1967-69, 1980-82
Ireland 1983-88
Italy 1957-59, 1962-69, 1972-77, 1982-84, 1987-89
Netherlands 1961-66, 1970-75, 1980-85, Ch 1984
New Zealand 1966-71, Ch 1969
Norway 1955-57, 1972-74, 1986-88
Portugal 1979-81
Spain 1966-68, 1984-86
Sweden 1966-68, 1977-79
Turkey 1954-56, 1962-64, 1970-78
United Kingdom 1947-78, 1980-87
United States 1947-89, Ch 1947-50

# Appendix C:
# Symbols of Commission Documents and Publications

The U.N. Commission on Human Rights and the Sub-Commission on Discrimination and Minorities have produced records that now fill several hundred bound volumes in the archives. Except for universities and others serving as United Nations' depositories, few research libraries hold all the official records, even on microfiche. This appendix serves as both a reference aid for those wishing to locate documents cited, as well as a key for the general reader desiring to understand the unfamiliar classification symbols used in the notes.

The United Nations codes documents with symbols composed of letter and arabic numerals separated by oblique strokes (/). Roman numerals were used before 1978 to identify resolutions from sessions I through XXXIII. The mimeographed records bear the same symbol and date in each language edition. Two symbols appear on documents printed as sales publications and on reports from the Commission to ECOSOC, and from the Sub-Commission to the Commission.

The first element in a symbol associates the document with one of the five principal U.N. organs:

A/    General Assembly
E/    Economic and Social Council
S/    Security Council
ST/   Secretariat
T/    Trusteeship Council

Commission documents begin with the symbol of its parent organ, E/-. ECOSOC numbered all documents in sequence from 1946–1977. Since 1978 all ECOSOC documents give the year and begin a new sequence annually. For example:

- U.N. Doc. E/5927 Report to ECOSOC of the Commission's 33rd session in 1977.
- U.N. Doc. E/1982/12 Report of the Commission's 38th session in 1982.

In the official records, those same documents are also identified as 62 U.N. ESCOR Supp. No. 6 and 1982 UN ESCOR Supp. No. 2.

The Commission's annual report to ECOSOC contains all the resolutions adopted, a separate section of draft resolutions recommended for adoption by ECOSOC, as well as appendices listing documents and members, observers, and NGOs participating. Resolutions are numbered in the order adopted by the Commission and identified by either a Ronam Numeral or, since 1983, the year of the session:

- CHR Res. 3(XXXIII) (1977)
- CHR Res. 1984/3

Until 1984, the annual Commission reports summarized the statements made during the debate on each agenda item. After years of lengthy disputes over political bias in the summaries, members agreed to an abbreviated report which simply identifies those who took part in the debate and records all roll call votes on each item.

Commission documents all bear the symbol E/CN.4/-., identifying their origin in the fourth Commission reporting to ECOSOC. The annual reports that became part of ECOSOC's official records identified above also have a Commission document number, E/CN.4/1257 (1977) and E/CN.4/1982/30. (1982 is the first year in which Commission document symbols indicate the year.)

Records from the Sub-Commission on Prevention of Discrimination and Protection of Minorities all have a third element. E/CN.4/Sub.2/-. For over thirty years, the Commission has had only one Sub-Commission, but the element Sub.1 was permanently assigned to the short-lived Sub-Commission on Freedom of Information and of the Press. Since 1982 all Sub-Commission document symbols give the year. For example:

- E/CN.4/Sub.2/495 Report of the Sub-Commission's 34th session in 1981 to the Commission. (The same document is identified as part of the Commission's records E/CN.4/1512.)

Table C.1 gives the symbols for all reports by the Commission and the Sub-Commission through 1986.

The general series documents issued for the Commission and Sub-Commission bear consecutive numbers and include the meeting agenda (provi-sional and annotated), memos from the Secretary-General, communications

TABLE C.1
U.N. Symbols for Reports of the Commission on Human Rights and
the Sub-Commission on Discrimination and Minorities, 1947-1986

| Year | Session | Commission on Human Rights Official Record | UN Doc. | Sub-Commission Session | UN Doc. |
|------|---------|--------------------------------------------|---------|------------------------|---------|
| 1947 | 1  | 4 UN ESCOR Supp. No. 3     | E/259     | 1  | E/CN.4/52     |
|      | 2  | 6 UN ESCOR Supp. No. 1     | E/600     |    |               |
| 1948 | 3  | 7 UN ESCOR Supp. No. 2     | E/800     |    |               |
|      | 4  |                            | E/1315    | 2  | E/CN.4/351    |
| 1949 | 5  | 9 UN ESCOR Supp. No. 10    | E/1371    |    |               |
| 1950 | 6  | 11 UN ESCOR Supp. No. 5    | E/1681    | 3  | E/CN.4/358    |
| 1951 | 7  | 13 UN ESCOR Supp. No. 9    | E/1992    | 4  | E/CN.4/641    |
| 1952 | 8  | 14 UN ESCOR Supp. No. 4    | E/2256    | 5  | E/CN.4/670    |
| 1953 | 9  | 16 UN ESCOR Supp. No. 8    | E/2447    |    |               |
| 1954 | 10 | 18 UN ESCOR Supp. No. 7    | E/2573    | 6  | E/CN.4/703    |
| 1955 | 11 | 20 UN ESCOR Supp. No. 6    | E/2731    | 7  | E/CN.4/711    |
| 1956 | 12 | 22 UN ESCOR Supp. No. 3    | E/2884    | 8  | E/CN.4/721    |
| 1957 | 13 | 24 UN ESCOR Supp. No. 4    | E/2970    | 9  | E/CN.4/740    |
| 1958 | 14 | 26 UN ESCOR Supp. No. 8    | E/3088    | 10 | E/CN.4/764    |
| 1959 | 15 | 28 UN ESCOR Supp. No. 8    | E/3299    | 11 | E/CN.4/778    |
| 1960 | 16 | 30 UN ESCOR Supp. No. 8    | E/3355    | 12 | E/CN.4/800    |
| 1961 | 17 | 32 UN ESCOR Supp. No. 8    | E/3456    | 13 | E/CN.4/815    |
| 1962 | 18 | 34 UN ESCOR Supp. No. 8    | E/3616    | 14 | E/CN.4/830    |
| 1963 | 19 | 36 UN ESCOR Supp. No. 8    | E/3743    | 15 | E/CN.4/846    |
| 1964 | 20 | 37 UN ESCOR Supp. No. 8    | E/3873    | 16 | E/CN.4/873    |
| 1965 | 21 | 39 UN ESCOR Supp. No. 8    | E/4024    | 17 | E/CN.4/882    |
| 1966 | 22 | 41 UN ESCOR Supp. No. 8    | E/4184    | 18 | E/CN.4/903    |
| 1967 | 23 | 42 UN ESCOR Supp. No. 6    | E/4322    | 19 | E/CN.4/930    |
|      |    |                            |           | 20 | E/CN.4/947    |
| 1968 | 24 | 44 UN ESCOR Supp. No. 4    | E/4475    | 21 | E/CN.4/976    |
| 1969 | 25 | 46 UN ESCOR Supp. No. 6    | E/4621    | 22 | E/CN.4/1008   |
| 1970 | 26 | 48 UN ESCOR Supp. No. 5    | E/4816    | 23 | E/CN.4/1040   |
| 1971 | 27 | 50 UN ESCOR Supp. No. 4    | E/4949    | 24 | E/CN.4/1070   |
| 1972 | 28 | 52 UN ESCOR Supp. No. 7    | E/5113    | 25 | E/CN.4/1101   |
| 1973 | 29 | 54 UN ESCOR Supp. No. 6    | E/5265    | 26 | E/CN.4/1128   |
| 1974 | 30 | 56 UN ESCOR Supp. No. 5    | E/5464    | 27 | E/CN.4/1160   |
| 1975 | 31 | 58 UN ESCOR Supp. No. 4    | E/5635    | 28 | E/CN.4/1180   |
| 1976 | 32 | 60 UN ESCOR Supp. No. 3    | E/5768    | 29 | E/CN.4/1218   |
| 1977 | 33 | 62 UN ESCOR Supp. No. 6    | E/5927    | 30 | E/CN.4/1261   |
| 1978 | 34 | 1978 UN ESCOR Supp. No. 4  | E/1978/34 | 31 | E/CN.4/1296   |
| 1979 | 35 | 1979 UN ESCOR Supp. No. 6  | E/1979/36 | 32 | E/CN.4/1350   |
| 1980 | 36 | 1980 UN ESCOR Supp. No. 3  | E/1980/13 | 33 | E/CN.4/1413   |
| 1981 | 37 | 1981 UN ESCOR Supp. No. 5  | E/1981/25 | 34 | E/CN.4/1512   |
| 1982 | 38 | 1982 UN ESCOR Supp. No. 2  | E/1982/12 | 35 | E/CN.4/1983/4 |
| 1983 | 39 | 1983 UN ESCOR Supp. No. 3  | E/1983/23 | 36 | E/CN.4/1984/3 |
| 1984 | 40 | 1984 UN ESCOR Supp. No. 4  | E/1984/14 | 37 | E/CN.4/1985/3 |
| 1985 | 41 | 1985 UN ESCOR Supp. No. 2  | E/1986/22 | 38 | E/CN.4/1986/5 |
| 1986 | 42 | 1986 UN ESCOR Supp. No. 2  | E/1986/22 |    |               |

from governments, committee reports and studies, and the annual final report. A final component of the general series symbol may designate additional text for the original document: -/Add.1, or correction: -/Corr.3, or Revision: -/Rev.1. Studies or reports from the general series published for wider distribution receive a sales number. Examples of general series documents:

- E/CN.4/Sub.2/462 Provisional Agenda for the 34th session of the Sub-Commission
- E/CN.4/Sub.2/1981/Add.1  Annotated Provisional Agenda for the Commission's 35th Session
- Sales No. E.86.XIV.1 *Exploitation of Labour Through Illicit and Clandestine Trafficking* (Originally E/CN.4/Sub.2/1986/6 by Halima Warzazi)

Limited series documents bear the designation -/L.- and include draft resolutions and proposed amendments submitted for consideration at a session. Where proposals involve financial expense, the Secretariat prepares and distributes an L. series document informing members of estimated financial implications. Reports and draft resolutions prepared for confidential review of Resolution 1503 situations in closed meetings are marked restricted and circulated only to members.

- E/CN.4/1984/L.21 Situation in Grenada - Nicaragua draft resolution

The nongovernmental organization series designated -/NGO/- also has limited distribution. Organizations in consultative status are permitted to make written submissions for translation and duplication if within a 2,000 word limit.

- E/CN.4/1982/NGO/2 Written statement submitted by the International Commission of Jurists

The separately bound summary records of the annual session provide detailed reports of the substantive debate and procedural decisions for each public meeting, but are not verbatim transcripts. The commission and Sub-Commission generally hold two daily meetings of about three hours duration; each meeting has its own -/SR.- number. In a six week annual session, the Commission may hold 50 public meetings for which summary records are available, and another ten private meetings to review confidential communications. Summary records for closed meetings devoted to confidential review under Resolution 1503 are numbered in proper sequence, but are marked (Restricted) and are distributed to members only. The annual report gives the meeting numbers when each agenda item was discussed. As an economy measure summary records were not produced in 1980 and 1981. The United

TABLE C.2
U.N. Symbols for Documents of
Selected Commission Working Groups and Committees

---

E/CN.4/AC.1/-. Drafting Committee [on the International Bill of
Rights] [1947--1948]
E/CN.4/AC.2/-. Working Group on the Declaration of Human Rights [1947]
E/CN.4/AC.3/-. Working Group on Convention on Human Rights [1947]
E/CN.4/AC.4/-. Working Party on Implementation of Human Rights [1947]
E/CN.4/AC.5/-. Ad Hoc Committee of Communications [1947--1948]
E/CN.4/AC.6/-. Sub-Committee Appointed to Examine the Human
Rights Yearbook, the Report of the War Crimes Commission and the
Study on the Evolution of Human Rights.
E/CN.4/AC.7/-. Committee on the Prevention of Discrimination and
the Protection of Minorities [1949]
E/CN.4/AC.8/-. Committee on the Yearbook on Human Rights [1949]
E/CN.4/AC.9/-. Committee on Communications [1949]
E/CN.4/AC.10/-. Committee on Trusteeship Questionnaire [1949]
E/CN.4/AC.11/-. Ad Hoc Commitee on Prevention of Discrimination
and Protection of Minorities [1950]
E/CN.4/AC.12/-. Ad Hoc Committee on the Yearbook [on human
rights] [1950]
E/CN.4/AC.13/-. Committee on Communications [1950] Restricted
E/CN.4/AC.14/-. Working Group on Economic, Social and Cultural
Rights [1951]
E/CN.4/AC.15/-. Working Group on Measures of Implementation of
Economic, Social and Cultural Rights [1951]
E/CN.4/AC.16/-. Committee on Communications [1958]
E/CN.4/AC.17/-. Committee on Periodic Reports [1962]
E/CN.4/AC.18/-. Committee on Periodic Reports on Human Rights [1964---]
E/CN.4/AC.19/-. Working Party on the Internationa Year for Human
Rights [1965---]
E/CN.4/AC.20/-. Ad Hoc Committee on Periodic Reports [1966---]
E/CN.4/AC.21/-. Working Group to Study the Proposal to Create the
Institution of a United Nations High Commissioner for Human
Rights [1966---]
E/CN.4/AC.22/-. Ad Hoc Working Group of Experts on investigation
of charges of torture and ill-treatment of political prisoners in
South Africa [1967---] Restricted
E/CN.4/AC.23/-. Ad Hoc Study Group to study the establishment of
regional commissions on human rights [1967---]
E/CN.4/AC.24/-. Ad Hoc Working Group Established under Resolution
8 (XXIII) to study the establishment of regional commissions on
human rights [1967---]
E/CN.4/AC.25/-. Committee on the Right of Everyong to be Free
from Arbitrary Arrest, Detention and Exile [1969---]
E/CN.4/AC.26/-. Special Working Group of Experts Established
under Resolution 6 (XXV) of the Commission on Human Rights [1969---]
E/CN.4/AC.31/- Working Group on Situations of Gross Violations
(Confidential)
E/CN.4/AC.33/- Group of Three under the Apartheid Convention

(cont.)

TABLE C.2 cont.

---

E/CN.4/Sub.1/-. Sub-Commission on Freedom of Information and of
the Press [1947--1952]
E/CN.4/Sub.2/-. Sub-Commission on Prevention of Discrimination
and Protection of Minorities
E/CN.4/Sub.2/AC.1/- Sub-Commission Working Group on
Communications (Confidential)
E/CN.4/Sub.2/AC.2/- Sub-Commission Working Group on Slavery
E/CN.4/Sub.2/AC.3/- Sub-Commission Working Group on Indigenous
Populations
E/CN.4/1266 Report of the Ad Hoc Working Group on Chile [1978]
E/CN.4/WG.1/-. Working Group on the Convention Against Torture
E/CN.4/1981/WG.4/-. Working Group on a Declaration Against
Religious Intolerance
E/CN.4/1982/WG.1/-. Working Group on a Draft Convention on the
Rights of the child
E/CN.4/1982/WG.3/-. Report of the Informal Open-Ended Working Group
on Further promotion and encouragement of human rights, . . .
programme and methods; . . . alternative approaches
E/CN.4/1982/L.42 Report of the Informal Open-ended Working Group on a
Declaration on Minorities
E/CN.4/1985/11  Report of the Working Group of Governmental Experts
on the Right to Development
E/CN.4/1986/15 Report of the Special Rapporteur on Torture
E/CN.4/1986/18 Report of the Working Group on Enforced or
Involuntary Disappearances

---

Nations Information Service issues detailed, consecutively numbered press releases (HR/-) for each Commisison meeting weeks before the summary records become available.

- E/CN.4/1982/SR.1-61 Summary Records of the Commission's 38th Session
- ECN.4/Sub.2/SR.895-934 Summary Records of the Sub-Commission's 34th Session (1981)

Working Groups and *ad hoc* committees of both the Commission and Sub-Commission may meet between, before, or during the regular sessions. Their reports, findings, and recommendations carry a separate designation, -/WG.- or -/AC.- and may be separately bound, if available. Working papers presented to a committee for its consideration are identified with -/WP-.

- E/CN.4/AC.22/-. Ad Hoc Working Group of Experts to study torture and ill treatment of political prisoners in South Africa

Table C.2 lists symbols for early committees and working groups and selected examples of more recent reports from the general series by groups and rapporteurs no longer identified by distinct symbols.

The Secretariat has published reports of advisory services seminars in two series designated ST/HR/TAO/HR/1–50 and ST/HR/SER.A/1—.

* ST/HR/SER.A/19 Seminar on international assistance and support to peoples and movements struggling against colonialism, racism, racial discrimination and *apartheid* —Cameroun, 1986

# Notes

## Chapter 1

1. Hersch Lauterpacht, *International Law and Human Rights* (New York: Frederick A. Praeger, Inc., 1950), p. 115–118.

2. Leslie Bethell, *The Abolition of the Brazilian Slave Trade: Britain, Brazil and the Slave Trade Question 1807–1969* (Cambridge: Cambridge University Press, 1970), pp. 12–18; see also Suzanne Meiers, *Britain and the Ending of the Slave Trade* (London: Longman, 1975).

3. James F. Green, *The United Nations and Human Rights* (Washington, D.C.: The Brookings Institution, 1956), pp. 6–7.

4. Marian Neal, "The United Nations and Human Rights," *International Conciliation* 489 (March 1953): p. 113.

5. See Green, *United Nations*, pp. 6–7.

6. See Archibald A. Evans, *Workers Rights are Human Rights* (Rome: IDOC International, 1981), pp. 5–9.

7. Percy E. Corbett, "Next Steps After the Charter: An Approach to the Enforcement of Human Rights," *Commentary* (November, 1945): p. 23.

8. Green, *United Nations*, p. 12. See generally Inis Claude, *National Minorities: An International Problem* (Cambridge: Harvard University Press, 1955); Oscar I. Janowsky, *Nationalities and National Minorities (With Special Reference to East-Central Europe)* (New York: Macmillan, 1945); Gilbert Murray, *From the League to the U.N.* (London: Oxford University Press, 1948); F. P. Walters, *A History of the League of Nations* (London: Oxford University Press, 1952).

9. Green, *United Nations*, p. 9.

10. Ibid, p. 14. Robinson traces the considerable wartime activities of nongovernmental organizations that planned for the peace and protection of human rights. Jacob Robinson, *Human Rights and Fundamental Freedoms in the Charter of the United Nations: A Commentary* (New York: Institute of Jewish Affairs, 1946). See also Edwin Borchard, "Historical Background of International Protection of Human Rights," *Annals of the American Academy of Political and Social Science* 243 (January 1946); pp. 112–117; Neal, "Human Rights," pp. 114–115.

11. Ruth B. Russell, *A History of the United Nations Charter: The Role of the United States 1940–1945* (Washington, D.C.: The Brookings Institution, 1958), p. 326.

12. Ibid., p. 329.

13. Paul G. Lauren, "First Principles of Racial Equality: History and the Politics and Diplomacy of Human Rights Provisions in the United Nations Charter," *Human Rights Quarterly* 5 (Winter 1983): pp. 9–12.

14. "With a view to the creation of conditions of stability and well-being which are necessary for peaceful and friendly relations among nations, the Organization should facilitate solutions of international economic, social, and other humanitarian problems and promote respect for human rights and fundamental freedoms." Chapter IX, Sec. A(1) of the Dumbarton Oaks Proposals, U.S. Department of State, Dumbarton Oaks Documents on International Organization, Publication 2192 (1944), p. 19 as cited by Green, *United Nations*, p. 16.

15. Russell, *History of Charter*, p. 215, n. 9. See also Robinson, *Fundamental Freedoms*, p. 32–34, which details the considerable efforts made by non-governmental organizations to influence United States planners; Commission to Study the Organization of Peace, *International Safeguard of Human Rights 4th Report* (1966), Part III.

16. "Round Robin Proposal of the Consultants to the American Delegation" in *The Jewish Position at the United Nations Conference on International Organization* (New York: 1945), pp. 77–78 as cited by Robinson, *Fundamental Freedoms*, p. 34. Secretary of State Edward Stettinius repeatedly paid tribute to the great impact of non-governmental organizations on the final human rights provisions of the Charter. Edward R. Stettinius, "The Commission on Human Rights," *Annals of the American Academy of Political and Social Science* 243 (January 1946): p. 1.

17. Russell, *History of Charter*, p. 610.

18. Ibid, p. 5.

19. Robinson, *Fundamental Freedoms*, pp. 22–23.

20. Russell, *History of Charter*, pp. 610, 792.

21. The provisions became Article 13 of the Charter.

22. Doc. 2, G/29, May 5, 1945 as cited by Robinson, *Fundamental Freedoms*, p. 27 (Documents of the United Nations Conference on International Organization, San Francisco, 1945, United Nations Information Office, New York). (Hereafter cited as *Doc.*)

23. Doc. 2, G/7(o), March 21, 1945, pp. 5–6 as cited by Robinson, *Fundamental Freedoms*, p. 29.

24. Robinson, *Fundamental Freedoms*, pp. 47–48.

25. Ibid., pp. 32–33.

26. See Lauren, "Racial Equality," p. 18.

27. Robinson, *Fundamental Freedoms*, p. 28.

28. U.N. Charter, signed 26 June 1945, entered into force 24 October 1945; 59 Stat. 1031, T.S. No. 933 (1945); reprinted in 1946–1947 U.N.Y.B., pt. 3, app. 1, arts. 55, 56 (hereafter cited as *Charter*).

29. Russell, *History of Charter*, p. 792.

30. M. Glen Johnson, "The Contributions of Eleanor and Franklin Roosevelt to the Development of International Protection for Human Rights," *Human Rights Quarterly* 9 (February 1987): pp. 19–48.

31. U.S. Department of State, "United Nations Conference on International Organization," *Bulletin* 12 (May 20, 1945): p. 928 (statement of Secretary of State Stettinius made at San Francisco). Stettinius had made a radio broadcast May 28 calling the human rights provisions as "of greatest importance." Robinson, *Fundamental Freedoms*, p. 37. United States delegates Harold Stassen and Dean Virginia Gildersleeve of Barnard strongly favored the provision to create a Commission on Human Rights.

32. Russell, *History of Charter*, p. 792; Robinson, *Fundamental Freedoms*, p. 48.

33. Charter, art. 68.
34. Robinson, *Fundamental Freedoms*, p. 50.
35. Doc. 861, II/3/55(1), June 8, 1945 as cited by Robinson, *Fundamental Freedoms*, p. 49.
36. Robinson, *Fundamental Freedoms*, pp. 31–32.
37. Charter, art. 39.
38. Robinson, *Fundamental Freedoms*, pp. 98–99, n. 7.
39. See Lauterpacht, *International Law*, pp. 374–378.
40. O. Frederick Nolde, "Possible Functions of the Commission on Human Rights," *Annals of the American Academy of Political and Social Science* 243 (January 1946): p. 147. Robinson quotes the extreme optimism of James Shotwell: "A magnificent victory for freedom and human rights," and Archibald MacLeish: "[A] great beginning, a beginning of which Jefferson and Lincoln and the other heroes of the endless struggle for human liberty would have mightily approved." Robinson, *Fundamental Freedoms*, p. 16, p. 6.
41. Corbett, "Next Steps," pp. 25–26.
42. Philip C. Jessup, "A Good Start," *Commentary* (January 1946): p. 56–57.
43. Nathaniel Peffer, "A Too Remote Goal," *Commentary* (January 1946): p. 59.
44. See Borchard, "Historical Background," pp. 116–117.
45. United States, *Congressional Record*, Vol. 91, No. 130, June 29, 1945, p. 7091 as cited by Robinson, *Fundamental Freedoms*, p. 14.
46. U.S. Department of State, *Charter of the United Nations, Report to the President on the Results of the San Francisco Conference by the Chairman of the United States Delegation, the Secretary of State, June 26, 1945*, Conference Series 71, no. 2349.
47. Stettinius, "Rights in Charter," p. 1.
48. See U.S. Department of State, "United Nations Conference," p. 929.
49. Report of the Preparatory Commission of the United Nations, Chapter III, Section 4, paragraphs 2, 15–17, 36–41 as cited by Robinson, *Fundamental Freedoms*, p. 96–97.
50. Ibid.
51. Ibid.
52. John P. Humphrey, *Human Rights and the United Nations: A Great Adventure* (Dobbs Ferry, New York: Transnational Publishers, Inc., 1984), p. 14.
53. Ibid., p. 27.
54. *Journal of the Economic and Social Council*, First Year, No. 14 (24 May, 1946), p. 164 as cited by Lauterpacht, *International Law*, p. 224.
55. Ibid., as cited by Lauterpacht, *International Law*, pp. 224–225.
56. *Journal of the Economic and Social Council*, First Year, No. 29 (13 July, 1946), p. 522 as cited in Lauterpacht, *International Law*, p. 225.
57. United Nations Economic and Social Council Resolutions 5(I) of February 16, 1946 and 9(II) of June 21, 1946 provide as follows: (See Appendix A for additional text.) "The work of the Commission shall be directed towards submitting proposals, recommendations and reports to the Council regarding: (a) An international bill of rights; (b) International declarations or conventions on civil liberties, the status of women, freedom of information an[d] similar matters; (c) The protection of minorities; (d) The prevention of discrimination on grounds of race, sex, language and religion; (e) Any other matter concerning human rights not covered by items [(a)–(d)]. The Commission shall make studies and recommendations and provide information and other services at the request of the

Economic and Social Council. The Commission may propose to the Council any changes in its terms of reference. The Commission may make recommendations to the Council concerning any sub-commission which it considers should be established."

58. Edgar Turlington, "The United Nations Commission on Human Rights," *American Journal of International Law* 39 (1945): p. 758.

59. Humphrey, *Adventure*, p. 17. See also Nabiel J. Fareed, "The United Nations Commission in Human Rights and Its Work for Human Rights and Fundamental Freedoms," (Ph.D. diss., Washington State University, 1977, University Microfilms).

60. Humphrey, *Adventure*, p. 17.

61. Rule 11, ECOSOC, Rules of Procedure of the Functional Commissions of the Economic and Social Council, U.N. Doc. E/5975 (1977) (hereafter cited as *Rules of Procedure*).

62. See Appendix B: State Members of the Commission, 1947–86.

63. Humphrey, *Adventure*, pp. 23–24.

64. Samuel Hoare, "The UN Commission on Human Rights," in *The International Protection of Human Rights*, ed. Evan Luard (London: Thames & Hudson, 1967), p. 61.

65. Humphrey, *Adventure*, p. 23.

66. Charter, art. 101, para. 2.

67. Humphrey, *Adventure*, p. 17.

68. Charter, art. 101, para. 3.

69. Charter, art. 100, para. 2.

70. Humphrey, *Adventure*, p. 338.

## Chapter 2

1. Charter (see chap. 1, n. 28), art. 70.

2. ECOSOC determined that a proposed Sub-Commission for women ought to be established as a full Commission in its own right.

3. Other petition procedures appear in the 1815 Congress of Vienna, 1878 Congress of Berlin, 1907 Hague Peace Conference, 1907 Treaty of Washington, and 1922 Geneva Convention on Upper Silesia. Donald P. Parson, "The Individual Right to Petition: A Study of Methods Used by International Organizations to Utilize the Individual as a Source of Information on the Violations of Human Rights," *Wayne Law Review* 13 (1967): pp. 678–687.

4. Charter, ch. VII.

5. Ibid., art. 87, para. b.

6. Ibid, art. 39.

7. ECOSOC Res. 9(II), 1946.

8. Ton J.M. Zuijdwijk, *Petitioning the United Nations: A Study in Human Rights* (New York: St. Martin's Press, 1982), p. 4.

9. CHR, *Report of the First Session*, U.N. Doc. E/259 (1947), para. 22.

10. Zuijdwijk, *Petitioning*, p. 4.

11. ECOSOC Resolution 75(V), 1947. ECOSOC authorized the Sub-Commission to review the confidential list, but did not grant the experts' request to review the original texts of communications alleging discrimination. Zuijdwijk, *Petitioning*, p. 9. ECOSOC also restricted review by the Commission on the Status of Women. Ibid., p. 29. See Appendix A, ECOSOC Res. 728(XXVIII)F.

12. ECOSOC Res. 116(VI), 1948.

13. James F. Green, *The United Nations and Human Rights* (Washington, D.C.: The Brookings Institution, 1956), p. 120, n. 1.

14. John P. Humphrey, *Human Rights and the United Nations: A Great Adventure* (Dobbs Ferry, New York: Transnational Publishers, Inc., 1984), p. 167.

15. See Green, *United Nations*, p. 124–125.

16. Humphrey, *Adventure*, p. 28.

17. U.N. Doc. E/CN.4/165 (1949) (Report of the Secretary-General on the present situation with regard to communications concerning human rights, presented to the Fifth Session of the United Nations Commission on Human Rights).

18. Humphrey, *Adventure*, p. 28.

19. CHR, *Report of the Fifth Session*, U.N. Doc. E/1371 (1949), para. 13.

20. Green, *United Nations*, p. 124.

21. Universal Declaration of Human Rights, adopted 10 December 1948; G.A. Res 217 A (III), U.N. Doc. A/810 (1948) (hereafter cited as *Declaration*). For more detailed analysis of the Declaration, see Helle Kanger, *Human Rights in the U.N. Declaration* (Uppsala: Skritter Utgivna Av Stratsvetenskapliga Forenign, 1985); Hersch Lauterpacht, *International Law and Human Rights* (New York: Frederick A. Praeger, Inc., 1950); L. Oppenheim, *International Law* 8th ed., ed. Hersch Lauterpacht (London: Longmans, Green and Co., 1955); Nehemiah Robinson, *The Universal Declaration of Human Rights: Its Origin, Significance, Application, and Interpretation* (New York: Institute of Jewish Affairs, 1958); Egon Schwelb, *Human Rights and the International Community: The Roots and Growth of the Universal Declaration of Human Rights, 1948–1963* (Chicago: Quadrangle Books, 1964).

22. Ruth B. Russell, *A History of the United Nations Charter: The Role of the United States 1940–1945* (Washington, D.C.: The Brookings Institution, 1958), pp. 326–327.

23. *United Nations Action in the Field of Human Rights*, U.N. publication, Sales No. E.83.XIV.2, p. 8.

24. Peter Meyer, "The International Bill: A Brief History," in *The International Bill of Human Rights*, ed. Paul Wiliams (Glen Ellen, California: Entwhistle Books, 1981), p. xxxix.

25. Humphrey, *Adventure*, pp. 31–32. Robinson lists twelve drafts that had been published by 1946. Jacob Robinson, *Human Rights and Fundamental Freedoms in the Charter of the United Nations: A Commentary* (New York: Institute of Jewish Affairs, 1946), pp. 98–99, n. 7.

26. *1947 Yearbook on Human Rights*, U.N. publication, Sales No. 49.XIV.1, p. 484. In addition, the Division supplied over 408 pages of documentation to the members. United Nations Department of Public Information, "International Bill of Rights to be Drafted," *United Nations Weekly Bulletin* (June 17, 1947): p. 639.

27. Humphrey describes Cassin's text as merely a revision, reorganization, and translation of the Secretariat outline. At the request of the French government, the United Nations later exhibited Cassin's handwritten draft as the "original" version of the Declaration. Humphrey, *Adventure*, pp. 42–43.

28. "A Statement on the Denial of Human Rights to Minorities in the case of Citizens of Negro Descent in the United States of America and an Appeal to the United Nations for Redress," prepared for the NAACP, October 23, 1947, Records

of the U.S. Mission, Record Group 84, U.S. Mission to the United Nations, 1945–49, National Archives.

29. Humphrey, *Adventure*, pp. 27, 40.

30. The ABA House of Delegates found the proposed Declaration and Covenants "not in contents or draftmanship suitable for approval or adoption." American Bar Association, "Declaration on Human Rights: Canadian, American Bars Ask for Delay of Action," ABA Journal 34 (October 1948): pp. 881, 885.

31. Roosevelt's 1941 state of the union address identified four freedoms, including economic well being.

32. Humphrey, *Adventure*, p. 40.

33. Ibid., p. 45.

34. "All human beings are born free and equal. . . . They are endowed with reason and conscience." Declaration, art. 1.

35. Ibid., art. 14.

36. Ibid., art. 17.

37. Ibid., art. 22.

38. Humphrey proposed the measure as a result of United States eighteenth century court rulings that barred slaves the right to appear in court.

39. Declaration, art. 19.

40. Ibid., art. 7.

41. Ibid., art. 29.

42. Ibid., art. 26.

43. Ibid., art. 25.

44. Ibid., art. 23.

45. Ibid., art. 24.

46. John Humphrey, "The Right of Petition in the United Nations," *Human Rights Journal* 4 (1971): pp. 464–465.

47. G.A. Res. 217B(III), 1948.

48. Richard Lillich and Frank Newman, *International Human Rights* (Boston: Little, Brown and Company, 1979), p. 53–121; Josef L. Kunz, "The United Nations Declaration of Human Rights," *American Journal of International Law* 43 (1949): p. 316; Egon Schwelb, "The Influence of the Universal Declaration of Human Rights on International and National Law," *American Society of International Law Proceedings* (1959): p. 217.

49. See International Commission of Jurists, "Montreal Statement of the Assembly for Human Rights, March 22–27, 1968," *Journal of the International Commission of Jurists* 9 (June 1968): pp. 94–95.

50. For a more detailed analysis of the covenants drafting see Nabiel J. Fareed, "The United Nations Commission on Human Rights and Its Work for Human Rights and Fundamental Freedoms," (Ph.D. diss., Washington State University, 1977, University Microfilms); Manouchehr Ganji, *International Protection of Human Rights* (Geneva: E. Droz, 1962); E. Lauterpacht, ed., *British Practice in International Law—1963* (London: British Institute of International and Comparative Law, 1965), p. 223; Gaius Ezejiofor, *Protection of Human Rights Under the Law* (London: Butterworths, 1964); Myres S. McDougal and Gerhard Bebr, "Human Rights in the United Nations," *American Journal of International Law* 58 (1964): p. 603; Symposium on the International Law of Human Rights, *Howard Law Journal* 11 (Spring 1965): p. 257.

51. In the Third Committee the Food and Agriculture Organization proposed language on freedom from hunger.

52. Humphrey, *Adventure*, p. 106. American Civil Liberties Union founder Roger Baldwin lobbied at the 1951 Commission session in Geneva. Ibid., p. 144.

53. Ibid., p. 88.

54. G.A. Res. 421E(V), 1950.

55. International Covenant on Economic, Social and Cultural Rights, opened for signature 19 December 1966, entered into force 3 January 1976; G.A. Res. 2200A (XXI), 21 U.N. GAOR Supp. No. 16, at 49, U.N. Doc. A/6316, art. 8, para. (d) (1966), (hereafter cited as *Economic Covenant*).

56. G.A. Res. 543(VI), 1952.

57. Humphrey, *Adventure*, p. 86. Seven Third World countries, Canada, and the Netherlands sought once again in the Third Committee to include the right to petition on the covenant itself. By a vote of 41 to 39 with 16 abstentions, the Third Committee decided instead to add the optional protocol. UN Doc. A/C.3/SR.1440 as cited by Manfred Nowak, "The Effectiveness of the International Covenant on Civil and Political Rights—Stocktaking After the First Eleven Sessions of the UN Human Rights Committee," *Human Rights Law Journal* 1 (1980): p. 141.

58. Although the Soviets have never accepted interstate complaints under Article 41 nor ratified the optional protocol, they did ratify both covenants and now publicly support the Declaration.

59. Congressional Quarterly News Features, "Bricker Treaty Amendment Debate," *Congressional Quarterly Almanac*, 83rd Cong., 2d sess., vol. X (1954), p. 254.

60. Optional Protocol to the International Covenant on Civil and Political Rights, adopted 16 December 1966, entered into force 23 March 1976; G.A. Res. 2200 (XXI), 21 U.N. GAOR Supp. No. 16, 59 U.N. Doc. A/6316, arts. 1–14 (1966).

61. Humphrey, *Adventure*, pp. 141–142.

62. Economic Covenant, art. 17, para. 3.

63. U.N. Doc. E/CN.4/1983/29, para. 7.

64. Economic Covenant, art. 2, para. 3.

65. The Resolution passed 33–9–10 in the Third Committee and 42–7–5 in plenary. Humphrey, *Adventure*, p. 163.

66. U.N. Doc. E/CN.4/L.24 (1952).

67. International Covenant on Civil and Political Rights, opened for signature 19 December 1966, entered into force 23 March 1976; G. A. Res. 2200A (XXI), 21 U.N. GAOR Supp. No. 16, at 52, U.N. Doc. A/613, art. 1, para. 2 (1966) (hereafter cited as *Political Covenant*).

68. Ibid., Article aa.

69. U.N. Doc. E/CN.4/SR.379 (1953), para. 14. The provision appears in the Political Covenant as follows: "Any advocacy of national, racial or religious hatred that constitutes incitement to discrimination, hostility or violence shall be prohibited by law." Political Covenant, art. 20, para. 2.

70. Ibid., art. 19, para. 3.

71. Ibid., art. 18, para. 3.

72. Ibid., art. 21.

73. Ibid., art. 4, para. 1.

74. The covenant's leading conservative foe in the United States, Senator Bricker, zealously denounced it as "a Covenant on Human Slavery," Congres-

sional Record, 82nd Cong., 1st sess., 1951, vol. 97, pt. 6, p. 8255. Bricker warned that the covenant would "betray the fundamental, inalienable, and God-given rights of American citizens enjoyed under the constitution." Congressional Record, 82nd Cong., 2d sess., 1952, vol. 98, pt. 1, p. 912. The ABA also opposed the covenants.

75. Senate Committee on the Judiciary, Subcommittee on Constitutional Amendments, *Hearings on S.U. Res. 1 and S.J. Res. 43, Treaties and Executive Agreements*, 83rd Cong., 1st sess., 1953.

76. Colonial powers unsuccessfully attempted to limit application of the declaration in their dependent territories.

77. A letter from Secretary of State Dulles to Mrs. Lord of April 3, 1953 appears in *Foreign Relations of the United States, `1952–1954*, vol. III (Washington: Government Printing Office, 1979), pp. 1564–1567.

78. Political Covenant, art. 50.

79. M. Glen Johnson, "The Contributions of Eleanor and Franklin Roosevelt to the Development of International Protection for Human Rights," *Human Rights Quarterly* 9 (February 1987).

80. Humphrey, *Adventure*, p. 85. See also Jason Berger, *A New Deal for the World: Eleanor Roosevelt and American Foreign Policy* (New York: Social Science Monographs, 1981). For the most extreme cold warriors, only communist governments committed human rights violations worth condemning.

81. UN Doc. E/C.2/SR84 (Restricted), 13 July 1950, p. 6 as cited by Chiang Pei-heng, *Non-Governmental Organizations at the United Nations: Identity, Role, and Function* (New York: Praeger, 1981), pp. 104–105.

82. ECOSOC Res. 1296(XLIV), 1968. The WIDF and IASL were unable to regain consultative status until 1967 when additional Third World members created a new voting majority on ECOSOC's NGO committee.

83. Charter, art. 100, para. 2.

84. Humphrey, *Adventure*, p. 171.

85. See Appendix: State Members of the Sub-Commission 1947–1983.

86. See ECOSOC Res. 9(II), 1946.

87. *The United Nations and Human Rights*, U.N. publication, Sales No. E.78.I.18, p. 26.

88. Meyer, *A Brief History*, p. xxxix. See also *The Impact of the Universal Declaration of Human Rights*, U.N. publication, Sales No. 1953.XIV.1.

# Chapter 3

1. O. Frederick Nolde, "Human Rights and the United Nations: Appraisal and Next Steps," *Proceedings of the Academy of Political Science* 2 (January 1953).

2. Norman Bentwich, "Human Rights in the Doldrums," *Contemporary Review* 1088 (August 1956): p. 79.

3. ECOSOC Res. 501C(XVI), 1953.

4. CHR, *Report of the Eleventh Session*, U.N. Doc. E/2731 (1955).

5. In 1967 the Commission added a fourth component, Regional Training Courses. CHR Res. 17(XXIII), 1967.

6. G.A. Res. 926(X), 1955.

7. John P. Humphrey, *Human Rights and the United Nations: A Great Adventure* (Dobbs Ferry, New York: Transnational Publishers, Inc., 1984), p. 204.

8. Ibid., pp. 205, 207.

9. CHR Res. VIII, 1955.
10. In 1958 the Assembly increased the annual appropriation to $100,000.
11. U.N. Doc. E/2573 (1954), para. 377.
12. CHR Res. II, 1956.
13. CHR, *Report of the Twelfth Session*, U.N. Doc. E/2884 (1956), para. 59.
14. CHR, *Report of the Sixth Session*, U.N. Doc. E/1681 (1950), para. 47.
15. CHR Res. I, 1956.
16. Humphrey, *Adventure*, p. 177.
17. See Ibid., p. 277. After his retirement, Humphrey refused to attend meetings in Manila in 1977 and 1978.
18. Ibid., pp. 279–280.
19. Ibid., p. 277.
20. U.N. Doc. E/CN.4/1192 (1976), p. 5.
21. Ibid.
22. U.N. Doc. ST/TAO/HR/1–50.
23. CHR Res. III, 1956.
24. Rosalyn Higgins, "Technical Assistance for Human Rights," *The World Today* 19 (May 1963): pp. 222–223.
25. Humphrey, *Adventure*, p. 277.
26. Ibid., p. 292.
27. The Commission made the addition to the advisory services program in 1967.
28. *United Nations Action in the Field of Human Rights*, U.N. publication, Sales No. E.83.XIV.2, p. 369.
29. U.N. Doc. E/CN.4/1192 (1976), para. 67.
30. U.N. Doc. E/CN.4/736 (1957), para. 16.
31. Higgins, "Technical Assistance," p. 220.
32. CHR Res. II, 1956.
33. U.N. Doc. E/CN.4/813/Corr. 1; *Study of the Right of Everyone to be Free From Arbitrary Arrest, Detention and Exile*, U.N. publication, Sales No. 65.XIV.2.
34. The draft principles appear in U.N. Doc. E/CN.4/826 (1962).
35. U.N. Doc. E/CN.4/996 (1969).
36. At that time the reports were consulted for drafting norms on torture and the rights of detainees.
37. U.N. Doc. E/CN.4/757 and Add. 1–7 (1958).
38. Nabiel J. Fareed, "The United Nations Commission on Human Rights and Its Work for Human Rights and Fundamental Freedoms," (Ph.D. diss., Washington State University, 1977, University Microfilms).
39. Moses Moskowitz, *The Politics and Dynamics of Human Rights* (Dobbs Ferry, New York: Oceana Publications, Inc., 1968), pp. 93–94; Samuel Hoare, "The UN Commission on Human Rights," in *The International Protection of Human Rights*, ed. Evan Luard (London: Thames & Hudson, 1967), p. 86; William Korey, "The Key to Human Rights—Implementation," *International Conciliation* 570 (November 1968): pp. 24–28.
40. ECOSOC Res. 9(II), 1946.
41. G.A. Res. 423(V), 1950, proclaimed December 10th as Human Rights Day.
42. G.A. Res. 1961(XVIII), 1963.
43. CHR Res. 6(XX), 1964.
44. International Commission of Jurists, "UN Commission on Human Rights," *International Commission of Jurists Review* 28 (June 1982): p. 38.

45. G.A. Res. 1386(XIV), 1959.

46. Declaration (see chap. 2, n. 21), art. 14.

47. Humphrey, *Adventure*, p. 264.

48. American Association for the International Commission of Jurists, *The Human Rights of All Persons in Prison or Detention: Draft Principles*, pamphlet by the American Association for the International Commission of Jurists, Inc.

49. Paul G. Lauren, "Human Rights in History: Diplomacy and Racial Equality at the Paris Peace Conference," *Diplomatic History* 2 (Summer 1978): pp. 258–259 citing F. A. McKenzie, *The Unveiled East* (London, 1907), p. 318, William Roberts, *The Mongolian Problem in America: A Discussion of the Possibilities of the Yellow Peril* (San Francisco, 1906), Madison Grant, *The Passing of the Great Race* (New York, 1916), p. 24, and United States, Congress, Senate, Immigration Commission, *Reports of the Immigration Commission*, 42 vols., 61st Cong., 3d Sess.

50. Lauren, "Racial Equality," p. 264 citing Conference de la Paix, 1919-1920, *Recueil des actes de la Conference*, 'Secret,' Partie 4, Commission de la Societe des Nations, (Paris, 1922), pp. 89–90.

51. Lauren, "Paris Peace Conference," p. 269 citing David Hunter Miller, *My Diary*, 1:243, 245.

52. Lauren notes that "on two other occasions (both of which were of concern to Wilson), the unanimity 'rule' had not applied at all." Lauren, "Paris Peace Conference," p. 272.

53. Paul Lauren, "First Principles of Racial Equality: History and the Politics of Diplomacy of Human Rights Provisions in the United Nations Charter," *Human Rights Quarterly* 5 (Winter 1983): pp. 10–12.

54. Lauren, "Racial Equality," p. 20 citing Discussion of 10 July 1945, Senate Committee on Foreign Relations, *The Charter of the United Nations: Hearing Before the Committee on Foreign Relations*, 79th Cong., 1st sess., July 1945, 311.

55. International Commission of Jurists, "U.N. Commission on Human Rights," *Bulletin of the International Commission of Jurists* 11 (December 1960), pp. 55–56.

56. Sub-Comm. Res. 3(XII), 1960 and CHR Res. 6(XVI), 1960.

57. Humphrey, *Adventure*, p. 293.

58. G.A. Res. 1904(XVIII), 1963. For the text see *Yearbook of the United Nations, 1963*, U.N. publication, Sales No. E.64/I.1, p. 330.

59. G.A. Res 2106 (XX) December 21, 1965. For more detailed analysis see Natan Lerner, *The UN Convention on the Elimination of All Forms of Racial Discrimination* (The Netherlands: Sitjthoff & Noordhoff, 1980); Bruno V. Bitker, "The International Treaty Against Racial Discrimination," *Marquette Law Review* 53 (1970): p. 68; T. Das, "Measures of Implementation of the Convention on the Elimination of All Forms of Racial Discrimination," *Human Rights Journal* 4 (1971): pp. 245–262. Frank C. Newman, "International Control of Racial Discrimination," *California Law Review* 56 (1968): p. 1559; Egon Schwelb, "The International Convention on the Elimination of All Forms of Racial Discrimination," *International and Comparative Law Quarterly* 15 (October 1966): p. 996.

60. Ian Brownlie, *Basic Documents in International Law*, 2d ed. (Oxford: Clarendon Press, 1972), p. 190.

61. G.A. Res. 1514 (XV), 1960.

62. International Convention on the Elimination of All Forms of Racial Discrimination, opened for signature 21 December 1965, entered into force 4

January 1969; 660 U.N.T.S. 195 (1969); G.A. Res. 2106 A (XX), 20 U.N. GAOR Supp. No. 4, U.N. Doc. A/6014, art. 2, para. 2 (1965) (hereafter cited as *Race Convention*).

63. Ibid., art. 1, para. 2.
64. Ibid., art. 1, para. 3.
65. Ibid., art. 1, para. 1.
66. Humphrey, *Adventure*, p. 332.
67. Race Convention, art. 4(a).
68. Ibid., art. 4.
69. Ibid., art. 2, para. 1.
70. Ibid., art. 3.
71. Ibid., art. 5.
72. Ibid., art. 7.
73. Ibid., art. 2, para. 2.
74. Humphrey, *Adventure*, p. 333.
75. Race Convention, art. 11.
76. Ibid., art. 9, para. 1.
77. Ibid., art. 14, para. 1.
78. Ibid., art. 9, para. 2. See for example, United Nations, "Committee on the Elimination of Racial Discrimination, twenty-fourth session," *Bulletin of Human Rights*, 33 (July–September 1981): p. 26.
79. By 1983 115 states had ratified the race convention, more than any other United Nations human rights instrument. The United States was one of nine additional countries that had signed without ratifying. *Human Rights International Instruments*, U.N. Doc. ST/HR/4/Rev.4, p. 18. Since the convention came into effect in 1969, the Committee has held two meetings a year in New York; the experts did not have jurisdiction to hear individual complaints until the tenth state declaration under Article 14 in 1982. The most common reservations repudiated the Committee's implied power to refer disputes to the International Court of Justice without prior approval of both parties. Race Convention, art. 22. Unlike the covenants, the race convention provides that two-thirds of the states parties may find a "reservation incompatible with the object and purpose of this Convention." Ibid., art. 20, para. 2.
80. See Declaration, art. 18; Political Covenant (see chap. 2, n.67), art. 18, para. 1.
81. Although French and British experts have been rapporteurs, Sub-Commission experts from the U.S. and U.S.S.R. have never had such responsibility.
82. *UN Action*, p. 169.
83. David Binder, "The Victor in the Nazi Trial Issue," *New York Times*, April 26, 1969, p. 9.
84. *The United Nations and Human Rights*, U.N. publication, Sales No. E.78.I.18, p. 39.
85. *UN Action*, p. 249.
86. G.A. Res. 2391 (XXIII), 1968.
87. Robert H. Miller, "The Convention on the Non-Applicability of Statutory Limitations to War Crimes and Crimes Against Humanity," *American Journal of International Law* 65 (1971): p. 501, n.143.
88. United Nations, *Human Rights*, p. 39.
89. European Convention on the Non-Applicability of Statutory Limitation to Crimes Against Humanity and War Crimes (Strasbourg Text in *International Legal Materials* 13 (1974): pp. 540–543).

90. *The Bulletin* (Bonn), September 13, 1979.

91. See Humphrey, *Adventure*, p. 296.

92. Norman Bentwich, "Doldrums," p. 76; Norman Bentwich, "Marking Time for Human Rights," *Contemporary Review* 1100 (August 1957): p. 80; Norman Bentwich, "Ten Years of Human Rights," *Contemporary Review* 1111 (July 1958): p. 23.

93. Article 14, adopted 21 December 1965, entered into force 4 January 1969, 660 U.N.T.S. 195. After the tenth state party declared a willingness to be bound, the procedure became effective in 1983.

94. Ton J. M. Zuijdwijk, *Petitioning the United Nations: A Study in Human Rights* (New York: St. Martin's Press, 1982), pp. 9–14.

95. ECOSOC Res. 728F (XXVIII), 1959.

96. GAOR, Third Committee, Fifth Session, 1959, para. 1.

97. Humphrey, *Adventure*, p. 296.

98. Roger Clark, *A United Nations High Commissioner for Human Rights* (The Hague, The Netherlands: Martinus Nijhoff, 1972), pp. 58–59; R. St. J. MacDonald, "The United Nations Commissioner for Human Rights," *Canadian Yearbook of International Law*, (1967): p. 84.

99. G.A. Res. 1761 (XVII), 1962.

100. The Western powers abstained in 1960 when the Assembly adopted the Soviet proposed Declaration on the Granting of Independence to Colonial Countries and Peoples.

101. G.A. Res. 1654 (XIV), 1961.

102. ECOSOC Res. 1102 (XL), 1966.

103. Zuijdwijk, *Petitioning*, p. 15.

104. U.N. Doc. E/CN.4/L.818 and L.825 (1966) (draft resolutions introduced by the Soviet and U.S. Representatives).

105. CHR Res. 2 (XXII), 1966.

106. ECOSOC Res. 1164 (XLI), 1966 and G.A. Res. 2144A (XXI), 1966.

107. U.N. Doc. E/CN.4/Sub.2/L.456/Corr. 1 (1967) (draft resolution).

108. U.N. Doc. E/CN.4/Sub.2/L.456/Corr. 1 (1967), para 5.

109. Sub-Commission Res. 5 (XXIX), para. 6 as cited by Zuijdwijk, *Petitioning* p. 18; Theresa D. Gonzales, "The Political Sources of Procedural Debates in the United Nations: Structural Impediments to Implementation of Human Rights," *New York University Journal of International Law and Politics* 13 (1981): pp. 450–451.

## Chapter 4

1. Sidney Liskofsky, "Coping With The 'Question of the Violation of Human Rights and Fundamental Freedoms'," *Human Rights Journal* 8 (1975): pp. 883–914.

2. Theo C. van Boven, "The United Nations Commission on Human Rights and Violations of Human Rights and Fundamental Freedom," *Netherland's International Law Review* 15 (1968): p. 383.

3. CHR Res. 9 (XXIII), 1967.

4. ECOSOC Res. 1235 (XLIV), 1967.

5. Ibid.

6. See Theresa Gonzales, "The Political Sources of Procedural Debates in the United Nations: Structural Impediments to Implementation of Human Rights," *New*

*York University Journal of International Law and Politics* 13 (1981): pp. 427–430.

7. U.N. Doc. E/CN.4/Sub.2/L.485 and Add.1 (1967) (draft resolution).
8. U.N. Doc. E/CN.4/SR.965 (1967), paras. 248–249.
9. U.N. Doc. E/CN.4/L.991/Rev. 1 (1968) (draft resolution).
10. U.N. Doc. E/CN.4/Sr.1474 (1978).
11. CHR, *Report of the Twenty-Fourth Session*, U.N. Doc. E/4475 (1968), paras. 192–193.
12. Reports of the Sub-Commission, *Twenty-second Session* (E/CN.4/1008) (1969), para. 225 and *Twenty-third Session*, (E/CN.4/1040 (1970)), p. 117. Sub-Commission Res. 6 (XXIII) as cited by Ton J. M. Zuijdwijk, *Petitioning the United Nations: A study in Human Rights* (New York: St. Martin's Press, 1982) pp. 25, 28.
13. Sub-Comm. Res. 2 (XXI), 1968.
14. CHR, *Report of the Twenty-Fifth Session*, U.N. Doc. E/4621 (1969), paras. 407–435.
15. Ibid.
16. Kent L. Tedin, "The Development of the Soviet Attitude Toward Implementing Human Rights Under the UN Charter," *Human Rights Journal* 5 (1972): p. 400.
17. ECOSOC Res. 1503 (XLVIII), 1970, para 8. (See Appendix A for the text of 1503.)
18. CHR Res. 17 (XXV), 1969.
19. U.N. Doc. E/AC.7/SR.637 (1970).
20. ECOSOC Res. 1503 (XLVIII), 1970, para 1.
21. *GAOR, XXV, Annexes, Agenda item 12* (A/8173/Add.1), paras. 21 and 22 (Report of the Third Committee) as cited by Zuijdwijk, *Petitioning*, p. 28.
22. See Richard L. Jackson, *The Non-Aligned, The UN and The Superpowers* (New York: Praeger, 1983).
23. See Chiang Pei-Heng, *Non-Governmental Organizations at the United Nations: Identity, Role, and Function* (New York: Praeger, 1981), pp. 171–172.
24. Ibid., pp. 174–175.
25. Philip Agee, *Inside the Company: CIA Diary* (New York: Stonehill, 1975), pp. 72–73.
26. Pei-Heng, *Non-Governmental Organizations*, p. 177.
27. ECOSOC Res. 1296 (XLIV), 1968.
28. Reportedly Argentina and Iran.
29. ECOSOC Res. 1919 (LVIII), 1975.
30. Pei-Heng, *Non-Governmental Organization*, p. 131.
31. Argentina named the World Conference of Religion and Peace, the International University Exchange Fund, Pax Romana, the International Federation for the Rights of Man, and the International Commission of Jurists.
32. Amnesty International, the International League for Human Rights, and the Anti-Slavery Society. Pei-Heng, *Non-Governmental Organizations*, p. 189.
33. International Commission of Jurists, *Uganda and Human Rights: Reports to the UN Commission on Human Rights* (Geneva: International Commission of Jurists, 1977).
34. CHR Dec. 12 (XXXV), 1979.
35. CHR, *Report of the Thirty-Third Session*, U.N. Doc. E/5927 (1977), paras. 72–78.
36. Richard B. Lillich and Frank C. Newman, *International Human Rights: Problems of Law and Policy* (Boston: Little, Brown and Company, 1979), p. 298.

37. Thomas Franck and H. Scott Fairley, "Procedural Due Process in Human Rights Fact-Finding by International Agencies," *American Journal of International Law* 74 (1980): p. 310. The authors' indicators of impartiality include: (1) choice of subject, (2) choice of fact-finders, (3) terms of reference, (4) procedures for investigation, and (5) utilization of product. Ibid., p. 311.

38. Helge Ole Bergeson, "The Power to Embarrass: The UN Human Rights Regime Between Realism and Utopia," paper presented to the International Political Science Association (IPSA) World Congress, Rio de Janiero, Brazil, August, 1982.

39. CHR Res. 2 (XXIII), 1967.

40. The Commission's Working Group discontinued its investigation when the Assembly created a Special Committee to investigate Israeli practices.

41. CHR Res. 2 (XXIII), 1967.

42. Ibid.

43. Franck, "Due Process," p. 318. The author praised as a "useful guide," procedural rules adopted during a 1963 United Nations mission to Vietnam. Ibid., p. 219.

44. The oath reads: "I swear to tell the truth, the whole truth, and nothing but the truth." "I solemnly declare, in all honour and conscience, that I will tell the truth, the whole truth, and nothing but the truth." U.N. Doc. E/CN.4/1985/8, para. 116, n.1.

45. John Carey, *UN Protection of Civil and Political Rights* (New York: Syracuse University Press, 1970), pp. 96–107.

46. In 1972 Ghana's motion to postpone narrowly passed, 11–9–8.

47. B. G. Ramcharan, ed., *International Law and Fact-Finding in the Field of Human Rights* (The Hague: Martinus Nijhoff, 1983).

48. At its 1980 Belgrade Conference the International Law Association adopted minimal rules of procedure for international human rights fact-finding missions, submitted to the Commission as U.N. Doc. E/CN.4/NGO/322 (1981).

49. CHR, *Report of the Thirtieth Session*, U.N. Doc. E/5464 (1974), pp. 56–57.

50. U.N. Doc. No. E/CN.4/1985/21, para. 34.

51. Manouchehr Ganji, *Study of Apartheid and Racial Discrimination in Southern Africa*, U.N. Doc. E/CN.4/979 (1970).

52. Two of the first five experts, Felix Ermacora and Branimir Jankovi'c of Austria and Yugoslavia, remained on the group 18 years later. An Indian became the sixth expert; appointees from Chile, Ghana and Zaire replaced members from Peru, Tanzania, and Senegal. In 1986 the Working Group of Experts included Annan Arkyin Cato, Chairman-Rapporteur, Ghana's permanent representative in Geneva; Branimir Jankovi'c, Law Professor from Yugoslavia, Mikuin Leliel Balanda of Zaire, Chile's Humberto Déiza-Casanueva, Austria's Felix Ermacora and India's Govinda Reddy.

53. See *United Nations Action in the Field of Human Rights*, U.N. publication, Sales No. E.83.XIV.2, pp. 283–284.

54. At the 1984 session speakers included special rapporteurs, 38 members, 14 observer states, and representatives of the OAU, the League of Arab States, the United Nations Committee on Apartheid, 4 liberation movements, and 7 NGOs.

55. In 1984 the speakers included 25 members, 17 observer governments, and representatives of the PLO, the League of Arab states and 3 non-governmental organizations.

56. The Charter states that the organization's goal "to maintain international peace," requires members to "settle their international disputes by peaceful means"

and prohibits the U.N. from intervening "in matters which are essentially within the domestic jurisdiction of any state." Charter (see chap. 1, n.28), arts. 1, para. 1, and 2, paras. 3, 7.

57. Ibid., art. 4, para. 1.

58. G.A. Res. 3379 (XXX), 1975.

59. International Convention on the Suppression and Punishment of the Crime of Apartheid, adopted 30 November 1973, entered into force 18 July 1976; G.A. Res. 3068 (XXVIII), 28 U.N. GAOR, Supp. No. 30, at 166, U.N. Doc. A/9030, art. 1, para. 1 (1974) (hereafter cited as *Apartheid Convention*).

60. U.N. Doc. No. E/CN.4/1497 (1982) and E/Cn.4/1983/38.

61. U.N. Doc. E/CN.4/Sub.2/1984/25, p. 11.

62. *Cincinnati Enquirer*, August 14, 1985, p. A–2; NBC Evening News Telecast, August 7, 1985.

63. U.N. Doc. E/CN.4/Sub.2/412 (Vols. I–IV) and Corr.1 (1978).

64. CHR Res. 6 (XXXIII), 1977.

65. ECOSOC Res. 1503 (XLVIII), 1970, para 1.

66. Sub-Comm. Res. 1(XXIV), 1971.

67. Ibid.

68. Hugh I. Manke, "The Exhaustion of Domestic Remedies in the United Nations Sub-Commission on the Prevention of Discrimination and Protection of Minorities," *Buffalo Law Review* 24 (1975): p. 643.

69. Resolution 1503 does not authorize a committee investigation if the situation is subject to other United Nations or regional procedures. For more detailed analysis of the rules on admissibility see Antonio Cassese, "The Admissibility of Communications to the United Nations on Human Rights Violations," *Human Rights Journal* 5 (1972): p. 375. Other accounts of the procedure by informed participants include: Jakob T. H. Moller, "Petitioning the United Nations," *Universal Human Rights* 1 (October–December 1979): p. 57; John Humphrey, "The Right of Petition in the United Nations," *Human Rights Journal* 4 (1971): p. 467. The most comprehensive guide is a 3 volume loose leaf reference: Maxine E. Tardu, *Human Rights: The International Petition System* (Dobbs Ferry, New York: Oceana Publications Inc., 1985).

70. M. E. Tardu, "United Nations Response to Gross Violations of Human Rights: the 1503 Procedure," *Santa Clara Law Review*, 20 (1980): p. 562.

71. See for example. Glenda da Fonesca, *How to File Complaints of Human Rights Violations, A Practical Guide to Inter-Governmental Procedures*, Commission of the Churches on International Affairs of the World Council of Churches (pamphlet No. ISBN 2-8254-0496-9, 1975). (1973). Malvina H. Guggenheim, "Key Provisions of the New United Nations Rules Dealing with Human Rights Petitions," *New York University Journal of International Law and Politics* 6 (1973): p. 427; Hurst Hannum ed., *Guide to International Human Rights Practice*, (Philadelphia: University of Pennsylvania Press, 1984).

72. International Commission of Jurists, "Disappointing Start to New U.N. Procedure on Human Rights," *International Commission of Jurists Review* 9 (December 1972): p. 7. For a different interpretation see F. Ermacora, "Procedure to Deal with Human Rights Violations: A Hopeful Start in the United Nations," *Human Rights Journal* 7 (1974): p. 670–686.

73. The Commission did ask ECOSOC to express hope that "adequate measures are being taken to provide remedy" to Jehovah's Witnesses who may have suffered injustices in Malawi. CHR Dec. 10 (XXXVI), 1980.

74. Hannum, *Human Rights Practice*, pp. 291–294 (Appendix C).

75. See Chapter III above.  See also Maya Prasad, "The Role of Non-Governmental Organizations in the New United Nations Procedures for Human Rights Complaints," *Denver Journal of International Law an Policy* 5 (1975): pp. 441, 460.

76. See David Weissbrodt, "The Role of International Nongovernmental Organizations in the Implementation of Human Rights," *Texas International Law Journal* 12 (1977): pp. 306–310.

77. Dinah L. Shelton, "Individual Complaint Machinery Under the United Nations 1503 Procedure and the Optional Protocol to the International Covenant on Civil and Political Rights," in Hannum, *Human Rights Practice*, pp. 59–73.

78. U.N. Doc. E/CN.4/1371 and Corr.1 (1980).

79. Kathleen Teltsch, "U.N. Unit Said to Report Greeks Violate Human Rights," *The New York Times*, September 21, 1972, p. 18.

80. Berlin, "U.N. Rights Unit to Prove Violations," *New York Post*, February 7, 1974, at 14.

81. Ibid.

82. R. B. Lillich, "The U.N. and Human Rights Complaints," *American Journal of International Law* 64 (1970): p. 610.  The complaint ultimately reached the United Nations through Amnesty International.  International Commission of Jurists, "Individual Petition and International Law," *International Commission of Jurists Review* 5 (March 1970): p. 23.

83. Press Release SG/SM/1200 of December 22, 1969, pp. 5–7.

84. Declaration (see chap. 2, n.21), arts. 12 and 19.  The Netherlands was commenting on the proposed Resolution 1503 procedure before final approval in 1970. Zuijdwijk, *Petitioning*, pp. 90–91.

85. ECOSOC Resolutions 270(X), 1950 and 474A(XV), 1953.

86. ECOSOC Res. 1503(XLVIII), 1970, para. 1.

87. Sub-Comm. Res. 2(XXIV), 1971.  Normally appointed by the Chair, in practice each regional group selects its own working group members.

88. Lillich and Newman *International Human Rights*, p. 365.

89. U.N. Doc. E/CN.4/SR.1618 (1981), para. 19, p. 5.

90. Shelton, "Individual Complaint," in Hannum, *Human Rights Practice*, p. 61.

91. CHR Dec. 4(XXXIV), 1978.  The Commission invited the Working Group's Chairman to attend.

92. Sub-Comm. Res. 7B(XXXI), 1978 and Sub-Comm. Res. 9B(XXXII), 1979.

93. Kathleen Teltsch, "U.N. Unit Said to Report Greeks Violate Human Rights," *The New York Times*, September 21, 1972, p. 18.

94. Sub-Comm. Res. 2(XXV), 1972.

95. *The New York Post*, September 3, 1974.

96. *Le Monde*, September 13, 1978, p. 3.  The Soviet representative introduced a resolution co-sponsored by experts from all regions asking the Secretary-General to investigate the source of the leak.  Although the Secretary-General's representative questioned the propriety of interrogating experts on the Working Group, the Sub-Commission adopted the request in Sub-Comm. Res. 10(XXXI), 1978.  In 1976 an enterprising reporter overheard the Group's 1976 discussions on press room earphones inadvertently left in service.

97. Ton Gardeniers, Hurst Hannum, and Janice Krueger, "The U.N. Sub-Commission on Prevention of Discrimination and Protection of Minorities: Recent Developments," *Human Rights Quarterly* 4 (Summer 1982): p. 368.

98. Sadi's 1978 proposal won five votes in 1978, U.N. Doc. E/CN.4/Sub.2/SR.821 (Restricted) (1978), para. 91, and Whitaker's 1983 draft has 8 votes in favor, 10 opposed and 3 abstentions, Sub.-Comm., *Report on its Thirty-Sixth Session*, U.N. Doc. E/CN.4/1984/3, para. 30 (vote on draft resolution U.N. Doc. E/CN.4/Sub.2/1983/L.5).

99. By a 5 to 5 tie vote with 11 abstentions the Sub-Commission failed to refer the communications on the United States to the Commission U.N. Doc. E/CN.4/Sub.2/SR.821 (Restricted) (1978), para. 115.

100. Uganda, Bolivia, Chile, Kampuchea, Paraguay, and Afghanistan. In 1982 Iran was the subject of both a public resolution on behalf of the Bahai's and a confidential referral. Sub-Comm. Res. 1982/25.

101. See U.N. Doc. E/CN.4/Sub.2/SR.821 (Restricted) (1978).

102. In 1972 the situations in Greece, Iran, and Portugal were all returned to the Group.

103. For example, U.N. Doc. E/CN.4/Sub.2/SR.821 (Restricted) (1978).

104. Mario S. Modiano, "Greece Frees Hundreds of Political Foes," *New York Times*, August 22, 1973, p. 3.

105. Lillich and Newman, *International Human Rights*, p. 361.

106. After the Commission initially refused to consider the Greek case under Resolution 1235 in 1968, the United Nations deferred to the Council of Europe which in 1970 found a violation of the convention of Rome.

107. Gillian Walker of the International Youth and Student Movement and Amnesty International as quoted in *The Times (London)*, Sept. 21, 1973, p. 7.

108. Vietnam and Korea.

109. Zuijdwijk summarizes press accounts for every year except 1975, and Liskofsky lists secondary sources for the same period. Lillich and Newman, *International Human Rights*, pp. 316–387 excerpted and republished materials connected with the investigation of Greece including: *The New York Times*, September 21, 1972, p. 18; *The Times (London)*, September 24, 1983, p. 7; *The New York Post*, February 7, 1974, p. 7; *The Times (London)*, February 27, 1975, p. 6. *See also The Guardian*, September 4, 1977, p. 5, col. 2; *Le Monde*, 13 September 1978; *Reuters*, March 9, 1978 as reported in *International Commission of Jurists Review* 20 (June 1978): p. 34.

110. Tardu, "The 1503 Procedure," p. 561.

111. The most detailed account of Commission practice under Resolution 1503 appears in the Report of Professor Fernando Volio Jiménez, Special Rapporteur appointed to study the human rights situation in Equatorial Guinea. U.N. Doc. E/CN.4/1371 and Corr.1 (1980). In 1979 the Commission concluded that non-cooperation by the Macias regime made futile any further deliberation under the Resolution 1503 procedure. As a result, the Commission appointed a Special Rapporteur under the public Resolution 1235 procedure and authorized disclosure of the previously confidential materials.

112. U.N. Doc. E/CN.4/1371 and Corr.1 (1980), p. 2.

113. Niall MacDermott, Secretary-General of the ICJ made interventions proposing the reform in 1975 and 1984.

114. International Commission of Jurists, "UN Commission on Human Rights," *International Commission of Jurists Review* 16 (June 1976): p. 26.

115. International Commission of Jurists, "UN Commission on Human Rights," *International Commission of Jurists Review* 18 (June 1977): p. 26.

116. Intervention by Niall MacDermot, Secretary-General of the ICJ. U.N. Doc. E/CN.4/1984/SR.61.

117. CHR Dec. 3, 1974.

118. In 1981.
119. CHR Dec. 14(XXXV), 1979; CHR Dec. 5(XXXIV), 1978.
120. See U.N. Doc. E/CN.4/SR.1515 (Restricted) (1979), para. 19.
121. U.N. Doc. E/CN.4/SR.1502 (Restricted) (1979), para. 21.
122. U.N. Doc. E/CN.4/1983/SR.33–40 (Restricted).
123. U.N. Doc. E/CN.4/1983/SR.35 (Restricted) (1983) (on Afghanistan 29–6–7).
124. E/CN.4/1371 and Corr.1 (1980), para. 9.
125. CHR Confidential Decision of 8 March 1979. U.N. Doc. E/CN.4/1371 (1980), Annex I.
126. CHR Dec. 10(XXXVI), (1980). In Decision 1984/102 the Commission telegraphed a public appeal to Malawi's President to suspend the death sentences of Orton Chirwa and his wife.
127. Section 23, *Proposed Programme Budget for the Biennium, 1984–85, Vol. III*, U.N. Doc. A/38/6 (1983), p. 81.
128. U.N. Doc. E/CN.4/SR.1624 (Restricted) (1981), p. 9.

# Chapter 5

1. Quincy Wright, "The Scope of International Criminal Law: A Conceptual Framework," *Virginia Journal of International Law* 15 (1975): pp. 572–573.
2. *Report of 1953 Committee on International Criminal Jurisdiction*, U.N. Doc. A/2645 (1954).
3. Convention on the Prevention and Punishment of the Crime of Genocide, opened for signature 9 December 1948, entered into force 12 January 1951, 78 U.N.T.S. 291, art. VI (hereafter cited as *Genocide Convention*).
4. *International Law Commission, Nuremberg Principles*, U.N. Doc. A/1316 (1950); *Draft Code of Offenses Against the Peace and Security of Mankind*, U.N. Doc. A/2645 (1954); John W. Bridge, "The Case for an International Court of Criminal Justice and the Formulation of International Criminal Law," *International and Comparative Law Quarterly* 13 (1964): p. 1255; John J. Parker, "An International Criminal Court: The Case for Its Adoption," *American Bar Association Journal* 38 (1952): p. 641; Vespasian V. Pella, "Towards an International Criminal Court," *American Journal of International Law* 44 (1950): p. 37. See generally Richard B. Lillich and Frank C. Newman, *International Human Rights: Problems of Law and Policy* (Boston: Little, Brown and Company, 1979), ch. XI.
5. John Carey, *UN Protection of Civil and Political Rights* (New York: Syracuse University Press, 1970), p. 67.
6. Dec. 16, 1970, arts. 2, 4, 7, 8, 22 U.S.T. 1641, T.I.A.S. No. 7192.
7. Sept. 23, 1971, arts. 3, 5, 7, 8, (1973) 24 U.S.T. 565, T.I.A.S. No. 7570.
8. Dec. 14, 1973, arts. 2, 3, 7, 8, (1977) 28 U.S.T. 1975, T.I.A.S. No. 8532.
9. Lillich and Newman, *International Human Rights*, pp. 811–812.
10. Carey, *Protection*, p. 64.
11. G.A. Res. 2145(XXI), 1966 and 2248(S–V), 1967.
12. Ibid.
13. GAOR Twenty-Sixth Session, Annexes, agenda item 54, U.N. Doc. A/8542, para. 32.
14. G.A. Res. 3068(XXVIII), 1973.

15. Apartheid Convention, (see chap. 4, n. 59), arts. 5, 12.
16. Ibid., art. 1, para. 1.
17. Ibid., art. 2.
18. Ibid., art. 3.
19. Genocide Convention, art. VI; Apartheid Convention, art. 5.
20. Ibid., art. 9, para. 1.
21. See Ibid., art. 7, para. 1.
22. Ibid., art. 10, para. 1.
23. Harry Scoble and Laurie Wiseberg, "Human Rights and Amnesty International," *Annals of the American Academy of Political and Social Science* 413 (May 1974): pp. 25–26.
24. See for example Hans Thoolen, "Thirty Years After the Universal Declaration of Human Rights: The Need for an International Convention Against Torture," *Background Information* 8 (1978) (Commission of the Churches on International Affairs of the World Council of Churches publication).
25. G.A. Res. 3452 (XXX), 1975.
26. World-wide seminars met in India 1968, Cameroon 1971, France 1971, Lesotho 1978, and Geneva 1979; a regional seminar also met in Geneva in 1979.
27. World-wide seminars in Cyprus 1969 and Geneva 1980, and regional meetings in Poland 1967 and Zambia 1970.
28. Cairo 1969, Tanzania, 1973 and Liberia 1979.
29. Approved by the Organization of African Unity in 1981.
30. CHR Res. 7(XXIII), 1967. The study appears in U.N. Doc. E/CN.4/979 and Add.1–8, Corr.1 (1969).
31. U.N. Doc. E/CN.4/1075 (1972).
32. U.N. Doc. E/CN.4/1426 (1980).
33. Ahmed M. Khalifa, *Study on Assistance to Racist Regimes in Southern Africa*, U.N. publication, Sales No. E.79.XIV.3.
34. U.N. Doc. ST/TAO/HR/42 (1971).
35. G.A. Res. 2784(XXVI), 1971.
36. Héctor Gros Espiell, *Study on the Implementation of United Nations Resolutions Relating to the Right of Peoples Under Colonial and Alien Domination to Self-Determination*, U.N. publication, Sales No. 79.XIV.5.
37. Aureliu Cristescu, *The Rights to Self-Determination: Historical and Current Developments on the Basis of United Nations Instruments*, U.N. publication, Sales No. 80.XIV.3.
38. See Peter Haver, "The United Nations Sub-Commission on the Prevention of Discrimination and the Protection of Minorities," *Columbia Journal of Transnational Law* 21 (1982): pp. 105–110.
39. U.N. Doc. ST/TAO/HR/23 (1965).
40. U.N. Doc. ST/TAO/HR/49 (1974).
41. *Protection of Minorities*, U.N. publication, Sales No. 67.XIC.3.
42. E/CN.4/Sub.2/384/Rev.1 (1979).
43. U.N. Doc. E/CN.4/Sub.2/351 (1975).
44. U.N. DOc. ST/TAO/HR/50 (1974) (preliminary report).
45. CHR Res. 21(XXXIV), 1978.
46. CHR Res. 25(XXXV), 1979.
47. Baroness Elles, *Study of International Provisions Protecting the Human Rights of Non-Citizens*, U.N. publication, Sales No. E.80.XIV.2.
48. CHR Res. 17(XXIII), 1967.
49. *United Nations Action in the Field of Human Rights* , U.N. publication, Sales No. E.83.XIV.2, pp. 361–362.

50. U.N. Doc. E/CN.4/1192 (1976), paras. 36–65.

51. U.N. Doc. E/CN.4/1983/30.

52. G.A. Res. 1710(XVI), 1961.

53. ST/TAO/HR/31 (1967) (entitled "The realization of economic and social rights contained in the Universal Declaration of Human Rights.").

54. Jacques Chonchol, "The Declaration on Human Rights and the Right to Development: The Gap Between Proposal and Reality," in *Development, Human Rights and the Rule of Law: Report of a Conference held in the Hague on 27 April–1 May 1981* (Oxford, Pergamon Press, 1981), pp. 110–111.

55. Ibid., p. 110.

56. See *Final Act of the International Conference on Human Rights*, U.N. publication, Sales No. E.68.XIV.2. The text of the Proclamation is reprinted in *Human Rights: A Compilation of International Instruments*, U.N. publication, Sales No. 83.XIV.1.

57. Manouchehr Ganji, *The Realization of Economic, Social and Cultural Rights: Problems, Policies, Progress*, U.N. publication, Sales No. E.75.XIV.2. Jack Donnelly, "Recent Trends in UN Human Rights Activity: Description and Polemic," *International Organization* 35 (Autumn 1981): p. 637.

58. U.N. Doc. E/CN.4/SR.1341 (1976).

59. U.N. Doc. E/CN.4/SR.1449 (1978).

60. U.N. Doc. E/CN.4/Sr.1326, 1364, 1368 (United States) E/CN.4/Sr.1448 (Sweden) (1978).

61. CHR Res. 4(XXXIII), 1977.

62. U.N. Doc. E/CN.4/1334 (1979). The Secretariat completed its work in two years, far less time than the Commission committees and rapporteurs assigned prior studies.

63. U.N. Doc. E/CN.4/966 and Add. 1.

64. The seminars met in Cairo in 1969, U.N. Doc. ST/TAO/HR/38 (1969); Dar-es-Salaam in 1973, U.N. Doc. ST/TAO/HR/48 (1973); and finally Monrovia in 1979 where the delegates proposed a Charter including an African Commission on Human and Peoples Rights: U.N. Doc. ST/HR/SER.A/4 (1979), *see also* A/34/359 and Add.1, Ann.1.

65. B. Obina Okere, "The Protection of Human Rights in Africa and the African Charter on Human and Peoples Rights: A Comparative Analysis with the European and American Systems," *Human Rights Quarterly* 6 (May 1984): pp. 149–152.

66. U.N. Doc. ST/HR/SER.A/2 and Add.1 (1978).

67. Theodor Meron, "Norm Making and Supervision in International Human Rights: Reflections on Institutional Order," *American Journal of International Law* 76 (1982): p. 754.

68. Louis B. Sohn, "Human Rights: Their Implementation and Supervision by the United Nations," in Theodor Meron, ed., *Human Rights in International Law vol. II* (Oxford: Clarendon Press, 1984), p. 369.

69. Meron, *Norm Making*, p. 775.

70. Moynihan resigned believing that the Republican administration opposed his statement out of a misplaced commitment to promoting friendly relations with both the Soviets and the Non-Aligned. Daniel P. Moynihan, *A Dangerous Place* (Boston: Little Brown and Co., 1978).

71. William Shawcross, Anthony Terry and Peter Pringle, "The Barbarism the World Ignores," *Atlas* 23 (June 1976): pp. 20–22 (excerpted and reprinted version of article that appeared in *The Times (London)*).

72. Donnelly, "Recent Trends," p. 4; Gerson Smoger, "Whither the Commission on Human Rights: A Report After the 35th Session," *Vanderbilt Journal of Transnational Law* 12 (1979): pp. 943–965.

73. See International Commission of Jurists, *Uganda and Human Rights: Reports to the UN Commission on Human Rights* (Geneva: International Commission of Jurists, 1977).

74. International Commission of Jurists, "Commentary: Commission on Human Rights," *International Commission of Jurists Review* 22 (June 1979): p. 34.

75. David Kramer and David Weissbrodt, "The 1980 U.N. Commission on Human Rights and the Disappeared," *Human Rights Quarterly* 3 (February 1981): p. 24.

76. Al-Jabiri's independence may have caused Iraq to replace him as representative to the Commission.

77. U.S. Congress, Committee on Foreign Affairs, Sub-Committee on International Organizations, *Review of the 36th Session of the United Nations Commission on Human Rights*, 96th Cong., 2d sess., 1980.

78. CHR, *Report of the Thirty-Fifth Session*, U.N. Doc. E/1979/36, p. 50.

79. ECOSOC Res. 1979/36.

80. Ibid.

## Chapter 6

1. The Peoples Republic of China, the only permanent member of the Security Council unrepresented on the Commission, sent its first observer in 1979 and was elected a member in 1982.

2. Jerome J. Shestack, "The Commission on Human Rights: Pitfalls, Progress, and a New Maturity," in *U.S. Policy in International Institutions*, ed. Seymour M. Finger and Joseph R. Harbert (Boulder, Colorado: Westview Press, 1982), p. 81.

3. Richard L. Jackson, *The Non-Aligned, the UN and the Superpowers* (New York: Praeger, 1983), pp. 66–69.

4. Thomas M. Franck, *Nation Against Nation: What Happened to the U.N. Dream and What the U.S. Can Do About It* (New York: Oxford University Press, 1985), pp. 224–228. This portion of Franck's book appeared as an article entitled "Of Gnats and Camels: Is There a Double Standard at the United Nations?" *American Journal of International Law* 78 (1984): p. 811. Votes on Morocco's illegal seizure of Western Sahara and Indonesia's conquest of East Timor demonstrated that Western rather than NAM members applied a double standard on principles on non-intervention. Despite obvious violations, many Western governments sided with the friendly, anticommunist governments of Indonesia and Morocco.

5. Felix Ermacora, *Report of the Expert on the Question of the Fate of the Missing and Disappeared Persons in Chile*, U.N. Doc. A/34/583 and Add.1 (1979).

6. Sub-Comm. Res. 5B(XXXII), 1979; Marc Bossuyt, "The Development of Special Procedures of the United Nations Commission on Human Rights," *Human Rights Law Journal*, 6 (1985): pp. 194–195.

7. See David Kramer and David Weissbrodt, "The 1980 U.N. Commission on Human Rights and the Disappeared," *Human Rights Quarterly* 3 (February 1981): pp. 18–33.

8. CHR Res. 20(XXXVI), 1980.

9. Al-Jabiri resigned, reportedly because Iraq disapproved of his active support for the initiative, and he did not return to the Commission's next session. Jordan, Pakistan and the Netherlands subsequently joined the group as representatives from the Asian and Western groups.

10. Members in 1985 included: Ivan Tosevski (Yugoslavia) Chairman/ Rapporteur; Toine van Dongen (Netherlands); Jonas K.D. Foli (Ghana); Agha Hilaly (Pakistan); and Luis A. Varela Quirós (Costa Rica).

11. Nigel Rodley, "U.N. Action Procedures Against 'Disappearances,' Summary or Arbitrary Executions and Torture" *Human Rights Quarterly* 8 (November 1986): pp. 700–730.

12. U.N. Doc. E/CN.4/1985/15 and Add.1, para. 84.

13. At a meeting in New York, an NGO pressed the group to recognize Soviet dissident Andrei Sakharov as disappeared.

14. U.N. Doc. E/CN.4/1984/15.

15. Angola, Guinea, Indonesia, Iran, Paraguay, Syria. Toine van Dongen, "In the Last Instance: Disappearances and the U.N.," *Human Rights Quarterly* 9 (1987).

16. U.N. Doc. E/CN.4/1986/18 and Add.1.

17. U.N. Doc. E/CN.4/1985/15 and Add.1, para. 90; CHR Res. 1986/55.

18. U.N. Doc. E/CN.4/L.1452 (1979); G.A. Res. 35/196, 1980.

19. CHR Res. 29(XXXVII), 1981.

20. U.N. Doc. E/CN.4/1503 (1982).

21. Bossuyt, "Special Procedures," p. 196.

22. Argentina lobbied effectively against reappointment and openly celebrated the decision. Van Boven also faulted the United States and believed that Washington disapproved of his active intervention in the Latin American situation.

23. CHR Res. 1982/29.

24. U.N. Doc. E/CN.4/1983/16. See also Political Covenant (see chap. 2, n. 67), arts. 6, 14, 15 (right to an appeal, representation by counsel, an opportunity to seek clemency, no execution under *ex post facto* criminal laws).

25. U.N. Doc. E/CN.4/1984/29.

26. Iran, Libya, and Malawi. U.N. Doc. E/CN.4/1985/17.

27. CHR Res. 1985/37.

28. U.N. Doc. E/CN.4/1985/17 (Bangladesh).

29. Angola and United Arab Emirates.

30. David Weisbrodt, "The Three 'Theme' Special Rapporteurs of the UN Commission on Human Rights," *American Journal of International Law* 80 (July 1986): p. 685.

31. U.N. Doc. E/CN.4/1985/SR.46.

32. Organization of American States, *Report on the Situation of Human Rights in Suriname, 1983*, OAS/Ser.L/II.61 Doc. 6 rev.1 (1983). The Inter-American Commission made its on-site visit six months after 15 opposition leaders were summarily killed.

33. U.N. Doc. E/CN.4/1985/17 and Annex V.

34. U.N. Doc. E/CN.4/SR.63 (1984), para. 48. A colloquium convened by the Swiss Committee Against Torture had made a similar recommendation in 1983.

35. CHR Res. 1985/33. ECOSOC, however, approved the resolution by consensus. CHR, *Report on the Forty-First Session*, E/1985/ss, para. 238.

36. CHR Res. 1985/33.

37. CHR, *Report on the Forty-First Session*, E/1985/22 and Ann.III, p. 244.

38. U.N. Doc. E/CN.4/1986/15.

39. The Sub-Commission has attempted to implement its own thematic approaches. A pre-sessional five member Working Group on slavery has received NGO complaints against numerous governments which have been asked to respond. Another Working Group has annually reviewed allegations about mistreatment of detainees. Despite NGO lobbying for a similar procedure on behalf of native peoples, the Sub-Commission Working Group on Indigenous Populations has restricted its activities to standard-setting and promotion.

40. Volumious summary records offer complete detail of individual speeches in the order made.

41. Rule 44, *Rules of Procedure* (see chap. 1, n. 60).

42. Howard Tolley, Jr., "Decision-Making at the United Nations Commission on Human Rights, 1979–1982," *Human Rights Quarterly* 5 (Winter 1983): pp. 42–43.

43. Since nearly all the proposals formally introduced are adopted, sponsors obviously make careful advance calculations.

44. "If two or more proposals, other than amendments, relate to the same question, they shall, unless the commission decides otherwise, be voted on in the order in which they were submitted. The commission may, after each vote on a proposal, decide whether to vote on the next proposal." Rule 65, para. 1, *Rules of Procedure.*

45. CHR, *Report on the Thirty-Eighth Session*, E/1982/12, paras. 266–280.

46. CHR, *Report on the Thirty-Sixth Session*, E/1980/13 and Annex V, para. 46–47.

47. Rule 52, *Rules of Procedure.*

48. CHR, *Report on the Thirty-Fifth Session*, E/1979/36, para. 134.

49. Interview with Munir Akram, delegation advisor, Pakistan Mission, Geneva, August 4, 1982.

50. Rule 58, *Rules of Procedure.*

51. CHR Res. 1982/26 (Poland) and 1982/27 (Iran).

52. CHR Dec. 12(XXXV), 1979; CHR Dec. 1984/102.

53. CHR Res. 1984/25. The more strongly worded Assembly resolution deplored the intervention of foreign forces. G.A. Res. 38/7, 1983.

54. CHR Res. 1984/13.

55. CHR Res. 1983/8.

56. CHR Dec. 1984/111.

57. CHR Res. 1984/10.

58. The Commission designated a special envoy to Bolivia, Héctor Gros Espiell, who detailed the government's acute needs for professional legal and economic aid. U.N. Doc. E/CN.4/1984/46.

59. U.N. Doc. E/CN.4/1983/NGO/4.

60. U.N. Doc. E/CN.4/1984/45.

61. CHR Dec. 12(XXXV), 1979.

62. U.N. Doc. E/CN.4/1984/30; U.N. Doc. A/29/635 (1984); U.N. Doc. E/CN.4/1985/19.

63. Nicaragua, Kampuchea, Guatemala, Iran, and Poland.

64. Equatorial Guinea, Chile, Guatemala and Afghanistan, Bolivia (Special Envoy), and El Salvador (Special Representative).

65. U.N. Doc. E/CN.4/1984/26. Iain Guest, *International Herald Tribune*, February 1984.

66. U.N. Doc. E/CN.4/1984/28; U.N. Doc. E/CN.4/1985/20.

67. U.N. Doc. E/CN.4/1985/SR.49.

68. The Bulgarian Chair explained why he had rescinded the appointment of Mrs. Elizabeth Odio Benito in U.N. Doc. E/CN.4/1983/43.

69. U.N. Doc. E/CN.4/1984/SR.42, para. 196.

70. U.S. Department of State, "Country Reports on Human Rights Practices for 1982," Report Submitted to the Committee on Foreign Relations, U.S. Senate and Committee on Foreign Relations, U.S. Senate and Committee on Foreign Affairs, U.S. House of Representatives, 98th Cong., 1st Sess.

71. U.N. Doc. E/CN.4/1984/20.

72. U.N. Doc. E/CN.4/1985/21, para. 34.

73. U.N. Doc. E/CN.4/1982/1500 and Corr.1 and Add.1, para. 28. See also Chapter (see chap. 1, n. 28), arts. 55, 56.

74. U.N. Doc. E/CN.4/1984/30, paras. 2–3.

75. U.N. Doc. E/CN.4/1985/21, para. 138.

76. U.N. Doc. E/CN.4/1983/18.

77. Legal Aid Service of the Archdiocese of San Salvador, "El Salvador: One Year of Repression," *Background Information* 1 (1981) (Commission of the Churches on International Affairs of the Council of Churches publication); Organization of American States, *Report on the Situation of Human Rights in the Republic of Guatemala, 1983*, OEA/Ser. L/II.61 Doc. 47 Rev.1 (1983).

78. Philip Alston, "Remedying U.N. Pussyfooting on Human Rights," *Human Rights Internet Reporter* 2 (June 1986): p. 7.

79. Americas Watch, Asia Watch, and Helsinki Watch Committees, *Four Failures: A Report on the UN Special Rapporteurs on Human Rights in Chile, Guatemala, Iran and Poland January 1986*, p. 13.

80. Ibid., p. 17.

81. U.N. Doc. E/CN.4/1984/25.

82. Helge Ole Bergeson, "The Power to Embarrass: The UN Human Rights Regime Between Realism and Utopia," paper presented to the International Political Science Association (IPSA) World Congress, Rio de Janiero, Brazil, August, 1982.

83. Bolivia, Guatemala, and El Salvador. Equatorial Guinea did not appear at the Commission but allowed a visit.

84. Costa Rica's former Foreign Minister, Fernando Volio Jiménez.

85. U.N. Doc. E/CN.4/1985/SR.18.

86. U.N. Doc. E/CN.4/1984/SR.31.

87. CHR Res. 1986/1A (at paragraph 12).

88. CHR Res. 1986/5 (adopted 29-5-8).

89. In 1984 the speakers included: 25 members; 17 observer governments; and representatives of the PLO; the League of Arab States; and 3 non-governmental organizations.

90. At the 1984 session speakers included: special rapporteurs; 38 members; 14 observer states; representatives of the OAU; the League of Arab States; the United Nations Committee on Apartheid; 4 liberation movements; and 7 non-governmental organizations.

91. In 1986 the Working Group included: Annan Arkyin Cato, Chairman-Rapporteur, Ghana's permanent representative in Geneva; Branimir Jankovi´c, Law Professor from Yugoslavia; Nikuin Leliel Balanda of Zaire; Chile's Humberto Djaaiaz-Casanueva; Austria's Felix Ermacora; and India's Govinda Reddy.

92. U.N. Doc. E/CN.4/1984/8, p. 97 (Progress Report of the *Ad Hoc* Working Group of Experts).

93. In 1983 the group of three included representatives of Zaire, Bulgaria, and Mexico; they reviewed reports of eight states parties. U.N. Doc. E/CN.4/1983/25.

94. Final Report on the Establishment of an International Criminal Court for the Implementation of the Apartheid Convention and Other Relevant International Instruments., U.N. Doc. E/CN.4/AC/22CRP.19/Rev.1 (1980), reprinted in *Hofstra Law Reivew* 9 (Winter 1981): p. 523.

95. CHR Res. 1982/12; CHR Res. 1983/12 U.N. DOc. E/CN.4/1984/48, para. 6.

96. U.N. Doc. E/CN.4/1985/SR.15, para. 77.

97. CHR Res. 5(XXXVII), 1981.

98. CHR Res. 1985/8.

99. CHR Res. 1985/11. Competing liberation groups such as the Pan-Africanist Congress complain when their members are ignored. U.N. Doc. E/CN.4/1984/SR.11, para. 14.

100. U.N. Doc. E/CN.4/1317 (1979) (Report of the Secretary-General).

101. U. N. Doc. E/CN.4/1317 (1979), paras. 30–36.

102. Section 23, *United Nations Proposed Programme Budget for the Biennium, 1984–85, Volume III*, U.N. Doc. A/38/6 (1983), p. 80.

103. U.N. Doc. E/CN.4/SR.1619 (1981), para. 19.

104. U.N. Doc. E/CN.4/1982/Sub.2/SR.27, para. 2.

105 Sofinsky, a member of the Soviet delegation to the Commission, was elected as a Sub-Commission expert with his own alternate in 1981 and 1984.

106. Sub-Comm., *Report on its Thirty-Second Session*, U.N. Doc. E/CN.4/1350 and Ann.I (1979) and Sub-Comm., *Report on its Thirty-Fourth Session*, U.N. Doc. E/CN.4/1512 and Ann.I (1981).

107. Later Sub-Commission Reports for 1982 and 1983 fail to note which members attended the Working group meetings.

108. U.N. Doc. E/CN.4/1982/Sub.2/L.6 (consideration was postponed by Sub-Commission Decision 1983/4); See also Antonio Cassese, "The Admissibil-ity of Communications to the United Nations on Human Rights Violations," *Human Rights Journal* 5 (1972).

109. U.N. Doc. E/CN.4/1982/Sub.2/L.6 (consideration was postponed by Sub-Commission Decision 1983/4).

110. U.N. Doc. E/CN.4/1512 para. 146 (1981). The Soviets repeatedly argue that the Resolution 1503 procedure is no longer required, since the International Covenant of Civil and Political Rights provides a petition system based on state consent. A 1976 Soviet proposal that ECOSOC review the 1503 procedure was amended to call for "improving the effectiveness of the United Nations efforts and machinery." Sub-Commission Resolution 1 (XXIX).

111. U.N. Doc. E/CN.4/1982/Sub.2/L.6 (consideration was postponed by Sub-Commission Decision 1983/4).

112. Sub-Comm. Res. 22 (XXXIII), 1980 and 23 (XXXIII), 1980.

113. The 1984 Working Group had representatives from Ireland, Bulgaria, Tanzania, Japan, and Cuba; in 1985 Representatives from Argentina and Jordan replaced the members from Japan and Cuba. U.N. press releases HR/1470 (1984) and HR/1529 (1984).

114. The Central African Republic, Uruguay, Venezuela, and Zaire. Three others had signed but not ratified as of 1982: The Philippines, El Salvador and Portugal. South Korea ratified after years of Commission scrutiny.

115. Of the 30 situations considered between 1978 and 1986, six governments charged were Commission members and another fifteen non-members sent representatives.

116. African governments have had the lowest response rate.

117. Malawi reportedly missed both sessions where the Commission reviewed a complaint on behalf of Jehovah's Witnesses. Equatorial Guinea sent a representative the first year its situation was considered, but missed the following two sessions.

118. Unpublished provisional lists of attendance at the Thirty-Ninth and Fortieth Sessions of the Commission on Human Rights.

119. Albania, Haiti, Paraguay, and Zaire.

120. Only one major NGO attempts to rate governments' human rights performance in a way that would permit comparison of the situations taken for review with the referrals disregarded. Raymond D. Gastil prepares the annual report: "The Comparative Survey of Freedom," published in *Freedom in the World: Political Rights and Civil Liberties* (Westport, Connecticut: Greenwood Press).

121. Gabon, Japan, Malaysia, Pakistan, and Venezuela sent representatives and were not kept under review. Apparently the members were satisfied with the governments' explanations.

122. Equatorial Guinea and Malawi.

123. CHR, *Report on the Forty-First Session*, E/1985/22, para. 277.

124. After release the detainee denied having met de Cuellar. Douglas Reichert, "38th Session of the U.N. Commission on Human Rights," *Human Rights Internet Reporter* (March–May 1982): pp. 680–683.

125. Foli concluded that the previously feared Tonton Macoutes had become a constructive forestry group.

126. The Human Rights Committee in 1979 found the government respon- sible for torture which had caused permanent physical damage. Amnesty Interna- tional had appealed for his release as a prisoner of conscience. *Amnesty Action*, May 1984.

127. CHR Dec. 1984/109.

128. U.N. Doc. E/CN.4/1984/SR.61 (MacDermott, 1984 Intervention).

129. Sub-Comm. Res. 23 (XXXIII), 1980; G.A. Res. 35/185, 1980; Comm. Res. 34 (XXXVII), 1981.

130. U.N. Doc. E/CN.4/1984/SR.63, para. 1. Previously both the Commis- sion and Sub-Commission had adopted public resolutions on self-determination in Afghanistan unrelated to the confidential situation.

131. The Sub-Commission had proposed the public resolution.

132. Amnesty International proposed to the Commission that it undertake a detailed study of the violations. Amnesty International, *Amnesty International Report 1980* (London: Amnesty International Publications, 1980), p. 88.

133. ECOSOC Dec. 1985/139 and ECOSOC Dec. 1985/156.

134. The assumptions made included the following: First, it can be assumed that if the Chairman announces that a state was subject to a decision in only one year, then the Commission decided not to keep that government under confidential review. If that government was also subject to a public decision in the same year, then the Commission apparently found no purpose for separate confidential review. Second, when the Commission had taken decisions affecting a government for several consecutive years, then the first decision was to keep the situation under review, and the last was to discontinue consideration.

## Chapter 7

1. Resolutions recommending general principles and standards express the prevailing majority view that states are encouraged to follow. Formal declarations are solemn instruments suitable for rare occasions that announce principles of great and lasting importance. There is a stronger expectation of compliance, and state practice may make widely honored declarations part of customary international law. Conventions when ratified become binding treaty obligations that can be amended or supplemented by protocols. Convenants are conventions establishing treaty commitments of the greatest import.

2. Amnesty International *Torture in the Eighties* (London: Amnesty International Publications, 1984), p. 2.

3. Personal interviews with Secretariat staff and nongovernmental participants, August 1982.

4. International Commission of Jurists, "Commentary: Commission on Human Rights," *International Commission of Jurists Review* 24 (June 1980): p. 36.

5. International Commission of Jurists, *Torture: How to Make the International Convention Effective* (Geneva: International Commission of Jurists, 1980).

6. U.N. Doc. E/CN.4/1983/L.2, paras. 21–22.

7. Ibid., para. 67.

8. CHR Res. 1984/21.

9. G.A. Res. 39/46 (1984).

10. U.N. Doc. E/CN.4/1987/SR.32 para. 94.

11. Draft Convention Against Torture and Other Cruel, Inhuman or Degrading Treatment or Punishment, arts. 1, 16, U.N. Doc. E/CN.4/1984/L2 Annex (hereafter cited as *Draft Convention Against Torture*).

12. Ibid., arts. 19–20.

13. Ibid., art. 28.

14. Ibid., arts. 21–22.

15. Ibid., arts. 3, 8.

16. CHR, *Report of the Fortieth Session*, U.N. Doc. E/1984/14, para. 469; CHR Res. 1984/19.

17. CHR Res. 1985/46.

18. G.A. Res. 1386 (XIV), 1959.

19. International Commission of Jurists, "UN Commission on Human Rights," *International Commission of Jurists Review* 28 (June 1982): p. 38.

20. Ibid. See U.N. Doc. E/CN.4/1982/30 and Add.1.

21. U.N. Doc. E/CN.4/1986/39 and Annex II.

22. U.N. Doc. E/CN.4/1986/39.

23. International Commission of Jurists, "The Convention of the Rights of the Child: Time for a New Look at Implementation," *International Commission of Jurists Review* 36 (June 1986): p. 33.

24. CHR Res. 1986/47.

25. U.N. Doc. A/140/605.

26. U.N. Doc. E/CN.4/1983/29. President Carter signed both covenants in 1977, but official ratification by the United States appears highly unlikely.

27. U.N. Doc. E/CN.4/1987 SR.26 para. 6. No states have brought complaints.

28. CHR Res. 1986/17.

29. CHR Res. 1986/18.

30. U.N. Doc. E/CN.4/SR.1592–1595 (1980).
31. U.N. Doc. E/CN.4/Sub.2/1985/57, para. 61.
32. Sub-Comm. Res. 1985/5.
33. CHR Res. 20 (XXXVII), 1981.
34. Declaration on the Elimination of All Forms of Intolerance and of Discrimination Based on Religion or Belief, art 8, adopted 18 January 1982, G.A. Res. 55, 36 U.N. GAOR Supp. (No. 51) at 171, U.N. Doc. Res 36/55 (1982) (hereafter cited as *Religion Declaration*).
35. Ibid., art. 1.
36. G.A. Res. 36/55 (1981).
37. Religion Declaration, art. 4.
38. Ibid., art. 5.
39. Ibid., art. 6.
40. Ibid., art. 7.
41. See comments by Mr. O'Donovan of Ireland.   U.N. Doc. E/CN.4/1983/SR.53, para. 55.
42. U.N. Doc. E/CN.4/1983/SR.50.
43. U.N. Doc. E/CN.4/1983/SR.49, para. 69.
44. CHR Res. 1983/40; CHR, *Report of the Thirty-Ninth Session*, U.N. Doc. E/1983/23, para. 509.
45. U.N. Doc. E/CN.4/1983/11 and Annex IV.
46. U.N. Doc. E/CN.4/1985/11 and Annex III.
47. U.N. Doc. E/CN.4/1489 (1982).
48. U.N. Doc. E/CN.4./1983/11.
49. U.N. Doc. E/CN.4/1984/13.
50. U.N. Doc. E/CN.4./1985/11 and Annex IX.
51. CHR Res. 1985/43.
52. U.N. Doc. A/C.3/40/L.53 (1983).
53. CHR Res. 1986/16. The United States voted against, and other Western members abstained.
54. U.N. Doc. E/CN.4/1986/43 and Annex.
55. U.N. Doc. E/CN.4/1983/L.5.
56. U.N. Doc. E/CN.4/Sub.2/1985/31 and Corr. 1.
57. U.N. Doc. E/CN.4/1986/43.
58. Political Covenant (see chap. 2, n.67), art. 27.
59. In 1971 Sub-Commission rapporteur José Martínez-Cobo began a study on discrimination against indigenous populations which took thirteen years to complete.   U.N. Doc. E/CN.4/Sub.2/476 (1981) and Add.1–6; U.N. Doc. E/CN.4/Sub.2/1982/2 and Add.1–7; U.N. Doc. E/CN.4/Sub.3/1983/21 and Add.1–5.
60. U.N. Doc. E/CN.4/Sub.2/1983/22.
61. Sub.Comm. Res. 1982/31; ECOSOC Res. 1985/38.
62. Sub-Comm. Res. 1985/22.   Annex II of the Group's fourth report, U.N. Doc. E/CN.4/Sub.2/1985/22, describes its standard-setting activities.
63. CHR Res. 23 (XXXVI), 1980.
64. CHR Res. 28 (XXXVII), 1981 and CHR Res. 1982/30.
65. CHR Dec. 1984/116.
66. CHR Dec. 1985/112.
67. The Group's first report in U.N. Doc. E/CN.4/1986/40.
68. CHR Res. 1986/44.
69. U.N. Doc. E/CN.4/Sub.2/1985/18.
70. Sub-Comm. Res. 9 (XXXI), 1978.

71. CHR Res. 19 (XXXVI), 1980. *See also* Richard B. Lillich, *The Human Rights of Aliens in Contemporary International Law* (Manchester, England: Manchester University Press, 1984), pp. 51–56 (UN Draft Declaration on the Human Rights of Non-Citizens).
72. U.N. Doc. E/CN.4/Sub.2/L.598 (1974). See José D. Ingles, *The Study of Discrimination in Respect of the Right of Everyone to Leave Any Country, Including His Own, and to Return to His Country*, U.N. publication, Sales No. 64.XIV.2.
73. CHR Res. 1986/30, U.N. Doc. E/CN.4/Sub.2/L.629 (1975) (published after ten years as U.N. Doc. E/CN.4/Sub.2/1986/6, Sales No. E.86.XIV.1).
74. U.N. Doc. E/CN.4/Sub.4/L.629 (1975) (published after ten years as U.N. Doc. E/CN.4/Sub.2/1986/6, Sales No. E.86.XIV.1). Halima Warzazi, *Exploitation of Labour Through Illicit and Clandestine Trafficking*.
75. G.A. Res. 34/172, 1979.
76. Lillich, *Rights of Aliens*, pp. 74–76.
77. See Lillich and Newman, *International Human Rights: Problems of Law and Policy* (Boston: Little, Brown and Company, 1979), pp. 183–261 (How Can the UN Create Human Rights Norms Other Than by the Treaty and Resolution Routes?).
78. Daniel L. Skoler, "World Implementation of the United Nations Standard Minimum Rules for the Treatment of Prisoners," *Journal of International Law and Economics* 10 (August-December 1975): p. 453.
79. Sub-Comm. Res. 5 (XXXI), 1978.
80. CHR Res. 17 (XXXV), 1979.
81. Sub-Comm. Res. 1985/26.
82. U.N. Doc. E/CN.4/Sub.2/1985/20; see Sub-Comm. Res. 1982/34.
83. CHR Res. 1986/12.
84. Ibid.
85. U.N. Doc. E/CN.4/Sub.3/1983/18; CHR Res. 1984/27.
86. CHR Dec. 10 (XXXVII), 1981.
87. U.N. Doc. E/CN.4/1075 (1972) and U.N. Doc. E/CN/4/1426 (1981).
88. CHR Res. 30 (XXXVII), 1981.
89. Ibid.
90. CHR Res. 1982/37.
91. U.N. Doc. E/CN.4/1983/31 and Add.1; U.N. Doc. E/CN.4/1984/45; U.N Doc. E/CN.4/1986/34 and Add.4.
92. U.N. Doc. E/CN.4/1439 (1980).
93. CHR Res. 31 (XXXVII), 1981.
94. U.N. Doc. E/CN.4/1494 (1981).
95. U.N. Doc. E/CN.4/1983/17.
96. U.N. Doc. E/CN.4/1983/NGO/4.
97. CHR Res. 1983/32.
98. U.N. Doc. E/CN.4/1986/34 and Add.2.
99. CHR Res. 1982/33 and 1983/34.
100. U.N. Doc. E/CN.4/1984/46.
101. CHR Res. 15 (XXXVII), 1981.
102. Sub-Comm. Res. 11 (XXX), 1977.
103. CHR Res. 13 (XXXIV), 1978.
104. G.A. Res. 33/174, 1978.
105. *Report of the Thirty-Seventh Session*, E/1981/25, para. 253; CHR Res. 5 (XXXVII), 1981.
106. G.A. Res. 5 (XXXV), 1979.

107. U.N. Doc E/CN.4/1983/SR.31, para, 32.  See E/CN.4/1984/19 (Fund Report).

108. CHR Res. 1985/26; CHR Res. 1986/52.

109. U.N. Doc. E/CN.4/1985/34 and Add.5.

110. CHR Res. 1986/52.

111. U.N. Doc. ST/HR/SER.A/6 (1980).

112. U.N. Doc. ST/HR/SER.A/16 (1985).

113. The motion to postpone debate on the resolution proposing the seminar carried 14–13–15.  U.N. Doc. E/CN.4/1985/SR.51.

114. U.N. Doc. E/CN.4/1986/34 and Add.5.  Governments had nominated 108 candidates.

115. U.N. Doc. E/CN.4/1985/SR.53.

116. CHR Res. 1985/49; CHR Res. 1986/54.

117. U.N. Doc. E/CN.4/1986/20 and Add.3.

118. Sub-Commission Res. 1983/10.

119. U.N. Doc. E/CN.4/Sub.2/1982/7.

120. U.N. Doc. E/CN.4/Sub.2/1983/6 and Add.1–2.

121. Geneva, U.N. Doc. ST/HR/SER.A/9 (1981).

122. G.A. Res. 3 (XXXIV), 1979.

123. A/CONF.119/26 (1983); G.A. Res. 38/14, 1983.

124. CHR Res. 1985/11.

125. U.N. Doc ST/HR/SER.A/17 (1985).

126. Held in Geneva in 1982, U.N. Doc. ST/HR/SER.A/14 (1982).

127. U.N. Doc. E/CN.4/1421 (1981); U.N. Doc. E/CN.4/1488 (1981).

128. U.N. Doc.  ST/HR/SER/A/15 (1983).

129. U.N. Doc.  E/CN.4/1984/12.

130. U.N. Doc.  E/CN.4/1983/SR.17-20.

131. U.N. Doc ST/HR/SER.A/8 (1980).

132. U.N. Doc. ST/HR/SER.A/9 (1981).

133. U.N. Doc. E/CN.4/1984/1 and Add.1, para. 22.

134. CHR Res. 4 (XXXV), 1979.

135. CHR Res. 5 (XXXV), 1979.

136. Ibid.

137. U.N. Doc. E/CN.4/1985/L.33/Rev.1.

138. CHR Dec. 1983/108.

139. See Jack Donnelly, "International Human Rights: A Regime Analysis" *International Organization* 40 (Summer 1986): pp. 599–642.

140. Thomas W. Netter, "U.S. is Said to Oppose U.N. Post for East German," *New York Times*, May 25, 1986, p. 6.  A Byelorussian representative became chairman in 1987.

141. CHR Res. 1983/51.

142. U.N. Doc. E/CN.4/1986/SR.3, para. 13.

143. *Human Rights and Scientific and Technological Developments* , and *The Role of Youth in the Promotion and Protection of Human Rights*, U.N. Doc. E/CN.4/1983/L.4, p. 3; CHR Dec. 1983/108.

144. U.N. Doc. E/CN.4/1424 (1980).

145. ECOSOC Res. 1983/184 (Section III).

146. U.N. Doc E/CN.4/1984/73.

147. U.N. Doc. E/CN.4/SER.A/12 (1982).

148. U.N. Doc. E/CN.4/1986/19.

149. U.N. Doc. A/36/440 (1981); U.N. Doc. A/38/416 (1983); U.N. Doc. A/39/556 and Add.1 (1984).

150. U.N. Doc. E/CN.4/1985/1 and Add.1, para. 4.

151. Roger S. Clark, *A United Nations High Commissioner for Human Rights* (The Hague: Martinue Nijhoff, 1972), pp. 39–54.

152. Sub-Comm. Res. 1983/36 (adopted 16–3–3).

153. Weissbrodt, "'Theme' Special Rapporteurs," p. 685.

154. G.A. Res. 37/437, 1982; G.A. Res 37/237 1982; U.N. Doc. E/CN.4/1984/L.3.

155. ABC News CLOSEUP, "Swords, Plowshares and Politics," 13 August 1982, Transcript, p. 7. Earlier, Van Boven refused to renew the contract of a Division employee suspected of recording one of the Director's phone conversations for the benefit of a member government. Personal interviews with Secretariat staff at the Centre for Human Rights, August 1982.

156. Personal interviews, Geneva, July 1982; see also CHR, *Report of the Thirty-Seventh Session*, U.N. Doc. E/1981/25, para. 234.

157. U.N. Doc. E/CN.4/WG.2/WP/6 (1981).

158. U.N. Doc. A/39/484 (1984).

## Chapter 8

1. John P. Humphrey, "The United Nations Sub-Commission on the Prevention of Discrimination and the Protection of Minorities," *American Journal of International Law* 62 (1968): pp. 869–870.

2. See CHR, *Report of the Second Session*, U.N. Doc. E/259 (1947), para. 20.

3. John P. Humphrey, *Human Rights and the United Nations: A Great Adventure* (Dobbs Ferry, New York: Transnational Publishers, Inc., 1984), p. 21.

4. CHR Res. 11 (XV), 1959 and ECOSOC Res. 728E (XXVIII), 1959. Humphrey suggests the change was made to create a seat for the Egyptian expert Mohammed Awad whose government had neglected to nominate him for reelection after he had served seven years on the Sub-Commission. Humphrey, *Adventure*, p. 83.

5. CHR Res. 4 (XXI), 1965 and ECOSOC Res. 1074G (XXXIX), 1965; and CHR Res. 9 (XXIV), 1968 and ECOSOC Res. 1334 (XLIV), 1968.

6. ECOSOC Res. 1334 (XLIV), 1968.

7. U.N. Doc. E/CN.4/SR.1474 (1978).

8. CHR Res. 1986/42.

9. Based on personal observation of the results announced by the Chair in the Fifty-Third meeting of the Fortieth Session on 13 March 1984. U.N. Doc E/CN.4/1984/SR.53.

10. Jonas Foli of Ghana, Ibrahim Jimeta of Nigeria, L. C. Mubanga-Chipoya of Zambia, Elizabeth Odio Benito of Costa Rica, Vsevolod Sofinsky of the U.S.S.R., Ivan Tosevski of Yugoslavia, and Munir Akram of Pakistan.

11. The Peoples Republic of China did not become a member of the Commission unti 1982 and made its first successful nomination to the Sub-Commission in 1984.

12. CHR Res. 17 (XXXVII), 1981.

13. CHR Res. 1983/21.

14. The United States expert, Ambassador Beverley Carter, died during his term.

15. Inis Claude, "The Nature and Status of the Subcommission on Prevention of Discrimination and Protection of Minorities," *International Organization* 5 (May 1951): p. 303.

16. International Commission of Jurists, "UN Sub-Commission on Discrimination and Minorities," *International Commission of Jurists Review* 23 (December 1979): p. 33.

17. Claude, "Status of Subcommission," pp. 303–304.

18. In 1973 the Sub-Commission lacked a quorum in the final session to adopt its report. International Commission of Jurists, "U.N. Sub-Commission on Minorities and Discrimination," *International Commission of Jurists Review* 11 (December 1973): p. 27.

19. U.N. Doc. E/CN.4/Sub.2/SR.787.

20. Claude, "Status of Subcommission," 304.

21. CHR, *Report of the First Session*, U.N. Doc. E/259 (1947), para. 19.

22. The Sub-Commission drafted the first paragraph of Article 2 which provides: "Everyone is entitled to all the rights and freedoms set forth in this Declaration, without distinction of any kind, such as race, colour, sex, language, religion, political or other opinion, national or social origin, property, birth or other status." The General Assembly drafted paragraph two and added "colour" to the Sub-Commission's list in the first paragraph. Humphrey, *Adventure*, p. 47, n.1.

23. CHR, *Report of the Fifth Session*, U.N. Doc. E/1371 (1949), para. 13.

24. Political Covenant (see chap. 2, n.67), art. 27.

25. Humphrey, *Adventure*, pp. 102–103.

26. Inis Claude, *National Minorities: An International Problem* (Cambridge: Harvard University Press, 1955), p. 152.

27. See Patrick Thornberry, "Is There a Phoenix in the Ashes?—International Law and Minority Rights," *Texas International Law Journal* 15 (1980): pp. 428–438.

28. The proposed definition provided: "[O]nly those non-dominant groups in a population which possess and wish to preserve stable ethnic, religious or linguistic traditions or characteristics markedly different from those of the rest of the population."

29. See Humphrey, "Sub-Commission," p. 872.

30. Ibid., pp. 874–876.

31. Humphrey, *Adventure*, p. 291.

32. Ibid., pp. 334–335.

33. Ibid., p. 310.

34. Humphrey, "Sub-Commission," p. 884.

35. Ibid., p. 885. "It was a disgraceful performance which showed quite clearly that the majority of the members were acting not as independent experts but as the representatives of their governments."

36. CHR Res. 13 (XXIII), 1967.

37. Theresa D. Gonzales, "The Political Sources of Procedural Debates in the United Nations: Structural Impediments to Implementation of Human Rights," *New York University Journal of International Law and Politics* 13 (1981): pp. 450–451.

38. U.N. Doc. E/CN4/Sub.2/1982/3 and Ann.III.

39. Humphrey, "Sub-Commission," p. 879.

40. Arabic 175, Chinese 120, English 1,700, French 750, Russian 225, and Spanish 350 copies. According to P. Malone, of the Centre for Human Rights, additional copies are run as needed.

41. U.N. Doc. E/CN.4/Sub.2/L.708 (1979) lists studies still in print and those out of stock.
42. Humphrey attributes the idea for the program of studies to his assistant, Edward Lawson. Humphrey, *Adventure*, p. 168.
43. Ibid., p. 182.
44. Charles D. Ammoun, *Study of Discrimination in Education*, U.N. publication, Sales No. 57.XIV.3.
45. Humphrey, "Sub-Commission," p. 877, n.24.
46. See Arcot Krishnaswami, *Study of Discrimination in the Matter of Religious Rights and Practices*, U.N. publication, Sales No. 60.XIV.2 and Hernan Santa Cruz, *Study of Discrimination in the Matter of Political Rights*, U.N. publication, Sales No. 63.XIV.2.
47. José D. Ingles, *Study of Discrimination in Respect of the Right of Everyone to Leave any Country, Including His Own, and the Return to His Country*, U.N. publication, Sales No. 64.XIV.2.
48. Sub-Comm. Res. 1982/23. The resolution passed with 11 in favor, 2 opposed and 6 abstentions. Sub-Comm., *Report of its Thirty-Fifth Session* , U.N. Doc. E/CN.4Sub.2/1982/43, para. 39. The Commission took no action on the recommended study.
49. Vieno V. Saario, *Study of Discrimination Against Persons Born out of Wedlock*, U.N. publication, Sales No. E.68.XIV.3.
50. Mohammed A. Rannat, *Study of Equality in the Administration of Justice*, U.N. publication, Sale No. E.71.XIV.3.
51. Hernan Santa Cruz, *Racial Discrimination*, U.N. publication, Sales No. E.76.XIV.3 (revised and updated version of previous study U.N. publication, Sales No. E.71.XIV.2).
52. Francesco Capotorti, *Study of the Rights of Persons Belonging to Ethnic, Religious and Linguistic Minorities*, U.N. publication, Sales No. E.78.XIV.1.
53. Expert Jules Deschênes proposed: "A group of citizens of a State, contituting a numerical minority and in a non-dominant position in that state, endowed with ethnic, religious or linguistic characteristics which differ from those of the majority of the population, having a sense of solidarity with one another, motivated, if only implicitly, by a collective will to survive and whose aim is to achieve equality with the majority in fact and in  law." U.N. Doc. E/CN.4/Sub.2/ 1985/31, p. 30, para. 181.
54. José R. Martínez Cobo, "Study of the Problems of Discrimination Against Indigenous Populations," E/CN.4/Sub.2/1983/21 Add. and 1–8 (1983).
55. Baroness Elles, *Study of International Provisions Protecting the Human Rights of Non-Citizens*, U.N. publication, Sales No. E.80.XIV.2.
56. U.N. Doc. E/CN.4/Sub.2/7 (1982).
57. Héctor Gros Espiell, *Study on the Implementation of United Nations Resolutions Relating to the Right of Peoples Under Colonial and Alien Domination to Self-Determination*, U.N. publication, Sales No. 79.XIV.5.
58. Aureliu Cristescu, *The Rights of Self-Determination: Historical & Current Developments on the Basis of United Nations Instruments*, U.N. publication, Sales No. 80.XIV.3.
59. Ahmed M. Khalifa, *Study of the Adverse Consequences for the Enjoyment of Human Rights of Political, Military, Economic and Other Forms of Assistance Given to the Colonial and Racist Regimes in Southern Africa*, E/CN.4/Sub.2/383.
60. Halima Warzazi, *Study of the Exploitation of Labour Through Illicit and Clandestine Trafficking*, U.N. Doc. E/CN.4/Sub.2/L.640 (1975).

61. International Commission of Jurists, "The UN Sub-Commission on Discrimination and Minorities," *International Commission of Jurists Review* 15 (December 1975): pp. 43–44.

62. The sales edition then appeared a decade after the study was completed. U.N. Doc. E/CN.4/Sub.2/L.629 (1975); E/CN.4/Sub.2/1986/6 (Sales No. E/86.XIV.1). Warzazi later collaborated on "Report of the Working Group on Traditional Practices Affecting the Health of Women and Children," U.N. Doc. E/CN.4/1986/42.

63. Abdelwahab Boudhiba, *Exploitation of Child Labour*, U.N. publication, Sales No. E.82.XIV.2 (1982). The United Nations printed nearly 5,000 copies in English and also issued an edition in Arabic.

64. Antonio Cassesse, *Study of the Impact of Foreign Economic Aid and Assistance on Respect for Human Rights in Chile*, U.N. Doc. No. E/CN.4/Sub.2/412 (1977). See Antonio Cassesse, "Foreign Economic Assistance and Respect for Civil and Political Rights: Chile—A Case Study," *Texas International Law Journal* \14 (1979): p. 251.

65. International Commission of Jurists, "Report of the Sub-Commission,," *International Commission of Jurists Review* 21 (December 1978): pp. 23–24.

66. Raul Ferrero, *The New International Economic Order and the Promotion of Human Rights*, U.N. Doc. No. E/CN.4/Sub.2/1983/24 and Add.1–2 (1983). U.N. publication, Sales No. E85.XIV.6.

67. Erica-Irene Daes, *The Individual's Duties to the Community and the Limitations on Human Rights and Freedoms Under Art. 29 of the Universal Declaration of Human Rights*, U.N. Doc. No. E/CN.4/Sub.2/432/Rev.2 (1983).

68. Erica-Irene Daes, *The Status of the Individual and Contemporary International Law*, U.N. Doc. No. /CN.4/Sub.2/1983/3.

69. Erica-Irene Daes, *Guidelines, Principles and Guarantees for the Protection of Persons Detained on Grounds of Mental Ill-Health or Suffering From Mental Disorder*, U.N. Doc. No. E/CN.4/Sub.2/1983/17 and Add.1.

70. Nicole Questiaux, *Study of the Question of the Human Rights of Persons Subjected to Any Form of Detention or Imprisonment* , U.N. Doc. E/CN.4/Sub.2/ 1982/15.

71. International Commission of Jurists, "Commentary: U.N. Sub-Commission on Human Rights," *International Commission of Jurists Review* 35 (December 1985): p. 16.

72. See U.N. Doc. No. E/CN.4/Sub.2/1983/30 (report to Sub-Commission).

73. Sub-Comm. Res. 1985/26.

74. Mohammed Awad, *Question of Slavery and the Slave Trade in All Their Practices and Manifestations, Including the Slavery-Like Practices of Apartheid and Colonialism*, U.N. Doc. E/CN.4/Sub.2/322 (1971).

75. Benjamin Whitaker, *Updating of the Report on Slavery Submitted to the Sub-Commission in 1966*, U.N. Doc. No. E/CN.4/Sub.2/1982/20 and Add. 1.

76. L. Singhvi, *Study on the Independence and Impartiality of the Judiciary, Jurors and Assessors and the Independence of Lawyers* , U.N. Doc. E/CN.4/Sub.2/ 1985 and Add. 5.

77. Nicodeme Ruhashyankiko, *Study of the Question of the Prevention and Punishment of the Crime of Genocide*, U.N. Doc. E/CN.4/Sub.2/416 (1979).

78. CHR Res. 1983/24.

79. U.N. Doc. E/CN.4/Sub.2/1985/6; International Commission of Jurists, "Commentary: U.N. Sub-Commission on Human Rights," *International Commission of Jurists Review* 35 (December 1985): p. 12.

80. Unlike the Sub-Commission, the Commission assigned its first two studies to a committee rather than to individual rapporteurs. *Study of the Right of Everyone to be Free from Arbitrary Arrest, Detention and Exile,* U.N. publication, Sales No. 65.XIV.2 and *Study of the Right of Arrested Persons to Communicate With Those Whom it is Necessary for Them to Consult in Order to Ensure Their Defence or to Protect Their Essential Interests,* U.N. Doc. E/CN.4/996 (1969) (prepared for the Commission on Human Rights by the Committee on the Right of Everyone to be Free from Arbitrary Arrest, Detention and Exile).

81. CHR Res. 1982/7.

82. CHR Res. 38(XXVII), 1981,; 1982/4; 1983/42.

83. International Commission of Jurists, "UN Sub-Commission on Discrimination and Minorities," *International Commission of Jurists Review* 17 (December 1976): p. 27.

84. The article by Isabelle Vichniac appeared in *Le Monde* September 13, 1978. See Sub-Comm. Res. 10(XXXI), 1978. Since the Commission began announcing which states have been the subject of decisions after its closed door review, there have been fewer press accounts of Sub-Commission deliberations.

85. Sub-Comm. Res. 7B(XXXIV), 1978; 9B(XXXII), 1979; and 27(XXXIII), 1980.

86. U.N. Doc. E/CN.4/Sub.2/1984/23.

87. Sub-Comm., *Report on its Thirty-Fourth Session,* E/CN.4/Sub.2/495 (1981), para. 280.

88. Ibid., para. 285.

89. U.N. Doc. E/CN.4/Sub.2/1982/33.

90. Sub-Comm. Res. 1983/37; ECOSOC Res. 1985/38.

91. U.N. Doc. E/CN.4/Sub.2/1985/22.

92. Sub-Comm. Dec. 1982/8.

93. Sub-Comm. Res. 17(XXXIII), 1980.

94. Sub-Comm. Res. 1982/10 (at paragraph 17).

95. Rules of Procedure (See chap. 1, n. 60), Rule 24, para. 2. See Annotations to the Provisional Agenda, U.N. Doc. No. E/CN.4/1983/1/Add.1. The Sub-Commission has created another unauthorized intersessional working group to promote ratification of international human rights instruments.

96. U.N. Doc. E/CN.4/Sub.2/1985/17.

97. ECOSOC Res. 1235(XLII), 1967.

98. Sub-Comm. Dec. 7, 1978.

99. Sub-Comm. Dec. 7, 1979.

100. Sub-Comm. Dec. 1(XXXIV), 1981.

101. Sub-Comm. Dec. 1982/2.

102. Abdelwahab Boudhiba and Halima Warzazi.

103. U.N. Doc. E/CN.4/Sub.2/1985/19.

104. U.N. Doc. E/CN.4/1261 (1977), paras. 14–15.

105. Sub-Comm. Res. 27(XXXIII), 1980. Adopted by fourteen votes in favor, one opposed and two abstaining.

106. Ibid.

107. Sub-Comm. Res. 19(XXXIII), 1980.

108. Sub-Comm. Res. 25(XXXIII), 1980.

109. Sub-Comm. Res. 22(XXXIII), 1980.

110. "Intervention by the representative of Brazil," Feb. 9, 1981, unpublished text of remarks delivered to the Commission on Human Rights at the Thirty-Fifth Session. As Chairman of the Commission at the 1980 session, Rodrigues did not deliver the prepared remarks himself.

111. U.N. Doc. E/CN.4/SR.1592–1595 (1981).
112. CHR Res. 17(XXXVII), 1981.
113. U.N. Doc. E/CN.4/Sub.2/1981/L.1.
114. U.N. Doc. E/CN.4/Sub.2/1982/L.3 introduced by Bossuyt, Carey, Daes, Eide, and Joinet.
115. CHR Res. 1983/21.
116. U.N. Doc. E/CN.4/Sub.2/1982/L.6.
117. Sub-Comm., *Report on its Thirty-Fifth Session*, U.N. Doc. E/CN.4/Sub.2/1982/43, para. 42.
118. Sub-Comm. Res. 1981/14.
119. Sub-Comm. Res. 1982/27.
120. E/CN.4/1983/L.42.
121. CHR Res. 1983/22.
122. CHR Res. 1983/22.
123. CHR Res. 1986/31.
124. Interview with David Weissbrodt, Amnesty International, September 19, 1986.
125. Interview with Hurst Hannum, Procedural Aspects of International Law Institute, September 20, 1986.
126. U.N. Doc. A/41/49 (1986).
127. Remarks by Mr. Fursland, U.N. Doc. E/CN.4/1983/SR.25, para. 106.
128. Benjamin Whitaker, "Why the U.N. Needs More Muscle to Guard Human Rights," *The Times (London)*, January 26, 1977, p. 7.

# Chapter 9

1. U.N. Doc. E/CN.4/1986/SR.1, para. 41.
2. Daniel P. Moynihan, "The Politics of Human Rights," *Commentary* 64 (August 1977): p. 19.
3. Hayward R. Alker, Jr., "Dimensions of Conflict in the General Assembly," *American Political Science Review* 58 (September 1964): pp. 642–657 as cited by Werner Feld, Robert Jordan with Leon Hurwitz, *International Organizations: A Comparative Approach* (New York: Frederick Praeger, Inc., 1983), p. 153. For reports on six earlier studies see Arend Lijphart, "The Analysis of Bloc Voting in the General Assembly: A Critique and a Proposal," *American Political Science Review* 57 (December 1963): p. 902; Bruce M. Russett, "Discovering Voting Groups in the United Nations," *American Political Science Review* 60 (June 1966): p. 327.
4. Jack Donnelly, "Recent Trends in UN Human Rights Activity: Description and Polemic," *International Organization* 35 (Autumn 1981): pp. 633–655.
5. Jeane J. Kirkpatrick, *Dictatorship and Double Standards: Rationalism and Reason in Politics* (New York: Simon and Schuster, 1982).
6. Thomas Franck, *Nation Against Nation: What Happened to the U.N. Dream and What the U.S. Can Do About It* (New York: Oxford University Press, 1985), pp. 238–242.
7. U.N. Doc. E/CN.4/1986/20/Add.2.
8. Michla Pomerance, *Self-Determination in Law and Practice: The New Doctrine in the United Nations* (The Hague: Martinus Nijhoff, 1982), pp. 24–28.
9. Two exceptions should be noted; the Commission has publicly condemned South African pass laws and privately scrutinized East Germany's emigration policies.

10. July 7, 1983 as reported in *Human Rights Internet Reporter* 9 (September-November 1983): p. 176.

11. The Ache-Guyaquis Indians. Richard Arens, *Genocide in Paraguay* (Philadelphia: Temple University Press, 1977).

12. Amnesty International, *Amnesty International Report 1980* (London: Amnesty International Publications, 1980), p. 35.

13. *Amnesty Action,* September 1983, p. 3.

14. While opposed to the whole concept of enforceable economic rights, the United States challenged an Assembly appropriation of $75 million for new conference facilities in Addis Ababa during Ethiopia's severe famine.

15. *Proposed Programme Budget for the Biennium 1982–83 Vol. 11*, U.N. Doc. No. A/36/6 (1981). That budget included $107,100 for travel expenses of Commission members and $300,000 for travel and stipends for experts on the Sub-Commission.

16. U.N. Doc. A/C.5/38/49/Add.23 (1983). During the 1980–81 biennium the Secretariat estimated at $2.4 million the "financial implications: of supplemental Commission requests. The $10.4 million in final appropriations for direct expenditures in that two-year period exceeded by $1.7 million the Centre's original budget estimate. It is unclear precisely how much additional expenditure was incurred for conference services and apportioned administrative overhead from other Secretariat departments.

17. U.N. Doc. E/CN.4/1985/SR.45–53.

18. In 1985.

19. David Weissbrodt, "The Three 'Theme' Special Rapporteurs of the UN Commission on Human Rights," *American Journal of International Law* 80 (July 1986): pp. 689–690.

20. Franck gives other examples of U.S. inconsistency. Franck, *Nation Against Nation,* ch. 12.

21. CHR, *Report of the Thirty-Sixth Session*, U.N. Doc. E/1980/13, para. 274. The vote was 24 to 16 with 3 abstentions.

22. Yugoslavia votes with the non-aligned.

23. Theo van Boven, *People Matter: Views on International Human Rights Policy* (The Netherlands: Muelenhoff Amsterdam, 1982), p. 83.

24. Franck, *Nation Against Nation,* pp. 244–245.

25. Lowell F. Schechter, "The Views of 'Charterists' and 'Skeptics' on Human Rights in the World Legal Order: Two Wrongs Don't Make a Right," *Hofstra Law Review* 9 (Winter 1981): pp. 364–365.

26. Dinah Shelton, "International Enforcement of Human Rights: Effectiveness and Alternatives," *American Society of International Law Proceedings* (April 1980): p. 6.

27. International Commission of Jurists, "Commentary: The Commission on Human Rights," *International Commission of Jurists Review* 24 (June 1980): p. 34.

28. U.N. Doc. E/CN.4/1371 (1980).

29. George A. Mudge, "Domestic Policies and U.N. Activities: The Cases of Rhodesia and the Republic of South Africa," *International Organization* 21 (Winter 1967): p. 55.

30. See Ozdemir A. Ozgur, *Apartheid: The United Nations and Peaceful Change in South Africa* (Dobbs Ferry, New York: Transational Publishers, Inc., 1982).

31. *The New York Times*, September 6, 1985, p. B6.

32. J. S. Watson, "Legal Theory, Efficacy and Validity in the Development of Human Rights Norms in International Law," *University of Illinois Law Forum* (1979): p. 609.

33. J. S. Watson, "The Limited Utility of International Law in the Protection of Human Rights," *American Society of International Law Proceedings* (April 1980): p. 1.

34. See Eric Lane, "Mass Killing by Governments: Lawful in the World Legal Order?" *New York University Journal of International Law and Politics* 12 (Fall 1979): p. 239–243.

35. On August 31, 1983 the Sub-Commission had cabled the government urging clemency for Professor José Luis Massera who was in poor health.

36. Statement by Mr. Caputo, Minister for Foreign Affairs and Religion of the Argentine Republic, U.N. Doc. E/CN.4/1984/SR.29, pp. 3, 5.

37. U.N. Doc. E/CN.4/1985/SR.47, paras. 7, 8, 14.

38. U.N. Doc. E/CN.4/SR/1626 (1981) (Restricted).

39. Amnesty International, *Amnesty International Report 1982* (London: Amnesty International Publications, 1982), p. 175; Amnesty International, *Amnesty International Report 1983* (Amnesty International Publications, 1982), p. 180.

40. M. E. Tardu, *Human Rights: The International Petition System* (Dobbs Ferry, N.Y.: Oceana, 1983).

41. Central African Republic, Uruguay and Venezuela.  As of 1982, three others, the Philippines, El Salvador, and Portugal, had signed without ratifying the protocol.

42. Equatorial Guinea, Malawi, Uganda, and the Republic of Korea.

43. E/CN.4/1984/SR.52.  The Commission only approved a carefully drafted public resolution concerning a state of siege, unrelated to the situation subject to a confidential decision.  Comm. Res. 1984/46.

44. David P. Forsythe, "The United Nations and Human Rights," *Political Science Quarterly* 100 (Summer 1985): p. 264–267.

45. U.N. Doc. E/CN.4/1424 and Annex 3 (1981).

46. Interview with Foreign Minister Roelof Botha, *Common Cause Magazine*, Vol. II, No. 3, 1985.

47. Theo C. van Boven, "The Right to Development and Human Rights," *International Commission of Jurists Review* 28 (June 1982): p. 49.

48. CHR Dec. 1984/102.

49. van Boven, "Right to Development," p. 49.

50. Philip Alston, "Prevention Versus Cure as a Human Rights Strategy," in International Commission of Jurists, *Development, Human Rights and the Rule of Law* (New York: Pergamon Press, 1981), p. 46.

51. U.N. Doc. ST/HR/SER.A/10 (1981) and U.N. Doc. A/37/42 (1982).

52. In 1952 the regular budget provided 34 professional posts in the Division of Human Rights.  In 1982 the Centre had 47 professionals and 33 general service staff, not counting seven "temporary" assistants.  The U.N. Secretariat had 3,426 employees in 1952 and budgeted for 11,243 in 1982.  U.N. Doc. A/1812 (1952) and A/36/6 (1981). The comparison slightly understates the growth of human rights personnel since the Secretariat transferred five professioanls from the unit servicing the Commission on the Status of Women from the Division in 1973.

53. U.N. Doc. A/36/6 (1981).

54. Personal interview with Toine van Dongen, Netherlands Ministry of Foreign Affairs, March 1986.

## Afterword

1. U.N. Press Release HR/3080, 16 March 1987.
2. U.N. Doc. E/CN.4/1987/15 and Corr.1 and Add.1.
3. U.N. Doc. E/CN.4/1987/13.
4. Libya co-sponsored the resolution at a time when the *New York Times* reported that that government had paid mercenaries in Chad.
5. U.N. Doc. E/CN.4/1987/8 and U.N. Doc. E/CN.4/1987/1.
6. U.N. Doc. E/CN.4/1987/L.10/Add.12.
7. Several nongovernmental organizations have filed petitions with the United Nations charging the United States with illegally detaining about 6,800 Cuban exiles in the United States. *New York Times*, April 14, 1987.
8. U.N. Doc. E/CN.4/1987/L.10/Add.12. The votes were 19-18-6 and then 17-15-11 with the Western bloc also voting against the motion to postpone a vote on the situation in the United States.
9. U.N. Doc. E/CN.4/1987/NGO/54. U.S. Congress. House of Representatives. Committee on Foreign Affairs. Sub-Committee on Human Rights and International Organizations. "Hearing to Review the U.N. Commission on Human Rights." 99th Cong., 2d Sess., June 25, 1986, Appendix 2, Statement by Russel L. Barsh "Making the United Nations Human Rights Machinery Cost Effective," p. 112.
10. *New York Times*, March 9, 1987, p. 5.
11. U.N. Doc. E/CN.4/1987/L.10/Add.1.

# Selected Bibliography

## Books

Amnesty International. *Amnesty International Report 1980*. London: Amnesty International Publications, 1980.

————. *Amnesty International Report 1982*. London: Amnesty International Publications, 1982.

————. *Amnesty International Report 1983*. London: Amnesty International Publications, 1983.

Berger, Jason. *A New Deal for the World: Eleanor Roosevelt and American Foreign Policy*. New York: Social Science Monographs, 1981.

Bethell, Leslie. *The Abolition of the Brazilian Slave Trade: Britain, Brazil and the Slave Trade Question 1807–1869*. Cambridge: Cambridge University Press, 1970.

Brownlie, Ian. *Basic Documents in International Law*. 2d ed. Oxford: Clarendon Press, 1972.

Carey, John. *UN Protection of Civil and Political Rights*. New York: Syracuse University Press, 1970.

Clark, Roger Stenson. *A United Nations High Commissioner for Human Rights*. The Hague: Martinus Nijhoff, 1972.

Claude, Inis. *National Minorities: An International Problem*. Cambridge: Harvard University Press, 1955.

Evans, Archibald A. *Worker's Rights are Human Rights*. Rome: IDOC International, 1981.

Esejiofor, Gaius. *Protection of Human Rights Under the Law*. London: Butterworths, 1964.

Franck, Thomas M. *Nation Against Nation: What Happened to the U.N. Dream and What the U.S. Can Do About It*. New York: Oxford University Press, 1985.

Ganji, Manouchehr. *International Protection of Human Rights*. Geneva: E. Droz, 1962.

Green, James Frederick. *The United Nations and Human Rights*. Washington, D.C.: The Brookings Institution, 1956.

Hannum, Hurst ed. *Guide to International Human Rights Practice*. Philadelphia: University of Pennsylvania Press, 1984.

Humphrey, John P. *Human Rights and the United Nations: A Great Adventure*. Dobbs Ferry, New York: Transnational Publishers, Inc., 1984.

International Commission of Jurists. *Development, Human Rights and the Rule of Law: Report of a Conference Held in The Hague on 27 April–1 May 1981*. Oxford: Pergamon Press, 1981.

————. *Uganda and Human Rights: Reports to the UN Commission on Human Rights*. Geneva: International Commission of Jurists, 1977.

Jackson, Richard L. *The Non-Aligned, the UN and the Super-Powers.* New York: Praeger, 1983.

Janowsky, Oscar I. *Nationalities and National Minorities (With Special Reference to East-Central Europe).* New York: Macmillan Co., 1945.

Kanger, H. *Human Rights in the U.N. Declaration.* Upsala: Skrifter Utgivna Av Stratsvetenskapliga Foreningen, 1985.

Lauterpacht, E., ed. *British Practice in International Law 1963.* London: British Institute of International and Comparative Law, 1965.

Lauterpacht, Hersch. *International Law and Human Rights.* New York: Frederick A. Praeger, Inc., 1950.

Lerner, Natan. *The U.N. Convention on the Elimination of All Forms of Racial Discrimination.* The Netherlands: Sijthoff & Noordhoff, 1980.

Lillich, Richard B. *The Human Rights of Aliens in Contemporary International Law.* Manchester, England: Manchester University Press, 1984.

Lillich, Richard B., and Frank C. Newman. *International Human Rights: Problems of Law and Policy.* Boston: Little, Brown and Company, 1979.

Luard, Evan, ed. *The International Protection of Human Rights.* London: Thames & Hudson, 1967.

Marie, Jean Bernard. *La Commission des droits de l'homme de l'Onu.* Paris: Pedone, 1975.

Meiers, Suzanne. *Britain and the Ending of the Slave Trade.* London: Longmans, Green and Co., 1975.

Moskowitz, Moses. *The Politics and Dynamics of Human Rights.* Dobbs Ferry, New York: Oceana Publications, Inc., 1968.

Mower, A. Glenn, Jr. *The United States, the United Nations and Human Rights: The Eleanor Roosevelt and Jimmy Carter Eras.* Westport, Conn: Greenwood Press, 1979.

Murray, Gilbert. *From the League to U.N.* London: Oxford University Press, 1948.

Oppenheim, L. *International Law.* 8th ed. Vol. 1. Edited by Hersch Lauterpacht. London: Longmans, Green and Co., 1955.

Ozgur, Ozdemir A. *Apartheid: The United Nations and Peaceful Change in South Africa.* Dobbs Ferry, New York: Transnational Publishers, Inc., 1982.

Pei-Heng, Chiang. *Non-Governmental Organizations at the United Nations: Identity, Role, and Function.* New York: Praeger, 1981.

Pomerance, Michla. *Self-Determination in Law and Practice: The New Doctrine in the United Nations.* The Hague: Martinus Nijhoff Publishers, 1982.

Ramcharan, B.G. *International Law and Fact-Finding in the Field of Human Rights.* The Netherlands: Martinus Nijhoff, 1983.

Robinson, Jacob. *Human Rights and Fundamental Freedoms in the Charter of the United Nations: A Commentary.* New York: Institute of Jewish Affairs, 1946.

Robinson, Nehemiah. *The Universal Declaration of Human Rights: Its Origin, Significance, Application, and Interpretation.* New York: Institute of Jewish Affairs, 1958.

Russell, Ruth B. *A History of the United Nations Charter: The Role of the United States 1940–1945.* Washington, D.C.: The Brookings Institution, 1958.

Schwelb, Egon. *Human Rights and the International Community: The Roots and Growth of the Universal Declaration of Human Rights 1948–1963.* Chicago: Quadrangle Books, 1964.

Sohn, Louis and Buergenthal, Thomas. *International Protection of Human Rights.* New York: Bobbs Merrill, 1973.

Tardu, M. E. *Human Rights: The International Petition System.* Dobbs Ferry, New York: Oceana Publications, Inc., 1982.

United Nations. *United Nations Action in the Field of Human Rights.* New York: United Nations, 1983.

———. *The United Nations and Human Rights.* New York: United Nations, 1978.

U.S. Department of State. *Foreign Relations of the United States, 1947–1954.* Vol. III. Washington, D.C.: Government Printing Office, 1979.

van Boven, Theo. *People Matter: Views on International Human Rights Policy.* The Netherlands: Muelenhoff Amsterdam, 1982.

Van Dyke, Vernon. *Human Rights, the United States and World Community.* London: Oxford University Press, 1970.

Walter, F. P. *A History of the League of Nations.* London: Oxford University Press, 1952.

Zuijdwijk, Ton J. M. *Petitioning the United Nations: A Study in Human Rights.* New York: St. Martin's Press, 1982.

## Articles

Alston, Philip. "Prevention Versus Cure as a Human Rights Strategy." In International Commission of Jurists, *Development, Human Rights and the Rule of Law,* 31–108. Oxford: Pergamon Press, 1981.

———. "Remedying U.N. Pussyfooting on Human Rights." *Human Rights Internet Reporter* 2 (June 1986): 7.

American Bar Association. "Declaration on Human Rights: Canadian, American Bars Ask for Delay of Action." *ABA Journal* 34 (October 1948) 881–885.

Bentwich, Norman. "Human Rights in the Doldrums." *Contemporary Review* 1088 (August 1956): 76–79.

———. "Marking Time for Human Rights." *Contemporary Review* 1100 (August 1957): 80–83.

———. "Ten Years of Human Rights." *Contemporary Review* 1111 (July 1958): 22–25.

Bitker, Bruno V. "The International Treaty Against Racial Discrimination." *Marquette Law Review* 53 (1970): 68–93.

Borchard, Edwin. "Historical Background of International Protection of Human Rights." *Annals of the American Academy of Political and Social Science* 243 (January 1946): 112–117.

Bossuyt, Marc J. "The Development of Special Procedures of the United Nations Commission on Human Rights." *Human Rights Law Journal* 6 (1985): 179–210.

Bridge, John W. "The Case for an International Court of Criminal Justice and the Formulation of International Criminal Law." *International and Comparative Law Quarterly* 13 (1964): 1255–1281.

Cassesse, Antonio. "The Admissibility of Communications to the United Nations on Human Rights Violations." *Human Rights Journal* 5 (1972): 375–393.

———. "Foreign Economic Assistance and Respect for Civil and Political Rights: Chile—A Case Study." *Texas International Law Journal* 14 (1979): 251–263.

Claude, Inis L. "The Nature and Status of the Subcommission on Prevention of Discrimination and Protection of Minorities. *International Organization* 5 (May 1951): 300–312.

Congressional Quarterly News Features. "Bricker Treaty Amendment Debate." In *Congressional Quarterly Almanac,* 83rd Cong., 2d sess., Vol X (1954): 254–262.

Corbett, Percy E. "Next Steps After the Charter: An Approach to the Enforcement of Human Rights." *Commentary* (November 1945): 21–29.

Das, T. "Measures of Implementation of the Convention on the Elimination of All Forms of Racial Discrimination." *Human Rights Journal* 4 (1971).

Donnelly, Jack. "International Human Rights: A Regime Analysis." *International Organization* 40 (Summer 1986): 599–642.

————. "Recent Trends in UN Human Rights Activity: Description and Polemic." *International Organization* 35 (Autumn 1981): 633–655.

Forsythe, David P. "The United Nations and Human Rights" *Political Science Quarterly* 100 (Summer 1985): 249–269.

Franck, Thomas M. and H. Scott Fairley. "Procedural Due Process in Human Rights Fact-Finding by International Agencies." *American Journal of International Law* 74 (1980): 308–345.

————. "Of Gnats and Camels: Is There a Double Standard at the United Nations?" *American Journal of International Law* 78 (1984): 811–834.

Green, James F. "Changing Approaches to Human Rights: The United Nations, 1954 and 1974." *Texas International Law Journal* 12 (1977): 223.

Gardeniers, Ton, Hurst Hannum, and Janice Kruger. "The U.N. Sub-Commission on Prevention of Discrimination and Protection of Minorities: Recent Developments." *Human Rights Quarterly* 4 (Summer 1982): 353–370.

Gonzales, Theresa D. "The Political Sources of Procedural Debates in the United Nations: Structural Impediments to Implementation of Human Rights." *New York University Journal of International Law and Politics* 13 (1981): 427–472.

Guggenheim, Malvina H. "Key Provisions of the New United Nations Rules Dealing with Human Rights Petitions." *New York University Journal of International Law and Politics* 6 (1973): 427–449.

Haver, Peter. "The United Nations Sub-Commission on the Prevention of Discrimination and the Protection of Minorities." *Columbia Journal of Transnational Law* 21 (1982): 103–134.

Higgins, Rosalyn. "Technical Assistance for Human Rights." *The World Today* 19 (May 1963): 219–224.

Humphrey, John. "The Right of Petition in the United Nations." *Human Rights Journal* 4 (1971): 463–475.

————. "The United Nations Commission on Human Rights and its Parent Body." *Rene Cassin Amicorum Discipulorumque Liber I* , Paris, (1969): 108–113.

————. "The United Nations Sub-Commission on the Prevention of Discrimination and the Protection of Minorities." *American Journal of International Law* 62 (1968): 869–888.

International Commission of Jurists. "The United Nations Commission on Human Rights." *Bulletin of the International Commission of Jurists* 11 (December 1960): 51–56.

Jessup, Phillip C. "A Good Start." *Commentary* (January 1946): 56–58.

Johnson, M. Glen. "The Contributions of Eleanor and Franklin Roosevelt to the Development of International Protection for Human Rights." *Human Rights Quarterly* 9 (February 1987): 19–48.

Korey, William. "The Key to Human Rights—Implementation." *International Conciliation* 570 (November 1968): 5–70.

Kramer, David and David Weissbrodt. "The 1980 U.N. Commission on Human Rights and the Disappeared." *Human Rights Quarterly* 3 (February 1981): 18–33.

Kunz, Josef L. "The United Nations Declaration of Human Rights." *American Journal of International Law* 43 (1949): 316–323.

Lane, Eric. "Mass Killings by Governments: Lawful in the World Legal Order?" *New York University Journal of International Law and Politics* 12 (Fall 1979): 239–280.

Lauren, Paul Gordon. "First Principles of Racial Equality: History and the Politics and Diplomacy of Human Rights Provisions in the United Nations Charter." *Human Rights Quarterly* 5 (Winter 1983): 1–26.

———. "Human Rights in History: Diplomacy and Racial Equality at the Paris Peace Conference." *Diplomatic History* 2 (Summer 1978): 257–278.

Lillich, Richard B. "The U.N. and Human Rights Complaints: U. Thant as Strict Constructionist." *American Journal of International Law* 64 (1970): 610–614.

Lijphart, Arend. "The Analysis of Bloc Voting in the General Assembly: A Critique and a Proposal." *American Political Science Review* 57 (December 1963): 902–917.

Liskofsky, Sidney. "Coping with the 'Question of the Violation of Human Rights and Fundamental Freedoms.'" *Human Rights Review* 8 (1975): 883–914.

MacDonald, R. St.J. "The United Nations Commissioner for Human Rights." *Canadian Yearbook of International Law* (1967): 84–117.

Manke, Hugh I. "The Exhaustion of Domestic Remedies in the United Nations Subcommission on Prevention of Discrimination and Protection of Minorities." *Buffalo Law Review* 24 (1975): 643–651.

Marie, Jean Bernard. "La Commission des droits de l'homme des Nations Unies a sa 29th Session." *Revue des droits de l'homme* 6 (1973): 369–433.

McDougal, Myres S. and Gerhard Bebr. "Human Rights in the United Nations." *American Journal of International Law* 58 (1964): 603–641.

Meron, Theodor. "Norm Making and Supervision in International Human Rights: Reflections on Institutional Order." *American Journal of International Law* 76 (1982): 754–778.

Meyer, Peter. "The International Bill: A Brief History." In *The International Bill of Human Rights,* edited by Paul Williams, xxiii–xlvii. Glen Ellen, California: Entwhistle Books, 1981.

Miller, Robert H. "The Convention on the Non-Applicability of Statutory Limitations to War Crimes and Crimes Against Humanity." *American Journal of International Law* 65 (1971): 476–501.

Moller, Jakob T.H. "Petitioning the United Nations." *Universal Human Rights* 1 (October-December 1979): 57–72.

Moynihan, Daniel P. "The Politics of Human Rights." *Commentary* 64 (August 1977): 19–22.

Mudge, George A. "Domestic Policies and U.N. Activities: The Cases of Rhodesia and the Republic of South Africa." *International Organization* 21 (Winter 1967): 55–78.

Nartowski, Andrzej. "Human Rights in the United Nations System." *V Polish Yearbook of International Law* 131 (1972-73).

Neal, Marian. "The United Nations and Human Rights." *International Conciliation* 489 (March 1953): 113–147.

Newman, Frank C. "International Control of Racial Discrimination." *California Law Review* 56 (1968): 1559–1611.

Nolde, O. Frederick. "Human Rights and the United Nations: Appraisal and Next Steps." *Proceedings of the Academy of Political Science* 2 (January 1953).

———. "Possible Functions of the Commission on Human Rights." *Annals of the American Academy of Political and Social Science* 243 (January 1946): 144–149.

Nowak, Manfred. "The Effectiveness of the International Covenant on Civil and Political Rights—Stocktaking After the First Eleven Sessions of the UN Human Rights Committee." *Human Rights Law Journal* 1 (1980): 136–170.

Okere, B. Obina. "The Protection of Human Rights in Africa and the African Charter on Human and Peoples' Rights: A Comparative Analysis with the European and American Systems." *Human Rights Quarterly* 6 (May 1984): 141–159.

Ostrovsky, Y. A. "International Protection of Human Rights: Non-Interference into Internal Affairs of States." *Soviet Yearbook of International Law* (1966–1967).

Parker, John J. "An International Criminal Court: A Case for Its Adoption." *ABA Journal* 38 (August 1952): 641–643.

Parson, Donald P. "The Individual Right of Petition: A Study of Methods Used by International Organizations to Utilize the Individual as a Source of Information on Violations of Human Rights." *Wayne Law Review* 13 (1967): 678–705.

Peffer, Natheniel. "A Too Remote Goal." *Commentary* (January 1946): 58–59.

Pella, Vespasian V. "Towards an International Criminal Court." *American Journal of International Law* 44 (1950): 37–68.

Prasad, Maya. "The Role of Non-governmental Organizations in the New United Nations Procedures for Human Rights Complaints." *Denver Journal of International Law and Policy* 5 (1975): 441–462.

Racklin, Lauren D. "Report of the 26th Session of the U.N. Commission on Human Rights." *Revue des Droits de L'Homme* 3(1970) p. 487.

Rodley, Nigel. "UN Action Against 'Disappearances,' Summary or Arbitrary Executions and Torture." *Human Rights Quarterly* 8 (November 1986): 700–730.

Russett, Bruce M. "Discovering Voting Groups in the United Nations." *American Political Science Review* 60 (June 1966): 327–339.

Schecter, Lowell F. "The Views of 'Charterists' and 'Skeptics' on Human Rights in the World Legal Order: Two Wrongs Don't Make a Right." *Hofstra Law Review* 9 (Winter 1981): 357–398.

Schoenberg, Harris. "The Implementation of Human Rights by the United Nations." *Israel Yearbook of Human Rights* 22 (1977): 22–52.

Schwelb, Egon. "The Influence of the Universal Declaration of Human Rights on International and National Law." *American Society of International Law Proceedings*(1959): 217–229.

———. "The International Convention on the Elimination of All Forms of Racial Discrimination." *International and Comparative Law Quarterly* 15 (October 1966): 996–1068.

Scoble, Harry and Laurie Wiseberg. "Human Rights and Amnesty International." *Annals of the American Academy of Political and Social Science* 413 (May 1974): 11–26.

Shawcross, William, Anthony Terry and Peter Pringle. "The Barbarism the World Ignores." *Atlas* 23 (June 1976): 20–22.

Shestack, Jerome J. "The Commission on Human Rights." In *U.S. Policy in International Institutions: Defining Reasonable Options in an Unreasonable World,* edited by Seymour M. Finger and Joseph R. Harbert, 71–82. Boulder, Colorado: Westview Press, 1982.

Simsarian, James. "Third Session of the UN Commission on Human Rights." *American Journal of International Law* 42 (October 1948): 879–883.

Smoger, Gerson. "Whither the Commission on Human Rights: A Report After the 35th Session." *Vanderbilt Journal of Transnational Law* 12 (1979): 943–968.

Skoler, Daniel L. "World Implementation of the United Nations Standard Minimum Rules for the Treatment of Prisoners." *Journal of International Law and Economics* 10 (August-December 1975): 453–482.

Sohn, Louis B. "Human Rights: Their Implementation and Supervision by the United Nations." In *Human Rights in International Law* Vol. 2, edited by Theodor Meron. Oxford: Clarendon Press, 1984.

Stettinius, Edward R. "Human Rights in the United Nations Charter." *Annals of the American Academy of Political and Social Science* 243 (January 1946): 1–3.

———. "Symposium on the International Law of Human Rights." *Howard Law Journal* 11 (Spring 1965): 257–263.

Tardu, M. E. "United Nations Response to Gross Violations of Human Rights: The 1503 Procedure." *Santa Clara Law Review* 20 (1980): 559–601.

Tedin, Kent L. "The Development of the Soviet Attitude Toward Implementing Human Rights Under the UN Charter." *Human Rights Journal* 5 (1972): 399–418.

Thornberry, Patrick. "Is There a Phoenix in the Ashes?—International Law and Minority Rights." *Texas International Law Journal* 15 (1980): 421–458.

Tolley, Howard, Jr. "Decision-Making at the United Nations Commission on Human Rights, 1979–1982." *Human Rights Quarterly* 5 (Winter): 27–57.

———. "The Concealed Crack in the Citadel: The United Nations Commission on Human Rights' Response to Confidential Communications." *Human Rights Quarterly* 6 (November 1984): 420–462.

Turlington, Edgar. "The United Nations Commission on Human Rights." *American Journal of International Law* 39 (1945): 757–758.

United Nations. "Committee on the Elimination of Racial Discrimination, Twenty-fourth Session." *Bulletin of Human Rights* 33 (July-September 1981): 26–44.

United Nations Department of Public Information. "International Bill of Human Rights to be Drafted." *United Nations Weekly Bulletin* (June 17, 1947): 639–643.

U.S. Department of State. "United Nations Conference on International Organization." *Bulletin* 12 (May 20, 1945): 928–931.

van Boven, Theo C. "The Right to Development and Human Rights." *International Commission of Jurists Review* 28 (June 1982): 49–56.

———. "The United Nations Commission on Human Rights and Violations of Human Rights and Fundamental Freedoms." *Netherlands International Law Review* 15 (1968): 374–393.

———. "The United Nations and Human Rights, Innovation and Stagnation." *SIM Newsletter,* No. 9, January 1985.

Watson, J. S. "Legal Theory, Efficacy and Validity in the Development of Human Rights Norms in International Law." *University of Illinois Law Forum* (1979): 609–641.
————. "The Limited Utility of International Law in the Protection of Human Rights." *American Society of International Law Proceedings* (April 1980): 1–6.
Weissbrodt, David. "The Role of International Nongovernmental Organizations in the Implementation of Human Rights." *Texas International Law Journal* 12 (1977): 293–320.
————. "The Three 'Theme' Special Rapporteurs of the UN Commission on Human Rights." *American Journal of International Law* 80 (July 1986): 685–699.
————. "The Forty-Second Session of the United Nations Commission on Human Rights, 3 February–14 March 1986." *International Lawyers* 20 (Fall 1986).
Whiteman, M. "Mrs. Franklin D. Roosevelt and the Human Rights Commission." *American Journal of International Law* (1968): 918–921.
Wright, Quincy. "The Scope of International Criminal Law: A Conceptual Framework." *Virginia Journal of International Law* 15 (1975): 561–577.
Zorin, V. "The UN and Human Rights." 36th Session of the UN Commission on Human Rights 6 *International Affairs* (Moscow) 89 (1978).

## Miscellaneous

American Association for the International Commission of Jurists. *The Human Rights of All Persons in Prison or Detention: Draft Principles.* American Association for the International Commission of Jurists, Inc. (pamphlet).
Americas Watch, Asia Watch, and Helsinki Watch Committees. *Four Failures: A Report on the U.N. Special Rapporteurs on Human Rights in Chile, Guatemala, Iran and Poland January 1986.* (Copies of report available from Watch Committees).
Commission to Study the Organization of Peace. *International Safeguard of Human Rights.* 4th Report (1966).
da Fonesca, Glenda. How to File Complaints of Human Rights Violations, A Practical Guide to Inter-Governmental Affairs. Commission of the Churches on International Affairs of the World Council of Churches (pamphlet, 1975).
Fareed, Nabiel J. "The United Nations Commission on Human Rights and Its Work for Human Rights and Fundamental Freedoms." Ph.D. diss., Washington State University, 1977, University Microfilms.
*Human Rights and Foreign Policy.* Ministry of Foreign Affairs of the Kingdom of the Netherlands. Presented to Lower House of the States General, 1979.
Thoolen, Hans. The Need for an International Convention Against Torture. Commission of the Churches on International Affairs of the World Council of Churches (pamphlet No. 8, 1978).

## United States Documents

U.S. Department of State. *Postwar Foreign Policy Preparation, 1938–1945.* Washington, D.C.: U.S. Government Printing Office, 1949.
————. The United Nations. *Dumbarton Oaks Proposals for a General International Organization.* Department of State Publications 2297, 1944.

————. *Charter of the United Nations, Report to the President on the Results of the San Francisco Conference by the Chairman of the United States Delegation, the Secretary of State*, June 26, 1945. Conference Series 71, no. 2349.

————. *The United Nations Conference on International Organization.* Washington, D.C.: U.S. Government Printing Office, 1946.

————. *The United Nations Conference on International Organization, San Francisco, California, April 25 to June 26, 1945, Selected Documents.* Washington, D.C.: U.S. Government Printing Office, 1946.

Congressional Record, 82nd Cong., 1st sess., 1951. Vol. 97, pt. 6.

"Adoption of Declaration of Human Rights." *Human Rights and Genocide* by Mrs. Franklin D. Roosevelt.    Department of State Publication No. 3643. Washington, D.C.: U.S. Government Printing Office, 1949.

U.S. Congress. House of Representatives. Committee on Foreign Affairs. Sub-Committee on International Organizations and Movements. "Hearing on the New UN Procedures for Human Rights Complaints." 93rd Cong., 1st sess., 1973.

————. House Committee on Foreign Affairs. *Review of the UN Commission of Human Rights.* "Hearings before the Sub-Committee on International Organizations and Movements." 93rd Cong., 2d sess., 1974.

————. Senate Foreign Relations Committee. Sub-Committee on International Operations. *Report.* 95th Cong., 2d sess., 1978.

————. House Committee on Foreign Affairs. Sub-Committee on International Organizations. *U.S. Participation in the United Nations and UN Reform. Hearings.* 96th Cong., 1st sess., 1979.

————. House Committee on Foreign Affairs. Sub-Committee on International Organizations. *Hearings.* 96th Cong., 2d sess., April 29, 1980.

————. House Committee on Foreign Affairs. Sub-Committee on International Organizations. *Review of the 37th Session and the Upcoming 38th Session of the UN Commission on Human Rights.* 97th Cong., 1st sess., 1981.

————. House Committee on Foreign Affairs. Sub-Committee on Human Rights and International Organization. *Review of the 38th and Upcoming 39th Session of the U.N. Commission on Human Rights.* 97th Cong., 2d sess., Dec. 10, 1982.

————. House Committee on Foreign Affairs. Sub-Committee on Human Rights and International Organizations. "Review of U.N. Commission on Human Rights." 99th Cong., 2d sess., June 25, 1986.

## Periodicals Most Frequently Reporting on the Commission

*American Journal of International Law*
*Human Rights Internet Reporter*
*International Studies Newsletter* of the International Studies Association
*The Review* of the International Commission of Jurists
*UN Monthly Chronicle*

# Index